The Promised Lands

THE MIDDLE AGES SERIES

Ruth Mazo Karras, General Editor
Edward Peters, Founding Editor

A complete list of books in the series
is available from the publisher.

The Promised Lands

The Low Countries
Under Burgundian Rule, 1369–1530

Wim Blockmans and Walter Prevenier

Translated by Elizabeth Fackelman

Translation revised and edited
by Edward Peters

PENN

University of Pennsylvania Press

Philadelphia

Originally published as *In de ban van Bourgondië* © 1988 by Fibula, Houten, the Netherlands.
English translation copyright © 1999 University of Pennsylvania Press
All rights reserved
Printed in the United States of America on acid-free paper

10 9 8 7 6 5 4 3 2 1

Published by
University of Pennsylvania Press
Philadelphia, Pennsylvania 19104-4011

Library of Congress Cataloging-in-Publication Data
Blockmans, Willem Pieter.
  [In de ban van Bourgondië. English]
  The promised lands : the Low Countries under Burgundian rule, 1369–1530 / Wim Blockmans and Walter Prevenier ; translated by Elizabeth Fackelman ; translation revised and edited by Edward Peters.
    p. cm.
  Includes bibliographical references and index.
  ISBN 0-8122-3130-9 (cloth : alk. paper). —
ISBN 0-8122-1382-3 (paper : alk. paper)
  1. Netherlands — History — House of Burgundy, 1384–1477.
2. Netherlands — History — House of Habsburg, 1477–1556.
I. Prevenier, Walter. II. Title.
DH175.B57 1999
949.2'01—dc21   98-48565
                                                              CIP

Contents

Editor's Note	vii
Preface	xi
The Dynasties of the Burgundian Low Countries	xv
1. Perspectives on the Burgundian Dynasty in the Low Countries	1
2. A New European Power in the Making, 1363–1405	14
3. Burgundian Interests in France and the Low Countries, 1404–1425	35
4. The Decisive Years, 1425–1440	72
5. The Difficult Path Toward an Integrated State, 1440–1465	103
6. The Promised Lands, 1440–1475	141
7. War, Crisis, and a Problematic Succession, 1465–1492	174
8. The Second Flowering, 1492–1530	206
9. The Burgundian Legacy	235
List of Abbreviations	243
Notes	245
Bibliography	265
Index	277

Editor's Note

In de ban van Bourgondië, first published at Houten in 1988, instantly became the best brief account in any language of the history of the Burgundian Low Countries from 1369 to 1530. Combining political, diplomatic, administrative, economic, social, artistic, and cultural history in a compact volume of fewer than two hundred pages, its authors, Wim Blockmans and Walter Prevenier, leading scholars in the great tradition of the University of Ghent, had used the most recent research on the subject, much of it their own, and produced a highly readable and accessible history.

This book had been preceded by the authors' classic, massive, and superbly illustrated *The Burgundian Netherlands*, which had appeared simultaneously in 1983 in Dutch (as *De Bourgondische Nederlanden*) and in French (*Les Pays-Bas bourguignons*). It appeared in an English translation in 1985, and in German as *Die burgundische Niederlande* in 1986. *The Burgundian Netherlands* is a great and wonderfully illustrated book, but the need for a shorter and more generally accessible version of the history was not met until the publication of Blockmans and Prevenier's second book on the subject, in 1988.

Characteristically on the part of the authors, in *In de ban van Bourgondië* they used research that had appeared after the publication of *The Burgundian Netherlands*, and for the present translation they have incorporated research that has been published since 1988, in several instances even while the present translation was being revised. Therefore, this is virtually a new edition of the Dutch original. Some of the revisions in this English version have been incorporated in the second Dutch edition, *De Bourgondiërs: De Nederlanden op weg naar eenheid, 1384–1530*, published in Amsterdam and Leuven in 1997.

In de ban van Bourgondië, like its longer predecessor, did not observe the older and erroneous convention of ending discussions of Burgundian rule in the Low Countries with the death of Charles the Bold in 1477. Instead it traced the history of the Burgundian Low Countries for three more generations of rulers, down to the death of the regent Margaret of Austria in 1530 and the increasingly imperial scope of the rule of her nephew, the emperor Charles V. For the present edition the authors have added several new themes, updated much of the research data, included notes, expanded the original bibliography, and oriented the book toward an international readership.

I have made three general kinds of revisions in this text. First, I have tried to group topics that were originally dispersed into a generally chronological sequence, adding subheads within chapters and dividing the original Chapter 4 into the two present Chapters 5 and 6.

Second, I have revised some of the style of the original work. The greatest difference between the original Dutch text and the present English text hinges on the backgrounds of the different audiences for which they are intended. *In de ban van Bourgondië* was written for a historically minded audience in the Low Countries, about its own national histories. That audience did not need the identifications and clarifications of points that it knew well, but that are generally unfamiliar to a more international audience. Individual persons and topics, too, could be treated briefly at one point, then reintroduced later in the text, and a regional audience that was at least generally familiar with them would have no difficulty in identifying them. Bryce Lyon has very kindly made many useful suggestions for revisions, and the authors and I have usually followed his advice.

The book was written in a lively, almost conversational Dutch, for which Elizabeth Fackelman provided an excellent literal translation, but also one that needed extensive revision for an Anglophone audience. The title, for example, means literally both "under the rule of Burgundy" and "under the spell of Burgundy," a perfectly appropriate ambivalence for Dutch readers but untranslatable in English. Moreover, the book traces the history between 1369 and 1530 of a dynastically ruled group of very diverse territories that survive today in the Netherlands, Belgium, Luxemburg, and parts of the modern French departments of Nord and Pas-de-Calais. To assemble such a "pragmatic empire" required both authority and persuasion—hence the double entendre of the Dutch title. Persuasion, the "spell," was no less important than authority and power—indeed, I have fallen under this sense of the *ban* myself. But the "spell" of the title is not at first self-explanatory. Hence the new title and the stylistic revisions.

Third, I have added identifications of people and places for the benefit of readers who may be unfamiliar with the world of northwestern France in the fourteenth, fifteenth, and early sixteenth centuries (or whose knowledge of that world may be based largely on Johan Huizinga's *The Waning of the Middle Ages*). Where it seemed necessary I have also given, at least at the first or most important citation, both Dutch and French names of individuals and places. Otherwise, I have retained conventional English usage where there is a convention — Ghent instead of Gent or Gand, Bruges instead of Brugge, Maas instead of Meuse, Louvain instead of Leuven, but also Mechelen instead of Malines. Generally, the term *Low Countries* is used here for the territories from Artois, Hainault, Luxemburg, and Namur north; the term *Netherlands*, which has modern political connotations that did not exist in the period covered by this book, appears very infrequently.

Professors Prevenier and Blockmans, who have been my friends for years and whose English is excellent, displayed remarkable patience and tolerance for revisions that must have often come as a surprise, but they have also read and approved every word of the present English version. Our collaboration has been a happy one. I undertook this work not only because of my affection and respect for the authors and the book, but also because of my gratitude for the kindness and hospitality shown me by Belgian, Dutch, and North American colleagues who work in the fields touched on in this book. I am grateful to my former colleagues at the Katholieke Universiteit Leuven — Werner Verbeke, Raymond van Uytven, Jan Goosens, Raphaël de Keyser, Daniel Verhelst, Eduard van Ermen, and Paul Trio; to friends and colleagues at the Universiteit Gent, not only the authors, but also Ludo Milis and Patricia Carson and Raoul van Caenegem. At the Katholieke Universiteit Nijmegen in the Netherlands, Hans Thijssen kindly showed me something of Gelderland and some of the Burgundian world outside Brabant and Flanders. Several American scholars very kindly read early versions of the Fackelman translation, especially Bryce Lyon and James Murray. The scholarship of David Nicholas has taught me very much. My own colleagues Ann Matter and Charles Minott helped and instructed me immensely, as we designed and jointly taught a course in three departments on the subject at the University of Pennsylvania in 1995 and 1997. Jerome Singerman of the University of Pennsylvania Press accepted the original idea of a translation and generously kept the project on his agenda during several long delays.

The affection and work of dedicated colleagues is one of the joys of the academic profession. My work on this book is a small acknowledgment of the character of an academic community that extends across several modern countries and one large ocean. Thanks to these international associations, contemporary boundaries fade, older communities with different geographical and cultural outlines become more clearly visible, and the ocean turns out not to be as large as it appears.

Edward Peters

Preface

This book is an account of one of the most striking political developments in the history of late medieval and early modern Europe: the formation of the state of the dukes of Burgundy in the Low Countries. The process of state formation began with the naming of Philip the Bold, son of King John II of France, as first peer of France and duke of Burgundy in 1363, and with his marriage in 1369 to Margaret of Male, heiress to the county of Flanders and other lands. With Philip's virtually independent financial and political power base in Burgundy and the wealth of the Flemish countship and cities, Philip and his descendants built an elaborate network of many principalities, diverse in their character and history but all united in the person of the duke. From its beginnings in Burgundy, the center of gravity of this network moved increasingly to the Low Countries. In the sixteenth century, much of this state followed the tangled pathways of inheritance into the Habsburg Empire of Maximilian I and his grandson Charles V, who organized the Low Countries into the Seventeen Provinces of the Netherlands in 1543 and the *Bourgondische Kreits*, the Burgundian Circle, a self-contained part of the Empire, in 1548. In turn, part of this was transformed into the Spanish-Netherlands Empire of Charles's son Philip II.[1]

The Seventeen Provinces of the Netherlands revolted against the absolutist regime of the king of Spain in the 1570s. The movement of revolution originated, not least for religious reasons, in the ten southernmost provinces of the seventeen, that is, principally in what is now Belgium. By 1585 these southern provinces had been reconquered by Spain with overwhelming military force. For that reason they remained in possession of the Spanish monarchy, and later the Austrian branches of the Habsburg dynasty, until 1794.

The seven provinces in the north, however, were able to win independence from the Spanish king, and, as the Republic of the United Provinces, entered their golden age in the seventeenth century. The Burgundian-Habsburg union in the Low Countries thus had the lasting effect of forming two states, artificially separated after 1585, which have since traveled further down their sundered paths, confessionally separated by the imposed predominance of Catholicism in the south and Calvinism in the north. One unmistakable consequence of this association of principalities, still independent of one another around 1380, under a single ruler was to keep this densely populated and prosperous territory, situated at the mouths of three great rivers, from being annexed by one of the powers surrounding it: France, England, and the German Empire.

The formation of the Burgundian state was a success owing largely to the shrewd manipulation of international politics and diplomacy on the part of the dukes, but this success was equally indebted to a well-considered domestic policy. However, the Burgundian dynastic triumph was achieved at the expense of many local and regional interests. Although the relationship between prince and subjects revealed a considerable number of common interests, it also laid bare an equal number of tensions.[2]

The time frame covered by this book is roughly 1369–1530, a period that we consider most illustrative of the Burgundian character of the Low Countries. In 1477 the heartland of the dynasty — the duchy of Burgundy — was detached from the union, and in that same year occurred the accession of the Habsburg dynasty. What remained — the Low Countries — had, meanwhile, evolved into a union sufficiently cohesive to survive this change of dynasty and diplomatic orientation without loss of identity. By 1530 the Spanish and imperial character of Charles V's dominion over the Low Countries had established itself so firmly that the memory of a Burgundian identity dwindled, and thus it ceases to be a meaningful focus for study.

But even during the first stages of the Seventeen Provinces' rebellion against the Spanish crown, many of the essential characteristics of Burgundian–Low Countries society were still very much in evidence, and its political structures remained functional. During the Burgundian period, the Low Countries surpassed the rest of Europe, with the exception of northern Italy, on both a cultural and economic level. It is the purpose of this book to describe and clarify the relation between that cultural and economic development and the political evolution of the region under the dukes of Burgundy.

The book is the work of two authors, celebrating more than thirty years of collaboration on the research topics treated here, first as teacher and student, later as colleagues. We have arrived at a fully shared vision of the subject of this book and have critically examined each others' chapters. Because of our different specialties, Chapters 1–4 were originally written by Walter Prevenier and Chapters 5–9 by Wim Blockmans. Our individual differences in style and emphasis will be less apparent in this English version, and we hope that the work as a whole expresses the vision of the Burgundian Low Countries that we both share.

Chapter 9, new paragraphs, and shorter additions have been written during the last year of this book's long genesis. These have been translated by Isola van der Hoven-Vardon, whose refined mastery of English and Dutch and historical interest made the new work very pleasant.

The authors wish to express their deep gratitude to Professor Ed Peters, who encouraged them to pursue the American edition of this work. He saw the need for an up-to-date overview, in English, of politics and society of the Burgundian Low Countries, in addition to the all-time classic that Johan Huizinga's *The Waning of the Middle Ages* is and will remain. Ed's painstaking efforts to restructure and reformulate the Dutch book in view of the needs of a foreign audience, and his additions and suggestions reshaped the text into a fairly new format.[3] His endeavors testify to deep friendship as well as a great intellectual spirit.

The Dynasties of the Burgundian Low Countries

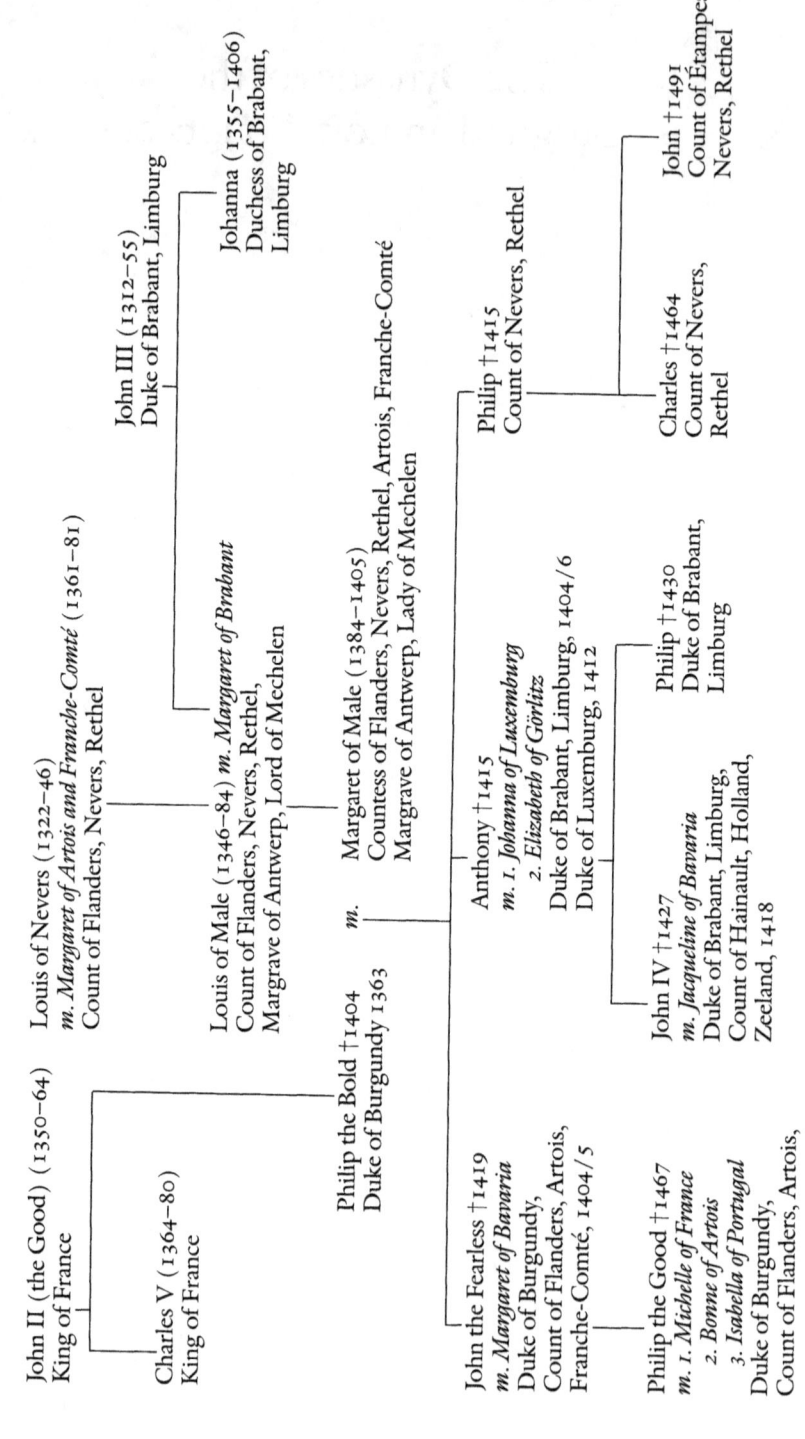

Franche-Comté,
Count of Namur 1429,
Duke of Brabant, Limburg 1430,
Count of Hainault, Holland,
Zeeland, 1427/1433,
Duke of Luxemburg 1443/51

Charles the Bold †1477
m. 1. *Catherine of France*
   2. *Isabella of Bourbon*
   3. *Margaret of York*
Same titles as Philip the Good,
with the addition of Duke of Lorraine,
Guelders 1473

Mary of Burgundy †1482
m. *Maximilian of Habsburg*,
Advocate and regent until 1493

Philip the Fair †1506
m. *Juana of Castile*
Ruler of the Netherlands, 1493
King of Castile, 1505/06

Margaret of Austria †1530
m. 1. *Charles of France*
   2. *Juan of Castile*
   3. *Philibert of Savoy*
Regent of the Low Countries (1507–15, 1517–30)

Charles V †1558

I

Perspectives on the Burgundian Dynasty in the Low Countries

When the story of the Burgundian Netherlands began in 1369, the "foreigner" Philip the Bold, son of the late French king John II and brother of the reigning king Charles V, had only six years earlier been named duke of Burgundy and first peer of France by his father. Now in 1369 he married Margaret, the only daughter and sole heiress of Louis of Male, count of Flanders. Margaret brought more in her dowry than the prospect of the territories ruled by her father—wealthy Flanders, Rethel, and the cities of Antwerp and Mechelen, the latter a seigneury enclaved in the adjacent duchy of Brabant but under Flemish rule since 1357. In addition, Margaret brought other territories bordering on both Flanders and Burgundy: the counties of Artois and the Franche-Comté and the county of Nevers, then ruled jointly by Louis of Male and his mother, Margaret of Artois. The marriage, of course, had been arranged for political purposes, by the respective families and by the French king. The prospects of drawing Burgundy and Flanders closer together—and closer to the French crown—appealed to both.

Louis of Male, with a French prince at his side as son-in-law, now stood in a strong position in the face of his arrogant Flemish cities, whose rebellious attitudes toward their counts had troubled Flanders throughout the fourteenth century. The king of France already envisioned his younger brother as the ruler of Flanders, a territorial principality that was nominally under French rule but had always been difficult to control. In addition, Flanders was economically prosperous and, consequently, fiscally attractive to the French royal treasury. On optimistic days the king tended to refer to it as a French conquest, as his predecessor Philip IV the Fair had done in 1301.[1]

In 1369, however, Philip the Bold, duke of Burgundy, was still only the son-in-law of the count of Flanders, an ambitious stranger with high hopes, ruler in Burgundy of the first in the hierarchy of French principalities. Yet Burgundy was still a largely agrarian and lightly urbanized territory, famed otherwise only for its wine. For all the splendor of the wedding feast of 1369 and the formal expressions of delight from all in attendance, Philip's prospects were still only prospects. The title to the county could not be instantly conjured out of the dower chest, since Louis of Male appeared in the pink of health. The marriage was only the first tentative scene in a play, the rest of whose script had not yet been written or even imagined.

Not even the next scene was clear, as servants removed the remains of pheasants and barrels empty of the heady Beaune wine (Burgundy's most important product) from the tables in the palace at Ghent on June 19, 1369. Might Duke Philip not prove merely a pawn of his illustrious and intelligent royal brother? As a young knight he had, indeed, so distinguished himself by his courage against the English on the battlefield of Poitiers in 1356 that thenceforth he had been known as the Bold. Might he, then, see every contact of the Flemish cities with England, even those of a purely economic character, as collaboration with France's archenemy? Or might Philip view himself as the lord of a new composite of territories, Burgundy-Flanders, which would further antagonize the independence-minded Flemish cities? Would and could he keep Flanders out of the turmoil of the Anglo-French war? Flanders had been a battlefield of that war more than once and had no interest in becoming one again. Radical sympathizers of the old anti-comital and Anglophile party, which dated from the heyday of the revolt under the leadership of Ghent's popular leader James van Artevelde in 1338–1345, probably still dreamed of forming a series of independent city-republics after the contemporary north Italian model. Throughout the history of the Burgundian Netherlands, Ghent remained the most volatile and rebellious of the Flemish cities.

Practical politicians among the Flemings acknowledged that there would be life after Louis of Male. They felt that their commercial interests would be best served by the continuity of the Flemish dynasty, even if it was now Valois-French in the male line, as long as it gave priority to the vital interests of the Flemish economy and respected urban autonomy, as well as the many privileges gained or extorted by the Flemings from their counts over the centuries. For its part, the new dynasty might consort with either the French or the English, as long as it ensured political and economic home rule in the county of Flanders.

Today, in our knowledge of the outcome of these possible scenarios, we may lose sight of the real uncertainty about the future that faced all the participants of the events of 1369. None of them could know that this marriage was to result in a sweeping process of unification that brought the whole of the Low Countries under a single crown and homogenized much of its institutional organization and culture, nor could they foresee that for generations this new dynasty would strive vigorously and sometimes successfully to create an evermore centralizing and unifying state. There was no way of predicting that in the first decades of the sixteenth century, this state would be absorbed into a yet greater whole — the far-flung empire of the direct successor to the dukes, the Habsburg emperor Charles V. Born in Ghent, Charles was to couple the Netherlands with the German (or Holy Roman) Empire, the crowns of Spain, and the New World. But even after it had been absorbed into the German and then the Spanish Habsburg empires, and in spite of the waxing power of the centralizing institutions of those empires and their rulers, the cities of the Burgundian Netherlands would continue to stamp their own mark firmly on the economy, on politics, on social structures, and on culture throughout the Low Countries.

In the first great age of northern European painting, in which the Burgundian Low Countries took pride of place, every picture depicted somewhere in the background a proud city hall, a town belfry, a tidy and ship-filled harbor, a great urban church, or, at the very least, a shop-lined street scene. These images gave the onlooker or the patron who had commissioned the painting a wondrously comforting feeling of recognition, by conjuring a world in which grand and often miraculous events out of the past were realistically located in a familiar landscape or townscape, where anyone might hope to attain wealth and status sufficient to commission and pay for such works of art. The works of the great Flemish painters were not the least important achievements of the world of the Burgundian Low Countries.

The Burgundian Low Countries were not brought into existence as a state by a single centralizing vision or a common cultural heritage. Both the dukes and the cities strove after 1369 to pursue their own goals. No single party determined the rest of the story. The princes and their dynastic ambitions and adventures tend to attract our attention first, since the scope of their ambitions, their notions of statecraft, and their strategies of unification were the most dynamic and successful of those of any European state. But even the dukes did not act alone. Major decisions always required that the duke consult with his seasoned courtiers, judicial and financial advisers, and ambassadors, who themselves did not necessarily share the same vision of life or of the state.

Nor was *subjects* a homogeneous category. The term was a collective name for Flemings, Brabanters, Hollanders, Zeelanders, Hennuyers (the population of Hainault), Artesians (residents of Artois), and Burgundians, and eventually for the people of Guelders, Liège, Groningen, and Utrecht as well. Within each of these territories, the term *subject* denoted a broad spectrum of social groups — nobles, clerics, farmers, petty landholders, farm laborers, wealthy burghers, textile and other craft workers, highly specialized craftspeople, and the poor supported by charity. These social differences created tangled, ever-shifting coalitions as well as recurring feuds and conflicts of interest.[2] The subjects of the dukes of Burgundy thus had their own frames of reference and quite diverse sentiments. They might, indeed, be prepared to submit to a certain degree of "burgundianization," but only when they saw it to their advantage to do so. They were equally prepared to resist and revolt, should they no longer be convinced that burgundianization still served their interests. With great ingenuity and equally great difficulty, these groups had, over time, devised systems of dispute settlement, mechanisms involving careful agreements as to the precise division of power and influence in their localities. Social harmony, to the extent that it existed, was achieved through agreements between employers and organized craftsmen. A form of social control was achieved by reserving assistance to the poor and creating social safety nets for those marginal parts of the population who were prepared to conform in their social conduct and to respect ecclesiastical rituals and the prevailing morality. The "Holy Ghost Tables," institutions that provided food for the deserving poor in the Flemish cities, represent one striking aspect of care for the poor.[3]

For both groups, the history of the century and a half following 1369 was one of temporary successes, compromises, and defeats. The most prominent participants were always in the foreground: the dukes and their counselors, the ambitious, proud, and wealthy urban merchant-politicians, the nobility. But even those well below these exalted social levels had a substantial role to play. The population of the Low Countries stood at 2.5 million in the fifteenth century, besides that of northern Italy the densest in Europe.[4] Such a large population brought with it problems of food supply and support for the needy that were far larger and more compelling than in most other European territories. These numerous and densely settled masses were a potential threat upon the occasion of any failure in the complex international economy that sustained them. Social control could not always be expected to work as its designers intended.

The peasant farmers had to exercise all their energy and ingenuity to extract the maximum from their land. Their very intensive and sophisticated agricultural techniques allowed the Low Countries to require only two farmers for each city dweller, as compared with three or four for each city dweller elsewhere in Europe. The massive imports of grain, chiefly from Artois and the Baltic regions, were still necessary to supplement the produce of Low Country agriculture, especially in years with lean harvests. Near the cities many varieties of vegetables were grown, as well as crops with purely industrial uses, including those used for the production of dyes and cloth. These rural populations were also so remarkably prolific—considering that they stood in proportion to the urban population at about 2 : 3 to 1 : 2 in the rest of Europe—that they consistently created a surplus rural population that then flowed into the cities, where a higher mortality rate made fresh blood desirable (indeed, a necessity) for maintaining an urban labor force. That labor force produced textiles and luxury products that were eagerly sought, from Königsberg in East Prussia and relatively nearby London to far-off Genoa and the ports of the Levant. But the rural population surpluses were achieved in the face of a capricious nature that could strike unexpectedly with crop failure or epidemic disease, especially plague. At the other end of the social scale, the ruling dynasty and the rest of the nobility were also vulnerable. There might be too many surviving children to provide for, or not enough children to carry on the line. A random accident might kill off a particular prince unexpectedly, or he might be cut down by a successful assassination.

In many respects, the prosperous towns and principalities on the golden delta of the great northern rivers might accurately be called the promised lands, the *terres de promission*, as the later court historian Philippe de Commynes termed them, on which the rest of Europe gazed with envy.[5] But in 1369 their promise was yet to be fulfilled. The "Great Duchy of the West" had yet to be created.

* * *

The future of the participants in the marriage celebrations of June 1369—the Flemings, their count and future countess, and the duke of Burgundy—and that of their descendants was also shaped by the circumstances that had originally brought them together.

From its earliest recorded territorial existence in the ninth century, Flanders, except for one small district east of the Scheldt known as Imperial Flanders, had owed its allegiance to the rulers of what became the kingdom of France. That kingdom had grown out of the disintegration of the Carolingian Empire. From the ashes of that empire, there arose eventually not only the two great kingdoms of France and Germany, but also a large number of smaller principalities located between them, such as the counties of Flanders, Holland, and Hainault, the duchy of Brabant, and the prince-bishopric of Liège. With the exception of Flanders and neighboring Artois, these all fell politically under the German king-emperors, by the late tenth and eleventh centuries as parts of the duchy of Lower Lorraine. But the bonds that held these territories under their respective royal rulers were more often chiefly juridical and theoretical in nature, leaving them considerable freedom to devise an autonomous foreign policy, their own specific administrative apparatus, and, above all, their own vigorous economic systems.[6] Only the power derived from their high level of economic and cultural development and the weakness or distraction of their nominal rulers allowed the principalities of the Low Countries such quasi independence.

They lay at the heart of a part of Europe that had already produced, even in the Carolingian period, an active trade and a universally respected culture. A highly developed center of metalwork flourished in the Maas region, especially at Dinant. Masterpieces of Romanesque and later Gothic church building arose in the Scheldt valley, and in thirteenth-century Brabant, William of Moerbeke began to turn the works of Aristotle into the foundation of the new scholastic philosophy. The metalwork of Liège[7] and the luxury textiles of Flanders, Artois, and Brabant reached a European public through their overland links with the oldest and most fertile of expanding commercial centers, Italy.[8] The yearly fairs of Champagne (at the halfway point between Flanders and Italy) grew into privileged and prosperous occasions for meetings and trade between Italy and the Low Countries.[9] In 1277, the first of the Genoese Atlantic galleys sailed out of the Mediterranean and then through the English Channel into the North Sea and moored at the Flemish city of Sluis, the outport of Bruges. Bruges began its career as the new hub of international trade between northern and southern Europe.

Bruges rapidly developed an open banking system for the benefit of those Italian and north German merchants, the latter organized since 1356 into the trade association known as the Hansa, who brought products from German territories as well as from Lithuania, Prussia, and Scandinavia.[10] Italians and Spaniards arrived in Flanders to sell Mediterranean wares, returning with cargoes of luxury products from the Low Countries. Bruges opened the first stock exchange in Europe in a house next door to the *loggia*, or residence, of the Genoese merchants. The centrality of the Flemish cities to the trade of both northern and southern Europe led to a precocious concentration of population in such cities as Ghent, with about 64,000 people around 1356, and Bruges, with 46,000.[11] These were, after Paris, the largest cities in Europe north of the Alps. The grand scale of Flemish urbanization spurred these cities to construct elaborate physical fabrics—impressive buildings for public use, ambitious urban churches, well-paved streets and squares, an impressive urban infrastructure of houses, markets, and water supply, proud halls, and massive roofed markets with tall belfries, like those that can be seen today in Bruges and Ypres. All these gave material expression to an emerging urban consciousness.

The Flemish cities, however, differed fundamentally from the contemporary northern Italian city-republics in that the counts of Flanders always remained in place as the ruling power. From the vigorous eleventh-century counts and the assassinated Charles the Good (1127) to the later more or less independently acting dynasties that succeeded them, the counts of Flanders asserted their ultimate authority in the political affairs of their principality continually, if not always successfully. Even the most Francophile and Franco-obligated of the counts remained conscious of their unique position in Flanders. So, eventually, did their Burgundian successors.

How strong a sense of unity existed in the societies of the various territories of the Low Countries during the thirteenth and fourteenth centuries? In general in Europe before the nineteenth century, groups tended to identify themselves first and foremost on a local level. One belonged primarily to a village or town community (or even to a subcommunity in a village or town), and was only more vaguely the inhabitant of a seigneury, county, or duchy. Moreover, the rulers and their subjects were linked by ties of personal loyalty, and, at least nominally, affection. These were usually formalized during the inauguration ceremonies of the rulers and sometimes in conjunction with the occasions known as the Blijde Inkomst, Joyeuse Entrée—the Joyous Entry—the formal entries of rulers into territories and cities. On these occasions, in each territory the ruler swore an oath to respect and protect the rights, privileges, and customs of his subjects, whereupon they, in turn, swore to serve him faithfully. Rulers who swore these oaths might even be considered the natural rulers, the *natuurlijke prinsen*, of these territories, even though they had been born and raised elsewhere.

The subjects themselves had no concept of a united state of the Low Countries. In the more urbanized and commercialized territories, there were intensive trade and financial relations that fostered a certain community of interests. There were also contrasts, such as those between town and country and between producer and consumer. Furthermore, such primarily rural territories as Namur and Luxemburg were considerably less well-integrated into the interregional economic system. Nor was there any linguistic unity: French dialects were spoken in the most southerly regions and variants of Low German in the northern sections, but the linguistic frontier ran right through Flanders, Brabant, Liège, and Luxemburg. The lack of linguistic unity did not create problems for the inhabitants, but problems did arise as soon as the Burgundian dukes made vigorous attempts to generalize the use of their French language in their official relations with their subjects.

Instead of the question of any political unity in the Low Countries, there was rather a heated rivalry among them. Louis of Male, count of Flanders (1346–1384), followed by his son-in-law Philip the Bold (1384–1404), was the most ambitious ruler in the Low Countries, and his county was the richest and most populous. But his rivals could also call upon substantial assets and forces. All of them engaged in military struggles, disputing one another's territorial claims. They concluded temporary and opportunistic alliances among themselves, often in the most capricious manner possible. With boundless cynicism they entered into continually shifting coalitions with foreign powers, in order to checkmate each other while safeguarding their own independence vis-à-vis other foreign powers. They all had to reckon with resistance from within, on the part of subjects with an acute awareness of any sign of princely weakness, demanding a greater voice and more respect for their traditions and privileges.

* * *

A brief survey of the situation of the Low Countries during the decade 1350–60 in the larger context of the great war between England and France may illuminate the problems faced by any ambitious and aggressive prince in the region in the late fourteenth century.

From the twelfth century on, the Low Countries, especially their southern parts, depended upon relative tranquillity among the neighboring great powers with which they usually traded. Even an apparently accidental and temporary troubling of that tranquillity might signal larger consequences. In 1273, for example, an English embargo disrupted the export of English raw wool to Flanders. It seemed only a momentary setback, but it heralded real troubles.[12] A new Anglo-French war that grew out of conditions that had nothing to do with Flanders caused a structural perturbation of trade routes starting in 1294, and it proved a lasting hindrance to the free trade on which the Flemings depended. In the years 1315–1317, Europe was subjected to a grain shortage and a terrible famine.[13] Population growth had caused too much marginal land to be put to agricultural use, and when that land failed, the consequences were felt throughout Europe, nowhere more than in import-dependent Flanders. At the same time, financially strapped French kings began to manipulate the metallic content of their currency, which disrupted monetary stability. Finally, in 1348–1350, the plague known as the Black Death caused such a panic as Europe had never known.[14] Demographic growth came to an abrupt halt after 1350, because of recurring outbreaks of the plague.[15]

The universal powers of the early fourteenth century were in no position to help. The papacy traditionally acknowledged a calling toward a universal role in European affairs, and prior to 1300, the popes were able to realize these ambitions, to some extent, by spreading the moral message of the Church, its charismatic and pastoral approach, and its intellectual and legal institutions. But in a series of disputed papal elections, the residence of the popes in Avignon from 1305 to 1376, the great Schism of 1378–1415, and papal conflicts with temporal powers led to local churches' looking more toward their kings than to the popes, and to the beginnings of "national" churches and the reduction of the temporal authority of the popes. In the German lands most effective imperial authority had disappeared, and political life and political ambitions had shrunk to the individual horizons of the four hundred principalities and city-states. Italy had an alluring economic potential but was politically divided into prosperous territorial states content to plant colonies in the Levant and on the Dalmatian coast, without great concern for the political troubles of northwestern Europe.

There remained England and France, both fully occupied with the construction of strong central states around London and Paris, administered uniformly through a network of judicial and financial technocrats, ideologically supported on the respective bases of English common law and Roman law.[16] Included in that process of construction were territorial integration and expansion into zones of influence, which they disputed. These lay on the northern borders and in the southwest of France, where the trouble spots were Aquitaine and Guyenne, which had fallen into the hands of the English king Henry II through his marriage in 1152 to the heiress Eleanor of Aquitaine. Notwithstanding the treaty of 1258 between Henry III and St. Louis, Guyenne remained a perennial source of conflict between the two crowns.[17] The confiscation of Guyenne by the French king Philip VI in 1337 led directly to the commencement of English military operations and to the start of the Hundred Years' War between the two monarchies, a war that did not end until 1453.[18] In this protracted conflict, the kings strove with variable success to gain influence over the county of Flanders. The Flemish cities, despite their allegiance to the king of France, resisted the French to such an extent that in 1340, they actually recognized the English king as their ruler.

The opening of the war against the background of economic and social disasters of the first half of the fourteenth century had great internal impact on the Low Countries. Monetary instability led to years of social tension over prices and wages in a largely wage economy. Different social groups also turned against each other in rivalry over local political power or against the magistrates in office and the prince, who were held accountable for everything that went amiss in the community and its fortunes. The magistrates and the princes were kept occupied with maintaining domestic control rather than foreign expansion. On occasion, this required all of their energy and resources as well as outside help. For example, the regime of Count Louis of Nevers of Flanders (1322–1346) faced a revolt in maritime Flanders in 1323–1328, sought the support of the French king, and then faced a revolt in Ghent that placed the popular leader James van Artevelde in power from 1338 to 1345 and swung Ghent temporarily toward an alliance with the English. The Ghent revolt was not forgotten, and not only in Flanders. In 1358 revolutionary fervor in Paris was stirred by Etienne Marcel, who adopted the war cry "Gand!" (Ghent) to remind his followers of the broad popular front that van Artevelde had been able to rally against the count in Ghent some twenty years earlier.[20]

Against this background, we may consider conditions in the Low Countries in the years 1350–60. Next to Flanders, the Avesnes dynasty that ruled the neighboring counties of Hainault and Holland-Zeeland undoubtedly enjoyed the most support from outside its own territory. This dynasty was also linked to the duchy of Bavaria, and this lent it prestige, connections, and an additional means of exercising power. In 1345 the male line of the Avesnes dynasty died out in Hainault. The eldest sister of the deceased count, Margaret, who was married to the German emperor Louis of Bavaria of the house of Wittelsbach (1314–1346), declared herself a candidate for the office of countess of Hainault, Holland, and Zeeland. The great powers and the neighboring principalities, alarmed at the prospect of the Wittelsbach dynasty intruding to such an extent, intrigued to prevent Margaret's succession. The opposition was particularly strong in Holland, and Margaret had to content herself with Hainault, reluctantly leaving Holland and Zeeland to her son William V, who succeeded her in Hainault upon her own death in 1356. Margaret's Wittelsbach support had vanished with the death of her husband, Louis, in 1346 and the rise of the rival Luxemburg dynasty to the imperial title. When Albert of Bavaria succeeded his mentally ill brother William V in 1358 as regent of Hainault, Holland, and Zeeland, he wisely decided against relinquishing his position as duke in Bavaria. The additional title lent him a much-needed psychological advantage over his restive subjects.[21]

The emperor Charles IV of Luxemburg (1347–1378), whose own dynasty had originated in the Low Countries, established a new imperial connection, this time with Brabant. Charles arranged a marriage between his brother Wenceslaus and Joan, eldest daughter of Duke John III of Brabant. As a matter of her own security, Margaret of Hainault now entered an alliance with both Brabant and the emperor. Charles IV himself did little, however, in either territory, because he was fully occupied with military operations on his own eastern borders and with building his great capital city of Prague. But Charles's assistance was not needed. One by one, Joan's brothers predeceased her, and Brabant passed to Joan and Wenceslaus in 1355. The occasion of Joan's and her foreign consort Wenceslaus's Blijde Inkomst, or Joyous Entry, into Brabant in 1356 reminded the Brabanters of the need to obtain a guarantee of respect for their own governmental institutions, and they elicited from the couple a charter that exacted from them firm principles of participation and control by representatives of their subjects.[22] Neighboring powers soon took advantage of what they understood to be a sign of weakness. In 1356 the count of Flanders marched into Brabant at the head of an army to enforce his own claims on the Brabant inheritance.[23] The count of Hainault also played a treacherous role in the proceedings by first supporting the existing agreement with Brabant, only to succumb to Flemish advances, even helping to negotiate the Treaty of Ath, favorable to Flanders, in June of 1357. By the terms of this treaty, Louis of Male acquired the cities of Antwerp and Mechelen (later parts of Louis of Male's daughter Margaret of Flanders's dowry), a heavy blow to the purse of Joan and Wenceslaus, since these cities were the most dynamic trade centers of their new duchy. Moreover, they were most reluctantly forced to recognize the succession rights of Margaret of Male to the whole of Brabant in the event that they died childless. Duchess Joan indeed remained childless, and her domestic authority crumbled even further in the wake of revolts in several of her cities. Brabant became an obvious target when Philip the Bold and Margaret succeeded to the county of Flanders in 1384.[24]

Neighboring princes had little to fear from Liège, a principality ruled by its bishop. Between 1331 and 1343, Prince-Bishop Adolph of Mark greatly provoked his subjects with his authoritarian policies. When Adolph died in 1345, the new bishop, Englebert of Mark, suffered a humiliating defeat at the hands of the citizens of Liège and Huy at Vottem in 1346. Once again internal signs of weakness were exploited by outside powers. The duke of Brabant immediately seized the city of St. Truiden. Englebert was forced to look on powerlessly in 1347 when the craftsmen of Liège, with their old privileges restored to them after Vottem, concluded a treaty of their own with the cities of Brabant. In the following decades, representative institutions were able to extend their political influence considerably at the expense of the central authority.[25]

* * *

Compared with these neighbors and rivals with their varied strengths and weaknesses, the Flemish count Louis of Male was in relatively good shape. Yet he, too, met with considerable resistance from his subjects. Since around 1297, a large portion of the Flemish population had favored a political coalition with England. They did so in part to counter the threat, real at the time, of outright annexation directly by the French king, but chiefly to safeguard their supply of English wool, the basic raw material for the Flemish textile industry.[26] The Flemish counts in the first decades of the fourteenth century had originally followed this course of action. But the revolts of 1323–1328 and the violent excesses of the radical weavers' party in Ghent during and after the revolt of van Artevelde in 1338–1345 led to a moderate trade agreement with England in 1338 and considerable support for the pacification policy of the new count, Louis of Male.[27] In its first phase, Louis's pacification policy achieved a degree of domestic peace in Ghent by granting the weavers a degree of political power in a new type of city government that, through proportional representation, maintained a balance between the various social groups. This domestic peace gave the count a free hand for the second phase of his program, in which he played the foreign powers off against each other by an opportunistic strategy designed to keep Flanders peaceful and out of the war.[28]

Within the Low Countries Louis was even able, through his shrewd manipulation of political and dynastic opportunities, to implement the policy of expansion that we have seen operate so successfully in Brabant, notably through the acquisition of Antwerp and Mechelen and the designation of his daughter Margaret as heir apparent of the duchy of Brabant. But his most spectacular diplomatic triumph was over England and France. Louis of Male had seen his father's unconditionally pro-French policy fail totally, and he had also realized the economic importance of good relations with England. He made peace with England as early as 1348. Then he began a more complicated game of playing the two powers off against each other. In 1351 he began negotiating an English marriage for his daughter Margaret, purely as a means of putting pressure on France. His strategem worked, because in 1355 Margaret married Philip of Rouvres, duke of Burgundy. When Philip died suddenly in 1361, Louis again opened negotiations, again first with England, arranging a marriage with the fourth son of Edward III, Edmund of Langley, then earl of Cambridge and later duke of York. For two years Louis of Male held the English king in suspense while he awaited a French offer. In 1364 Edward III offered Louis very attractive prospects of succession to Calais and to the nearby counties of Ponthieu and Guines, and even to Hainault-Holland, to which Edward III had a claim through his mother. But the pope, under pressure from the French, refused to grant the necessary dispensation for the marriage of the too closely related Flemish bride and English groom. Louis of Male did nothing to overcome this objection, since he had already planned a bold new scenario. For three years, from 1366 to 1369, he gave the French king time to come up with a counteroffer. He succeeded, reaching an agreement on April 12, 1369, by which Louis promised his daughter to the new duke of Burgundy, Philip the Bold, brother of the French king, on the condition that Walloon Flanders (consisting of the southern castellanies of Lille, Douai, and Orchies), lost to the county since 1305, be restored.[29] The marriage was duly and joyfully celebrated at Ghent on June 19, 1369.

In 1369 Philip the Bold's prospects indeed looked bright. His father-in-law was seated more firmly in the domestic saddle in Flanders than were his rivals in Hainault-Holland and Brabant, and he even had hopes of succession in Brabant. The succession to these prospects was now open to the ambitious young duke of Burgundy. He had worked very hard and had considerable good luck to acquire it.

2

A New European Power in the Making
1363–1405

Philip the Bold, a French Prince

Philip, later called the Bold, the fourth son of King John II of France and Bonne of Luxemburg, was born at Pontoise on January 17, 1342.[1] Although not expected to succeed to the throne, Philip, like any royal son, was expected to excel in military affairs and to demonstrate administrative competence, diplomatic ability, and cultural refinement. Training in these was readily available at the court of John II, and Philip appears to have made the most of it. John II was widely regarded as a model of the ideal of royal knighthood, and the French royal court was as good a place as any for a prince without expectation of succession to the crown to develop those skills that the crown could call into royal service.

But John II's interest in the complex rules of chivalric warfare did not serve him well when the Anglo-French war broke out with renewed ferocity in 1355. The most formal "rules" of chivalric warfare demanded that battles be fought on a "playing field" agreed upon by both parties well in advance, and rules of engagement were strict. Impulsive, heroic, and picturesque actions by individual knights were valued over the tactical deployment of massed troops, and degrees of proper respect were to be shown to victorious or defeated opponents. John was a mediocre strategist in any case, and the English had already developed new military tactics, though they, too, acknowledged the responsibilities of noble combatants. The first disaster of these competing styles of combat occurred in the battle of Crécy in 1346 and was repeated at the battle of Poitiers, on September 19, 1356, to which John II had brought the fourteen-year-old Philip. Both father and son displayed great personal courage, but they lost the battle. "*Mon père, regardez à gauche, regardez à droite!*" (Father, look to the left, look to the right!) Philip is reported to have warned his father in the heat of battle, but the English led them both away, to be held for ransom at Windsor during a long captivity.

Philip's courage in the field was acknowledged by the nickname the Bold, which he won at Poitiers. The appellation later served his reputation well, but he never took to warfare with quite the enthusiasm of his father. Although he later took part in some half-dozen battles, military life did not really suit him. In August 1369 near Calais, for example, entrusted with the command of an army assembled to invade England, Philip encountered a numerically inferior English force led by John of Gaunt. Rather than take advantage of his superior strength, Philip proposed a chivalric duel on a specified battlefield, but at the last moment he retreated even from this pseudobattle. He later encouraged many tournaments, indicating that he preferred war as theater rather than as massed combat.

Philip and his father were ransomed and released from English captivity in 1360. As a reward for his heroism and companionship, Philip received from his father the duchy of Touraine, thus becoming formally a royal vassal. In 1363 he exchanged this modest duchy for the lieutenant-generalship of Burgundy, and later in the year for the ducal title of Burgundy, more prestigious than that of Touraine. Burgundy had escheated to the crown of France in 1361 upon the death of its last Capetian duke, Philip of Rouvres, ending a dynastic line that had ruled the duchy since 1032. The king of France might simply have retained Burgundy, but instead he chose to give it as an *apanage* to his son Philip. In the fourteenth century the apanages were fiefs that usually were given to royal male children, under the condition that they would revert to the crown if the family should die out in the male line. This did occur, eventually, in the case of Burgundy, but not until 1477, when then-king Louis XI denied the duchy to the only heir, Mary of Burgundy (see Chapter 7). As long as the duchy remained an apanage, however, the king could expect and exert indirect control over the region, while giving its inhabitants the illusion of at least partial autonomy. This practice was also used elsewhere in the kingdom, especially in border areas, the idea being to provide the various members of the royal family with administrative experience that could prove useful in royal service, while at the same time assuring the king of the loyalty of a close family member ruling a distant territory. The idea usually worked, at least for the first generation. The apanages were, obviously, not intended to encourage any vassal to build up a personal regime independent of the crown, but this is what Philip the Bold did.

In 1364 John II died at the age of forty-five, and Philip's older brother Charles V (1364–1380) succeeded to the French crown. Charles confirmed Philip's titles, including that of lieutenant-general of Burgundy. Charles and Philip seem to have gotten on well together, for throughout his reign, the new king called upon Philip for assistance in all major affairs of state, both domestic and foreign. This mutual trust was based, no doubt, upon a series of shared character traits, both negative and positive. Neither Charles nor Philip was enchanted by the clatter of weapons (Charles never participated in a single military campaign). Both were fascinated by the ideological foundations of state authority and by the practical and effective exercise of power through personal charm and astute diplomacy. They both took pleasure in associating with intellectuals and artists.

Immediately upon his accession and within the framework of his defense policy, Charles V added to Philip's responsibilities the supervision of the territories of the bishoprics of Lyon, Mâcon, Autun, Chalon, and Langres. In 1366 Charles granted Philip authority over Champagne, and in 1369 over Picardy. Shortly after, Charles began negotiating a marriage for Philip, bidding for the niece of the king of Hungary in 1365, and for the daughter of Galeazzo Visconti, Prince of Pavia, in 1367. In 1369 he finally succeeded in arranging a marriage with Margaret of Male, the only daughter of the count of Flanders, which gave Philip the prospect of inheriting this rich and unstable principality. All of Charles's marriage plans fit neatly into the framework of royal diplomatic strategy, and Charles must have believed that what was good for Philip was good for France: a stronger Burgundian-Flemish union under a French prince was a means of securing a firmer hold over the French northern frontier territories.[2] The king was even prepared to cede Walloon (French-speaking) Flanders, which had been directly ruled by the French crown since 1312, to the current Flemish count Louis of Male as the price for this desirable marriage. Philip, the potential heir, swore two secret oaths: one to Charles V that Walloon Flanders would be restored to France after the death of his father-in-law, the other to Louis of Male that it would not.[3] Philip, even at this early stage in his career, could thus act without scruples both as a loyal French prince and as a territorial lord who anticipated standing on his own. In 1369 he probably assumed that he had enough time that he would have to deliver on only one or the other of these promises. As things turned out, he was right.

Philip's activities nominally in the service of France also reflect this mixture of loyalty and self-interest, on the one hand, and his skillful use of pomp and ceremony on the other. In 1375, at the request of his brother and to impress the English, Philip brought to Bruges a splendid company of councillors, courtiers, and minstrels. He brought tapestries that were works of art to please the eye and provide better acoustics, famed vintages from Beaune to loosen tongues and render spirits more malleable, and tournament performers to demonstrate chivalric ideals.[4] In 1376, Philip, also at the request of Charles V, attempted to persuade Pope Gregory XI not to desert Avignon for Rome. Characteristically, he sailed down the Rhône to Avignon with thirty-six casks of wine and many delicacies in his baggage to bestow as gifts on key papal advisers. The Avignon mission was clearly in the French interest, but the English mission at Bruges in 1375–1377 was in both the French and the Flemish interests. The Avignon mission failed, but the English mission, at least, led to a temporary truce, if not to the enduring solution that Charles V had wished for. It is difficult to know how enthusiastically Philip acted in these cases, in the light of his own self-interest. At the same time, Philip lent support in 1375–1376 to a number of pretenders to rulership outside of France — the Viscontis in the duchy of Milan and Prince Ladislas in the kingdom of Poland. This support also may reflect his own, rather than France's interest.

Philip's political persona was also shaped by the intellectual climate of the French court in which he lived and worked. Charles V was in many ways the model Philip most admired. It was not often that a king of France turned out to be an intellectual and an aesthete, fond of beautiful manuscripts illuminated by gifted miniaturists like the Fleming John of Bruges. Charles V was the first sovereign in the late Middle Ages to found a full-fledged royal library, organized and directed by a true librarian, with the express condition that it be maintained intact after his death. But Charles was not merely an artistic bibliophile; he was also fascinated with the contents of his manuscripts. The king read philosophers, such as William of Moerbeke, and astrologers, although his adviser Nicholas Oresme counseled against the latter. He read and listened to jurists, financial experts, Oresme (who also translated Aristotle into French for him), and the traveler and socially engaged thinker Philippe de Mézières. Together they provided him with the theoretical foundations for his vision of the state as a highly centralized polity (the word *politique* entered the French language during Charles's reign) with a powerful monarch who, nevertheless, ought to rule in harmony with and affection for his subjects, and who must learn to distinguish his affairs as a private person from his public responsibilities. This was a principle that had hitherto rarely been espoused by medieval kings.[5]

Charles also served as the model of the ideal administrator for Philip: he ensured a sturdier financial base for the monarchy by creating "extraordinary" finances alongside the traditional taxes and demesne income of the crown.[6] Although he was no soldier, he realized the implications of the fact that the long conflict with England was no longer war as it had been in his father's and grandfather's day, and that new weapons and tactics were necessary, as well as fortifications adequate for the cities to withstand long sieges.

Diplomacy also became more professional, although this process had begun in the reign of Charles's illustrious predecessor, Philip IV the Fair (1285–1314).[7] Charles engaged jurists to examine the rights to the French crown that the French Valois and the English Plantagenets disputed, in order to combat point by point the Treaty of Brétigny of 1360, through which so many French territories had been lost. His jurists also had to show that the English king Edward III (1327–1389) was nothing but a brutal usurper. Charles's sending Philip on diplomatic missions to Avignon and Bruges reminds us of Philip's prominent role in Valois diplomacy.

Finally, Charles developed the social and cultural life of the French court as a model of how one could present the monarchy as an impressive show, what historians have come to call a theater state. The nature and exercise of the prince's authority was embodied in the rituals and solemnities of tournaments, banquets, and Joyous Entries, which gave both the average subject and the self-interested courtier a concrete visualization of the majesty of kingship. With the money, manpower, and courtly style of Charles V, Philip the Bold learned at court and in the course of diplomatic missions how to impress and outbluff a political or diplomatic opponent. His barrels of Beaune in Avignon and his minstrels in Bruges were his own resources, but he had learned to use them at the court of Charles V.

Territorial Ruler in Burgundy

The duchy awarded to Philip the Bold was the territorial outcome of a series of divisions of the old Frankish kingdom that had begun in 843. These divisions were not stabilized until 1032, by which date Burgundy had come to consist of two parts, the county of Burgundy (Franche-Comté, later the Franche-Comté of Burgundy), under the rule of the German king-emperors, and the duchy of Burgundy proper, under the kings of France.[8] In 1369 the Franche-Comté was ruled by Margaret of Artois and her son

Louis of Male, also, of course, count of Flanders. When Margaret died in 1382, Louis alone held the Franche-Comté, and when Louis himself died in 1384, Philip inherited in right of his wife, Margaret of Male.[9] The aggressive noble families of the Franche-Comté, not held in check by a strong central authority, had long taken an independent diplomatic line in regard to the neighboring French kingdom, even to the extent of maintaining good relations with its arch foe, the English. Their military operations disrupted the affairs of the neighboring duchy of Burgundy, itself also often disrupted by roaming armed "companies" of unemployed soldiers who had pillaged and plundered freely during truces in the war between England and France, since the death of Odo IV of Burgundy in 1349. Whatever degree of law and order remained in the two Burgundies necessarily emanated from Paris. King John II, who saw most problems in a military light, considered the appointment of Philip of Rouvres, and afterward of Philip the Bold in 1363, as a means of keeping the eastern border regions of his kingdom under his immediate control. But Philip the Bold's interests remained in Paris, rather than in his new duchy. In his first few years as duke, he spent less than four months of the year in Burgundy.[10]

Charles V steered a different course from that of his father, and Charles's new diplomatic approach suited Philip much better. At the request of the king, Philip undertook to negotiate with Margaret of Artois, countess of Franche-Comté, and with the turbulent and hostile nobility of the county. By July 1364, Philip had reached an agreement with the nobility, ratified in September of that year. Already wise in the tactics of diplomatic charm typical of the French court, Philip was able to sit down in January 1371 with the most rebellious of the nobles of Franche-Comté at a banquet in Auxonne, as if there had never been even the suspicion of earlier hostility between them. Once again the Beaune wines performed their service of rinsing away enmity.[11] Even the countess Margaret of Artois was won over by Philip. After his marriage to Margaret of Male in 1369, he completely won Margaret of Artois's trust, concluding a new peace treaty with her and with the count of Savoy, his neighbor to the south, in the same year.[12]

After 1369, with the succession in Flanders, Franche-Comté, Artois, Rethel, and Nevers (once attached to the duchy but separated in the thirteenth century and now in Margaret's dowry) as real possibilities, Philip the Bold must have felt himself as much (if not more) a potential territorial ruler as the king's lieutenant-general and duke. The territories he expected to acquire through Margaret certainly had, from a fiscal point of view, ten times the revenues of the Burgundian lands. Moreover, his ducal function in Burgundy was his first confrontation with subjects of his own. Philip now seized the opportunity to put to the test the ideas and practices he had learned in France under Charles V. After 1363 Philip the Bold was a prince learning his trade, a trade he later put to successful use in dealing with his Flemish subjects in the years 1379–1385.

Burgundy was a good place to practice the princely trade in the late fourteenth century. Still largely agrarian, with its excellent wines easy to ship to Paris along the Seine, Burgundy had no great cities. Its only town of any stature, Dijon, could boast only around ten thousand inhabitants, and it would have no bishop until the eighteenth century. The duchy's religious authorities were the neighboring bishops of the even smaller towns of Autun, Auxerre, Chalons-sur-Saône, Langres, Mâcon, and Nevers. Still, Burgundy was worth the conflict between the citizens of Dijon — wishing to protect their autonomy in administration, justice, and finance — and the new duke, advocating a centralized system of ducal government. On Philip's side were the institutions, particularly the financial ones, that John II had slyly introduced into Burgundy after the death of Odo IV in 1349. The highest administrative organ was the autochthonous and traditional Council of the Duke. In order to increase its efficiency and better align it to a centralizing ducal government, Philip established specialized chambers within the council, first one for judicial matters and, in 1364, one for finance. In the judicial chamber, magistrates from the Parlement of Paris, the highest judicial body of the kingdom of France, sat, on occasion, to lend an intellectual hand.[13] The second was entrusted with the financial supervision of all the lower-echelon officials. These reforms resulted in the appearance of two fully fledged chambers by 1384. But much earlier, the young duke's subjects felt the weight of his new model government. The first clash between the city of Dijon and the new ducal justice dates from 1366. By 1376 the city had to fight to retain the right of freely electing its mayor. By 1395 Philip dared to go so far, against all local tradition, as to have his bailiff imprison citizens of Dijon. Princely centralization struck ever harder.

A French Prince in Flanders

The marriage of Philip and Margaret of Male in 1369 represented a considerable challenge for Philip. For him, it shaped an entirely new set of expectations. Burgundy was not, after all, a vital center of the European economy. Flanders, on the other hand, was economically, culturally, and in all other respects at the forefront of European development. In Burgundy, Philip had acquired useful experience in his clashes with the nobles of Franche-Comté and with the citizens of Dijon. The major Flemish cities were, however, four to six times larger than Dijon and far wealthier, more powerful, and restive. Their struggle for a measure of independence from their count and his suzerain, the French king, had long since been given form and substance by the formation of a representative institution, the Members of Flanders, dominated largely by the three great cities of Ghent, Bruges, and Ypres. More than once, in 1323–1328 and again in 1337–1345, revolts had forced the count onto the sidelines or even driven him out of the county.

When Philip arrived in Ghent for his marriage, Flanders was temporarily pacified in the aftermath of the intense social tensions of 1359–1360. In Bruges and Ypres, Louis of Male had managed to place magistrates into office who were favorably inclined toward him. In Flanders, as a whole, he implemented a policy of centralization upon which Philip could later build, but always on the condition that he and his subjects understand and respect each other.

Philip also realized that he ought to take advantage of the relatively long period he expected to have before his eventual succession to Flanders and his father-in-law's other territories. As a Burgundian French prince, he needed to gain a certain level of acceptability — even popularity — in order to bind his future subjects to him personally. He also needed to familiarize himself with the complex economy that had created and sustained the county's — and the count's — prosperity. Until 1369 Philip had associated chiefly with eminent prelates at Avignon, jurists and diplomats at the courts of Paris and Dijon, and military men. International mercantile society must have seemed very unfamiliar to him in 1369.

In Burgundy, both industry and agriculture had stagnated after the plague of 1348, and the population had decreased dramatically. In Flanders, on the other hand, Philip encountered a remarkably dynamic society; even the successive waves of plague had failed to slow its momentum. The export of luxury textiles formed the most important sector of the economy. The textile industry was highly international, and, for precisely that reason, extremely vulnerable. Philip soon realized that good relations with foreign powers were of the utmost importance, particularly those with the primary wool supplier, England. As a French prince, he thus found himself in a difficult position. His efforts in the years 1375–1377 to bring an end to the Hundred Years War must be understood, at least in part, as an attempt to safeguard the economy of his future Flemish subjects.

Aside from the peace negotiations with England, there are many other indications that Philip was both fascinated by and concerned with the fortunes of Flanders well before his succession in 1384. His wedding feast in Ghent was also a display of power and accessibility with which he began to bind the Flemish nobles more closely to him, aided by chests full of gifts. The Flemish clergy saw in him the sort of powerful patron who might intervene at the papal court in Avignon to help them obtain coveted promotions. Nor did Philip ignore the urban patriciate. He paid the mayor of Bruges, Tideman van der Berghe, the great honor of entering his house as a guest. The other rulers in the Low Countries, those of Brabant and Holland, were also included in this courtship. In 1376, as a token of his ambition to play political arbiter in this part of Europe, Philip hosted a lavish banquet for them at Ghent. His connections with the French crown and with Flanders gave the duke of Burgundy greater opportunities than any other prince in the Low Countries.[14]

The Revolt of the Flemish Cities

The diplomacy of the count and his son-in-law pacified Flanders for a decade, from 1369 until 1379. But that pacification was only temporary; from 1379 to 1385, Flanders endured a long period of bitter and open conflict involving the cities. This time the conflict did not begin in a clash of count and cities, but as a feud between the two greatest cities, Ghent and Bruges. At stake was the extent of their respective spheres of influence over the surrounding rural districts (*castelries*). For a long time, the city of Ghent held the "staple" of all goods shipped on the Lys/Leie and the Scheldt. The terms of the staple allowed Ghent to collect a tax on all goods shipped through it and also to command for itself a fixed portion of the total import, thus assuring Ghent of a steady grain supply and considerable commercial advantages as well.[15] Bruges had begun excavating a new canal that would enable it to avoid shipping grain from Hainault and Artois via the Lys and the Scheldt, thus avoiding the staple at Ghent. Ghent at once organized its militia for one of its familiar raids, causing the work crews from Bruges to lose all interest in further digging. The count, who had backed the Bruges initiative, had one of the leaders of the Ghent faction arrested. But in doing so, he violated the custom that dictated that the city itself was exclusively responsible for all judicial processes involving its own citizens. The count's action was regarded by the people of Ghent as sufficient reason for them to murder the count's bailiff who had arrested their fellow citizen. But such an act was, in turn, an encroachment on the majesty of the ruler. Thus Flanders was once again caught up in a widening spiral of escalating violence and rebellion.[16]

All of these events were charged with symbolism. The arrest was not simply an attack on the cities, but on the towering and precious structure of privileges and juridical doctrines that custom had erected into a common law, for which the cities demanded unconditional respect. Behind the arrest there lay also the count's ambition to demolish this structure, initially by means of military suppression of the revolt, as had happened in 1328. In 1379 a second concern dominated the minds of Flemish citizens: the passionate desire to safeguard free trade with England.[17] Troubled already by the failure of Philip the Bold to gain more concessions from the English during the negotiations of 1375–1377, the Flemings realized that the truce could be violated at any moment, hurling trade and the textile industry once more into chaos. The Ghent War of 1379–1385 was thus a sharp warning issued by the Flemish political elite to the old count, but it was addressed even more sharply to his son-in-law. The French prince must not be allowed to think that he could jeopardize good relations with England or encroach upon the achievements of urban autonomy. The outcome of the war would determine how far both prince and people might go in asserting their respective spheres of authority.

But neither was the war simply a duel between prince and people. As the brother and ambassador of Charles V in the 1375–1377 negotiations at Bruges, Philip the Bold had necessarily to take into account the interests of the French crown. And the population of the Flemish cities did not consist solely of patrician elites. In Ghent, for instance, besides the international merchants and great property owners, numerous smaller merchants and craftsmen worked for the local market, as did thousands of textile workers whose interests and incomes varied enormously, and some of whom (the fullers) were in the employ of others (the weavers). The revolutionary stimulus in earlier revolts in Ghent had lain with the radical wing of the weavers. In 1338–1349 they had been the architects of a broad front of all social groups as well as a league of Flemish cities, and they aired their wishes through the eloquent Ghent politician James van Artevelde. The English king's brutal cutoff of the wool supply and the consequent threat of economic catastrophe for the Flemish textile industry had, by then, convinced even the moderates that the only course open to them was a more autonomous stance in regard to the count and the French king and a pro-English policy that, under the guise of neutrality, would make possible a trade agreement with England. In 1379 the embers of autonomy, still smoldering, again flared up. Once again the actions of the count enabled the radicals to toy with the idea of a front of city-republics such as existed from time to time, although in a different context, in Italy.[18]

The three Members of Flanders—Ghent, Bruges, and Ypres—announced on December 1, 1379, the formation of a commission that was to examine the actions of the count's officers and that subsequently banished a number of them.[19] But the cities were also internally vulnerable to social unrest caused by the friction between different social groups. In Ghent the intolerance of the weavers angered the fullers, who constituted the second largest craft guild. The arrogance of the textile workers, stemming from their recently acquired power, proved equally unpalatable to the patriciate and to the middling group of small businessmen and lesser craftsmen. The situation in 1379 and the years following began to look ominously like the darkest days of the weavers' dictatorship between 1345 and 1349. The difficulties in Ghent led to the withdrawal from the league of the other two members, Bruges and Ypres, in August 1380.

Only Ghent persisted in the revolt and sought military support in England. The weavers backed James van Artevelde's son Philip as their leader, a conscious echo of the events and the most evocative name of 1337. But the echoes and evocation failed, since Philip was too closely identified merely as the leader of one of the many factions then tearing Ghent asunder, rather than as a leader of the whole city.[20] In May 1382, Ghent won a costly victory over the count's army and seized the city of Bruges, but six months later it suffered a terrible defeat at Westrozebeke by a coalition of the forces of the count and the French king, mobilized by Philip the Bold. But even Philip's mobilization of the comital and royal forces at Westrozebeke may reflect the diplomat rather than the soldier. Philip had left the actual request for French troops, always a thorny problem, to his father-in-law, Louis of Male. Philip also refrained from striking any military blows at the city of Ghent itself. But even this tactical restraint had a price: the Ghent revolt smoldered for many years to come.

The Arts of Power

Philip the Bold and Margaret of Male succeeded Louis of Male in Flanders, Franche-Comté, Rethel, Antwerp, Mechelen, Artois, and Nevers in 1384.

There were fewer territorial rulers in Europe as well prepared as he to develop the arts of power required to rule such a range of different lands. His six years of experience in Burgundy, followed by his fifteen years as both duke of Burgundy and apprentice count in Flanders, his diplomatic experience, and his intimacy with the French king had all prepared Philip to wield his authority and prestige with a strong hand and to bring his diverse subjects under his personal and institutional rule. Tactfully he filled many traditional offices, but he often undermined the new officeholders by creating new offices or subordinating old offices to others. He considered regional institutions within their traditional jurisdictions, but he also prepared them for a later integration. The process proceeded most smoothly in Burgundy itself, where Philip had already laid the foundations for the formal inauguration in 1384 of a central judicial tribunal and a chamber of accounts. Franche-Comté and Nevers, whose administrative institutions were even less well developed, were placed under the control of Dijon in 1386. But the process of centralization was never entirely completed. The great distance separating Burgundy from the Low Countries stood in the way of such a step. For this reason, in 1386 Philip created a second center in Lille, much like the administrative center in Dijon but independent of it, to coordinate the finances of his northern holdings in the same way as Dijon did in Burgundy, Franche-Comté, and Nevers. The Chamber of Accounts in Lille was able to audit all ducal financial operations in Flanders. Philip also established a central comital court of appeals for the smaller cities and the countryside. By this means he removed these from the stranglehold of the three great cities of Ghent, Bruges, and Ypres, at the same time removing one of the pillars that supported the old hegemony of the great Flemish cities over the smaller ones and over the countryside. Later, in 1390, Philip appointed a *procureur-général* to act as the count's prosecutor. This official channeled many cases to the count's tribunal that would previously have fallen under the jurisdiction of the great cities, thus breaking the judicial monopoly the cities held over the rest of Flanders.[21] Philip thus created two nerve centers for his dominions, increasing the efficiency of his government but not offending regional sensibilities by trying to rule every territory directly from Dijon.[22]

Philip then turned to his own staff. In 1385 he appointed Jean Canard, previously a capable advocate at the Parlement of Paris, as his chancellor, an office that eventually grew into the position of virtual prime minister, with authority over all the duke's territories and immediate responsibility for all higher officials.[23] The ducal council also dealt with all the territories, dispatching ambassadors who could speak in the duke's name all over Europe. Even for finances, a receiver "for all finances" was appointed, whose duties were to centralize the income from all territories, though this eventually proved unmanageable in practice. The duke still ruled personally in each of his lands, but he had laid the foundations for the beginnings of the Burgundian state as a federation of all those lands.

But the new regime first had to consolidate its position in each of its territories individually. After the battle of Westrozebeke in 1382, Philip preferred the techniques of diplomacy once again. He realied that, in spite of the conflicts between them, he shared substantial common interests with his Flemish subjects. His own representatives and the moderate factions of Ghent worked patiently on a compromise that would enable both sides of the conflict to save face, finally concluding the Peace of Tournai on December 18, 1385.

Both the duke and the urban patriciates were still real powers, ducal centralism balancing urban particularism. In order to preserve their respective power bases, each side had to take into consideration the interests of the population as a whole. In the Peace of Tournai, Philip generously ratified all of Ghent's historic privileges without — as had sometimes been done by victorious counts in the aftermath of earlier revolts — abolishing any of them.[24] The experienced city clerks of Ghent and the wily jurists of the duke knew very well that their agreement did not preclude a continuation of their duel. When city and prince later clashed over their respective jurisdictions, the duke could always dismiss Ghent's position as a bad, later custom, and Ghent could readily reply that this customary law had also been ratified in the course of the peace negotiations at Tournai. The winner in any of these later conflicts won less as a matter of juridical legitimacy than as the key to the balance of power existing at the time of the dispute.

Ghent's military connections with England during the revolt of 1377–1385 were obviously high treason from the French point of view. As a French prince, Philip also forced the city to make a clean political break with England and to acknowledge that England was excluded from the many trade privileges accorded by the duke to foreign nations between 1384 and 1387. But these steps were not as consequential as they might appear. In fact, Philip made them as a concession to the anti-English party in Paris so as to avoid jeopardizing his position at court in the aftermath of the death of Charles V in 1380. At the same time the pragmatic duke turned a blind eye in 1387 to those merchants from Bruges who, like Lubrecht Scutelaere, concluded their own private English trade agreements, virtually ignoring the Hundred Years War. All of these steps enabled Philip to arrange a summit conference in 1396 between the English and French kings that resulted in a truce, and to establish trade commissions that eventually reached an Anglo-Flemish trade agreement, in 1407.[25] Thus Philip was able to neutralize the pro-English political faction in Flanders, leaving the much less dangerous commercial dimension to be solved by his skillful manipulation of the different priorities of the major cities. Ghent continued to favor political alliance, where Bruges and other cities had trade agreements as their primary objective. The new count continued to learn to manipulate the complex structure of his county.

Differences of this kind between the great cities also played into Philip's hands with respect to the Western Schism, the division of Christian Europe into two parts as the result of the disputed papal election of 1378, with half of Europe accepting the pope in Avignon, Clement VII, and the other half accepting the one in Rome, Urban VI.[26] As a vassal of Charles V, Philip the Bold was pro-Avignon, but in the peace of Tournai in 1385, he granted their own choice to his pro-Roman Flemish subjects, who, in this case, took the same line of allegiance as the English. However, Philip also embarked on a shrewd propaganda campaign featuring theologians from the University of Paris, who argued in Flanders in favor of the pope at Avignon. By the end of 1393, the whole of Flanders, with the exception of Ghent, had "converted" to the Avignon obedience. But when Philip proposed that it would be best if both popes were to step down in order to resolve the problem (a possibility that had existed in canon law explicitly since 1298), he proved to be considerably ahead of his time. Only in 1417, long after Philip's death, did the Council of Constance settle the schism with methods very close to those Philip had proposed.

In these aspects of his early reign, Philip's centralization of his many holdings was more far-reaching than his subjects perceived — or cared to admit. He had begun to master the arts of power.

European Ambitions

The urban patricians of Flanders and their new count-duke both had European as well as local Flemish interests. The strategy of the cities was to keep all of Europe, as much as possible, one free market. The count-duke's strategy was more complex. Until 1380 Philip had, in partnership with his royal brother, exercised his entire repertoire of diplomatic skills at various European courts and trade centers. He discovered the ease with which he could make people fall under his spell. At the death of Charles V in 1380, Philip stood at a crossroads in his career. His first option was to continue to work within the framework of the interests of the French crown. The second was to conduct himself as befit a nonroyal Flemish-Burgundian territorial prince. The third was to set his own independent goals for himself and his dynasty, and to regard his possessions (his *Hausmacht*) as the foundation of an ambitious Burgundian state whose possibilities were limitless, not excluding even a crown for its ruler.[27]

In 1380, however, the last of these was the least likely, at least in the short term. There were far too many other dynasties firmly in power in the various territories of the Low Countries and in the lands between the Low Countries and Burgundy for Philip to envision either a united realm in the Low Countries or a Flemish-Burgundian state that might resemble the old Carolingian Middle Kingdom. His Flemish interests were more immediately pressing. Throughout the century the cities in Flanders and, for thirty years, those in Brabant had given evidence of substantial pro-English sympathies, of firm resistance to any attempt at annexation on the part of France, and of a proud and businesslike consciousness of their own vitality and autonomy. Philip recognized the value of this position. In 1377 and afterward he attempted to restore free trade with England.

And he began to patronize Flemish artists, first at Dijon and later elsewhere throughout his dominions. He commissioned a remarkable altarpiece from the Flemish sculptor Jacques de Baerze, the outer panels of which were painted by Melchior Broederlam. It was fully assembled by 1399, for the Carthusian monastery at Champmol, outside Dijon. From the sculptor Klaas Sluter from Haarlem in Holland, Philip commissioned, also for the Charterhouse at Champmol, the majestic figures of prophets on the great *Well of Moses*, which were painted and gilded by the Nijmegen artist Jan Maelwael. Sluter also executed the great figures for Philip's tomb in Dijon. These commissions began the great association of the dukes with the most talented artists of northern Europe, an association that lasted beyond the end of the dynasty.

Philip also perceived the depth of the stubborn spirit of independence in Flanders and in his other territories, a spirit that explains why those tiny countries on the North Sea are still, to this day, sovereign states. It was clear to Philip in 1380 that the hunger of the great powers to gain control of the Low Countries had to be held in check, and his best guarantee of this was to maintain by diplomacy the continuity of a carefully measured balance of power among several power blocks. He preferred to manage this balance himself, and thus he became the champion of the interests of other princes in the Low Countries, with the intention of strengthening both their and his own positions. In 1375 he had already acted as negotiator for a marriage between a daughter of the French king and the heir of Hainault and Holland-Zeeland.

His greatest coup in this regard, however, was the double wedding in Cambrai in 1385 of the male heirs of Burgundy-Flanders-Artois and Hainault-Holland-Zeeland with each other's sisters, an event of enormous political significance. With the weddings there emerged a peaceful alliance between the two most powerful ruling dynasties in the Low Countries, and through them it united spheres of influence in the German Empire and in France. Such a momentous union had to be celebrated sufficiently lavishly to convince all contemporaries of the significance (and the authorship) of the event. The seventeen-year-old French king Charles VI (1380–1422) came to Cambrai to attend the wedding of his two nieces. Philip and Margaret's daughter, Margaret of Burgundy, barely ten years old, married the twenty-year-old William of Bavaria; Philip and Margaret's son, John of Burgundy, was thirteen and married the twenty-two-year-old Margaret of Bavaria. Clearly, interests of state and dynasty outweighed the age differences of the couples.[28]

The abbot of the Augustinian convent at Cambrai, whose buildings housed the numerous high-ranking guests, has left a description of the festivities. According to his estimate, as many as twenty thousand interested spectators had journeyed to Cambrai, many of them housed in the six thousand tents that had been set up in the surrounding villages. "Gates, theaters, and arches of triumph" were also erected for the greatest "feast and triumph the city had seen in 500 years."[29]

For contemporaries, the first remarkable feature of the celebration was the presence of such a large number of prominent foreign guests. The splendor of their attire also made a great impression. Albert, duke of Bavaria and *Ruwaard*, or regent, and after 1389 count of Hainault and Holland-Zeeland, and father of one of the grooms, was clad in white robes embroidered with eagles and golden griffins. His daughter, one of the brides, wore a red gown decorated with tiny golden birds. For the occasion, enormous sums were disbursed for gems either worn as jewelry or sewn onto the rich fabrics of their raiment.[30] Garments were not only commissioned and purchased, but also borrowed. Duke Philip the Bold himself borrowed some clothing from his royal nephew and from his brother the duke of Berry. The rulers of Holland requested the loan of crowns from the queen of England and the countess of Blois, even though the latter was actually of lower rank than were they.

The celebration lasted a week. On the first day there took place the solemn arrival and entry of the king of France, greeted by a procession from the town. The nuptial mass was followed by a lavish feast at which the king, surrounded by the newlyweds and their mothers, was served by all the other dukes, princes, and lords, seated on their tall chargers. The poet Jan van Mechelen describes how an entremets appeared in the form of a castle. It was defended by four wild beasts against half-Moorish, half-barbarian attackers. Two little maidens held above the castle a marvelous crown and the French fleur-de-lis, above which shone a white hart with silver wings.

There followed two days of jousting, tournaments, and races, with a winner proclaimed and awarded a prize for each event. The festival of courtly chivalry cost the princely fathers and their subjects a fortune. Philip the Bold's expenses were at least four times those of his counterpart from Holland. Gifts account for half of Philip's expenditures, being the means par excellence by which the Burgundian duke made a deep impression on the public, won friends, and bound people to him. Although Albert of Bavaria did the same thing on a much more modest scale, he still went deeply into debt in order to maintain his status. The cities of Hainault and many Lombard bankers helped him to cover his expenses, which totaled the whole of his revenues from Holland in a normal year. It is understandable that Albert had to compromise a bit for several years in order to recover financially from his share of the wedding festivities. He even had to slow down the development of his capital at the Hague. But he had gained greatly in prestige and won a staunch ally in Philip the Bold.

Philip thus took up the role of the *grand seigneur* in the Low Countries, occupying the limelight by the splendor of his patronage of the arts and by his magnificent feasts and banquets. But behind these scenes, he cunningly and patiently wove a web of favorable connections for his dynasty.

Between the two territorial blocks brought together by the double wedding of 1385 lay Brabant, ruled by the elderly and childless duchess Joan. Philip the Bold supported her in a conflict with the neighboring duchy of Guelders, but at the same time he put her under so much pressure for his support that in 1387, she ceded to Philip the income and in 1396 the lordship of the tiny duchy of Limburg. In 1390 she secretly designated Philip as her successor in Brabant. After negotiations with the reluctant Estates of Brabant, which had elicited the restricting terms of the Joyous

Entry from Joan thirty-four years earlier, Philip's younger son Anthony was designated heir of Brabant. Although Philip was strongly tempted to annex Brabant to Flanders via a personal union under Philip himself, the Brabanters were too strongly attached to their own territorial independence, which had been confirmed to them in the past. Moreover, the normal administrative language of Brabant was Dutch, a rule also confirmed in the privileges; here even more than in Flanders, a francophone administration would encounter fierce opposition. Young Anthony represented an infiltration of Brabant by the Burgundian dynasty, but he did not add it yet to the dynastic union. This compromise actually made possible a very subtle form of burgundianization. Not long after his accession to Brabant in 1404, Anthony introduced several Burgundian-inspired administrative institutions into both Brabant and Limburg and certainly initiated a style of administration that later permitted smooth unification.[31] The Estates of Brabant took the defense of their "national" rights very seriously.[32]

But beyond Hainault and Holland-Zeeland and Brabant, Philip had other broad concerns. On the English question, he could steer neither a purely French nor a purely Flemish territorial course. He permitted Flemish business circles to take all initiatives and then followed where they led. For all of his Low Country and commercial interests in England, Philip also aspired to a prominent role in the politics of the French kingdom.

Charles V had died on September 16, 1380, leaving an eleven-year-old prince, Charles VI, to succeed him. A regency obviously had to be arranged. Charles V had decided to avoid a dangerous concentration of power in the hands of a single regent by placing the care of his son in the hands of a council made up of members of the royal family. Louis, duke of Anjou, became its head, and the dukes of Burgundy, Berry, and Bourbon the members.[33] The plan appeared logical and workable, but it raised conflicts of interest in the case of each of its members.

On the one hand, in order to remain legitimate in the eyes of the king's councillors, the Parlement of Paris, the University of Paris, the Parisian commercial world, and various high-ranking officials, the members of the council were obliged to play the roles of disinterested uncles whose sole interest was the well-being and instruction of the young king. But at the same time, they were also individual territorial princes. They realized that their function as regents would last only a few years, whereas their territorial jurisdictions and Hausmacht were theirs for life, could be handed down to their own sons, and might even serve as stepping stones to yet higher posts, as they already had in the case of Philip the Bold. The temptation was great to put the interests of their territories and dynasties ahead of those of the French crown.³⁴ All of them shamelessly plundered the royal treasury to further their own provincial interests. Philip the Bold used it in 1382 for the military reconquest of his domains in Flanders; the duke of Berry attempted to improve his position in Languedoc; the duke of Anjou had devised an even costlier project. In 1382 he marched with French troops into Provence and Italy, hoping to add the kingdom of Naples to his French holdings and to become preeminent among the princes. But Louis of Anjou fell ill and died in Italy in 1384.³⁵

Philip the Bold then emerged as the strongest figure among the council of regents, and in 1385 he was able to open his campaign to charm the Bavarian Wittelsbachs of Hainault and Holland-Zeeland into the grand weddings at Cambrai. Having transformed both the Bavarian house and the French crown from potential rivals into allies, Philip had neutralized them politically. After the double wedding at Cambrai, he arranged the marriage of the young Charles VI himself to Isabela of Bavaria, but more in the interest of equilibrium in the Low Countries than in France. Even the father of the bride, Stephen III, duke of Bavaria and brother of Albert, now count of Hainault and Holland-Zeeland, was not particularly elated. For Charles married Isabela without either a contract or a dowry, and Stephen was forced to accede most reluctantly to the ritual of having his daughter inspected by the ladies of the French court by means of a portrait, for which she had to pose virtually nude.

In 1388 Charles was considered of age and therefore capable of ruling on his own. But around him there arose a struggle for power and influence, as a result of which a number of officials from the royal government and former members of Charles V's entourage, particularly Olivier de Clisson, again seized the reins of power and forced Philip the Bold to relinquish his primacy to the party of Louis of Touraine.³⁶ During these years it became clear that each of the regents was no more than the hub of a clan, and, like all clan leaders, could be excluded or eliminated. In 1392, when the first signs of mental instability began to appear in the king, the regents once more assumed their former roles, and the centralists of 1388 were ousted.³⁷ The regents now began to extend their power bases outside of Paris. Louis of Touraine, later duke of Orléans, became head of the council; the dukes of Berry and Burgundy once more became members. Berry was more or less content to play the role of patron of the arts (for which he is still known), commissioning the brothers Limburg to create his brilliant manuscript *Book of Hours*, with its unique illuminated miniatures. Louis of Orléans and

Philip the Bold were the real rivals vying for public favor in Paris and for power outside Paris.[38]

To further their political ends, they assembled groups of followers, often with paramilitary trappings, as a defense against the forces backing the mayor of Paris (the *prévot des marchands*) and the royal tribunal, the Parlement.[39] Philip outraged his enemies in 1393 by eliminating the popular provost Jean Jouvenel, symbol of Parisian urban autonomy.[40] Louis of Orléans lost respect through his extravagance, by financing his private interests at the papal court and in Naples with funds from the French treasury and by the indelicate manner in which he organized expensive banquets with his mistress, Charles VI's queen Isabela of Bavaria.[41] After 1394, Philip the Bold acted far more skillfully and insinuated himself securely into the machinery of state by providing generous gifts to everyone, up to and including the royal chancellor, chairmen, and advocates of the Parlement of Paris in exchange for services to be rendered to him when he needed them.[42] Both princes were able to lure the intellectual elites into their camps by their patronage of artists: Philip the Bold commissioned Christine de Pizan to write tracts in praise of women and sensual poetry.[43] Louis of Orléans commissioned erotic ballads from Eustache Deschamps.[44] On their more serious days, Philip conversed with the theologian Jean Gerson and Louis corresponded with members of the papal court at Avignon and with the humanist poet Petrarch, then in residence at Avignon. In the more turbulent years that followed, between 1395 and 1402, their rivalry erupted into civil war.

* * *

Philip the Bold's succession to Burgundy in 1363 and to Flanders in 1384 had opened a new political world. After 1384, Philip and the Flemish cities, his most important assets and opponents, set out on an uneasy journey together, Philip bringing with him the glory of the royal house and his wealth of experience as a European diplomat, and the cities their immense economic resources, administrative routine, contacts in far-flung cities, and, always, the threat of revolt against their ruler. They were linked uneasily together, and they faced common questions: how deeply to commit themselves to the ambience and danger of Parisian society, what to do about England, how independent to permit the city-republics to be. What was to be Philip's prime concern—power in Paris or in the Low Countries and Burgundy?

Philip could now envisage the control of a large part of Europe by his dynasty. Within his territories he had begun a streamlined, centralizing system of government, finance, and law in which the ruler professed responsibility for the commonweal and in which the people were to be "the obedient servants of the ruler." Fundamentally, this was the ideology of an identity of interests among prince, state, and subjects.[45] As in the time of Charles V, the Parisian intelligentsia provided this philosophy of state with firm theoretical foundations. But the Flemish cities also defended their own conception of the commonweal, defined as that of their own citizens. Both Philip and his various territories entered the fifteenth century with these often conflicting concerns.

3

Burgundian Interests in France and the Low Countries 1404–1425

John the Fearless, Heir-Apparent and Crusader

Philip the Bold died at Hal, near Brussels, on April 27, 1404. His body was taken to Dijon, where it was buried in the Carthusian house of Champmol, eventually in the tomb commissioned by him and designed by the sculptor Klaas Sluter. His widow, Margaret of Male, continued to rule over her hereditary domains of Flanders and Artois until her death in 1405. Their eldest son, John the Fearless (1371–1419), already count of Nevers, now became duke of Burgundy. John's brother Anthony, already count of Rethel, became regent of Brabant for his aunt the duchess Joan, and then duke when Joan died in 1406. But for all of his glorious prospects, John had not been quickly initiated into governmental affairs. His father had taken him along on his military campaigns against Guelders in 1388, but as late as 1391, Margaret had still considered him — at the age of twenty — too inexperienced to be formally proclaimed her heir in Flanders and in her other possessions. Philip the Bold had been preoccupied with French political affairs during much of John's youth, and not until 1394 had John been given an opportunity to make a name for himself — and then not primarily in Flanders or in Burgundy, but in the prospect of the Crusade.

In the early fourteenth century, the Ottoman Turks had extended their rule into much of Asia Minor, and beginning in 1348 they conquered a great deal of Thrace, most of Bulgaria, and Serbian Macedonia. After their victory at Kossovo in 1389 they controlled most of the Balkans, and they invaded the Peloponnese in 1394. The new Muslim threat in vulnerable southeastern Europe alarmed both the popes and the royalty and much of the nobility of Europe. In 1395, a lull in the Anglo-French war permitted the formation of a great league against the Turks by France, England, Hungary, Venice, and Burgundy.[1] Philip the Bold was its most vigorous promoter, and he organized Burgundian participation in the plans for the new Crusade. In order to finance his share of the crusading costs, Philip had begun to negotiate with the Flemish cities and clergy for a very steep extraordinary tax. Philip chose John as his negotiator and designated him as the Burgundian leader of the Crusade.

John had his work cut out for him. The many letters he exchanged with his father during 1394–96 indicate the meticulousness that he applied to the project. He carried out ducal instructions "just as you and your chancellor advised me, my beloved lord and father." He exhibited considerable diplomatic adroitness in taking aside the representatives of Ypres, who were proving obstructive, "lest the other cities follow the example of their unfavorable response . . . I even explained to them in Flemish, as well as I could," the reasons why their contribution was essential. So successful was John that he wrote to his father, "you would be most surprised should Ypres prove unwilling to submit to your will on a matter so near your heart, and of such importance to all of Christendom, a matter touching both your honor as a knight and my own."[2] John's negotiations finally brought about a compromise that granted a sum larger than what the cities had originally been prepared to grant.

Philip saw the advantages for John that a heroic reputation in the service of Christendom might provide. But John acquired that reputation in an unusual way, leading the Burgundian forces to the military disaster at Nicopolis in 1396. John's personal courage during the battle indeed won him considerable renown, and, as it turned out, John proved to be the most militarily talented ruler of his dynasty. Taken prisoner and held for an enormous ransom by the Turks until 1398, John also acquired something of an air of martyrdom. Like his father's bravery at Poitiers and long captivity in England, John's bravery at Nicopolis and his own long confinement considerably enhanced his reputation, giving him his own nickname: Jean sans Peur, Jan zonder Vrees, or John the Fearless. In 1398, a triumphant John was able to thank his future subjects at Dijon and in Flanders in person for their generous donations to his ransom.[3]

After 1398, Philip began to initiate John into the complexities of the Parisian political world in which he played such a prominent role. For many months, John was able to observe his father's deft diplomacy and his conduct of the many intrigues entailed by the continual mental relapses of Charles VI. Like his father, John perceived the opportunities that the king's illness offered to ambitious princes of the blood, particularly that of milking the royal treasury to ensure the prosperity of their own territorial states.

From 1399, with Philip preoccupied with French politics and Margaret of Male attending to the northern part of the Burgundian state from the city of Arras, John the Fearless began to live for longer periods in Burgundy, presiding in his father's name over the ducal council at Dijon and outlining regional policy for the duchy. But he neglected Flanders, rarely visiting it between 1398 and 1405. His Flemish subjects expressed their apprehension about John's absences; they preferred rulers and heirs-apparent who resided in Flanders, not in Paris or Dijon. But the dukes of Burgundy, especially Philip the Bold and John the Fearless, had compelling interests in French political affairs, and these had to be considered before turning to ducal interests in Burgundy, Flanders, the other Low Countries, and Europe.

Burgundian Ambitions in France, 1404–1419

In order to maintain his power and income in France, Philip the Bold lived almost continuously in Paris during the last years of his life. After Philip's death, John the Fearless attempted to resume his father's role — without significant experience in the complexities of French royal court life and without those personal ties, laboriously established at great expense by his father, with influential officials at the University of Paris and the Parlement of Paris.[4] Nor was John close to Charles VI, to whom he was merely one cousin among many.[5]

Because of his poor health, Charles was able to rule only sporadically and was always assisted or replaced temporarily by a council of regents.[6] Among the latter Louis of Orléans, brother of the king, was the most ambitious.[7] He assumed Philip the Bold's position as the chief power behind the throne upon Philip's death in 1404. And he had already increased his influence by making the queen, Isabela of Bavaria, his mistress.[8] Isabela had also been afflicted by the king's illnesses, neglected both emotionally and sexually. Her highly unstable royal husband was unable, most of the time, to act normally as either husband or political leader. The fact that Isabela and Louis of Orléans became lovers would not have unduly shocked their contemporaries, for their affair was by no means unique. But the consequences of the affair on their collaboration on the political level soon made them extremely unpopular with the Parisian public.⁹ They greatly increased the level of taxation in France to further the private goals of Louis of Orléans rather than the *bien commun*, the common weal of France. Their cultivation of the Avignon pope Benedict XIII also angered those who accused the pope of acquiring large amounts of French tax revenues for the benefit of the papal treasury in return for his promises of a kingdom in Italy for Louis.¹⁰ Louis of Orléans and Isabela also arranged several marriages that appeared to benefit only the house of Orléans, such as the marriage of Louis's son Charles to the daughter of Isabela and King Charles VI.

In these unfavorable circumstances, it was essential that John the Fearless strengthen his role at the French court. More was at stake than the prestige of the ducal house of Burgundy. In 1394–1396 the royal "gifts and pensions" amounted to one-fifth of all the duke's revenues. When Philip died in 1404, his properties and territories were divided among his three sons — John the Fearless, Anthony of Brabant, and Philip of Nevers — thus substantially reducing John the Fearless's income compared with that of his father. The ducal yearly gross income from domains and aids in 1394–1396 had amounted to 350,820 ecus (of 40 groats). By 1419 this sum had dropped by 40 percent, to 210,146 ecus. The territorial division of Nevers, Rethel, the Champagne territories, and Limburg among the brothers reduced John's ordinary income by 14.3 percent. The aids he was able to levy in Burgundy fell to one-third of their former levels, and the alienation of his Flemish domains implied a 29 percent reduction. Moreover, between 1404 and 1407, the transfers from the French royal treasury had virtually ceased. Louis of Orléans was the primary beneficiary, thus posing a direct threat to the financial stability of the Burgundian state. John, of course, had no prospects of succeeding to the throne of France, as his father had occasionally had, but the advantages of a stronger position at the French court were still attractive, particularly if it could be used to strengthen the Burgundian state and its finances in the event that all French financial support might eventually be withdrawn. In these matters, John the Fearless proved astonishingly successful. By 1419 he built up his revenues from the French royal treasury to the level of 197,000 ecus, which, combined with his profits from the royal mintage, added another 191,000 ecus to that sum. In short, John the Fearless brought the share of French royal resources in his total revenue for 1419 to the amazing level of 65 percent.

Finally, a prominent role in Paris still won prestige in Europe, lending advantage to any prince in his relations with prominent figures from England, Germany, and Italy. In order to improve his status in Paris, John chose two courses of action: that of public opinion and that of military intervention. Louis of Orléans was the chief representative in France of a policy of peace with England, but also a symbol of royal centralization and the heavy fiscal burdens associated with a strong central authority in the kingdom. John began to portray himself as the opponent of these policies, as the champion of social discussions, of a "contract with the subjects," of judicial reform in the name of the *bien commun,* and of fiscal reform against the extravagance of his rival.[11] Prominent members of the Parlement of Paris wrote memoranda noting how touched they were by John's "affecting sympathy for the social situation of the people."[12] In the commercial circles of Paris, John's arguments along these lines made him appear an attractive alternative to Louis of Orléans. John also managed to attract the theologians and other scholars of Paris to his side, by supporting their sharp criticism of the strong-willed pope Benedict XIII, criticism that had led to the remarkable withdrawal of French obedience in 1398 and the long siege of the papal palace at Avignon in 1398–1399. John even demonstrated his willingness to enter into negotiations with the Roman pope Innocent VII. In his influential and well-attended speeches, Jean Gerson, chancellor of the University of Paris, lashed out against absolutist traits in domestic policy, an unmistakable allusion to Louis of Orléans.[13]

John's second course of action was to gain control of the king and the still very young Dauphin. In July 1405, John agreed to a tripartite alliance in the Low Countries with his brother Anthony, governor of Brabant, and his brother-in-law William VI, count of Hainault and Holland-Zeeland. A large, secretly armed force of the three allies' contingents set out in August 1405 to threaten Paris, where Louis of Orléans had also set his own troops in readiness. The confrontation, however, was confined to a war of words and pamphlets. Although John did succeed in bringing the Dauphin under his tutelage and thus presenting himself as the "protector of the French royal dynasty," he still needed a stronger position from which to bargain. In January 1406, John finally succeeded in regaining his father's place in the regency council, although the council was still dominated by the duke of Orléans.[14]

During 1406 and 1407, the two protagonists managed to maintain a precarious balance of power. To avoid losing the favor of public opinion, both were forced to devise military plans against England in which neither really believed. John pushed ambition and cynicism so far as simultaneously to prepare to lay siege to the English-controlled Calais and bring about an Anglo-Flemish trade agreement. The duke of Orléans, however, continued to control the French treasury, and he interfered in the Low Countries by supporting John's enemies in Liège. He drastically reduced the number of Burgundian partisans in the king's council, leaving only two, whereas the Orléanist party numbered more than twenty members.

On November 23, 1407, John's hired assassins murdered Louis of Orléans in Paris. Public opinion, already critical of the duke of Orléans, chose to interpret the assassination as a matter of personal rather than political hostility. Louis was said to have kept a portrait gallery depicting the objects of his amorous conquests. When John paid an alleged visit to the gallery he was reported to have discovered the portrait of his own wife, Margaret of Bavaria, among them. The assassination thus became refigured as a matter of personal honor. The story was all the more persuasive because of John's circumstances and Louis's temperament. It is possible that John had not shared the marriage bed all that often. John had been married to Margaret in the great double wedding of 1385. Their first son, later Philip the Good, was born in 1396. Three subsequent children were born to them, all daughters. John also had four illegitimate children — two more than his father, but twenty-two fewer than his son! It is possible, too, to see the appeal of such a seduction to Louis of Orléans, as the most dishonoring form of revenge upon his rival. Whether the story, or any part of it, is true is impossible to say, and in any case the political motives of John the Fearless were certainly foremost. That the story was widely believed is evidence that public opinion attributed to John both a capacity for cold, political calculation and a passionate impulsiveness.[15]

Following the assassination, John fled to Flanders to avoid retaliation and to strengthen his image in France. In Paris the angry widow of the duke of Orléans, Valentina Visconti, set in motion a judicial inquiry into the killing.[16] The other members of the regency council were divided in their opinions on the facts of the case and did nothing. The dukes of Anjou and Berry were reluctant to oppose John the Fearless and tried to open lines of contact with him.[17] To strengthen his position at home, John first assured himself of the support of his Flemish subjects and of his allies since the treaty of 1405, the rulers of Brabant and Hainault and Holland-Zeeland. With this backing, John traveled to Amiens to discuss the situation with his fellow members of the regency council. Evidently he was able to explain his way out of the affair, probably because the regents were themselves relieved by the removal of the troublesome duke of Orléans. By February 1408 John was able to make a public return to Paris, where he was greeted as a hero.

John now set about the task of convincing prominent members of the

Parisian political public that the assassination had been an act essential for the maintenance of the public welfare of the kingdom. The most remarkable product of this process was Jean Petit's four-hour speech, delivered on March 8, 1408, to an audience of jurists and officials of the royal court. Petit, an extremely capable theologian, was acting as advocate for John the Fearless. His speech was a masterpiece of political manipulation disguised as political philosophy. Petit"s "Justification," copies of which were circulated throughout Europe in the form of manuscripts illuminated with miniatures, was a shrewd, learned, and inflammatory piece of theological casuistry, laced with citations that reveal an astounding knowledge of civil and canon law. Jean Petit's thesis argued that the assassination of the duke of Orléans was justified because the duke had been a tyrant and disloyal to the king, whose life he had even attempted to end. The last accusation stemmed from an incident at a masked ball in 1393, when Louis of Orléans had been accused of having attempted to set the king's clothing on fire, with the treasonous intention of setting himself upon the French throne with the support of his ally Pope Benedict XIII. Jean Petit's argument was sufficiently philosophical and emotional that the Parisians accepted it, as did Charles VI himself. The Visconti inquest ended with John's exoneration.[18]

But the opposition to John did not vanish. In 1408, Valentina Visconti married her son Charles of Orléans to the daughter of the count of Armagnac and thus created a new anti-Burgundian coalition, one that survived the death of Valentina in 1409. The party that emerged came to be called that of the Armagnacs and was joined by the dukes of Bourbon and Berry. In March 1409, the Armagnacs and Burgundians agreed to a truce at the Peace of Chartres, mediated by John's brother-in-law William VI of Hainault and Holland-Zeeland, blood relative of the French queen Isabela.[19] William's daughter Jacqueline of Bavaria was also married to Isabela's son John of Touraine. Isabela herself seems to have come to be resigned to the supremacy of John the Fearless. On March 17, 1409, John the Fearless made a triumphal entry into Paris, and within a few months he was able to purge the royal council of anti-Burgundian elements and to surround the Dauphin with trusted Burgundian partisans who kept him securely under control. Once again money flowed unchecked from the royal treasury to the Burgundian. John maintained his popularity by depicting the Armagnac party as the continuation of Louis of Orléans's policies of high taxation and indifference to the welfare of the subjects of the king of France. He suggested to the Estates General the idea of taxing higher incomes at a higher rate than others, and he instituted measures to combat corruption among public officials. As a symbolic gesture of his influence, John married his eldest daughter Margaret to the Dauphin, Louis of Guyenne, in 1412.

But John was not free of opposition. Although he managed to avert a civil war launched by the Armagnacs in 1411, he miscalculated in 1413 when he threw his support behind a new group of rebels, the Cabochiens, who proposed to reform the state in a drastic fashion, alarming both the burghers of Paris and the nobility.[20] The revolt committed considerable excesses that were widely publicized and sometimes exaggerated, and the Armagnacs now stepped forward as the party of law and order. Their intervention permitted the Dauphin to free himself from the tutelage of John the Fearless and forced John to flee once more to Flanders, in August 1413. The Burgundians were now replaced by Armagnacs in the French government, and a new political climate emerged in which rougher and blunter tactics of influencing support by the clash of intrigue and propaganda determined the outcome of rivalry between contending parties in France. Enemies circulated forged letters reputedly sent by partisans of their opponents, and parties accused each other of making secret treaties with the kingdom's enemies.

The new rulers in Paris represented two different points of view concerning John the Fearless. One position took a more pacifist view of affairs and was prepared to talk with the duke of Burgundy. The other, however, was the hard line taken by the most aggressive of the Armagnacs and implacably hostile to Burgundy and its duke. Encouraged by the division, John fabricated a letter, allegedly from the Dauphin, appealing to him for help and providing him with a pretext for marching on Paris in February 1414. At the last moment, however, John reluctantly declined to attack the city. The Armagnacs responded just as fiercely, making a public spectacle of the burning of Jean Petit's "Justification" as a symbol of Burgundian perfidy. In September 1414, a military clash between the two factions took place near Arras. The truce that followed was characteristic of the political relations of the two factions: in the official text John agreed to cede Arras to the Armagnacs; in a secret article, the Armagnacs agreed to leave the city in the hands of their rival.

The English, while displaying considerable ambivalence, speculated on the possible advantages to them of the discord in France. One group of nobles surrounding King Henry V and the duke of Bedford was inclined to come to terms with John the Fearless, although other nobles preferred dealing with the Armagnacs. Opposition English "parties" negotiated with opposition French "parties" in a general atmosphere of caution and profound mistrust. In May 1414, Henry V tried to lure John into a military coalition, an invitation that provoked the Armagnacs into circulating in Paris a treaty alleged to have been signed by the English king and the Burgundian duke. It was merely an unapproved and unsigned draft agreement with a summary of objections and conditions that further exposed the deep mutual mistrust that existed not only between rival parties in France, but also between the English and the Burgundians.

Henry V finally decided to use his own troops to restore English authority on the Continent. On October 25, 1415, he won a resounding victory over the French at Agincourt. Although John the Fearless had personally promised the Dauphin that he would support the French with a strong army, his forces somehow failed to reach the battlefield on time.[21] But John's failure was clearly not Burgundian policy: John's brother Anthony of Brabant fought and was killed in battle, as was another brother, Philip, count of Nevers. From John's perspective, these personal losses may have been offset by the destruction and capture of most of the Armagnac chiefs. But John's hopes for a return to Paris came to nothing: there was no popular or governmental sympathy for him, and in December the Dauphin, Louis of Guyenne, who had been at least willing to talk to the Burgundian faction, died.

But John's prospects were not utterly obliterated. John's brother-in-law and ally William VI of Hainault and Holland-Zeeland arranged with his cousin Queen Isabela to name as the new Dauphin and hence formal heir her son John of Touraine (married to William's daughter Jacqueline of Bavaria). The Armagnacs planned stiff resistance to the appointment, but it was not needed. Both the new Dauphin and the architect of the plan, William VI, died at the beginning of 1417. In his renewed propaganda campaign, John the Fearless accused the Armagnacs of having arranged the murders of two Dauphins in quick succession and of having themselves agreed to the treaty with the English that they had circulated against John a few months earlier.

John now chose a military course of action. He won city after city from the Armagnac party around Paris: Mantes, Beauvais, Senlis, Provins, and Chartres. France had splintered into three territorial parts: the English king controlled Guyenne and Normandy; the Armagnacs and the new Dauphin Charles (later Charles VII) controlled Paris and the south of the kingdom; John the Fearless controlled the north and east and maintained a cordon around Paris itself. John even extricated Queen Isabela from the city and formed with her a government in rivalry to that of the Dauphin. On May

29, 1418, the Burgundian army seized Paris itself, and on July 14, 1418, John and Isabela triumphantly reentered Paris together and gained control of King Charles VI and the royal treasury.[22] The Dauphin Charles, however, had fled the city before it fell to John and Isabela, not to return until 1437.

But there was no significant acclaim from the Parisian political factions or the people. Civil war and vicious propaganda campaigns had helped discredit anyone claiming political legitimacy. With three claimants — the English king; the Dauphin, away at Bourges; and Charles VI, controlled by Isabela and John the Fearless — there was no clear winner. John did not command the financial, military, and psychological resources to dominate both his Burgundian lands and Paris or to neutralize the Armagnacs and the English. He could, however, negotiate an agreement that reduced the field from three rivals to a coalition of two against one, and he began negotiations for an Anglo-Burgundian joint rule and for a division of France between Burgundians and Armagnacs. The Armagnacs and the Dauphin, however, envisioned a simpler solution. They arranged for a conference to be held at Montereau on September 10, 1419, and when John arrived, their assassins cut him down in a carefully planned ambush. The news of the murder of John the Fearless on the bridge at Montereau circulated quickly and widely. It must have seemed an echo of that earlier murder of Louis of Orléans, contrived by John the Fearless in Paris twelve years before.[23]

The murder at Montereau both isolated the Dauphin and moved Charles VI toward a diplomatic settlement with the English and the Burgundians. The Dauphin Charles remained isolated in Bourges. He had sanctioned the murder of John the Fearless and proclaimed himself regent for his incapacitated father, Charles VI, which was technically an act of treason. Charles VI accepted the Anglo-Burgundian Treaty of Troyes in May 1420, married his daughter Catherine to Henry V of England, and acknowledged Henry V as regent and heir to the throne of France.

Ducal Rule in Burgundy and Flanders, 1404–1419: Centralism and Resistance

Like his father, John the Fearless favored a strong, centralized administration and an autocratic form of government in his own territories, of which Flanders and Burgundy were the most important. His deep involvement in international politics, particularly those of the kingdom of France, and the ambitions that drove him to become a leader and mediator for the whole of the Low Countries, left him insufficient time, energy, and resources to implement his domestic policies fully. The political opposition within his territories eagerly seized every opportunity by John's temporary weaknesses to regain lost political terrain. During the early years of the reign, John was able to show a consistently strong hand, but his centralizing efforts were clearly hindered in the years 1411–19 by his weaker position in international affairs. He was thus both obliged and prepared to grant concessions to his subjects.

Following his father's death, John was able to assert a political identity of his own. His reputation in the wake of the Crusade of Nicopolis had been that of a military leader. But now he revealed himself as an astute political ruler and a clever and capable centralizer in Flanders and Burgundy. He did not act with the impulsiveness that is sometimes ascribed to him, but rather with a degree of deliberation that formally respected the rights of local representative institutions, while at the same time steering politics and decision making in the direction of a more authoritarian exercise of power. Only in his interventions outside Flanders and Burgundy, as in his repression of resistance in Liège in 1408, did he commit himself outright to the use of military force.

One of the complaints most frequently made by the subjects of Philip the Bold, especially in the later years of his reign, had been his absence from Flanders and Burgundy. John the Fearless also spent much of the period of 1399–1405 in Burgundy and Paris, but not in Flanders. After 1405, however, John departed radically from this course, dividing his time equally among the various nerve centers of his dominions: as a young duke he resided an average of two months of the year in Burgundy, two to six months in Flanders, and the rest of the time in Paris, where he was, at least, equidistant from his Flemish and Burgundian subjects.[24] This policy was tactical. In most of medieval Europe, power was only effective when visibly and locally exercised. The display of a visible dynasty going about its business in the places upon which its power depended was also reflected in the way John more systematically relied on the constructive use of family members in his own absence than had Philip the Bold. Beginning in 1407, for example, John was more or less permanently represented in Burgundy by his son Philip, count of Charolais and later Philip the Good, and in later years chiefly by his wife, Margaret of Bavaria.

John's confrontation with the Flemings, always the least tractable of his subjects, represented a particularly challenging test for his policy of dialogue and personal contact. At Easter 1405, John had made his Joyous

Entry into Ghent. At the Prinsenhof, his palace in Ghent, he received with great pomp the highest representative body of the county, the Four Members. These were the representatives of three great cities of Ghent, Bruges, and Ypres, plus an extensive and prosperous rural district, the Bruges Free Quarter (the Franc of Bruges), which had won a voice in this college in the fourteenth century. The Members presented John with a list of their most urgent complaints, as was the custom in Flanders and elsewhere in the Low Countries at any Joyous Entry. They demanded, among other things, the rapid conclusion of a trade agreement with England; the transfer of the central ducal tribunal, the Council of Flanders, from French-speaking Lille to the Dutch-speaking part of Flanders, where its proceedings should be systematically conducted in the Dutch language; the regular presence of the duke in Flanders; and the removal of non-Flemish officials.[25] Thus, early in his reign, John encountered a taste of the stiff particularism of his Flemish subjects, as well as a forceful criticism of Philip the Bold's centralizing governmental policies. John countered calmly, with assurances couched in diplomatic terms suggested to him by advisers familiar with the Flemish style of dealing with its dukes.[26]

The success of the Joyous Entry of 1405, indeed, was translated into hard reality. The duke and his family resided for nine weeks in the county during the months following Easter 1405, and for six months in 1407. This was a considerable change from the period before Easter 1405. Only weeks after the Entry, the Council of Flanders had already begun meeting in Dutch-speaking Oudenaarde, and in 1407, as an extreme token of accommodation, it was transferred to Ghent, a city that only twenty years before had waged an all-out war against its Burgundian ruler.

In the following years, John continued to implement this policy of silken goodwill and strove to project the image of a dutiful steward furthering the interests of his Flemish subjects, particularly on the economic front. It was vital to the Flemish textile trade and industry that the import of raw materials from England be safeguarded despite the continuing Anglo-French war. The duke was still hampered — as his father had been before him — by the anti-English obligations he was forced to assume in order to prevent his position in Paris from eroding. But, also like his father, John was perfectly capable of simultaneously promoting conflicting interests. He was able, as a French prince, to expel the English troops that had landed in Flanders, and at the same time to smoothly negotiate a trade agreement with the English. An agreement was finally reached in 1407, with the secret stipulation that it continue in force even in the event of war between France and England.[27] In 1408, John's reform of the Flemish fiscal system meshed perfectly with this streamlining of social and economic life. By recalculating the percentages for the distribution of the tax obligations of the cities and rural districts, the duke brought about a more equitable distribution of the tax burden, thus making it possible to collect virtually all of the tax revenues due.

In the years 1405–7, John the Fearless established a reputation as an efficient manager of the Flemish economy while at the same time displaying a meticulous respect for institutional traditions. At the same time, his successes at the French royal court and elsewhere in the Low Countries (see next section) enhanced his reputation at home. From these years on, John could afford to take the risk of assuming the role of a strong prince at home. In 1407 he began to limit the military autonomy of the Flemish cities by forbidding at least one city, Bruges, to assemble armed contingents from the craft guilds without his consent. The inhabitants of Bruges contemptuously christened the ordinance proclaiming this restriction, the *Calfvel* ("calfskin," a trivializing reference to the fact that it was only a piece of parchment). In fact, the duke was not risking much with this action against one city, since the Flemish cities often disagreed among themselves on many issues and were unlikely to close ranks against John in this case.[28]

A tough general law followed, in 1409. In it the duke revealed the entire spectrum of his centralizing notions of governing Flanders. This new ordinance was designed to bring both the cities and the ducal officials to heel, and in it, John subtly took back with one hand what he had appeared to give with the other. In the Council of Flanders, French was again spoken, but behind closed doors. In public sessions, Dutch speakers were to receive answers in their own language. The council was granted broader jurisdiction over conflicts between the Flemish cities and between the cities and the rural districts, as well as over problems stemming from the trade privileges given to foreign merchants. It was precisely these latter that chilled the Flemish cities to the marrow, because they had already developed their own jurisprudence in international trade. They had developed effective measures and procedures to resolve cases quickly and with considerable expertise. The obligation of having foreign merchants appear before the comital magistrates at Ghent meant delay and inflexibility, but it also meant increased control by the count.

If the duke's firm hand had been directed only against the cities, it would surely have led to increased tensions and hostility. But John the Fearless was adroit enough to take an equally hard line with respect to his own officials and to forbid them—in that same year of 1409—to continue their practice of forcing marriages through the exertion of moral pressure in the name of the government. He also empowered the Council of Flanders to exercise stricter supervision over the ducal officeholders. The Council of Flanders was thus assigned, in addition to its traditional role of regional tribunal for the duke, a new intelligence function. This task involved a permanent surveillance of officials and monitoring the meetings held by the Four Members. On the surface, the duke's stronger policing powers and stronger political grip on Flemish society lent him a certain mystique as the defender of the general welfare, of individual freedoms, and of what was then rather vaguely known as the *bien commun*.[29]

John's curb on urban autonomy by no means restricted the freedom the duke granted to the Flemish commercial community on the international level. A weak economy would yield the state no revenues. A well-filled treasury was the essential prerequisite for the recruitment of a large army in support of the duke's ambitions in regard to neighboring powers. It also provided the economic basis for a civil service and for a professional judicial system capable of maintaining strong internal authority. Tax revenues also paid for the continuous festival of the Burgundian theater-state: feasts at court, patronage of the arts, and Joyous Entries with colorful retinues of luxuriously clad councillors and ladies-in-waiting. Such ceremonies were not, of course, an exclusively ducal creation. The Flemish cities had long been noted for their own rich festivals, employing painters, musicians, and performers. The dukes, wisely, added yet another layer upon the elaborate festive life of prosperous Flanders.

Increased economic activity in Flanders was thus advantageous for its prince, specifically through indirect toll revenues. But John the Fearless applied all his ingenuity toward finding a means of increasing the central government's share of these extra profits in the cities. A simple formula would have been the introduction of a direct, personal tax on his subjects, to be paid directly to the central government. But this would have gone too much against the grain of the long-standing Flemish tradition stressing indirect taxes. Beginning in 1407—the same year as the introduction of the harder political line by the duke—the duke experimented with indirect taxes by insisting, at least in Bruges, that a fixed percentage of the city's revenues be reserved for the state treasury. Specifically, a seventh of the proceeds from such indirect taxes as those on the sale and transport of a number of key consumer products was to go to the state. He was able to win that concession in exchange for the resumption, essential for Bruges, of trade with England. The exchange became possible because of the Anglo-Flemish trade agreement in the same year. But such policies could not be established everywhere; in Ghent, only in 1453, after the great revolt, was John's successor, Philip the Good, able to introduce an analogous measure.[30]

Such steps as these offered the duke an opportunity to undermine, at least in part, the power that urban politicians had been comfortably exercising for centuries. The unlimited monopoly on the administration of city revenues that they had enjoyed prior to 1407 had given them power over both the prince and the city. The magistrates not only decided just how much money the city might allocate to the central government, but also awarded contracts for public works, appointed lucrative public positions, and gave gifts for goodwill. The duke's new grip on the city's treasury after 1407 thus enabled him to curb the fiscal and political power of the urban elites.

But the duke also needed to rely on that same elite, however curbed, as an intermediary to maintain the political and social harmony within cities that was necessary for the implementation of his plans abroad. John the Fearless cultivated a Burgundian clientele among the urban patriciate, granting his clients many favors and ducal protection, but also encouraging intermarriage between the Flemish urban notables and others already incorporated into the ducal family: at court, in the civil service, and among the nobility. Similar social networks were also woven among the nobility and the clergy. Scarcely a single office of bishop or abbot could be filled in the Burgundian territories without the successful candidate's having earlier become associated with the ducal clan. This form of interference by lay rulers in the appointment to high ecclesiastical office was greatly facilitated, of course, by the Great Schism (1378–1415) and the existence of two claimants to the papacy at the same time (and, from 1409 to 1415, three), with corresponding divisions of recognition and obedience that further complicated European diplomacy.

This ducal strategy was intended to limit the autonomous power of the great cities, but not to break the power of the elites within each city. Resistance to the Burgundian dynasty in Flanders was greatly reduced by the discreet mustering of support from the top layers of the city magistrates and thus, indirectly, within the Flemish representative body, the Members of Flanders, individual members of which were recruited from among the city aldermen. Influence within the Four Members was essential for the duke, because this representative body was the spearhead of resistance to centralist governmental policies and the struggle for autonomy. Its sessions were from time to time extended, to include delegates from the smaller cities and rural districts. The meetings were also sometimes held jointly with the nobility and clergy and were then called the Estates of Flanders; in these a number of nobles and clerics from the pro-ducal clans participated, although they were generally unable to breach the particularism of the Four Members. The Members provided a real political counterweight in Flanders at the beginning of the fifteenth century.[31]

John the Fearless seemed to grip the reins less firmly after 1411. John's years of involvement in the French civil wars and struggles for power in Paris, and not any lack of interest in or attention to Flemish affairs, were the real cause, absorbing the greater part of his time, money, and energy. Financing these operations was most difficult during the period 1413–1418, when his exclusion from Paris deprived him of transfers of funds from the French to the Burgundian treasury. This loss weakened the duke in his own territories and obliged him to make both diplomatic and political concessions that would have been highly unlikely in the years 1407–1411. In 1411, it became apparent that John needed to devote all his time and energy to French politics. Under the circumstances it was logical for him to establish his son, Philip, count of Charolais and heir-apparent, as his representative in Flanders, at the Prinsenhof in Ghent. There Philip was surrounded by councillors familiar with the local situation and able to steer him clear of, at least, the worst sort of mistakes that a prince, reared in Burgundy like his father, might make. The regime of the duke and his son built up goodwill in Flanders, by wooing merchants and artisans and by maintaining a trade policy designed to reopen or improve relations with England, France, the German Hansa, Brabant, and Holland after years of disruption and, thus, restore industrial production and export to their normal and necessary levels.

Still, the change of regime was often an occasion for signs of resistance. The first violent sign came in 1411 from the artisans of Bruges, who had never forgotten the humiliation dealt them by the Calfvel of 1407. At the duke's request, Bruges provided a militia that participated in the expedition against the Armagnacs in September 1411. After more than a month of unsuccessful campaigning, however, the Brugeois deserted their duke at Montdidier and, disillusioned by their low pay, returned to the city of Bruges. But the army refused to enter the city until the city government met its list of seven demands. Philip of Charolais and the ducal councillors advised their supporters in the magistracy of Bruges to concede the four points over which the city had direct competence — such as extra pay for the militia—in order to prevent a worse uprising. But the ducal party held fast to the remaining three points, namely those fundamental, in the long run, to centralistic governmental policy—such as the demand to abolish the ruler's fixed portion of the city's taxes, one-seventh of the total.

The militia did concede this point. But the government had, cleverly, made another concession that, though strongly imbued with symbolism, did not touch the essence of the matter in dispute. The despised Calfvel was revoked. Philip had caused the document to be sent from the central archives to Bruges, where a spectacle was made of its being torn to pieces by the people. Shortly afterward, Philip took yet a second psychologically astute step, by dismissing from office two of the ducal officers in Bruges with whom the rebels had violently clashed.

In 1414, it became the turn of the Four Members to take the lead in the confrontation with the duke at a moment when, besieged at Arras by the Armagnacs, he was even more vulnerable. This time the Four Members, and no longer only guildsmen in the Bruges militia, presented him with a twelve-point list of demands compiled by the whole of the Flemish political elite as a condition for raising troops and subsidies. The *cahier de doléances*, or list of grievances, as such petitions were called, demanded the retraction of virtually all of the centralized institutions and taxes introduced during the first ten years of John's reign. Although the duke was prepared to concede eight or nine of these points, the parties could not reach agreement, and both continued to debate the requested subsidies for years afterward.

In July 1417 while John was, once more, fully occupied by military operations in France, the Four Members again demanded concessions, this time with a revised five-point list: the appointment of native officials in Flanders, an Anglo-Flemish trade agreement, free trade with France, a voice for the Members in any new currency adjustment, and the abolition of the board of commissioners established the preceding February and armed with a mandate to deal with any irregularities in the financial and judicial affairs of Flanders. The Members correctly considered this board of commissioners as a measure chiefly intended to erode further the power of the great cities. Once more, as in 1405, John the Fearless saw to it that his concessions of 1417 were carried out in practice, since this was a point of honor for him. It is remarkable that the Flemish cities accomplished their aims solely on the basis of their intrinsic power and through diplomatic negotiation, and not on the grounds of any constitutional texts, as had been the case in Brabant, where the Joyous Entry of 1356 had long proved instrumental in limiting the power of the ruler.

The Duke in Burgundy

Burgundy went through a process of ducal centralization and resistance analogous to that in Flanders, but less forcefully and in a less spectacular manner. The social and economic situations, and hence the political situation, were considerably different from those of Flanders. Burgundy had no great urban centers with a city-republic mentality like those in Flanders. John the Fearless had begun his reign in Burgundy with attention to the regularizing of state finances. The Chamber of Accounts was a central institution based at Dijon with supervisory powers over the collection and administration of state finances; its officials were informed in no uncertain terms, by an ordinance of March 1409, that they risked dismissal from office if they failed to turn in their accounts on time. For twenty-two of them such failure did, indeed, result in suspension. The duke applied pressure on the judicial level as well. In 1405, the duke's judicial officers in Burgundy were given the authority to act on their own initiative, ex officio, rather than wait for a complaint from an injured party or for an initiative from the urban tribunals. This was the Burgundian stage of a broad European trend among centralized states to replace private justice pursued by rival families with uniform judicial action on the part of the government. The movement, based on Roman and canon law and generally designated the *Ius Commune*, had begun in the city-republics of northern Italy and had reached France in the late thirteenth century.

In the years 1404–1409, the rumblings of war were sufficiently stilled so that in 1408, John the Fearless was able to convert his military budget in Burgundy from the expenses related to a wartime offensive to those entailed by an ambitious defensive building plan, for the consolidation of his borders and to discourage internal unrest. Hundreds of repairs were made on ducal castles and other military facilities. These activities notably increased the influence of ducal power, and at the same time they provided the duke's subjects with a feeling of security under a self-confident and successful ruler.

Also as in Flanders, the duke made extensive use of the clientele system in Burgundy. In the only large city, Dijon, he provided members of the principal families with respected and well-paid positions. Here, too, the duke had an established representative belonging to his own family: Duchess Margaret, who presided over the ducal council from her palaces at Rouvres and Dijon, attended the meetings of the Estates of Burgundy in order to obtain subsidies, appointed ducal officials, and kept her busy husband informed. She asked (and received) his advice by letter. In 1414, Margaret succeeded in finally acquiring for Burgundy the territories of Tonnerre and Beaujolais as a shield against the Armagnacs. Just as in Flanders, the emphasis on the defense of the territory and the concerns over the civil war between contending French political factions were responsible for setbacks in the duke's political program of increasing centralization. Above all, John the Fearless never succeeded in implementing his plans of 1415 for administrative reform in Burgundy, intended to reorganize the civil service and to reduce extravagant salaries.

Both Flanders and Burgundy emerged in 1419 from a fifteen-year tug-of-war with John the Fearless over centralization and regional autonomy. The duke's initiatives for the construction of a stronger and more centrally controlled government in both territories were inherently rational, and they corresponded to efforts made by other contemporary rulers toward the same goals. However, the growth of a unified state governed by central institutions was not steady or consistent. The duke's involvement in international conflicts prevented him from ever fully implementing his policies. Any future duke would require years of peace in order to accomplish these goals.

But if John the Fearless never fully accomplished his purposes in Burgundy and Flanders, he nevertheless continued and advanced many of the policies of his father. And as the second generation of the Valois dynasty in both Burgundy and Flanders, John also had a considerable impact in the rest of the Low Countries.

Ducal Ambitions in the Low Countries Outside Flanders, 1404–1419

Like the inhabitants of Flanders and to a greater degree than those of Burgundy, the regions of Brabant, Hainault, Holland-Zeeland, and Liège possessed a well-developed consciousness of their own political autonomy and were reluctant to see their own princely houses absorbed into the Burgundian state, either directly or indirectly. This particularism influenced even those members of the Burgundian ducal house who acquired power in these territories by marriage, designation, or inheritance. In essence the aim of John the Fearless was not to annex neighboring territories, but to keep all of the principalities of the Low Countries out of the hands of other European powers and, at the same time, to play the role of an active political architect building strong political ties among these territories. This second goal was achieved chiefly by insinuating members of his own family, whenever possible by means of matrimony or succession, into the rule of these territories. At the very least, these policies helped to develop a network of territories in the Low Countries sympathetic to Burgundian ducal policy.

From the end of the fourteenth century, Philip the Bold and John the Fearless had created a network of influential Burgundian councillors in these states, lured into Burgundian sympathies by the payment of substantial pensions by the dukes. This external and internal influence on neighboring territories created a balance of power and solidarity within the Low Countries that proved to be of substantial benefit to the duke's international policies and, to a certain extent, to his military operations. On the one hand, his alliances with the friendly princes of the Low Countries strengthened his position in Paris; on the other, his prominence in Paris and his access to the French royal treasury elevated him to a yet more prominent position in the Low Countries. John was able to consolidate this position by showing in turn first one face and then the other: alternating between the velvet glove of diplomacy and the iron hand of arms, a policy leading him first to strengthen his allies, then to weaken them until he again needed their strength.

The Brabant Succession

The duchy of Brabant is an appropriate case for a closer examination of the subtle processes that introduced various forms of burgundianization into a stubbornly (and constitutionally) independent principality. In Brabant the sense of regional autonomy was exceptionally well developed, as the regulations of the Joyous Entry of 1356 prove. Any action on the part of the dukes of Burgundy in respect to influencing Brabant was inherently suspect, partly because the French origins of the ducal house conflicted with the interests of these subjects of the German king-emperors. In 1390 the childless Brabantine duchess Joan decided to take steps to safeguard the future of her territory. She wished to cede Brabant entirely to her niece Margaret of Male and to Margaret's husband, Philip the Bold, but Joan had to do so secretly in order to avoid protests on the part of her subjects, the emperor, and rival pretenders. Since Joan retained the rule of Brabant until her death in 1406, she was able to keep her secret. But before Joan died, her sister the duchess of Guelders made her own claims on the Brabant inheritance. Joan then publicly invited Anthony of Burgundy, the second son of

Philip the Bold, to reside at her court to be coached as a possible successor. Such a policy was more acceptable to her Brabant subjects, and when Joan finally formally abdicated in 1401 in favor of her niece Margaret of Male, she stipulated that Margaret was to be succeeded by her son Anthony in both Brabant and Limburg. This plan of succession was arranged under pressure from the Estates of Brabant, who maintained that their opinion on the succession, as well as the wishes of the duchess, should play a decisive role in the choice of a successor.

But Joan and the Estates were not the only voices to be heard in the matter of succession. The emperor and other relatives in the Bavarian male line also contested Joan's arrangements. The emperor considered Brabant *heimgefallen*, that is, as having reverted to the empire in the absence of a direct male heir.[32] Anthony's prospects brightened, however, because Brabantine public opinion required the duke to live permanently in the duchy, something that neither the Burgundian duke nor the emperor could do. With a duke in residence, Brabant could then preserve its own institutions staffed by native personnel, also a provision of the duchy's territorial charter, the Joyous Entry of 1356. Brabant was one of the few regions in the Low Countries with such a written constitutional basis for the preservation of its own identity.[33]

But Anthony of Burgundy soon gave Brabanters reason to fear for that identity by his creation, while still regent for Joan, of a centralized financial department at Brussels as early as 1404. The department was modeled after the Chamber of Accounts for Flanders, established by Philip the Bold at Lille in 1386, itself based on earlier Burgundian-French models. The appointment to the Brussels chamber of a treasurer from Lille, David Bousse, and the temporary residence in Brabant of capable Flemish jurists and officials like Simon Formelis and Jacob van Lichtervelde must have struck the Brabanters as a violation of their long-standing rights. Not surprisingly, upon the death of Duchess Joan in 1406, the Estates of Brabant demanded and obtained from John the Fearless the formal cession to Anthony of all rights that John claimed to hold over the duchy through his mother, Margaret.

The rule of a territory of one's own soon changes the perspective of a prince, regardless of the policies he may have brought with him when his reign began. Philip the Bold had originally come to Flanders as an instrument of the French king, but he developed an independent perspective and independent policy once he became both duke of Burgundy and count of Flanders. In short order Anthony also developed a distinctively Brabantine style of rule. In 1409 he chose to marry Elizabeth of Görlitz, a niece of the German king and heiress to Luxemburg, a marriage indicative of a more independent course of action than the Burgundian dukes might have wished, perhaps even of territorial ambition of his own.[34] But Anthony was also a vassal of the French king, and he was killed in the king's service at the battle of Agincourt in 1415.

For a short time John the Fearless could dream once more of a personal union of Brabant and Flanders by setting himself up as regent for Anthony's young son John. But the Estates of Brabant proposed their own regency council without the Burgundian duke. John the Fearless came in person to Brussels and Mechelen to negotiate, accusing the Brabantine cities of excuses and delaying tactics and threatening them with ultimatums, all to no avail. He was forced to accept the inauguration of his nephew as duke John IV. Brabant had once more succeeded in preserving its own dynasty. But indirect burgundianization also continued; the regency council was composed not only of representatives of the major cities, but also of influential Brabantine nobles belonging to the Burgundian party.[35]

Regardless of his failure to secure Brabant by acquiring the regency, John the Fearless no longer allowed any power to share his role as arbiter of the affairs of the Low Countries after 1415. The powers that most concerned him were France and the German emperor. In 1418 John succeeded in arranging the marriage between John IV of Brabant and Jacqueline of Bavaria, the only daughter of his brother-in-law and ally William VI of Holland-Zeeland-Hainault, a union vainly opposed by the emperor Sigismund. Independent though it may have been, Brabant was nevertheless subject to a scion of the Burgundian dynasty, now joined to the only other dynasty of importance in the Low Countries, that of Bavaria. By this means the personal union of Brabant and Luxemburg, realized up till that point by the late duke Anthony's marriage to Elizabeth of Görlitz and very strongly inclined toward Germany, was broken. By marrying John IV to Jacqueline of Bavaria, John the Fearless attached the Bavarian house of Holland-Zeeland-Hainault even more securely to the house of Burgundy than had the double wedding of 1385. The new marriage also lessened the influence of Queen Isabela of France, who, as a member of the Bavarian dynasty, had been an unwelcome rival to the Burgundian duke in this affair. Jacqueline of Bavaria had been married to Isabela's son, the French Dauphin John of Touraine, from 1409 until John's death in 1418. From the perspective of John the Fearless, Jacqueline's first marriage had been an extremely dangerous alliance.[36]

The House of Bavaria

The second factor in the growth of Burgundian influence in the Low Countries was the relationship of the Burgundian dukes to the Bavarian royal house. The Bavarians were both formidable allies and formidable opponents. Since 1345 (see Chapter 1), both Hainault and Holland-Zeeland had been partially under the control of the house of Wittelsbach, which ruled Bavaria and also held the German imperial crown. The precise position of the house of Wittelsbach in the European structure of power depended on its possessions and influence in the Germanic world, much as did the position of the dukes of Burgundy in the French world. And just as the Burgundians owed much of their power to the possession of the economically prosperous county of Flanders, so the Wittelsbachs owed much of their power to their control of Hainault and Holland-Zeeland. In many respects the two dynasties were well matched. In marrying two of his children to the Wittelsbach Bavarian House in 1385, Philip the Bold chose the security offered by good neighborly relations over the hazards of more ambitious, but also more dangerous, marriages. But it is not likely that in 1385 Philip had any idea of eventually absorbing Hainault and Holland-Zeeland into the Burgundian territories (this only happened in 1433 – see next chapter). The double wedding of 1385, together with existing family connections to the Brabantine ducal house, were definitely conscious creations of a union of princes in the Low Countries, related by both family ties and common interests. By 1418 this union consisted of the three blocks with nuclei in Flanders, Hainault and Holland-Zeeland, and Brabant.

As early as 1405, the implicit understandings of 1385 became explicit with the treaty between John the Fearless, Count William VI of Hainault and Holland-Zeeland, and Anthony, then regent of Brabant. Such an alliance certainly put a damper on the ambition of any foreign princes to attempt the annexation of any of these territories. It is ironic that the champions of Low Country independence, the Burgundians and the Bavarians, owed their power in large measure to the use they could make of their respective positions in French and German political milieus. And the treaty of 1405 was no mere formality – between 1405 and 1407 the rulers of Hainault and Brabant repeatedly provided troops, lending force to a show of power by John the Fearless in his conflict with the duke of Orléans. In 1408 the prince-bishop of Liège, John of Bavaria, appealed successfully for help to his relatives, the rulers of Brabant and Hainault and Holland-Zeeland, as well as to John the Fearless. The coalition of 1405 proved remarkably sturdy. Moreover, their cooperation was not exclusively military. In more peaceful periods, the alliance functioned as an efficient board of arbitration for the resolutions of political differences within the Low Countries. It also played a crucial role in the international forum of diplomacy. As has been seen already, the negotiating talent of William VI effected a compromise in 1409 between the Armagnacs and the Burgundians.

This peace-promoting mechanism was dealt a disabling blow by the deaths of Anthony of Brabant in 1415 and of William VI in 1417. A new equilibrium was not easily and everywhere attained, in the wake of two such losses. In Brabant the problem was solved relatively simply: the Burgundian John IV became duke in 1415 and in 1418 married Jacqueline, the only daughter of William VI. Such a marriage lay perfectly in the line of the old coalition of 1405.

Hainault and Holland-Zeeland

But the case of Hainault and Holland-Zeeland involved greater complications. William VI was survived by his daughter Jacqueline and his brother John of Bavaria, prince-bishop of Liège. Both claimed rights of succession, and John was even prepared to set aside his title of bishop and in fact proved himself an able strategist. He won the support of the emperor Sigismund, who saw in him a means of checking the Franco-Burgundian advance in the Low Countries. Sigismund also protested the marriage of Jacqueline to John IV of Brabant on the grounds that with the end of the male line in Hainault and Holland-Zeeland, the counties reverted to the empire, and on the grounds that the couple were related within the fourth degree — Philip the Bold had been the grandfather of both.

Sigismund's protests failed, and the marriage was celebrated in March 1418. Jacqueline and John IV became count and countess of Hainault, Holland, and Zeeland and were expected to continue to play the Burgundian hand. But John of Bavaria refused to abandon his claims and began military operations designed to contest their claims on the county of Holland. John the Fearless once again asserted his role as chief arbiter in the Low Countries in February 1419, when he forced John of Bavaria into a compromise with the Treaty of Woudrichem. But John and his German supporters were not totally defeated. The treaty provided that John of

Bavaria and John IV of Brabant were to act as regents of Holland in the name of Jacqueline for five years, and that John of Bavaria was to be Jacqueline's heir should she die without issue.

The Bishoprics of Liège and Utrecht

As ecclesiastical territories, the principalities of Liège and Utrecht enjoyed a special status. They were principalities ruled by bishops, in cooperation with chapters of cathedral canons made up exclusively of clerics and simultaneously holding spiritual and temporal authority. The Burgundian interest in Utrecht became apparent only much later, but the prince-bishopric of Liège came under the influence of Burgundy late in the fourteenth century. Then Liège was torn by intense partisan conflict between two warring factions. One of these — the Haydroits — wished to confine the bishop essentially to the ecclesiastical sector, and the more moderate party was prepared to accept the bishop as both a spiritual and a temporal ruler.[37] Supporters of the Haydroits were to be found primarily in the craft guilds of Liège, although they could also be found among some of the nobility. In 1390 John of Bavaria, brother of Count William VI of Hainault and Holland-Zeeland, managed to have himself elected ruler of the prince-bishopric by the cathedral chapter of Liège without the election's being followed, as would normally have been the case, by ordination and coronation.[38] The new prince-bishop encountered "popular" opposition directly after his election, when he evinced a desire to create a more authoritarian state, reducing the influence of the city aldermen in what had traditionally been a land of self-conscious, autonomous cities.

A second source of tension was the result of the Great Schism. The Avignon pope Benedict XIII, at the instigation of Louis of Orléans, put forward another candidate for the prince-bishopric. This maneuver was another of those designed by Louis to thwart the role of John the Fearless, Louis's chief rival in French politics, in his ambition to act as mediator in the Low Countries. At the same time, of course, the second nomination undermined the authority of the first prince-bishop-elect, John of Bavaria, to such an extent that in 1408, at the height of the conflict, John was obliged to appeal to John the Fearless and William VI of Hainault and Holland-Zeeland. With the armies of his allies, the rulers of Brabant and Hainault — who were, respectively, the nephew and brother of the bishop-elect of

Liège—John the Fearless marched on Othée, where, on September 23, 1408, he crushed the forces of the Haydroits of Liège. John of Bavaria mounted the bishop's throne once more, but he needed the consent of John the Fearless to open negotiations with his subjects, since the duke of Burgundy had unilaterally appointed himself protector of the prince-bishopric. In this capacity, without even consulting the prince-bishop, John the Fearless pronounced in Lille a devastating sentence that dismantled the craft guilds of Liège and imposed a crushing fine on the principality. Liège became virtually a Burgundian protectorate. The victory at Othée also represented a distinct humiliation for the party of the duke of Orléans, which had supported the rebellious Haydroits. It was thus both a demonstration of John's military power and a display of his influence in the wider European theater.

The adventure of Liège, more than any other action, exposed the hitherto veiled ambitions of the Burgundian duke to achieve political domination in the Low Countries. His plans were no longer directed solely against France, but now against the German emperors as well. With the exception of Artois and most of Flanders, the Low Countries were subject to the German king-emperors, and the dukes of Burgundy had not expected significant opposition from the German quarter. At the beginning of the fifteenth century, the empire was fragmented into a multiplicity of several hundred virtually autonomous states under different dynasties, independent urban authorities, and a number of prince-bishoprics, becoming a series of atomized aristocratic powers in which the crown enjoyed great prestige but little authority. From 1400 to around 1410, the crown itself was disputed between two claimants. But with the accession of Sigismund, imperial authority was considerably strengthened. Sigismund presided over the Council of Constance (1415–1417), which settled the papal schism and considerably enhanced his prestige. Sigismund also perceived the threat posed by Burgundian ambitions on the western edges of his realm. In order to counter these and reduce or eliminate Burgundian influence in Brabant and Luxemburg, Sigismund sought a rapprochement with the anti-Burgundian party in France and supported John of Bavaria in his dispute with John the Fearless regarding his aspirations to the succession in the county of Holland. But Sigismund ultimately lacked the resources to assert his own influence throughout the Low Countries nearly as successfully as had Philip the Bold and John the Fearless. After 1417 the emperor concluded a truce with John the Fearless, whose influence in the Low Countries outside his hereditary lands remained undiminished.

Philip the Good and the Burgundian State in Europe, 1419–1425

The assassination of John the Fearless in September 1419 dramatically changed both the life of Philip of Charolais and the political and diplomatic options open to Burgundy. Now duke of Burgundy and soon to acquire the nickname Philip the Good (1419–1467), the twenty-three-year-old Philip was certainly struck by the news of his father's murder. But he also faced the pressing need to devise a political strategy that would preserve the power of Burgundy in the Low Countries, so slowly built up by his father and grandfather. To what extent should he pursue a policy in France similar to that of John the Fearless? Could he realistically challenge the claims of the French Dauphin or the military supremacy demonstrated by the English at Agincourt? Further, the prospect of the loss of income from the French royal treasury, virtually certain once Charles VI died and was replaced by a more competent heir, was substantial and severe. England was now so strong that it was imperative to remain on friendly terms with Henry V. Retribution for the assassination, however badly Philip may have wanted it, would have to wait.

The Parisian political world held few attractions and fewer prospects for Philip the Good. John the Fearless had been so deeply involved in that world that he resided in a specially equipped tower fortress at the Hôtel d'Artois. But Philip the Good's longest visit to the city consisted of only most of one year in Paris, 1420, time enough to make some necessary political arrangements in the wake of the Treaty of Troyes—which had designated Henry V of England as regent, son-in-law, and successor of Charles VI. Afterward, Philip used his short visits more for amusement than for politics. Philip's social style was a far cry from the relentless seriousness of his father. During one of the many balls that he organized during his visits, Philip seduced, among others, the countess of Salisbury, wife of one of the most prominent members of the English delegation, to the great displeasure of her noble husband. The chronicler Chastellain, a fine psychologist, remarked at the ease with which Philip the Good got on with people, "aux femmes surtout" (especially with women), a judgment attested to by Philip's twenty-six illegitimate children.

Also unlike his father, Philip was not particularly fond of battle. In 1421 he allowed himself to be persuaded by his entourage into a few *prouesses* (feats of arms) against the Armagnac forces in a battle at Mons-en-Vimeu, though it cost the Burgundian propaganda machine a great deal of effort to characterize such modest actions as a strategic tour de force by the son and heir of John the Fearless. But if Philip the Good had no Poitiers or Nicopolis to his credit, neither did he experience captivity. And his diplomacy was more than the equal of that of his father and grandfather.

Philip's first diplomatic policies had to deal with France—or rather with three Frances—controlled respectively by the English king Henry V, the Dauphin at Bourges, and Charles VI and Queen Isabela. The France controlled by Charles VI and Isabela at Paris, until recently in collaboration with the Burgundian duke, was still administered by a Burgundian political-administrative group of officials based at Troyes in Champagne. But neither the legal title to the French crown nor any overwhelming public opinion in their favor gave decisive advantages to any of the contending parties. Dynasties and ambitious individuals struggled with each other, and each of them had the support of some portion, at least, of the French population. Although he had fewer ambitions for a powerful role in French royal politics than his father, Philip the Good was equally unwilling, if only because of the emotions aroused by the assassination at Montereau, to concede victory to the Dauphin, who was attempting to become king with the support of the Armagnacs. Philip chose to deal with the French legacy of his father through diplomacy and marriages.

For the first few years after 1419, Philip the Good strove to isolate the French Dauphin by courting public opinion and the English alliance. This form of psychological warfare took place on several different levels simultaneously. The Dauphin was depicted in Burgundian propaganda as a common criminal, the murderer of Montereau. In all the cities of France and the Low Countries, in Paris, Troyes, Navarre, the German principalities, Rome, and Avignon, Burgundians distributed memoranda describing the allegedly true "facts" about the assassination at Montereau and demanding legal punishment of the Dauphin. A Burgundian jurist worked for months to prepare a document that the future chancellor of the duke, Nicholas Rolin, used as an act of indictment. It demanded that the Dauphin acknowledge his guilt by making a penitential procession through the streets of Paris, that a memorial church be built at Montereau, and that a written confession be posted in six European cities. Although none of this was feasible, the charges did make a significant impression, as did Philip the Good's quartering of an alleged accomplice of the Dauphin before the gates of Dijon. Philip's diplomacy also held the Armagnacs at bay and secured the frontiers of Burgundy by treaties of cooperation with the neighboring principalities of Bar, Bourbon, Lorraine, and Savoy, as well as by a marriage alliance with the duke of Brittany.

In France, Philip's policy was shaped by the Treaty of Troyes, which had been signed on May 21, 1420, and shortly after ratified by the Parlement of Paris. According to its terms, Henry V of England, in his capacity as husband of Catherine, daughter of Charles VI (the marriage took place at Troyes on June 2, 1420), was regent of France and sole heir to the French crown.[39] The Dauphin Charles (later Charles VII, 1422–1461) was repudiated and disinherited by the treaty. The parties to the treaty, Henry V and Philip the Good, further pledged not to enter into separate negotiations with the Dauphin. Henry V was now committed to establishing royal rule throughout France, a prospect whose military and financial costs proved daunting. But Henry was also committed to supporting the royal government, in which the French political and social elite at Paris retained the same high judicial, economic, and administrative positions they had held before the treaty. This ruling elite recognized the personal union of the two crowns in the person of Henry V, just as it had formerly approved the control of the French court by John the Fearless. The English king was represented in Paris by his brother John, duke of Bedford and husband of Philip the Good's sister Anne. Between them Henry V and Philip the Good controlled the French crown, and "Burgundian France" and "Lancastrian France" were fused into a single block. When Henry V died on August 31, 1422, the duke of Bedford immediately became regent for Henry's successor, Henry VI (1422–1461, 1470–1471), who also succeeded to the throne of France upon the death of Charles VI on October 21, 1422.

Even the death of Charles VI did not bring Philip the Good to Paris, suggesting that Philip's interests had become concentrated in the Low Countries. Philip entrusted his adroit chancellor Nicholas Rolin with negotiations involving the duke of Bedford and the Dauphin, the latter now claiming the throne as Charles VII.[40] By balancing the English interests against those of the Dauphin, Philip found himself in an enviable bargaining position.

Philip desperately needed that position, because of the considerable financial difficulties raised by the death of Charles VI and the succession of Henry VI. French royal funds had constituted 65 percent of the ducal income of John the Fearless. All these flows suddenly ended after the murder at Montereau, leaving Duke Philip with the relatively modest income of his own domains and aids from Flanders, Artois, and Burgundy. His options in

France being severely reduced, he had to turn to other horizons to seek means to keep up the high ambitions of his predecessors. That horizon would be found in the Low Countries, in territories formally depending on the Holy Roman Empire of the German Nation.

Brabant

In order to increase Burgundian interests in the Low Countries, Philip first turned to the familial networks with ruling houses that had worked so well in the past. In the case of Brabant, this may have appeared deceptively simple. Philip expected to keep the ineffectual duke John IV and his wife, Jacqueline of Bavaria, firmly under his influence as loyal allies. Therefore, he kept nearly half of the councillors of Brabant on his payroll, sustaining the clientage that his grandfather had created in the form of fief-rents, or incomes in return for service and loyalty.[41] Although Philip's views and those of the Estates of Brabant were diametrically opposed, the Estates accepted the marriage of John IV and Jacqueline and saw in it — and in the apparent strengthening of the dynasty with the counties of Hainault, Holland, and Zeeland — a guarantee of their continued independence.

But the marriage of John IV and Jacqueline had already soured by April 1420, probably as a result of the incompatibility of Jacqueline's raging temper and ambition with John's lethargic temperament. The Estates of Brabant, rather than the duke himself, took the lead in the struggle to defend his dynastic claims to Holland and Hainault. But the Council of Brabant was itself divided into pro-Burgundian and pro-imperial factions. The latter urged John IV to compromise with John of Bavaria, eroded his already uncertain power base, accused him of repeated infractions of the Joyous Entry of 1356 that he had sworn to respect, and even appealed to John's brother Philip of Saint-Pol, in whom they saw their only chance of preserving their regional autonomy. The situation was further complicated by social unrest in Brussels and by the continuing pressure exerted by the king of the Romans, Sigismund (elected emperor in 1433), who supported an unsuccessful attack on the city aimed at eliminating Burgundian influence.[42] A popular movement led by the craftsmen of Brussels against John IV and the legal opposition raised by the Estates of Brabant against his evident incapacity to rule further undermined the duke's position. John IV lived out his reign under severe restrictions that placed effective power in the hands of the council.

In 1422 John IV was compelled to swear an oath to respect twenty-eight articles considered as an extension of the old Joyous Entry of 1356, the solemn territorial charter that John had sworn to uphold at his inauguration as duke of Brabant. This Nieuw Regiment, or New Government, secured the Estates' control over the composition and the functioning of the duke's council, his officials and judges, the appointment of urban magistrates, the payment of his debts, the maintenance of internal peace, and the integrity of the territory. One article even recognized the right of the towns to resist in the event of their being invaded by the duke and foreign troops, as John had attempted with the support of some German princes in 1421. These restrictions did not please Philip the Good, and both the marriage difficulties between John and Jacqueline and the curbing of John's authority by the Estates suddenly made Brabant a much greater problem than it had seemed just a few years earlier. In the long term, it was of the utmost importance that Brabant remain under Burgundian influence, because it was through his connections to the Brabantine branch of the family that Philip the Good was later able to make the claims on Hainault, Holland, Zeeland, and Luxemburg that constituted the great territorial breakthrough of his reign.[43]

Holland-Zeeland

The troubles of John IV of Brabant and Jacqueline of Bavaria also spilled over into the county of Holland. The conflict between Jacqueline and her uncle John of Bavaria were only momentarily settled by the terms of the Treaty of Woudrichem of February 1419. Holland was an attractive prize, and John of Bavaria refused to let it go lightly. From the emperor's perspective, Holland was too valuable a prize to fall into Burgundian hands. The county of Holland in the early fifteenth century had acquired a new economic importance: the heavy migration, then just beginning, into its urban centers was the result of a large portion of its arable land becoming unfit for cultivation of wheat and rye. With the influx of this new urban labor force, the cities of Holland became potential rivals to the great cities of Flanders.[44] What made the case of Holland even more complex, however, was the mix of political influences brought to bear on its affairs. John IV and Jacqueline of Bavaria consistently displayed an unpredictable temperament, ranging from inaction to furious and usually futile intervention; at the same time, the mighty patrons of both them and of John of Bavaria, the emperor and the duke of Burgundy, also used their influence on the contending parties.

And there was a new element in these struggles: the violent tension between contending political factions in Holland. In none of the areas of previous Burgundian involvement outside Flanders had party divisions among the subjects played such an active role as in Holland. In order to understand these divisions, it is necessary to consider the history of the county in the second half of the fourteenth century.

In 1345 the county of Holland-Zeeland was riven by the struggle between two broad groups of burghers and nobles, the Hooks (*Hoeken*) and the Cods (*Kabeljauwen*).[45] The origins of these divisions lay in feuds among the nobility, but over the years, alliances changed and the division became associated with a wide range of political issues. The rift lay between noble families who were linked to different groups of urban elites. The parties were thus led by nobles but found their followings in all layers of Holland society. The local power bases of these parties remained largely stable, and in the cities, groups in conflict with each other for virtually any reason found it attractive to range themselves with one or another of the local versions of the Hooks and Cods.[46] Through much of the later fourteenth century these groups, heavily armed and each clad in its own specific raiment, were an all too visible symbol of social and political division.

The issues in debate were even more complex. In the industrial city of Gouda, for instance, the majority belonged to the Hook party. In Amsterdam the international merchants were Cods, whereas the city's inhabitants, more concerned with the local market and with investments in land, were more likely to be Hooks. In Leiden, the division was one of Hook artisans against a Cod merchant elite. There were also profound divisions between the urban populations—who as a group decided questions of governmental taxation in the representative bodies—and the rural population, which, although just as heavily taxed, had no voice in the matter.

Legally, Jacqueline of Bavaria had the strongest claim for the succession in Holland, since her father, William VI, had left her as his only heir. But William's brother John of Bavaria, as has been seen, also made a strong claim and took an energetic stance, attracting the support of Sigismund. As in Brabant in 1405 and Luxemburg in 1412, Sigismund considered that the county should revert to the empire in the absence of a direct male heir, and he supported the claim of John of Bavaria. Jacqueline spent far too much time in Hainault and Brabant to contest John's operations in Holland. She was, moreover, extremely unpopular in Cod public opinion, since her father had waged open war throughout his reign upon the great Cod seigneurs. These wars had proved extremely costly, and the costs had been borne largely by the cities.⁴⁷ Relations had been further strained by William's partisan appointments, exclusively of Hooks, to administrative offices in most cities. The chief city of Holland, Dordrecht, had for this reason refused to recognize the succession of Jacqueline as countess. John of Bavaria took advantage of this refusal, was acclaimed in Dordrecht, and became the leader of the Cod party. He charmed the elites of Holland by his active patronage of the arts at his court. He began a propaganda campaign in the cities, for which he conjured up hopes of economic advantage. He played upon Holland's fears of union with Brabant, and the fears also that its trade centers of Antwerp and Mechelen would be favored and more advanced economic competitors.

Jacqueline of Bavaria and the Politics of Frustration

Philip the Good, obliged to rely on the unstable Jacqueline and John IV of Brabant to counter the opposition of John of Bavaria and the emperor Sigismund, attempted to limit the damage to the Burgundian dynasty by mediating between the pretenders. But John IV proved so politically inept that he was driven to the Treaty of Woudrichem and lost further when John of Bavaria remitted payments agreed to in the terms of the treaty. Jacqueline of Bavaria was enraged at John IV's many tactical blunders and at the circumstances of a badly frayed marriage. She complained with some justice of the discourteous treatment accorded herself and her ladies in waiting at the Brabant court, possibly at the instigation of political opponents. John IV did little to stop this, and his continuing hesitation turned out to be the last straw in the marriage. On April 11, 1420, Jacqueline left Brussels and her husband, a decision that began her remarkable emotional and political adventures. John IV was subordinated to a regency by the Estates of Brabant.

The chronicler Chastellain described Jacqueline as "lovely, very lively, and very strong of body." At the age of nineteen she already had two arranged marriages behind her.⁴⁸ Her departure from Brussels and John IV was also a revolt against that world of men that had manipulated her, and against the Burgundians who seemed to see her only as a useful pawn. Jacqueline fled to England, where Henry V received her with all due honors—but also with a few ulterior motives. Henry saw in Jacqueline's flight to England an interesting opportunity to establish a new English influence on the Continent, no longer only in Lancastrian France, but also close to the very heart of the lands of the duke of Burgundy. Although Philip the Good and Henry V became allies at the Treaty of Troyes a month after Jacqueline's flight, Henry showed no qualms in arranging a new marriage for Jacqueline with his elegant, learned, and charming youngest brother, Humphrey, duke of Gloucester, in October 1422. Even though the validity of this marriage was immediately contested, it was for Jacqueline an attractive sexual and political alternative to the misery of her previous marriages, neither of which may even have been consummated.

With Jacqueline in England and no useful rapport possible to establish with John IV of Brabant, Philip the Good had no alternative but to approach the childless and perhaps now more tractable John of Bavaria. Philip's diplomacy worked; in April 1424, John named the duke his heir for those of his possessions in Holland that were held as private domains. Philip's damage control was threatened, however, in July 1424, when the duke of Gloucester and Jacqueline made ready to land troops on the Continent to recover "their" Holland from John of Bavaria. Philip the Good and his son-in-law the duke of Bedford, for many years his trusted English ally in French politics, strove to prevent the landing. But in October 1424, Humphrey and Jacqueline landed at Calais and soon had all of Hainault under their military control. Their reception in Hainault was not a friendly one, however, and only a fraction of the Estates recognized them as regent and countess. Jacqueline's explosive personality also appears to have alienated the duke of Gloucester, because at the beginning of 1425 he abruptly departed for England, taking with him not Jacqueline, but one of her ladies-in-waiting, Eleanor Cobham, whom he then married.

From her "false and treacherous city of Mons," Jacqueline appealed to her wayward husband in a moving letter, dated June 6, 1425, "for help to your sorrowful creature, if you do not wish to lose me forever. I have hopes that you will do this, for I am fully prepared to accept death for love of you, so much does your noble dominion please me." But she also wrote, with considerable justification, "it appears to me that you have banished me wholly from your thoughts."

On January 6, 1425, John of Bavaria died. Legally, Holland-Zeeland should have gone either to the now-estranged Jacqueline and John IV or to one of the two, with Jacqueline having the better claim. But Jacqueline was now alone in Hainault, and John, as usual, was unable to exert himself, even on his own behalf. Philip the Good took no chances. He captured Jacqueline and imprisoned her in Ghent. With Jacqueline temporarily removed from the scene, Philip opted for a provisional formula that required John IV to turn Holland-Zeeland over to him as a pledge in July 1425. But in September, Jacqueline escaped from Ghent with the aid of Hook partisans and reached Gouda, hoping for the return of the duke of Gloucester and the recovery of her vanished inheritance. She could not hold out in Holland unaided, and in 1428 she formally recognized Philip the Good as regent and heir of Hainault and Holland-Zeeland. When John IV's younger brother died in 1430, Philip the Good became duke of Brabant. A new episode in the expansion of the Burgundian state had begun, in which Holland-Zeeland and Hainault definitively entered the Burgundian sphere of influence.

Namur

Philip the Good also made other gains in these years, with far less difficulty than he experienced with Holland-Zeeland. The county of Namur was of great strategic importance to Philip, because it bordered on Liège, Brabant, and Hainault. In 1420, the childless count John III, who was in financial difficulties, offered to sell his territory to Philip for the unusually high price of 132,000 golden crowns. Philip immediately accepted, although he had to accept John III's continued retention of the county for the remainder of his life. John died in 1429. Philip had already spared himself any possible resistance on the part of his new subjects by assuring himself of his acceptability to the Estates of Namur, prior to the purchase. In 1421 he purchased the county of Béthune, again with far less difficulty than he had encountered in Holland.

The Politics of Culture in the Burgundian Netherlands

One of the most distinctive features of the exercise of political power in late medieval Europe was the dominant role played by the court. With the decline of the court at Paris, the court of the dukes of Burgundy, especially under Philip the Good, became the most admired in Europe. Its household accounts and ordinances, the former surviving from 1426, are the most complete in Europe. Court officials organized the formal details of the daily life of the ruler and his entourage from the levels of accommodation, food, billeting, and entertainment, to the highest level of ceremonial and functional intimacy with the prince. The prince's safety; his ability to impress rivals, subjects, foreign visitors, and ambassadors; his display of power and wealth at weddings, Joyous Entries, tournaments, banquets, and festivals; and the daily routines of governance and administration all flowed from the organization of the court. The protocols of court life regulated relations between contending social elites by serving as a distribution center for revenues, offices, pensions, and gifts. The court's members consisted not only of the ducal family and the duke's officials, but also the nobility, regional elites, prelates, and patricians of Flemish, Dutch, and Brabantine cities, as well as jurists, theologians, financiers, medical personnel, poets, musicians, artists, and official and unofficial historians of the dynasty.

The court life of the dukes of Burgundy was also linked to the elaborate ceremonial life of the Flemish and other Low Country cities, which itself had developed from the twelfth to the fifteenth centuries. The cities developed festive occasions in order to assert their sense of dignity, independence, and sacrality. Cities, too, rang their bells; sponsored processions of costumed musicians and singers through elaborately decorated streets and squares; and celebrated Joyous Entries and ducal or urban victories, funerals, and the births of ducal or comital heirs.

With the link between court life and political image firmly established, the personal influence of an artistically inclined ruler was crucial. When Louis of Orléans was assassinated in 1407, for example, the Armagnacs did not succeed in holding together the creative Parisian world of humanists and men of letters that had surrounded that ambitious prince. The Burgundian dynasty, on the other hand, was able to preserve both its own continuity and the continuity of Burgundian court life and artistic patronage. Philip the Bold was an intellectual and a lover of the arts. John the Fearless appears at first to have been somewhat less so, but even in the whirlwind of his military, political, and diplomatic activities, John found time and money for the completion of his father's mausoleum at Champmol, for the court chapel, and for the expansion of his father's library by two hundred manuscripts.

Burgundian court culture, heavily influenced by French court culture, was also imitated elsewhere in the Low Countries. It was introduced into predominantly French-speaking Liège by John of Bavaria immediately following his accession in 1390, and he took it to the Hague in 1417, when he made his claims on the county of Holland. In Holland John was able to build on the earlier efforts of Albert of Bavaria, the father of William VI, who had developed his court at the Hague. John enabled it to become a center of vernacular Dutch literary and musical creativity, encompassing a broad range of literary genres and styles. Dutch-language courtly literature, however, disappeared in Holland after the Burgundian conquest. The end of an independent court deprived it of the necessary creative stimulus.⁵⁰ But culture at the court of Hainault-Holland before the transfer of power to Philip the Good should not be disparaged, in spite of its political turbulence. It appears that Jacqueline of Bavaria devoted attention to music, for example; in 1423, she possessed a lute, a clavichord, and a harp, and she presented her lover, Humphrey of Gloucester, with a harp as well.

The case of Jan van Eyck is symbolic of this displacement of cultural and political centers. In 1422, John of Bavaria attracted this not-yet-famous painter to his court at the Hague. But Philip the Good, recognizing and appreciating van Eyck's vast talent, lured him in 1425 to the Burgundian court as a very generously paid valet de chambre, or chamberlain. At Ghent and Bruges, both inside and outside the duke's service and even on journeys to distant lands, the brothers Hubert and Jan van Eyck peerlessly captured the essence of contemporary Low Country society in their portraits — such as those of clerics like the Bruges canon van der Paele, the chancellor Nicholas Rolin, a wealthy Italian merchant, and well-to-do Flemish ladies. Philip the Good even sent Jan van Eyck to Portugal to paint a portrait of the princess Isabella, whom Philip was considering marrying. Although none of van Eyck's work for the duke has survived, such masterpieces as his portraits and the great *Adoration of the Lamb* altarpiece in Ghent suggest the sure eye and judgment of Philip the Good. From the Baerze-Broederlam altarpiece and the Sluter well and tomb at Champmol to the ducal service of great Netherlands painters like van Eyck, the dukes of Burgundy displayed a considerable sensitivity to both the visual and the literary arts, as well as to their role as instruments of culture in the service of political power.⁵¹

4
The Decisive Years
1425–1440

Dynastic Marriage and Statebuilding

One of the most useful aristocratic and royal means of obtaining allies and furthering dynastic interests was the carefully planned marriage. In 1385 Philip the Bold had arranged two such key marriages between his own dynasty and the Bavarian house of Wittelsbach, which then held the imperial crown (see Chapter 2). Such marriages sometimes provided extraordinary opportunities for those poised to take advantage of them. One member of the Wittelsbachs, for example, Albert of Bavaria, was even able in 1358 to combine the office of duke in Bavaria with that of regent, Ruwaard, and, after 1389, with that of count of Hainault, Holland, and Zeeland. Albert vigorously undertook to establish the Hague as his capital, expanded the old Knights' Hall into his palace of the Binnenhof, and both patronized and inspired a new and original phase of Middle Dutch literature. Albert's daughter Margaret of Bavaria married Philip's son and successor John the Fearless in 1385. These alliances assured Philip the Bold of stable relations with the neighboring states in the Netherlands and with the crown of France. John the Fearless had then increased his own opportunities in France, by marrying his son Philip the Good to Michelle, daughter of Charles VI and Isabela of Bavaria, in 1409. Philip the Good followed a similar policy in the first years of his reign, although with a notable tactical shift in the direction of an Anglo-Burgundian alliance aimed at securing control of the French throne. In order to outmaneuver the Dauphin and the other pretenders to the French throne, the English king Henry V married Catherine, another daughter of Charles VI and Isabela, and was proclaimed the French king's sole heir by the Treaty of Troyes in 1420. Philip the Good, for his part, married two of his sisters respectively to the brother of the duke of Brittany and to the duke of Bedford, brother of the English king. The duke and duchess of Bedford settled in Paris, as both a symbol and a guarantee of the Anglo-Burgundian coalition.

Michelle of France died in 1422, and Philip the Good then married Bonne of Artois, countess of Nevers, another marriage into the French line. After the unexpectedly early death of Bonne in 1425, however, Philip's plans took on an entirely new dimension. He realized that his own interests would best be served by keeping aloof from the Anglo-French conflict, but he remained saddled with the inheritance from his father of the Anglo-Burgundian alliance. One way to create some distance between himself and the Anglo-French conflict might be to marry again, this time outside the orbit of the contending powers. Philip's councillors and his Flemish subjects also pressed strongly for a new marriage, one with better prospects of producing offspring.[1] Long negotiations ensued with the king of Portugal for the hand of his daughter Isabella, negotiations that included sending the painter Jan van Eyck to Portugal to paint a good likeness of the prospective bride.[2] The marriage agreement was signed at Lisbon in July 1429, and, after the long sea voyage, the wedding of Philip the Good and Isabella of Portugal took place at Sluis on January 7, 1430.[3] It was followed by a week of festivities at Bruges, with culinary extravagances and spectacles, among them a wedding cake containing a sheep.[4]

The lions spouting wine, the fanfare of seventy trumpeters, and the bright banners representing all the duke's territories so impressed his contemporaries that they nearly missed the essential message of this particularly lavish Burgundian spectacle. For the first time, the Valois duke had married outside the dynasties of the great powers. The third marriage of Philip the Good reflected his desire to create a strong centralized structure of ducal authority, a unified, self-supporting state ruled by a prestigious dynasty that the people of Europe would have to respect, one with its own cultural identity, acknowledged as new and original.[5] The choice of a Portuguese bride was not without political calculation. Isabella was not only the daughter of the king of Portugal; she was also the granddaughter of John of Gaunt, son of Edward III of England and duke of Lancaster. After two French marriages, Philip's third could be considered a sign of the survival of the Burgundian-English affinity.[6] This third marriage also produced Philip's only legitimate heir, Charles, later called the Bold, in 1433. The court life of Burgundy under Philip and Isabella became a prototype for all of Europe, a model for imitation.[7]

The Order of the Golden Fleece

The most dramatic indication of Philip's decision to establish himself firmly in the courtly culture of the European aristocracy was his founding of the Order of the Golden Fleece at Bruges on January 10, 1430, in the midst of his wedding festivities.[8] Knightly orders, the most prestigious of which was the English Order of the Garter, appeared throughout most of Europe in the fourteenth century, the last medieval embodiment of the traditional ideals of a warrior elite, doomed to disappear with the development of new military techniques and the appearance of the centralized monarchical state.[9] But for more than a century, the Order of the Golden Fleece served its purpose well. Like other orders, that of the Golden Fleece was a select association designed to honor the duke's most noble subjects and his foreign allies. The order also underlined the bonds between the ducal dynasty and its historical antecedents. The emblem of the order, the fleece of a ram, was a reminder of the legend of the Argonauts, the heroic mariners of Greek mythology who took ship, led by Jason, son of Iolchos in northern Greece, and sailed for the east coast of the Black Sea to bring back the Golden Fleece, which would allow Jason to restore the political power lost by his father. The fleece also became part of the political symbolism employed by the Burgundian dukes to lend substance to their claim to be descendants of the mythical Trojans, a common northern European idea that was echoed by both France and England.[10] In the Low Countries, as early as the late thirteenth century the dukes of Brabant claimed that their dynasty was descended via Charlemagne from the heroes of Troy. But the fleece also had biblical connotations, since it recalled the heroic story of Gideon and his destruction of the Midianites (Judges 6:36–40), a symbol preferred by some of Philip's clerical advisers and, in any case, easily compatible with classical mythology.[11]

Originally the order consisted of twenty-four knights, all of whom had to be of legitimate birth and descended from nobility through all four lines of parents and grandparents. In the first years after its foundation in 1430, the membership of the order originated predominantly from Burgundy and the northern French and Flemish border regions; only one-third came from "the lands over there." From 1440 onward, however, the share of the duchy and free county of Burgundy fell to one-fourth and one-fifth, and after 1478 to only a very few. At the same time, the number of knights from Holland and Zeeland rose from three in the 1440s and 1450s to seven in 1505. Although the members of the order (the number was later expanded) were to be skilled in the use of various weapons suitable for nobles in combat and tournament, as well as in the courtesies of courtly love, in view of the ages of the first members, these latter requirements must have been largely symbolic. The order possessed its own detailed rules and costumes, the most conspicuous of which were the brilliant red robes and the emblem of the golden ram's skin suspended from a richly-worked chain around the neck of the knight. The formal meetings of the order were marked by elaborate ceremonials with the duke of Burgundy as the so-called sovereign of the order. For the duke, the annual chapter meetings of the order provided an ideal opportunity to integrate and bind to himself the nobility of recently acquired regions and new allies. Among members, personal and political conflicts could be treated in a dignified and, therefore, acceptable manner. Chivalric symbolism also served very practical and immediate political interests.[12]

The Duke of Burgundy and the Anglo-French Conflict

In spite of the apparent and unavoidable continuities between the policies of Philip the Good and those of his father and grandfather—the common concern for centralizing their rule over a number of diverse states, their patronage of the arts, certain institutional practices, political networks that furthered cohesion within the Low Countries territories, and the furtherance of dynastic interests—by 1430 Philip the Good had gained control over far more of the Low Countries than had his predecessors, and the possibilities for centralizing his authority were substantially increased. Philip the Good also expanded the ducal patronage of the arts in the service of public relations. Under Philip the Bold and John the Fearless, culture and patronage had been essentially limited to the court and the person of the duke. For many years, Philip the Bold had supported Klaas Sluter and his associates in their work on the construction of the Moses Fountain at the Charterhouse of Champmol, a building and artistic complex that was originally intended to serve as a ducal mausoleum. Philip the Bold was also an avid collector of manuscripts and enjoyed conversing with Parisian intellectuals and artists.

Philip the Good, on the other hand, took pains to cast the spell of his Burgundian court over a larger and much more international audience. Not only did he patronize first-rate artists like Jan van Eyck, but he immediately established van Eyck and others as cultural diplomats. Finally, neither Philip the Bold nor John the Fearless had considered France as a foreign country. They defended to their utmost their own positions in that kingdom, upholding them even at the risk of losing their other territories. Philip the Good regarded foreign territories, including France, as adversaries to be neutralized in order to gain a free hand for the "real" political work, reversing the traditional political agenda of the dynasty. Under Philip the Good, the consolidation of his own internal Burgundian affairs was most important, in order to reappear on the European stage in a much stronger and autonomous position, as an independent power beholden to none for his authority.[13]

Part of Philip's policy shift was triggered by circumstances. His chances of exercising substantial power in France diminished considerably in 1422 with the death of Charles VI, and with that of his English rival Henry V. The French monarchy gradually recovered its position, gaining considerable impetus in this direction with the military victories of Joan of Arc over the English in 1429 and 1430.[14] Thus, while the Burgundian prospects in France were much reduced, the duke observed a number of opportunities for consolidating his position in the Low Countries in those principalities belonging to the German Empire. From 1430 on, the formation and consolidation of a Burgundian territorial princely complex took place at the expense of its great neighboring states.

But the task was not easy. The Hundred Years War between France and England had entered a decisive phase, with the tide turning in favor of France. Increasing French strength in the west was paralleled by the growing strength of the German emperor to the east, now once again in a position to exercise his authority in areas where he found the dukes of Burgundy to be irksome rivals who did not hesitate to appropriate, without his permission and against his will, such imperial territories as Hainault, Holland-Zeeland, and Brabant. Philip the Good inherited enemies on both sides of his domains. The great powers begrudged Philip both his free hand and his success. They ruthlessly sabotaged his carefully engineered political balances.

In France Philip had to deal with the former Dauphin, now Charles VII, who reigned from 1422 to 1461. Philip had publicly held Charles responsible for the murder of his father, John the Fearless, who himself had driven the Dauphin from Paris to Bourges in 1418, and Charles had been forced to remain there until 1429. Philip's only chance for influence in Paris lay with the Parlement, which was also an occasional court of appeal for Flemish, Artesian, and Burgundian subjects in conflict with each other or with the duke.[15] Since this appeal had more to do with political opposition on the part of recalcitrant opponents of ducal central government and with the meddling of the French king than it did with juridical necessity, the Parlement had been courted by Philip and his predecessors with gifts of money and favors. But precisely in these years, the judges in the Parlement began to take a far more independent stand regarding Philip the Good than they had with his predecessors, who had supported an expensive clientele among the judges. In the early 1420s, the number of cases brought in appeal from Flanders to the Parlement rose suddenly, mainly as a consequence of the increasing pressure from the duke's court, the Council of Flanders. Individual subjects and even the large cities sought protection of their interests against their direct lord in the Parlement, which obviously was seen as an independent — indeed, sovereign — court.[16] Around 1440, the Parlement dealt regularly with nearly forty Flemish cases per year. By that time, the high professional standards of the Parlement also prevented the king of France from using these appeals as the occasions of purely political interference in the principality of his vassal. In 1430 the rebellious inhabitants of the Flemish rural district around Cassel managed to win their case against Philip the Good, suggesting that his influence even in Parlement had greatly weakened.[17] One can interpret the behavior of Philip the Good in this sector as part of his policy of centralization.[18] It had quickly become evident to Philip that he badly needed to normalize his relations with Charles VII. In order to develop his own power and effectiveness of rule in the economically prosperous Netherlands, Philip needed at least the neutrality of his neighbors, especially France. He also wanted to distance himself from the brutal methods, false propaganda, and military interventions upon which John the Fearless had relied.

The first signs of rapprochement with France date from 1424. Philip voluntarily refrained from attacking the episcopal see of Tournai, which was located geographically inside Hainault but was politically an enclave dominated by the French king.[19] Philip negotiated a substantial annual payment from the city in return for his favor. In the same year Philip also reached an agreement with Charles VII at Chambéry, according to which Charles pledged to discontinue military operations along the Franco-Burgundian frontier from Auxerre to Lyons. In exchange Philip agreed explicitly to recognize Charles VII as king, even though he had already acknowledged the English claims at the Treaty of Troyes four years earlier. In 1429 the Chambéry agreement was extended by an analogous treaty, dealing with the frontiers of the northern portion of the Burgundian territories. With these steps, Philip had already distanced himself from the murder of John the Fearless at Montereau and also from the unconditional alliance with England.

The rapprochement with France, however, also entailed a new element of risk. Philip still had to maintain good relations with England. After all, Philip's sister was married to the second most powerful noble in England, the duke of Bedford, regent of France and Philip's loyal and long-standing friend, one who had faithfully defended the interests of England and Burgundy in Paris.[20] Bedford was also Philip's best safeguard against the new plots of Bedford's brother, Humphrey, duke of Gloucester and regent of England, who had already, during his brief marriage to Jacqueline of Bavaria, toyed with the idea of acquiring for himself part of the Low Countries possessions of the duke of Burgundy. In regard to England, of course, Philip had other troublesome issues with which to contend. A number of his advisers still favored military collaboration with England, and a number of Flemish cities had crucial economic relations with England.

In 1429 Joan of Arc persuaded the Dauphin Charles to undertake a more vigorous political course, even having himself crowned as Charles VII in the city of Reims as a lesson to the English "usurper." Once more the English government found it necessary to intervene militarily in France. On the basis of the Treaty of Troyes of 1420, Philip the Good was promptly appointed royal lieutenant of the English king Henry VI on French soil. The English made plans to reinforce Paris, which they still held, surrounded by the forces of Charles VII, who was already besieging St. Denis in preparation for an attack on Paris itself. An English military operation in the southwestern part of France around Guyenne was designed to divert some of the attention and resources of the French king. The English also made plans for a march on Reims. Philip, very ambivalent about these operations, somewhat reluctantly set forth in the summer of 1430 to besiege the town of Compiègne, seventy-five kilometers north of Paris, where he met with no success. "I only came to war at your request," he wrote to his royal English ally in a letter that he would probably rather have signed with some other formula than the flowery "vostre humble et obeissant oncle" (your humble and obedient uncle).[21] In other correspondence, Philip complained endlessly about the absence of English subsidies for his troops and about the economic damage to his territories caused by the war. He threatened Bedford and Henry VI with the conclusion of a separate peace with France, and he carried out his threat to the extent of agreeing to a truce with France in September 1431.

Recognition by Pope and Rejection by Emperor: The Council of Basel and the Treaty of Arras

Philip's marriage to Isabella of Portugal in 1430 had signaled another dimension of his new policy: neutrality with respect to France and England and the ambition to demonstrate to the rest of Europe that the Burgundian state itself had achieved the status of a great power. In both respects Philip encountered considerable opposition. He did his utmost to remain neutral in the Anglo-French conflict, as well as in the great struggle within the Church that broke out in 1431 between the new pope Eugenius IV (1431–47) and the clergy gathered at the Council of Basel.[22] The quarrel concerned the question of whether the Church would remain a centralized institution in which political decision making lay essentially with the pope and curia (the papal administrative staff), or whether the Church should adopt a conciliar form of government, providing for substantial and regular involvement on the part of the cardinals and other clergy. The Council of Constance had ended in 1417 with a compromise on this question, placing the authority of the council above that of the pope. This had been promulgated as canon law by the conciliar canons *Haec Sancta* of 1415 and especially *Frequens* of 1417.[23]

From the moment of his accession in 1431, Pope Eugenius IV made it clear that he wished to reassert the authority of the papal office. As a counterweight to the influence of the cardinals and other conciliar theorists, he sought support among the lay princes. He succeeded admirably with Philip the Good by promising to intervene with the German emperor to ensure Philip's continued rule in Brabant and Holland-Zeeland, and by appointing to bishoprics in the Burgundian territories only those clerics who were nominated by the Burgundian duke because of their favorable attitude toward his regime.[24] Since virtually all of the European lay rulers, including Charles VII, supported the conciliar group, which promised greater influence to the growing "national" churches of Latin Europe, Philip had to do his utmost to remain neutral. He had other objectives at Basel besides papal support.[25]

One of these objectives is illustrated by the long procedural battle over the proper seating of the many lay delegates within the cathedral of Basel. Jean Germain, Philip's ambassador, demanded a seat adjoining those of royalty, as had been the case of the Burgundian ambassador at the Council of Constance.[26] Germain argued his case on May 26, 1433, with a well-documented speech in which his duke was portrayed as a descendant of Charlemagne and of the Trojan heroes of antiquity. Such matters as the order of seating at ecclesiastical and other assemblies were not a matter of vanity, but a reflection of the proper ordering of powers in the world and of the world's recognition of that order.[27] The ambassador was testing Philip's acceptance as a respectable European sovereign at the royal level. But Sigismund rejected Germain's claim, declaring that the council had more important work than that of catering to the wishes of the duke of Burgundy. The emperor's dismissal of Germain's arguments should be understood less as a reflection of the emperor's idea of proper world order than as the result of imperial resentment of Burgundian incursions into imperial territories in the 1420s. The imperial-Burgundian feud was never settled at the Council of Basel.[28] After a humiliatingly long wait, a compromise was reached in May 1434, seating Philip's ambassador next to the king of Scotland. Philip had not yet attained the position he claimed in the hierarchy of European sovereign houses.

The emperor was not the only ruler who opposed Philip the Good. Charles VII of France, hoping to force Philip out of his neutrality, managed to maneuver the duke of Austria, Frederick IV, into invading Burgundy. In 1432 the French army itself attacked the Burgundians in the neighborhood of Auxerre, to the northwest of the duchy of Burgundy. In 1434 Sigismund launched a *Reichskrieg*, a formally declared imperial war, against Philip, having finally freed his hand by crushing the heretical Hussite rebellion in Bohemia.[29] On May 8, 1434, Sigismund even formed an alliance with Charles VII against Philip, the "disobedient rebel." But the lack of imperial resources and French royal diplomacy prevented the alliance from invading Burgundy, and the German cities, dependent on good commercial relations with the prosperous Burgundian territories, refused to levy troops for the emperor. At the same time, Charles VII of France, with apparent generosity, offered Burgundy an alliance that would remove the danger of a Franco-imperial encirclement.

Reluctant to abandon his policy of neutrality between France and England, and aware that his old ally Bedford lay dying at Rouen, Philip nevertheless had to choose a side in the conflict. The German threat suggested that he side with France, as did the rest of Charles VII's policy. Charles had also spent a great deal of money to persuade some of the duke's chief advisers to support a French alliance. Charles's bribery had reached even Philip's closest councillors, including the chancellor Nicholas Rolin[30] and

Philip's favorites, the lords of Croy (see Chapter 5).[31] Charles seems even to have persuaded duchess Isabella in favor of the treaty he concluded on September 21, 1435, in the city of Arras, by means of which France and Burgundy became allies once again.[32]

The Congress of Arras has often been termed the first international peace conference, attended and influenced by representatives of both Eugenius IV and the Council of Basel, as well as by delegations from England, France, and Burgundy, including both noble laity and high clergy. The Congress was held in the great monastery of St. Vaast, and in spite of the animosity between the English and French delegations (who tried to avoid meeting face to face throughout the two months during which the Congress was in session), the Congress appears to have done its business in a remarkably peaceful fashion. The treaty between Philip the Good and Charles VII was thus arranged in the midst of the most solemn circumstances that northern Europe had ever witnessed.

Philip's territorial gains from the treaty were not substantial. According to the treaty, Philip received from France the city of Péronne on the Somme, along with its surrounding territories. He also received land around Auxerre and Mâcon, areas over which, by that time, France had no de facto control in any case. He received Ponthieu, a seigneury to the southwest of Artois, and other cities along the Somme located from the southwest of Hainault, along the southern border of Artois, to the English Channel. This was done as a pledge, which Charles VII reserved the right to redeem. In the event, the French crown did not redeem the Somme towns until 1463 (see Chapter 5).

More important to Philip's prestige were those clauses of the treaty that gave him moral satisfaction, and those pertaining to religious foundations made in atonement for the murder of his father at Montereau. Most important was Philip's personal release from all obligations of a vassal of the king. No longer a vassal, Philip could begin laying the groundwork for replacing the appellate authority of the Parlement of Paris over his subjects in Flanders and other French fiefs within the Burgundian state by his own Burgundian Great Council, gradually built up into a full-fledged central high court and eventually renamed the Parlement of Mechelen, in 1473.[33] Although the agreement between France and Burgundy remained in place, Philip's strategic position was not strong enough to enable him to conclude a peace between France, England, and Burgundy. He had to settle for only the Franco-Burgundian treaty because of English resistance. After Arras, Henry VI of England bluntly referred to Philip the Good as "the rebel."

English Revenge and Imperial Hostility

The Treaty of Arras represented the recognition of Philip the Good as a prince of European stature. Thenceforth France and England had to deal with him as an equal. In the long run, then, the treaty worked to the advantage of Burgundy, but it also had distinct disadvantages in the short term. It posed a threat to Philip's cherished policy of neutrality and led inevitably to a beach in relations with England, and thus to a conflict with Philip's Flemish and Dutch subjects, economically dependent on England.[34] And it had done nothing to solve the problem of Burgundian-imperial relations.

Philip's concerns with England were sharpened by the death of Bedford in September 1435. Bedford's brother, Humphrey, duke of Gloucester, still rancorous over his earlier clashes with the Burgundians, deemed the time ripe for further intervention in Burgundian affairs and formed an anti-Burgundian alliance on the Continent toward the end of 1435.[35] The alliance consisted largely of Philip's old enemies: Jacqueline of Bavaria, who was just as vindictive toward Philip as was her former husband; the German emperor Sigismund; Arnold of Egmond, the duke of Guelders and an ally of the emperor; and the count Palatine of the Rhine.

Philip decided to strike first. In January 1436 he attacked Calais, the English enclave on French soil just southwest of Flanders. Calais was a staple town, enjoying the benefits of a commercial privilege stipulating that the entire English export of wool and sheepskins to the Continent had to pass through the city, and that taxes levied on this trade by the English crown were to be collected there. Calais was thus of the utmost strategic and economic importance to England, given its location on French soil at the narrowest part of the English Channel. Hoping to mount a successful campaign against Calais, Philip the Good appealed primarily to Flemish urban militias, which, as usual, proved to be both undisciplined and unruly. En route to Calais, the militias amused themselves by widespread pillaging without ducal permission, and when they arrived at the siege of the city, they achieved virtually nothing. Their most important achievement was the construction of a wooden watchtower on a hillock, promptly razed by the English.

Because of its coastal location, Calais could only be taken if the fortress was also assaulted from the sea, or at least blockaded effectively enough to prevent any fresh supply of goods and troops from arriving by sea. Philip knew that he needed a fleet, but to obtain one, he had to have new ships built in Brabant and others hired and armed in Zeeland and Holland. Such a complicated land and sea campaign of infantry attack and naval blockade required detailed coordination, and, in this case, coordination failed. The Burgundians' lack of experience with large naval enterprises may help to explain why the fleet did not arrive until weeks after the ground troops and was thus entirely ineffective. In addition, a desperate plan to block the harbor of Calais by sinking a ship in it failed utterly. The entire experience of the siege of Calais was a concatenation of serious strategic and logistical blunders on the part of the Burgundian leaders.[36] The militia of Ghent, in particular, were so thoroughly demoralized by the failed campaign that they returned home after four weeks at the siege. The duke accused them of desertion and cowardice, but they quickly pointed out the deficiencies of the equally ineffectual ducal officers.

The men of Ghent had other reasons to break off the siege, and these reasons reveal the absence of any serious support in Flanders for a war against the English. All Flemish cities feared the disruption of trade relations with England, particularly at a time when it was becoming apparent that the towns in Holland, untouched by the war, were profiting from the displacement of the English trade. On the occasion of a later attack launched by Philip upon an English fortress on the Somme, Le Crotoy, even knights of the Golden Fleece and other nobles were conspicuous by their absence. In the small southern Flemish city of Poperinghe, where Humphrey of Gloucester arrived in the course of his anti-Burgundian expedition on the Continent, the burghers went so far as to acclaim him as count of Flanders on August 15, 1436. But if the Flemings did not want war with England, neither did they support Humphrey with much enthusiasm. After a single destructive raid through Flanders, he prudently withdrew. The English had no more desire than did the Flemings to disrupt their lucrative trade wth Flanders.

The alliance of 1435 between Humphrey of Gloucester and the emperor Sigismund quickly dissolved, but the emperor continued his strikes against Burgundian territory from the east. In 1437 he authorized the Landgrave Louis of Hesse, one of many small German territorial states, to recover on his own account all the imperial territories that had fallen into Philip's hands by inheritance, purchase, or annexation. But the inhabitants of Brabant and Hainault were sufficiently realistic about their own best interests as to refuse to commit themselves to Louis's enterprise. The death of Sigismund in December 1437 put an end to the imperial attempt to redraw the map of northwestern Europe.

Philip needed someone capable of assessing his position and options in the face of English and imperial hostility, especially since the loyalties of even his most trusted councillors were, obviously, divided. On September 10, 1436, in the wake of the shameful affair of the siege of Calais, Hugh de Lannoy, Philip's ablest councillor, addressed just such a memorandum to the duke, giving a shrewd analysis of the political situation. Lannoy first proposed a general peace between France, Burgundy, and England. The war and its ravages in the Flemish coastal area, and its disruption of the trade routes to England, was a luxury that neither the Burgundian state nor the Flemish cities could afford. Continuing such a war would spur the cities to rebellion and lead to a loss of confidence in the ruler. Trade and industry were of greater importance to Philip's subjects than were political and military actions. Only as peacemaker could the duke gain popularity.[37]

> You must have appreciated, during the siege of Calais, what harm was done by the lack of finance, and it is to be feared that the war has only just begun. If you need to raise finance in Brabant, Holland, and other lands of yours, it can only be with the consent and good will of the people, especially when they see that you are at war [with England] and that the Flemish seem likely to revolt against you at any moment. If the truth be told, you have no territory whose populace is not hard pressed financially; nor are your domains, which are mortgaged, sold, or saddled with debts, able to help you.
>
> Again, you have seen how agitated your Flemish subjects are; some of them, indeed, are in armed rebellion. Strange and bitter things have been said about yourself, your government, and your leading councillors; and it is very likely that, having got as far as talking in this way, they will soon go further than mere talk. Moreover, if you pacify them by kindness and by accepting their demands, other towns, which have similar aspirations, will rebel in the hopes of getting similar treatment. On the other hand, if you punish and repress them, it is to be feared that they will make disastrous alliances with your enemies. If by chance they start pillaging and robbing, it is possible that every wicked person will start plundering the rich. Covetousness exists among the well-off; you can imagine how much worse it is among the populace. In this matter, there is much cause for anxiety.
>
> I note that, according to reports, the English are planning to keep a large number of ships at sea in order to effect a commercial blockade of your land of Flanders. This is a grave danger, for much harm would result if that country were deprived for any length of time of its cloth industry and commerce. And you can appreciate how much it would cost to send a fleet to sea to protect this commerce and resist the enemy. Moreover, if Holland and Zeeland continue their trade with the English, and they will probably want to do this, the Flemish, finding themselves without commerce, without their cloth industry, and involved in war on sea and land, will probably make an alliance with the English, your enemies, which could be very much to your prejudice and dishonor.[38]

In fact, in Artois, Flanders, Brabant, Zeeland, and Holland, the effects of privateering and of the blockade disrupting the English wool export had dire results. Moreover, the Dutch towns simply ignored the duke's ban on English trade, while the administrations of the cities immediately pressed him to open negotiations. Unemployed artisans became rebellious, particularly after the price of grain rose to crisis levels in 1437 and 1438. In the spring of 1437, the cities and the ducal council sought discreet contact with England.

In spite of the restrictions imposed by the enduring terms of the Peace of Arras, Philip the Good virtually was obliged to open a diplomatic offensive in favor of peace with England and wisely placed its design in the hands of the anglophile Hugh de Lannoy. By May 1438, negotiations began in earnest for a trade agreement and a truce, which took effect in September 1439 and was afterward extended regularly for a year at a time. Burgundy and England could not risk an official peace treaty in light of the Peace of Arras, but neither could they continue to be at odds with each other, because that would have inflicted too much damage upon both of their economies. As Hugh de Lannoy reminded Philip, such conflict also held political implications for the Low Countries. Conferences held in 1439 revealed further English resistance, but Lannoy's diplomacy led in July 1439 to a Flemish-English and a Dutch-English trade agreement, separately from the purely political negotiations concerning the war.[39]

By 1440, Burgundian relations with France and England had, thus, returned to approximately the position they had been in at the very beginning of the fifteenth century, when Philip the Bold had held the reins of power. On the one hand, the Burgundians were at something of a disadvantage, since their great resource of the earlier period—the ability of using French public finances to the advantage of the Burgundian duke and state—had disappeared by 1440. But overall the Burgundian position was considerably stronger, for in the intervening period, the Burgundian dynasty had acquired control over seven territories. In comparison with the four it had held in 1419, this meant a considerable increase in international prestige. The new territories had also shifted the center of Burgundian power to the Low Countries and to the principalities that were, technically, within the empire. The "lands from here onward," *landen van herwaerts over, pays de par deça*, as the Burgundian dukes had come to call their Low Countries possessions, now formed a geographically contiguous and economically coherent whole. The original Burgundian lands became "the lands over there," *landen van derwaerts over, pays de par de-la*. It stood to reason that the duke would now direct his attention primarily to the consolidation of this considerable territorial acquisition and even plan to forge it into a single unified state. Philip thus established something of a "cold peace" with France and England, relieved by trade agreements. By 1440 he had come to owe his power to neither France nor England, and his conflict with the empire had come to an end with the death of Sigismund.

The 1430s were, thus, decisive years. But the transition to nonaligned international status and the increasing international prestige of Burgundy might have been more rationally and diplomatically managed, nor did Burgundy emerge from it unscathed. The princes of Europe had certainly placed substantial obstacles in the path of Burgundian ducal ambition. For a time in the 1430s, Philip the Good paid a stiff price in domestic unrest, particularly in Flanders, for his ineptitude in international relations. But on the whole, Philip had done better than any contemporary ruler except Charles VII.

And when he turned to consolidating his own territories in the Low Countries, Philip opted for gradual change. He patiently built up goodwill and laid almost imperceptible structural foundations. By diplomacy and charm, and only occasionally by a show of power, he managed to cast the Burgundian spell over the autonomous inhabitants of Namur, Brabant, Hainault, and Holland-Zeeland, and to gain their reluctant acceptance of annexation, and a place in the Burgundian constellation of territories.

Jacqueline of Bavaria in Hainault and Holland-Zeeland

The most reluctant territories were Hainault and Holland-Zeeland. At the death of her uncle John of Bavaria in 1425, John's niece Jacqueline of Bavaria, theoretically, held the upper hand as the legitimate heir and successor to her father, William VI of Bavaria. Needing external support as well as legitimacy, Jacqueline hoped to gain the former from her third marriage, to Humphrey of Gloucester. But that hope vanished with Humphrey in 1425, when he left her alone and embittered in Mons, capital of Hainault. Nor could Jacqueline secure Holland-Zeeland. In a land divided by partisan strife between Hooks and Cods, Jacqueline was a Hook, whereas a large portion of the population were Cods and willing to recognize Philip the Good's right to inherit, which he had cleverly insinuated into his earlier agreements with John of Bavaria and John IV of Brabant in 1424–25.

But not all inhabitants of Holland-Zeeland were equally willing to accept Philip, whom they regarded as an ambitious duke from the south.

They had no knowledge of Philip's plans for Holland, nor did they know whether the taxes they paid to the duke would be spent for the protection of their own agriculture, industry, and trade, or flow imperceptibly into the single great treasury of the Burgundian dynasty, to be squandered on magnificent feasts and fanciful projects that the sober Dutch farmers and merchants were unlikely to appreciate — especially if these feasts and spectacles were to be produced in Brussels, Bruges, or Dijon. In the first phase of his acquisition of rule in Holland-Zeeland, from 1419 to 1425, Philip did not envisage an outright annexation, having more in mind a scenario that entailed indirect control and a process of burgundianization similar to the one previously enacted in Brabant. But the death of his ally John of Bavaria seems to have changed his plans. Philip's pawns, John IV of Brabant and Jacqueline of Bavaria, had proven either insufficiently vigorous or untrustworthy. Jacqueline's private ambitions and English plans to make use of the duke of Gloucester, separated but not yet divorced from Jacqueline, threatened Philip's earlier plan. Philip then changed to a plan allowing him to take over the administration of Holland-Zeeland and channel the financial yield of this prosperous territory more efficiently into his own treasury. But in order to accomplish this, Philip also needed to appear to his new subjects as a "desirable prince"; he needed to win hearts and minds to obtain titles and taxes. And first of all, he needed to neutralize Jacqueline of Bavaria and Humphrey of Gloucester.

At the news of the death of John of Bavaria, Jacqueline ensconced herself in Hook-dominated Gouda and waited for support from England. A year later Humphrey of Gloucester finally sent a fleet and an army of two thousand men. Both were soundly beaten by Burgundian troops at Brouwershaven in Zeeland, Philip having been advised of Humphrey's move in advance by none other than Humphrey's own brother and Philip's faithful ally, the duke of Bedford. Humphrey's English archers proved to be no match for Philip's heavily armed knights.

Philip also managed to capture Jacqueline and confine her in Ghent, only to learn of her escape back to Gouda in September 1425. Jacqueline immediately assumed the leadership of the resistance to Philip in Holland-Zeeland, and three long years of bitter warfare followed. A great deal of blood was spilled, a great deal of material damage was done, many trade routes were temporarily but thoroughly disrupted, and enormous sums were drained from the treasuries of all parties involved. Philip took the challenge seriously and sacrificed nearly three full years to lead the military operations himself, meanwhile neglecting his other political objectives in

France and his other territories. In order to convince the Dutch cities of the sincerity of his intentions, he had the Four Members of Flanders participate in negotiations; they were thus present at his formal inauguration as heir to Holland in Den Briel on March 25 and 26, 1426. The sympathies of the population, partly because of the civil war between Hooks and Cods, were initially ambivalent and quickly shifting, as were the fortunes of war. In October 1425, Jacqueline inflicted a defeat on the Burgundian army near Alphen on the Rhine, between Gouda and Leiden, in her own territory. In April 1426 she won again at Alphen, this time with the support of the Dutch town of Alkmaar and that of the farmers of Kennemerland, a district in North-Holland whose legal and political interests were closely tied to those of Frisia, and, therefore, that had often been in conflict with the counts of Holland over legal rights.

In July 1426, Philip struck back hard. Driving Jacqueline's forces from the field and separating her allies, he undertook a policy of brute terror, comparable to that of his father at the battle of Othée in 1408. The conquered farmers of Kennemerland, already frustrated by what they perceived as an unjust fiscal burden imposed by the cities, were saddled with a fine of one hundred thousand gold crowns, along with an annual hearth tax (a tax on each residence), and they lost the right of their aldermen to administer justice autonomously. Alkmaar lost its walls and its privileges. These steps were uncharacteristic of Philip, generally, and did not contribute to his earlier plan of pacification; as soon as the storm died down, he began to restore many of the rights he had taken away. On several occasions Philip was even able to appear in the role of peacemaker. While he was besieging the Dutch town of Zevenbergen, a quarrel arose between the military leaders of the garrison and the urban population over the provisioning of foodstuffs. The duke was able to mediate between the two Zevenbergen parties so effectively that the town acknowledged him as count and its inhabitants declared themselves his loyal subjects.

The Peace of Delft and the Last of Jacqueline of Bavaria

April 1427 saw the death of the ineffectual John IV of Brabant. Although Jacqueline of Bavaria had been the undisputed countess of Hainault up to that point, Philip the Good now saw an opportunity to lay his own hands on the county. Jacqueline rallied to her cause a number of Philip's enemies: her conniving mother, Margaret of Burgundy, grandiosely calling herself duchess of Bavaria as well as countess of Hainault, Holland, and Zeeland; and her English husband, Humphrey of Gloucester. But English ships proved unsuitable for navigating in the sandbars of the Dutch waters, while Philip had the advantage of being able to hire local flat-bottomed vessels.[40] The actual leader of the English forces in the field was the duke of Salisbury, who had had a personal score to settle with Philip ever since Philip had seduced Salisbury's wife at a ball in Paris in 1424. But Jacqueline's great plans never materialized, because Bedford rejected them as too dangerous to the Anglo-Burgundian alliance and to English interests in France. Moreover, in January 1428, Eugenius IV declared Jacqueline's marriage to Humphrey invalid. Gloucester thus obtained his freedom, married Eleanor Cobham, and promptly cut off the last of Jacqueline's English subsidies.

Disillusioned at last by Humphrey's faithlessness and faced with the failure of her last alliance, with Rudolph of Diepholt, bishop of Utrecht, Jacqueline was reluctantly forced to accept Philip's terms. In July 1428, Philip and Jacqueline agreed to the Peace of Delft. Philip recognized Jacqueline as countess of Hainault, Holland, and Zeeland, on the conditions that she refrain from appealing the papal ruling on her marriage to Gloucester, accept Philip as her heir and governor over her lands, and, above all, promise not to marry again without Philip's consent. Philip was to appoint six members of the comital council of Holland and Jacqueline three, and the revenues were to be shared.

Philip's dominance was now both formally and materially established. His victory had come about because of the wealth of resources upon which he could draw, by his astute diplomacy with the towns of Holland and Zeeland, and by the support of Bedford. On her part, Jacqueline's Hook power base proved inadequate and her masculine allies unreliable. More fundamental was the deep division into two warring factions in Holland-Zeeland, which had resulted in a rift extending through all strata of society. These divisions offered a made-to-order power base for any strong opponent of the legitimate count. In this context, it is understandable that Philip's first concern following his victory over Jacqueline was the healing of the social rift.[41]

Even before his victory, Philip had begun to initiate a gentler process of burgundianization in Holland-Zeeland.[42] As early as 1426 he had added a Flemish captain-general to the Council of Holland, the highest judicial and governmental body of the county.[43] Immediately after the Peace of Delft, the Council of Holland was reestablished and, by way of reconciliation, filled with a carefully measured balance of former Hook and Cod adherents. The use of these faction names, however, was thenceforth prohibited in an attempt to prevent a resurgence of destructive factionalism. In October 1430 Philip made an additional gesture to his subjects in Holland-Zeeland, farming out the government of the county for a period of eight years to the native van Borselen clan in order to give at least the appearance of autonomy to the county. But this experiment soon went awry: in 1432 Philip learned in the Hague that one of the van Borselens, Frank, had secretly married Jacqueline of Bavaria, thus abrogating both the agreement with the van Borselens and the conditions of the Peace of Delft.[44] Philip immediately imprisoned Frank van Borselen and, in order to free her husband, Jacqueline permanently ceded all her rights in Holland-Zeeland to Philip.

Jacqueline's fourth marriage did not last long, nor did she long survive it: she died in 1436. She had had a remarkable political and marital career, defending her claims to legitimacy against the most powerful and ambitious men of her age. Her career echoes the prominence of strong feminine figures in much of the literature of the late fourteenth and fifteenth centuries. But neither Jacqueline's ambitions nor her abilities were acknowledged in pictorial representations, in which she was treated with scornful criticism of her quest for new marriage partners (without whom, it may be added, she would have been unable to accomplish as much as she did). Was hers a romantic and adventurous approach to political activity, or a calculating series of marital alliances designed to further her own plans? In the event, Gloucester failed her and Philip the Good proved even more calculating than she.

A complete process of burgundianization could now proceed in Holland-Zeeland. Philip's loyal councillor Hugh de Lannoy from Walloon Flanders, became *stadtholder* of Holland-Zeeland, and, as president of the Council of Holland, his appointment ensured that this body became, in fact, a dependency of the Great Council of the duke of Burgundy, with the result that ultimate decision making took place outside Holland-Zeeland. Financial policy, too, passed entirely under the external control of the ducal Chambers of Accounts at Brussels and Lille.

In Dutch commercial circles, Philip gained considerable gratitude through Hugh de Lannoy's successful negotiation in 1438 of a Dutch-English trade treaty in the aftermath of the Anglo-Burgundian hostilities of 1436. In the same year, the duke managed to increase his hold over his Dutch subjects by skillfully negotiating wth the Hanseatic cities in the matter of the problem of piracy in the Sont, the sea straits between Denmark and Sweden. But the agreement remained unsatisfactory for the expansionist Dutch shippers. They launched a sea war on their own initiative against the Hanse, enforcing their share of the Baltic trade by the Treaty of Copenhagen in September 1441.[45]

The Acquisition of Brabant

Following his successful annexation of Hainault, Holland, and Zeeland in 1428, the purchase of the county of Namur in 1429 (see Chapter 3), and the conclusion of a treaty of friendship with his former opponent and Jacqueline of Bavaria's former ally Rudolph of Diepholt, bishop of Utrecht, Philip the Good had yet another stroke of luck in 1430. Philip of St. Pol, the childless duke of Brabant, son of Anthony of Brabant and younger brother and successor of John IV of Brabant, died suddenly and unexpectedly in 1430. Philip of St. Pol had already acknowledged Philip the Good as his successor, but his death occurred so suddenly that some contemporaries suspected Philip the Good of murder — chance appeared to have to have played its role too well and in too timely a manner. Although the suspicion appears to have been groundless, Philip the Good did not succeed to Brabant without other opposition. The German emperor, Sigismund, cherished the ambition of effectively reincorporating Brabant into the empire; and, besides two other German princes with claims on the duchy, there was another candidate closer to home in the person of Philip's aunt Margaret of Burgundy, who had also stood in his way as the intriguing mother of Jacqueline of Bavaria in the matter of succession to Holland-Zeeland. The Estates of Brabant, however, had the final decision, and they chose Philip the Good after he successfully pleaded his case before them at Louvain. In October 1430, Philip celebrated his Joyous Entry as duke of Brabant.

From 1404 to 1430, Brabant had been ruled by a younger branch of the Burgundian dynasty. There was no reason to assume that the line would die out, nor that it would prove such an important link in the growth of the political power of the senior branch of the family. Relations between the two other branches had not always been cordial. Philip, count of Nevers, the third son of Philip the Bold, for example, had followed an independent policy because his line was more dependent on the French crown. Although good relations with Brabant had been restored during the reign of Philip of St. Pol, there was no indication that this crucial central territory would willingly drop like a ripe fruit into the lap of Philip the Good. The acquisition of Brabant simultaneously brought Philip three ducal titles: that of Brabant; that of Limburg, which had long been linked to it; and that of Lotharingia, a purely theoretical title from the glorious Carolingian past that the Brabantines had cherished since the thirteenth century.[46] The last of these ducal titles allowed Philip the Good to assert his independence from both the king of France and the emperor, since Charlemagne's imperial title had been bestowed on his son Louis the Pious and then on his grandson Lothar, whose brothers had received the rulership of West Francia and East Francia. The dukedom of Lotharingia, according to the historical reading of Philip the Good, was thus independent of the successor-rulers in those territories.

Centralizing Ambition and Social Harmony

The unification of a number of economically distinct territories within a single Burgundian federation made the Burgundian complex as a whole much less vulnerable to fluctuations in the international market and to crop failures. The different territories of the Burgundian state, varied in their economic structures, were also economically complementary. In normal years there was always at least one territory with an agricultural surplus. Any temporary shortage of a particular product in one region could be compensated for by a surplus in another. In the Burgundian complex, there were both rich grain-producing regions and dynamic textile-producing cities, as well as areas rich in forests and metallic ores. The complex enjoyed easy and protected access to the sea and was connected by good overland roads and waterways. Merchants from the Baltic, England, and the Mediterranean considered Bruges the ideal place for doing business, a city in which an ambitious company had to establish at least an agency if it proposed to play a significant role in European commerce. When Philip the Good paid a formal visit to Bruges in 1440, he was greeted by a cosmopolitan procession that included representatives of the Hanseatic cities, Catalans, Luccans, Florentines, and others.

The context of this prosperity, consolidated by social harmony, provided ample opportunity for a clever ruler to establish a firm central authority. Philip the Good wished to be both loved and feared by his various subjects, and this ambition is evident in the salutations of letters addressed to him. He had a powerful personality and held the reins of state firmly in his own hands until very near the end of his reign, although it had been very difficult for him to do this during the first two decades of his reign. Just as John the Fearless had been forced to limit his centralization policy from 1411 to 1419 because of his deep involvement in French royal politics, Philip himself was deterred from consolidating his rule between 1419 and 1440.

Between 1425 and 1428, Philip devoted his energies to the annexation of Hainault, Holland, and Zeeland. From 1430 to 1440, his time was occupied far more than he wished with military operations not of his own devising, first against the German emperor, then against the French king, then, in 1436, against the English, and finally, in 1438, against the Wendish Hanseatic cities (the six cities around Lübeck), which were at odds with his Dutch subjects.[47] Although Philip tried to impose his own peace, he lost control over the Dutch shippers, who, on their own initiative, began a privateers' war. The seafaring burghers had their own methods of settling disputes with their trading competitors, and the Burgundians had neither the experience nor the means of stopping them. The Dutch simply ignored Philip's diplomacy, and Philip found himself unable to impose it on them.[48] Philip also complained that his allies tried to persuade him, against his better judgment, to attack French cities in 1430. On the other hand, his Flemish and Dutch subjects objected to his siege of English Calais in 1436, on the grounds of the excessive expense it entailed and of the economic damage it incurred. For this reason, Philip could not be persuaded to mobilize troops against the English in 1449, when Charles VII requested his help. He was unwilling, principally for economic reasons, to risk having his relations with the great wool supplier threatened anew. Thereafter, Philip engaged in a cautious balancing act between the crowns of England and France.

The Administration of the Burgundian Complex

Despite these difficulties, Philip the Good had devised a workable plan to create the strong state he envisioned. His administrative plan moved toward the centralization of the ducal government as well as that of the governments within each of the territories that constituted the Burgundian complex. The coordinating strategy for all the Burgundian lands was planned by the members of the ducal council, which proved an effective means of limiting local and regional autonomy. Between 1435 and 1445, the Great Council was detached from the ducal council in order to serve as a specialized court of higher justice. The Great Council thus came to function as a rival to the Parlement of Paris, by then so deeply under French royal influence that Philip the Good thought it to be no longer an acceptable court of appeal for his subjects. Philip also developed a coordinated strategy of interregional popular representation. In 1427 he summoned the Estates of all his northern territories to participate with him at a meeting of the Estates of Hainault, in order to give broader legitimization to his coup in Hainault. This meeting may be considered a first—albeit tentative—manifestation of the Estates General in the Netherlands.[49] Philip also had the Members of Flanders accompany him to the 1427 dedication at Zierikzee, in order to gain Zeeland's cities' acceptance of his succession.

Within each of the regions, Philip's centralization policy made two principal changes: it replaced the alderman's tribunals of the great cities with the ducal council chamber in each territory as a court of appeals for all of the populace, and it ensured the regular transfer of a large part of the cities' public revenues to the central treasury. With this extra income added to the various revenues already collected by the duke in his capacities as private owner of manors and a ruler enjoying the profits of justice, mintage, and tolls, Philip was able to implement his own policies as dictated by his changing political circumstances on the basis of a larger regular income, independent of each particular territory.

One of the duke's means of implementing these policies was the absorption of competent administrators from the town governments into the central government. Simon van Formelis, city clerk of Ghent until 1404, was able to make good use of his administrative experience after he became councillor to the duke in Brabant and later president of the Council of Flanders, the highest ducal tribunal in the county.[50]

But the duke's administrative centralization also had to take into account the substantial and self-conscious power of his subjects. This power varied among different groups—well-to-do merchants and industrial entrepreneurs, specialized artisans producing for local markets, or manual laborers from the great export industries in the textile-producing cities. Each group had its own specific organizations and interests. Active and ambitious inhabitants of the cities and countryside held in their hands the means of maintaining the level of the state's gross product through their talent as successful businessmen and bankers, or as skilled and productive workers in manufacturing or agriculture. The most determined among them built up social and political networks, through which they were able to control appointments to public office and the distribution of financial resources in the cities. As city aldermen, they decided upon the allocation of public funds and decided how much, if any, should be turned over to the prince.

Their decisions mattered. In the period 1439–1449 the patrimonial income of the dynasty in Flanders alone brought in an annual income of 151,000 pounds *parisis*, whereas the subsidies, or aids, paid by the duke's Flemish subjects provided 127,000 pounds, accounting for nearly half the state's budget in their county. The granting of these subsidies at the level of the county was the responsibility of the representative institutions, the Estates, and provided the duke's subjects with an occasion for some political leverage. These representative institutions, existing in each of the regions of the Burgundian state and known as the Estates of Flanders, Estates of Holland, and Estates of Brabant, formed a powerful collective body that often determined whether or not the duke's requests would be honored. Within these Estates, the cities constantly strove for greater autonomy. But even the least economically powerful workers, by virtue of their sheer numbers and political volatility, were not without their own influence; they often challenged the urban and central governments by organizing strikes and rebellions, or by merely threatening to do so.[51]

The duke had to play his hand to his own best advantage against these various social and economic interest groups. He had to appease urban merchants and workers by safeguarding their trade relations abroad. After the Peace of Arras in 1435, for example, he continually negotiated trade agreements with England and the Hanseatic cities in the name and in the interests of his Dutch, Brabantine, and Flemish subjects. He was able to influence the political elites of the cities by binding them to him personally using the advantages he could offer, by generous gifts, and by ennobling outstanding citizens. His control over the urban networks gave him a foothold in each of the regional representative bodies, such as the Estates of Flanders, and even in the politically more potent college of the great Flemish cities, the Four Members of Flanders. The greatest threat to this stability was posed by revolts. When these occurred, the prince was left no alternative but to make a spectacular show of military power in the hope that its demonstration would suffice, without actual resort to arms and violence.

After the introduction of the Burgundian dynasty into Holland and Zeeland in 1425, for example, we find striking examples of these strategies. Philip the Good managed to attract the elite, although many of the great Dutch families remained suspicious and fearful. When necessary, he ruthlessly implemented a policy of repression, as in the case of the recalcitrant Kennemer peasants. But even in those regions that had been absorbed into the Burgundian state long before, there were occasional setbacks in the years from 1420 to 1440. These usually stemmed from the duke's being forced by external military or diplomatic circumstances to grant concessions to his subjects, who were always quick to come forward with a list of demands whenever the duke was involved in foreign diplomatic or military activities.

Urban Uprisings

Social and political revolts in late medieval European cities usually involved questions of social inequality and its political and economic consequences, and often they included wage demands, in cases when some sudden change in the value of currency or the imposition of higher taxes or rising food prices threatened social expectations. Whether the duke chose the side of the elites in power or that of the poorer laborers in these conflicts was determined exclusively by opportunism and a strategy that strove either to undermine a given group or to support it, for reasons often having little to do with the immediate situation. In most cases, however, the duke strove to promote social harmony in his territories, in cooperation with the urban land-owning, mercantile, and manufacturing elites. The duke generally got on remarkably well with the urban aristocrats, because of the considerable similarity in their lifestyles, social ambitions, and interests. Apart from these affinities, there was also the practical consideration that the urban aristocracy was easier to court by the tried and true method of granting it substantial material advantages, something that the duke could not afford to do with the lower classes.[52]

In 1430 and 1432, revolts broke out among the lower social classes in the Flemish cities of Geraardsbergen and Ghent, both in protest against the monetary policy of the duke and against the aldermen's manipulation of the cities' public finances. These revolts placed the urban aristocracy and the duke on the same side, and, predictably, the city aldermen consistently called upon the duke for help in suppressing these revolts. It is noteworthy that the spokesmen for the city of Ghent, when called upon to explain the disturbances to the duke and the highest ducal tribunal, the Council of Flanders, laid the entire blame for the unrest upon the heads of the local "rabble," the lower social classes, claiming that they represented merely a minority in a city predominantly loyal to the duke. The duke, in turn, decided that given the circumstances, he could "generously" take the risk of pardoning those involved in the revolt. In response to the demands of the Flemish representative body, the Four Members of Flanders, he established currency regulations that ensured twenty years of monetary stability and alleviated much of the discontent. The preamble to the act of monetary reform cites such considerations as the furtherance of trade, social harmony, and "the Public Weal," expressions that were more than mere attempts to gain popular goodwill. They were also expressions of a real social policy that recognized social harmony as a requisite condition for the forging of a stronger and more stable state. The opportunity afforded by this measure to establish a uniform currency in Flanders, Brabant, Holland, Zeeland, and Hainault was ably exploited by the centrist-minded duke, who lost no opportunity for promoting social peace.

The grand confrontation between ruler and subjects came in 1436. It unmasked the conflicting ambitions and desires of the duke as well as those of the urban elites and those of the more radical members of the craft guilds. The timing was no accident. Philip the Good's march against the English at Calais had just ended in a fiasco, resulting in the futile expenditure of a great deal of money on the part of the duke upon the poorly motivated urban guild militia. On arriving at the gates of Bruges in August 1436, when the urban guild militia refused to disband unless a number of its demands were met, the scene resembled that of 1411, when, after the equally disastrous military campaign mounted by John the Fearlesss and the Flemish urban militias against Montdidier, those militias also refused to disband. A militia in arms was a powerful and dangerous force at the gates of its own city, regardless of how well or poorly it had conducted itself in actual combat.

What had begun as a small-scale riot on the part of badly paid and inadequately disciplined amateur soldiers soon mushroomed into a full-scale social revolt. That autumn in Bruges the laborers called for a general strike, with disastrous consequences for the manufacturing entrepreneurs as well as for the trade and industry of Bruges. The artisans immediately made the duke and the city magistrates responsible for all that had gone amiss. When the duchess, Isabella of Portugal, in the course of the riot smuggled out of the city in her baggage the wife of Roland van Uitkerke, the despised ducal captain of Sluis, even she became persona non grata. Sluis, the outport of Bruges, had long been a thorn in the flesh of the inhabitants of Bruges. They wanted complete domination of all the towns along the Zwin, the waterway that linked Bruges to the sea, in order to retain the city's position as the commercial center of Flanders and northern Europe.

The confrontation came at a particularly bad moment for the duke, and the commoners of Bruges were well aware that they had caught him at a disadvantage. He had already lost face with the futile siege of Calais, and he had also had to deal with the depredations of unemployed and unpaid mercenary troops in Burgundy itself. They also knew that the political elite of Bruges feared the loss of its privileged position, through a strike that would undermine the financial and economic foundations upon which its power rested. They, too, remembered the circumstances of 1411, when the artisans had forced John the Fearless to revoke the ducal edict, the hated Calfvel, the "calfskin" (see Chapter 3). Medieval urban memory was much more tenacious than is usually imagined.

The radical leaders of the uprising viewed the duke and the urban patrician elite as a coalition, and they treated them as a single entity in the execution of several spectacular acts of violence that were steeped in symbolism indicating the rage of the people. One of the most visible officials of the duke, the *schout*, or sheriff, of Bruges, entrusted, among his other functions, with the detection of criminals and with summoning suspects before the urban tribunal in the duke's name, was murdered in a fundamental dispute over his jurisdiction. The radicals arrested all the city receivers and local political leaders who had been in power for the past thirty years, and against whom there were serious grounds for suspicion of corruption. The effect of the strike as an economic measure had been correctly calculated. Foreign merchants acted as intermediaries in the negotiations that brought about a temporary peace. It was so successful that Philip the Good was even able to celebrate Christmas safely in Bruges.

But the truce did not hold much longer. The conflict broke out again in April 1437. This time assassins murdered the mayor of the city, Morisses van Varsenare, who was suspected of concocting with the duke a plan to repress the "common folk" of Bruges. Van Varsenare, the liaison between the urban elite and the duke, was the symbol par excellence of the coalition and of the oppressive policy of the city administration. The foreign merchants now abandoned the city in panic, leaving the duke with few options. The inadequacy of his network of political connections with the urban elite as instruments of social control became apparent. The social policy of the government, of which the monetary measures of 1433 were a part, also had insufficient impact to guarantee peace. The duke considered a show of power—preferably without bloodshed—as he had used at Zevenbergen in 1427. He also considered retaliation at the cost of many lives, as at Othée in

1408. In May 1437, the duke marched on Bruges in person, but the citizens suspected him of planning the military subjugation of the city and permitted only a small portion of his troops to enter the city gate. In the extreme confusion that ensued a skirmish began, and the city gates were closed to prevent the main part of the army from joining the duke. Philip found himself caught in a trap, barely escaped with his life, and was forced to take ignominious flight from the city. His highest officer, the lord of l'Isle-Adam, hero of the Holland campaign, lost his life. Twenty-two of his men — Picard soldiers especially detested by the people of Bruges — were captured and publicly executed.

Philip the Good's humiliation was great, and his vengeance was proportionate. In February 1438, Bruges was finally forced to come to terms with him at Arras and to accept humiliating terms for a peace. The infamous gate, site of the coup, was to be razed, and a penitential chapel erected in its place. An enormous fine of 200,000 *riders* was imposed, and forty persons were to be surrendered for execution. Finally, at the next visit of the duke to Bruges, the city administration was to appear barefoot and bareheaded to pay him honorable amends.

In Ghent, Philip had to deal with no fewer than four revolts of the "commons" between 1432 and 1436. These, too, had a socioeconomic background and stemmed from the anti-English policy that the duke had adopted since 1430, and that had proved particularly disadvantageous for the city. On September 3, 1436, the very day that the magistrature was arrested in Bruges, Philip's bodyguard was disarmed in Ghent and Philip himself held captive until he agreed to a list of demands. His humiliation was even greater than in Bruges. Nevertheless, Philip made no comparable move against the impertinence of the Gentenaars: the risks were too great. Ghent had been ruled for decades by a stable coalition of masters from the important craft guilds and the wealthy, land-owning bourgeoisie, the *poorterij*. This system guaranteed social peace, but it offered the duke little opportunity to intervene in urban affairs. Aside from an immediate concern for his own physical safety, Philip could not easily act against the proud city of the Arteveldes. Nor could he challenge his two greatest cities at the same time. Following the line of least resistance, therefore, he confronted the artisans at Bruges. Although the repression carried out against Bruges in 1438 could easily be seen as a rehearsal of what Philip might have had in store for Ghent, he delayed his revenge on that city until after the revolt of 1453 (see Chapter 5).[53]

Patron and Clients

The duke's strategy in handling these volatile cities when they were not in revolt consisted in converting the powerful urban elites into a kind of clientele in the service of the central government.[54] He could not have eliminated them, since he needed them to achieve some social control over the craft guilds, the magistrates, and the general population, which could, because of its sheer numbers, pose a threat to the Burgundian peace.

Clientage was consolidated by the continual negotiation of marriages between patrician families and Burgundian courtiers and civil servants, strengthening mutual interests and creating personal as well as political relationships. Although this practice was effective in some respects, it had drawbacks in others. Closer ties among the ruling groups of the state created the practice of mutual protection, which permitted fraudulent and criminal practices to flourish with virtual impunity. Because of these opportunities, alliances with the magistrates and officers of justice were much sought after. Even the duchess applied herself industriously to promoting marriages between respectable families and members of the Burgundian court, so as to broaden the ruler's "clan." But such marriages required the cooperation of both parties; others tried to marry into the Ghent patriciate by more devious and violent means. In 1438, Philip the Good acceded to a request by the patricians and aldermen of Ghent for a stricter legal decree against those social climbers who resorted to the kidnapping and rape of rich daughters in order to force marriages into wealthy Ghent families. For all the advantages to be gained by marriage into the Burgundian court, the Ghent social elite also needed to protect itself from the intrusion of undesirable persons from the lower social orders into their political, economic, and domestic milieus.[55]

Clientage was not limited to the urban elites. It was just as eagerly embraced to strengthen ties among the nobility and the clergy. The nobility was bound to the Burgundian dynasty through countless court offices, functions in the ducal council, and ambassadorial missions. These tasks, which required knowledge of courtly etiquette and of the elaborate European codes of chivalric behavior generally modeled on those of the French royal court, were especially suited to members of the traditional noble families. But for such functions, the clergy also proved valuable. In earlier centuries, clergy had carried out the more demanding intellectual work at the courts of medieval rulers. The Burgundian dukes, too, recognized the value of clerical talent, and some higher clerics had been appointed chancellors to the dukes. The dukes of Burgundy also exploited the divisions within the higher clergy, as in the consequences of the Great Schism of 1378–1415, to a greater degree than had their predecessors. As resolute supporters of the popes at Avignon, the dukes were in a position to apply pressure for the appointment of their favorites, to the extent that virtually all of the higher ecclesiastical hierarchy in the Burgundian state consisted of political appointees who owed their high offices to a deft collaboration between the popes and the dukes. These clerics neglected no opportunity of returning the favor to the duke on a political level. The ducal influence over the network of higher clergy also enabled him to exercise a greater-than-usual influence on the moral and mental perceptions of his lay subjects.[56]

As a result of the dukes' affiliations with the urban patriciates, the nobility, and the higher clergy, the Burgundian administrative and political elite took the form of a huge super-clan. The patronage system was strongly personalized in the figure of the duke. The prospect of the extra compensation and attractive appointments granted to those who proved valuable in the duke's service generated increased loyalty and gratitude. Such bonuses supplemented the generally low salaries of ordinary ducal offices. The practice of extra rewards left a good deal of room for the recognition and compensation of extraordinary services, but it could also encourage the sort of fraud that might easily take advantage of innocent and frustrated subjects. Burgundian ducal patronage was effective, but it was not perfect.

Fraud and maladministration were a continuing weakness of the Burgundian state. In many respects, that state was a giant with feet of clay. In order to prevent the worst excesses, the duke had introduced firm checks, but even these did not always work. In each of the territories, there was a functioning ducal council and a Chamber of Accounts. The council was a high court that served as a court of appeal as well as a court of first instance. It also carried out various administrative tasks in the name of the duke. The Chamber of Accounts exercised permanent supervision over all the lower echelons of financial administration and services, centralized the ducal revenues, and authorized direct expenditures. Above these territorial institutions there was the Great Council, with judicial and administrative jurisdiction that, in theory, should have provided the duke with the information to detect abuses and trace financial fraud. But even this system could not restrain an official who was determined to enrich himself illegally at someone else's expense. After a revolt in Rotterdam in 1439, the local sheriff and general treasurer of the county of Holland, William of Naaldwijk, was able to set up a system whereby he managed to pocket ten pounds in bribes from each of the banished participants in the revolt who wished to return to the city.

An important factor in the success of the Burgundian political elite was the dukes' sensitivity to regional diversity. In each of the regional territories of the Burgundian state, officials and councillors were appointed who were familiar with the region and had firm political ties there. But the dukes were always careful to place a check on these regional officials, by balancing them with a sufficient number of officials from other territories who were loyal to the central government. Thus, when he annexed the county of Namur in 1429, Philip the Good left all of its political and administrative mechanisms in place. However, he also brought in a number of his own intimates from outside the county, to introduce new and particularly Burgundian ideas of governance. This became a general policy. In newly acquired territory, the dukes appointed loyal officials from territories already fully incorporated into the state. Many Flemings, for example, served in high offices in Holland, but the ducal administrative corps was chiefly peopled by men from Burgundy, Artois, and Hainault. These were mostly Francophone officials, a fact that later provoked resistance in the Dutch-speaking territories.

This single great governing clan thus shaped prevailing social and political attitudes throughout the Burgundian complex of territories and took the lead as patrons of the arts as well as leading participants in what has often been called the Burgundian theater-state.[57]

5

The Difficult Path Toward an Integrated State
1440–1465

Following the significant expansion of the Burgundian territories in the years 1425–35, the conclusion of a lasting peace with a recovering France, and the establishing of repeated truces in the wake of the war with England, Philip the Good's attention focused primarily on the internal consolidation of his possessions. Each of the principalities had its own individual tradition of autonomy, and so there could be no question of a unified Burgundian "state" in 1440. The constellation of territories could best be described as a personal union, a composite — or "pragmatic" — empire, in which two totally different territorial complexes, themselves made up of a variety of smaller regions, came under the authority of a single ruler. In light of the increasingly centralist structure of the French kingdom, which Philip knew intimately and probably still regarded as a model, it was evident that he would attempt to bring more uniformity to the administrative institutions of his territories and endeavor to strengthen his control over local and regional administrations. To this end, the duke employed three complementary methods. First he created a number of coordinating institutions, with authority over either all the principalities or all those in the Low Countries. Second, he brought more uniformity to the internal administration of different regions. Finally, he strove to break local resistance through the offer of personal advantages to local potentates, or, if necessary, by armed repression of resistance. The period from 1435 to 1476 was characterized by a vigorous development of the monarchic authority of the dukes. But that development also encountered stiff resistance.

Peace on the Borders: Luxemburg, the Empire, and the Quest for a Crown

Around 1440, the duke of Burgundy no longer faced dangerous rivals of any significance in the Low Countries. Moreover, he also enjoyed the prospect of succeeding to yet another valuable contiguous territory, the neighboring duchy of Luxemburg, the homeland of a dynasty of German emperors that had ruled from 1346 to 1437. In the early fifteenth century the duchy of Luxemburg was ruled by Anthony, duke of Brabant, by right of his wife, Elizabeth of Görlitz, niece of the emperor Sigismund and granddaughter of the emperor Charles IV. Anthony, who was also Philip the Good's uncle, had been killed at Agincourt in 1415. Elizabeth remarried, this time to John of Bavaria, who abandoned his episcopal see in order to pursue the acquisition of Holland and Zeeland at the expense of his cousin, Jacqueline of Bavaria (see Chapter 4). Neither of Elizabeth's marriages produced offspring. If either had, one of two alternatives might have occurred. If the marriage with Anthony had had issue, a cadet branch of the Burgundian dynasty would have been able to erect a territorial complex consisting of Brabant-Limburg-Luxemburg as a counterweight to Flanders-Artois-Burgundy. If the second marriage had had issue, the house of Bavaria would have been able to erect a complex consisting of the whole of Hainault-Holland-Zeeland-Luxemburg.

In the event, the childless Elizabeth continued to rule the duchy, acknowledging Philip the Good as her heir and appointing him regent of the duchy in 1441. But there were other claims on the duchy besides those of Philip. The king of Bohemia claimed the duchy, and, after his death, Frederick of Meissen, duke of Saxony, took over the claim with the support of Frederick III (at the time, king of the Romans and prospective emperor), King Charles VII of France, and a small part of the native nobility of Luxemburg. Frederick of Meissen quickly established Saxon garrisons in the city of Luxemburg, and not until the night of 21–22 November 1443 were the Burgundians able to take the city, drive out the occupying forces, and temporarily buy off the claims of the Saxon duke. The Saxon claim against Luxemburg, however, persisted for a long time after 1443. Upon the death of Elizabeth of Görlitz in 1451, the Estates of Luxemburg formally acknowledged the succession of Philip the Good. Unable to assume direct rule of the duchy, however, Philip continued to hold the duchy as pledge until the claims of the duke of Saxony and the concerns of the new German ruler, Frederick III (1440–93), could be resolved in his favor. In the meantime, Philip created a new administrative council for Luxemburg with its own governor, Anthony of Croy, the duke's most trusted adviser, whose brother held a similar post in Hainault.

The claims of the duke of Saxony and Frederick III were aired at a meeting between the king and the duke of Burgundy at the imperial city of Besançon in 1442. Although the two parties did not reach agreement, they did establish somewhat more cordial relations. Unlike his predecessor Sigismund, Frederick III had wider and more sympathetic interests in Burgundy. He foresaw the attractions of a series of dynastic marriages: between his brother Albert and a female relative of Philip the Good, and between his daughter Elizabeth of Austria and Philip the Good's son and heir Charles, count of Charolais. In 1447, Frederick's chancellor, Kaspar Schlick, even proposed to erect either Friesland or Brabant to the status of a kingdom, with Philip as king.[1] Philip, however, insisted that all of his territories be included in the new kingdom, along with the neighboring German territories of Cleves, Jülich, and Berg. However attractive the prospect of a royal crown may have been, Philip refused to accept one on any terms but his own. But the German ruler did not accede to his demands, and the plan was dropped in 1448.

King or not, it was clear that Philip of Burgundy had become one of the most powerful princes of the empire. Holding the duchies of Brabant, Luxemburg, and Limburg and the counties of Burgundy (Franche-Comté), Hainault, Holland, Zeeland, and Namur, all of which owed allegiance to the empire, Philip found that he owed fealty to the German ruler for the majority of his titles. Scion of the French royal dynasty of Valois and duke of Burgundy, the oldest and most respected duchy in France, the first peer and highest nobleman in the French kingdom, Philip could now nevertheless consider himself an autonomous sovereign at the head of his own dynasty. By affiliating himself with the empire, he accentuated his independence from France, from which his dynasty and his first titles had come. The central control that any emperor might exercise was so weak that, aside from the prestige of the highest worldly title in the west, there was little power that the emperor could use to overawe so mighty a vassal.

Philip's independence, even from the emperor, is indicated by the alacrity with which he accepted the invitation of Frederick III in 1454 to participate in a Reichstag at Regensburg. There Philip could flaunt his prestige before the other imperial princes, not only as their equal, but as the real ruler of Luxemburg. The failed negotiations of 1442 at Besançon over Luxemburg, as well as the stalled imperial acknowledgment of Philip's right to Hainault, Holland, and Zeeland, were also on Philip's mind at the prospect of the Reichstag, and perhaps also the possibility of securing the title of king on more favorable terms than those of 1447–48. Philip also came to Regensburg triumphant. In 1453 he had inflicted a decisive defeat on Ghent, the greatest city in his territories, after years of rebellion, and in February 1454, during a sumptuous banquet given at Lille, Philip proposed to take the cross in order to regain Constantinople from the Ottoman Turks, who had captured the great city in May 1453. The banquet was called the Feast of the Pheasant, after the main representation presented to the duke, in which "a pheasant which had a gold collar around its neck, decorated with rubies and fine, large pearls" had been brought in by two knights of the Order of the Golden Fleece and two damsels, who asked the duke to make a vow to undertake the Crusade. The vow was later known as the Vow of the Pheasant.

This was not Philip's only, or earliest, interest in the idea of a Crusade. In 1432 he had sent one of his most able advisers, Bertrandon de la Broquière, on a long journey through the Middle East to obtain information that might help guide a new Crusade. Bertrandon's report, *The Journey Across the Sea*, is a remarkable account of his experiences. Twenty-one years later, in 1453, with Constantinople now lost, Philip had agreed to go on Crusade, providing that the king of France and other powerful Christian rulers would do the same. A hundred nobles from Philip's entourage had followed his example and strove to outdo their seigneur in the boldness of their own vows.[2]

In fact, the main purpose of the Reichstag at Regensburg in 1454 was the emperor's consultation with the imperial princes about the proposed Crusade. But nothing came of Frederick's interest, and Frederick himself left Regensburg hurriedly, called to deal with severe internal dissension in Hungary and to provide support to the regent, John Hunyadi, in the wake of the terrible Hungarian defeat at Varna in 1444 at the hands of the Ottoman Turks.

In 1463 Frederick III again suggested a crown for Philip the Good, as part of the negotiations for a marriage between Frederick's son Maximilian and Philip's granddaughter Mary of Burgundy, daughter of Charles the Bold. Frederick was supported by Pope Pius II, even offering Philip the office of imperial vicar over the left bank of the Rhine. But again Philip declined. Negotiations for a crown were reopened with Charles the Bold in 1467, 1469, and 1473 — but to no end, except for the final agreement with Frederick III at Trier in 1473, when Frederick and Charles agreed to the betrothal of their respective heirs, Maximilian and Mary of Burgundy. It was a marriage that was to prove decisive for the later history of the Low Countries and of the Habsburg dynasty (see Chapter 7). For all of Philip the Good's prestige at Regensburg in 1454 and his real power as the greatest prince in the western part of the empire, his triumph was not to be signaled by a crown for Burgundy. And after twenty years of interrupted negotiations, Frederick III finally managed to achieve what Sigismund and he had been trying unsuccessfully to do for much of the fifteenth century — bring the Low Countries decisively into the political orbit of the empire.

Disorder within Regions: Holland-Zeeland

Although Philip the Good was the personal ruler of a host of diverse territories, these territories were not themselves always internally unified. In Holland, for example, the city of Dordrecht refused to support Amsterdam in its dispute with the Hanse over trade and transport rights in the Baltic region. In turn, Dordrecht, the oldest city in the county, drew little sympathy for its own interests, because of its attempts to maintain its traditional staple rights on all river trade. In 1444, the city was condemned for rebellion and for contempt of the ruler's authority, and it lost its staple rights with respect to the other towns of Holland, though it persisted in its refusal to contribute its share of the county's taxes.

In addition to these intra-regional conflicts of interest, Holland had suffered regularly from outbursts of factional strife since 1350. Sometimes these conflicts were merely feuds between powerful local families. In other cases, however, such conflicts merged into the general duel between Hooks and Cods (see Chapter 4), with one faction supporting and another opposing the legitimate count.

In the course of his attempts to annex Holland, Philip the Good was inevitably forced to take sides in the Hook-Cod dispute. Since most of Jacqueline of Bavaria's supporters were Hooks, her rivals John of Bavaria and Philip the Good naturally took over leadership of the Cods. But once in power, Philip the Good attempted to banish this large-scale factional strife in the name of public order. In 1428, the Peace of Delft prohibited the further use of party names, the wearing of special clothing indicative of party sympathies, and the carrying of long knives. These prohibitions had to be repeated many times, because such practices had been deeply rooted in local custom. When he officially took office in 1433, the duke replaced the city administrations of Dordrecht, Amsterdam, and Alkmaar. In general, the duke strove to achieve peace by allowing both parties equal representation in the city administrations. He also appointed foreigners, who were presumed to be neutral, as his stadtholders (lieutenants). The first of the duke's appointees to that office was Hugh de Lannoy, lord of Saintes, a member of the high nobility of Walloon Flanders with close ties to the powerful Croy family of governors and councillors. Hugh had already proven his worth in the negotiation of truces and trade agreements with England in 1435–37 (see Chapter 4). From 1440 to 1445, the office was held by William of Lalaing from Hainault, and from 1448 to 1462, it was held by John de Lannoy, a nephew of Hugh and the husband of Joan of Croy.

But stadtholder William of Lalaing's impact on domestic administration was unfortunate. Everywhere he appointed Hooks who had done him various financial favors at the expense of the cities. In Amsterdam, between 1443 and 1445 he appointed exclusively Hook aldermen who had never held that office before. In turn, and contrary to city law, they appointed three Hook treasurers, whose duties had traditionally been performed by the mayors. Over the protests of the mayors, they spent substantial sums on militia, who expelled the Cods from the city. With the support of the stadtholder, Hooks also took power in Haarlem and Leiden, where they executed all sorts of irregular financial maneuvers in William's favor. William was finally removed from office in April 1445, after complaints from the Cods. It was no coincidence that Reinoud van Brederode, member of a leading noble family with Hook sympathies, was married in November 1445, to Yolanda of Lalaing, daughter of the former stadtholder William.

The dismissal of the pro-Hook stadtholder did not, however, end factional conflict. In 1445 riots occurred in Leiden on Whitsunday and again on the first of July. The two parties fought in the streets, shouting out the names of the two leading families, van Zwieten and van Poelgeest, in order to avoid the forbidden party names. A peace mission led by Duchess Isabella of Portugal—whose successful negotiation of a trade agreement with England had won her great prestige in Holland—did not bring about the wished-for peace. Only a show of armed force by the duke himself was able to bring the Cods once more within the city walls and impose an equitable division of the administrative posts between the two parties. Once more stipulations were made banning the use of the party names Hook and Cod, the singing of party songs, the wearing of party symbols and costumes, such as red hats (for the Hooks) and gray hats (for the Cods). Stringent regulations were imposed regarding the wearing of armor and weapons within the cities. In Leiden some 130 Hooks were convicted, and three of the leaders were executed. In 1449, the duke granted an amnesty on the occasion of the inauguration of a city council with forty members. Within this council, however, the Cods acquired a substantial majority.

The duke's measures restored order to the county for a long time, although partisan rivalry by no means disappeared. The most remarkable feature of this rivalry was the cooperation between the urban patricians and nobles from both the immediate neighborhoods and more distant regions. The century-old tradition of feuds between the noble clans and their followers, and the symbols associated with them, had begun to serve as models for the behavior of the urban elites. This helps to explain the repeated outbursts arising from local circumstances. Over time, the antagonism between artisans and entrepreneurs gave rise to the old slogans and formerly noble party names to designate conflicts among new and continually shifting urban coalitions.

In most cities, the duke created councils of eighty, forty, or twenty-four notables, and the councils were named after the number of their members. Each year they were to draw up a slate of candidates for office, listing twice the number needed for aldermen. The stadtholder and the Council of Holland (the highest court and administrative college of the county) chose from this slate only moderate Hooks and Cods. The system functioned well until 1472, until Duke Charles the Bold reserved the appointment entirely to himself, for reasons of financial advantage. This led to the appointment of a disproportionate number of Hooks, once more giving rise to partisan conflicts. As often happened, history seemed about to repeat itself.

Utrecht, Guelders, and the Bishoprics of Thérouanne and Tournai

Philip was more fortunate in his attempts to gain control of the prince-bishopric of Utrecht and other ecclesiastical lordships. The bishop of Utrecht had exercised spiritual authority over Holland, Zeeland, and the small territory known as the Four Offices (Vier Ambachten) in the north of Flanders. It was important for the secular lord of any territory to maintain good relations with the ecclesiastical authorities that governed its spiritual life, because the influence of ecclesiastical authorities also extended to the appointment of favorites, relatives, and all sorts of other clients to the countless ecclesiastical offices and dignities endowed with attractive incomes. In addition, the bishop of Utrecht acted as the secular lord of the Sticht, a territory roughly corresponding to the present-day Netherlands province of Utrecht, and the Oversticht, which included the present-day Netherlands provinces of Overijssel and Drenthe, as well as part of the province of Groningen.

These two territories were separated by a portion of the duchy of Guelders, particularly the regions around Zaltbommel and Tiel, and the city of Nijmegen. Guelders was both a nuisance and an attraction. Its location commanded all the great rivers of the northern Low Countries: the Maas, the Waal, the Rhine, and the IJssel, and it bordered not only on Utrecht but also on Brabant, Holland, and Liège. Territorially, the duchy of Guelders consisted of a series of scattered territories with imperfectly integrated administrations. Warring factions among the nobility found support from various groups of cities, and these factions also influenced the often hostile relations between the dukes and their successors. The duchy's lack of cohesion and the friction between the dukes and the main cities of Nijmegen, Arnhem, Zutphen, and Roermond posed a potential threat to the stability of the entire region. During the fifteenth century, the duchy itself was ruled by the Egmond dynasty, not always friendly to the dukes of Burgundy.

Guelders was also tied dynastically to the duchy of Cleves, in which Philip the Good also had an interest. In 1406 Philip's sister Mary of Burgundy was married to Adolph, duke of Cleves. Catherine, the daughter of Mary and Adolph, was married in 1430 to Arnold of Egmond, duke of Guelders, who nevertheless became an ally of the emperor Sigismund against Philip the Good in 1435. But in the 1450s, Philip the Good took the part of Adolph, son of Arnold of Egmond, against his father. In 1459 the dukes of Burgundy and Guelders reached an agreement by which Adolph acquired lordship over Nijmegen, the most important city of the region, and its surrounding area, the most crucial parts of Guelders as far as the problem of Utrecht was concerned. Adolph also secured the support of most of the cities. In 1461, Philip the Good admitted him into the Order of the Golden Fleece and arranged a marriage between him and Catherine of Bourbon, a sister-in-law of Charles the Bold. In 1470 Adolph of Ravenstein, a younger son of Duke Arnold of Cleves, married Anne of Burgundy, an illegitimate daughter of Philip the Good. Adolph of Ravenstein became a loyal vassal of the dukes of Burgundy and rose to the office of stadtholder-general under Charles the Bold (see Chapter 8). Thus, the succession in Guelders was slowly turned to the advantage of the dukes of Burgundy. The dispute between Arnold and Adolph continued until the old duke's death in 1473 (see Chapter 7). The duchy was drawn closer to Burgundian interests, although the dukes of Guelders themselves did not enter into exclusive alliances with Burgundy. Instead, they tried to preserve their independence with a number of other alliances.

Philip the Good had already made one attempt in 1423 to have his own candidate appointed to the bishopric of Utrecht, but he received insufficient support. In the years following, Philip's attention was diverted to the conquest of Holland. At the end of that process, at the Peace of Delft in 1428 (see Chapter 4), Philip for tactical reasons gave priority to making peace between the contending parties in Holland. These included his old enemy Rudolph of Diepholt, who had been the successful candidate at Utrecht in 1423. When Rudolph died in 1455, Philip's military operations, undertaken for purely dynastic reasons in the Rhine area, had rendered him extremely unpopular with the people of Utrecht. Accordingly, the cathedral chapter of Utrecht, empowered to choose a new candidate, nominated almost unanimously the provost of the cathedral, Gijsbrecht van Brederode. Although Brederode had received the title of ducal councillor from Philip, who had also admitted his brother Reinoud to the Order of the Golden Fleece, the name Brederode was still synonymous with Holland's struggle for independence from Burgundy. By reiterating his vows to undertake a Crusade for the liberation of Constantinople, however, Philip was able to persuade the pope, Nicholas V, to appoint Philip's own illegitimate son David as bishop of Utrecht. But the matter remained complex, since the Estates of the Sticht had already recognized Gijsbrecht van Brederode as their worldly lord and protector.

Philip transferred his court to the Hague for several months to negotiate with Brederode, but in July 1456, he decided to assemble an army. This convinced the provost, who agreed to withdraw his claim on the bishopric in return for an equivalent appointment as dean of the wealthy and prestigious chapter of St. Donatian at Bruges and for compensation amounting to nine hundred times the yearly wage of a skilled craftsman, as well as yearly rents worth seventy-five such annual earnings. The duke accepted the offer and triumphantly entered Utrecht, accompanied by an impressive military escort. The new bishop, who had previously held the much more modest bishopric of Thérouanne, followed in Philip's wake.[3]

The events at Liège and Utrecht, as well as those in Liège in later years, indicate the extent to which power politics could dominate both the spiritual function of episcopal churches and the rights of electors to high ecclesiastical office. The institution of the prince-bishopric naturally entailed the confusion of secular and spiritual affairs. The desire of the ecclesiastical hierarchy for political power, however, often undermined its ability to fulfill its spiritual mission adequately and credibly.

Liège, Utrecht, and Thérouanne were not the only episcopal sees over which the dukes of Burgundy attempted to extend their power. Between 1410 and 1483, the dukes were able to arrange the situation at Tournai, a small French episcopal enclave between Flanders, Hainault, and Artois, in such a way that the office of bishop of Tournai was continuously held by the president of the Burgundian Great Council, the highest official after the ducal chancellor. Arras and especially the bishoprics in and around Burgundy itself were held almost exclusively by protégés of the dukes. These choices were not always justifiable from an ecclesiastical standpoint. John of Burgundy, the illegitimate son of Duke John the Fearless, who was appointed bishop of Cambrai in 1439 and whose temporal power included only a small holding in imperial territory between Hainault and Artois, appeared officially in his see only once in forty years. But through him the duke was able to intervene in the administration of Cambrai, which had spiritual authority over parts of Artois, Brabant, Hainault, and Flanders.

In the years between 1440 and 1465, Burgundian power continued to expand in the Low Countries, although sometimes in a cautious and indirect fashion. The duke's rivals in Luxemburg and Utrecht were bought out, under various combinations of a military show of force and lucrative bribes. In addition, Philip the Good pursued a policy directed at winning as many allies as possible, by placing his own trusted men in strategic offices. His systematic intervention in ecclesiastical appointments was a favorite means to this end, but by no means was it the only one.

Changing Relations with France

The caution with which Philip the Good operated after 1440 is best explained not through his personality—since he had often taken aggressive action before 1440—but by the necessity of taking foreign powers into account. The German emperor's reluctance to recognize Philip's conquests forced him to exercise caution, as he did in Luxemburg. Philip also strove to increase his influence in France, but even his most energetic diplomacy failed to change the French balance of power in his favor. The duke of Burgundy remained the French king's most powerful rival after the Peace of

Arras in 1435, and certainly after the English were finally defeated, in 1453. But the king of France now had the insight and the means of resisting Philip's influence. He countered Philip's attempts at dynastic influence and in the area of ecclesiastical appointments; he even countered Philip inside his own court.

Philip's interests in influence in France were signaled by his early marriage policies for his heir, later Charles the Bold. The first two marriages of Charles, to Catherine of France in 1440 and to Isabel of Bourbon in 1454, were characteristic of this policy. Philip hoped to win Charles, duke of Bourbon, over to his side against Charles VII of France. The duke of Bourbon, a powerful territorial lord, was an attractive ally, especially in coalition with Burgundy. The admission of the dukes of Orléans, Brittany, and Alençon to the Order of the Golden Fleece in the 1440s should also be seen in the context of this policy. But the Bourbon alliance proved costly.[4] In hopes of obliging his powerful Bourbon ally and serving his own interests at the same time, Philip secured the appointment of the eighteen-year-old and frivolous Louis of Bourbon as bishop of Liège. Philip also hoped to establish Louis as his own puppet ruler of this crucial region, since the bishop's spiritual authority extended over large portions of the duke's own territories. The move, however, backfired against Burgundy, for the new bishop immediately and repeatedly engaged in conflict with his subjects, who were determined to preserve their autonomy and therefore sought the support and protection of the French king. Charles VII eagerly seized the excuse provided by the unrest in Liège to block further Burgundian expansion in an area outside of France where Charles could exert considerable influence. Louis had moved from being Philip's pawn to being that of Charles VII.

Charles also used bribery to play upon the ambitions of the Croy clan, Duke Philip's most influential councillors, but also a clan whose largest holdings lay in the Picard-French region.[5] Anthony of Croy was governor of Luxemburg, Namur, and Boulogne; his brother John was captain-general and high bailiff of Hainault, and he was succeeded in that office by Anthony's nephew Philip. The Croy thus held sway over the southern flank of the Low Countries and remained on excellent terms with the king of France, increasing their personal fortunes as well as their standing at the French court. But the very fact of the Croy divided allegiance also helped to avert any head-on confrontation between Burgundy and France. When Charles the Bold finally banished them from his court and from their offices in 1464–65, the buffer between the two powers vanished with them, and continuous war followed.[6]

Fathers and Sons in France and Burgundy

The troubled relations between France and Burgundy were echoed in the troubled relations between Charles VII and his son, later Louis XI (reigned 1461–83), and between Philip the Good and his son, Charles the Bold (reigned 1467–77). The two sons then became, in turn, even greater antagonists than their fathers had been, and their long conflict laid the groundwork for the reshaping of the Burgundian domains after Charles's death in 1477.

Charles the Bold was born in 1433 and was made count of Charolais, the conventional title that designated the successor of the duke of Burgundy. But Charles grew to resent a number of aspects of his father's rule. Not only did Charles and Philip confront each other as aging father and ambitious son, but Charles was also attached more closely to his mother, the intelligent and capable Isabella of Portugal, who also grew estranged from Philip after too many mistresses and Philip's twenty-six illegitimate children. Charles also resented the enormous influence exerted by the Croy family over Philip the Good, particularly because he considered the Croy responsible for the humiliation that his father had suffered at the hands of the king of France. A spectacular quarrel between Charles and Philip led to a bitter power struggle at the Burgundian court in 1457. This caused the removal of the chancellor Nicholas Rolin and the council president Jean Chevrot, with the Croy emerging more powerful than ever. Charles left the court and retired to his personal estates at Le Quesnoy in Hainault and at Gorkum in Holland, where he extended his castle with the Blue Tower and carried out occasional minor tasks at his father's request, such as the negotiation of a subsidy from the cities of Holland in 1462. But when Charles tried to make use of this occasion to gain formal recognition of his status as heir of Philip from the Estates of the Burgundian territories, Philip peremptorily cut off Charles's allowance, obliging him to request loans from the cities of Holland to maintain himself. This, in turn, bound Charles the Bold to the local elites, particularly the Hook nobility. After 1457 Charles could only bide his time, as Philip the Good ended his rule without his successor at hand.

Louis XI had a similarly checkered career, in France. Born in 1423 (thus ten years older than Charles the Bold), Louis had been raised apart from his father and, as defender of Languedoc in 1439, had participated in the short-lived revolt against Charles VII known as the Praguerie. Briefly reconciled with his father, he again fell out with him after the death of Louis's mother,

Queen Margaret of Scotland, in 1445. Louis subsequently retired to his own province, the Dauphiné, in 1447. In the Dauphiné, Louis developed skills as a reformer of provincial government that later proved valuable to his administration of the kingdom. Yet another conflict, this time over Louis's marriage to Charlotte of Savoy, of whom his father strongly disapproved, led to Louis's flight to the court of Philip the Good at Brussels in the crucial year 1457.

Duke Philip saw in his "troublesome" guest an ideal opportunity to begin healing the breach with France, and he pampered the Dauphin in every possible manner, demonstrating an absurd degree of humility before his royal guest and refusing all of Charles VII's requests for Louis's extradition. Charles VII is reported to have commented that "My cousin of Burgundy is keeping a fox there that will eat all of his chickens." Philip indeed underestimated the Dauphin; once crowned, Louis XI pursued his father's policies with even greater determination, as well as the advantage of having spent his five years in exile in Brabant, Bruges, and Arras at the ducal court. Louis made extensive personal contacts at the Burgundian court during the years 1457 to 1461, and he shaped these into a pro-French faction there, weaving an international web of anti-Burgundian alliances that served him well when he became king of France and even further alienated from the Burgundian house.

Charles the Bold, already concerned with the French influence over the Croy family, grew further alienated from his father over Philip's embarrassingly humble demeanor toward the Dauphin. But the event that triggered Charles's anger took place in the autumn of 1463. Invoking a clause in the Treaty of Arras of 1435, which allowed for the French recovery of the Somme towns upon the French payment of a cash indemnity, Louis redeemed the towns for France by paying 400,000 gold écus to Philip the Good. While this represented a staggering sum, it also represented a fundamental political gain for France. Louis's network of personal contacts at the ducal court, and particularly his cultivation of Anthony of Croy, certainly smoothed the way for this achievement, but it also contributed to Charles the Bold's profound mistrust of his father's advisers and his bitter resentment toward France and his rival, its new king, whom Charles both hated and feared. Charles's outrage at Philip's loss of the Somme-Picard lands was so great as to lead him in 1465 to force the return of Picardy to the duke of Burgundy at the treaty of Conflans, with the stipulation that France could not redeem the new pledge until after Charles the Bold's own death. Although much of Charles's reign and foreign policy was focused on his eastern borders and the empire, he retained his hostility toward Louis XI and France, and that hostility helped to shape Franco-Burgundian relations until the Peace of Cateau-Cambrésis in 1559 (see Chapter 7).

* * *

In support of the diplomatic and political policies of Philip the Good and Charles the Bold, there emerged the mechanics of a working state that represents — in both its strengths and weaknesses — the character and expression of Burgundian ducal power in the mid-fifteenth century. That state can be examined in terms of its uses of justice, currency, language, and administrative practices, its ability to tame local resistance, its weaknesses, and its self-representation to its subjects and outside powers as a theater-state that used the imagery of power to almost as great a degree as it used power itself. The theater-state is not the least useful innovation of the dukes of Burgundy in the Low Countries.

The Working State: Justice, Currency, Language, and Administration

Like the duke's financial resources (see Chapter 6), justice, too, was gradually but determinedly institutionalized at the central level. But, also like the duke's finances, centralization encountered stubborn opposition. One of the most distinctive features of medieval communities was their claim to possess their own local customary law, recognized as having existed for a long time (whether locally generated or long ago granted by a superior or borrowed from elsewhere), applied peacefully and uninterruptedly by local community leaders, approved by community consensus — and, hence, opposed to both legislation and learned law. Many communities even recognized a common interest in postponing a local decision in unusual cases, and sending them to a neighboring, often larger and more experienced community for settlement. The early fifteenth-century Flemish jurist Jan van den Berghe emphasized that a knowledge of customary law could be acquired only by practice and by listening to the advice of experienced people.

A good example of the place of law in local loyalties is the resistance offered to Philip the Good in 1425 by the farmers of Kennemerland (see Chapter 4), who followed a number of specific Frisian legal customs and defended these against the courts of Holland and against Philip himself. In fact, historical customary law in the fourteenth and fifteenth centuries is better understood as the law that the people of a district recognized as applicable to themselves at any given time, regardless of its historical origin, which could have lain in borrowing from the customs of another district, or in earlier legislation, or in local adoption of an element of learned law, long since forgotten. Customary law thus had the advantage of satisfying local communal consciousness, while at the same time being extremely flexible in both its substance and its application. It was usually applied by respected local people, often the aldermen of a town or the representatives of the lord of a region. Individual manors or lordships also possessed their own customs.

Customary law possessed these advantages in part because it was unwritten, and it was, therefore, preserved in the creative memory of those who applied and acknowledged it. During the fifteenth and sixteenth centuries, most customary law in northern Europe underwent the process of homologation, the official recording of customs in writing and their subsequent application as a written body of law. But homologation also had the effect of "freezing" a kind of law that had long been characterized by its unconscious flexibility and its adaptation to contemporary circumstances and values. In a world of generally limited, or at best practical, literacy and a relatively finite spectrum of conflicts and disputes, oral custom generally worked well on the local level and in the limited circumstances where it was always applied. But new kinds of conflicts and claims based on another kind of law that professed superior authority greatly challenged customary law, and such conflicts and assertions about the law increased throughout northern Europe during the fourteenth and fifteenth centuries.

The challenge of authority came from two sources, often allied: the exertion of ducal authority over local districts and the increasing application of learned law. The latter had grown up in the twelfth century, based on the study of the Roman law of late antiquity and on that of the canon law of the Latin Christian church. During the thirteenth century, learned law influenced the growth of the *Ius Commune,* a common learned law applied throughout most of continental Europe. Although much of the learned law was usually remote from the routine affairs of villagers and townsfolk, it appealed to centralizing higher authorities, both the administrations of the great northern Italy city-republics and ambitious princes and kings, as an instrument of increasing their own authority in the legal sphere as well as in fulfilling their own ideas of their responsibilities to administer justice. In general, the establishment of new central courts by fourteenth- and

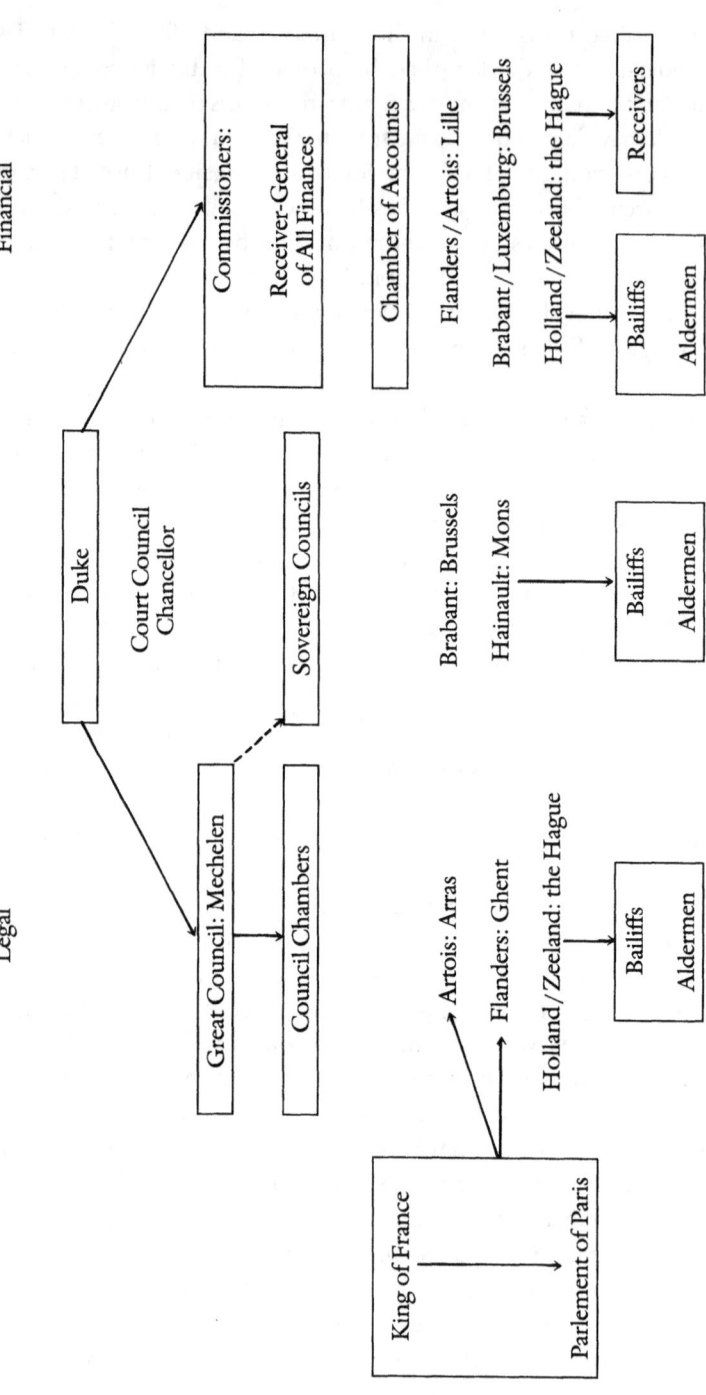

Figure 1. Ducal Institutions

fifteenth-century rulers served as a sign of the arrival of the learned law in a principality. That law confused and conflicted with the customary law of many districts. In the case of the Low Countries, however, learned law served the princes less well. It did not reach the county of Holland during the fifteenth century, and when it appeared in the sentences and pleadings of the Great Council it was usually marginal, initially limited to procedural matters that learned jurists liked to designate with French terminology, a demonstration of academic learning by jurists who continued to base their arguments on the customary law of the place or district.

Between 1435 and 1445, the duke of Burgundy established a college separate from the ducal council, to function as a central high court. Because of the territorial expansion of the Burgundian complex, the duke's own councillors (in any case not always legally proficient) were overburdened by all sorts of increasingly complex litigation. It was the express intention of the government to use its own administration of justice, and to impose in the various territories a unity and consistency of law and legal authority over all local and regional laws. The new college, known as the Great Council (*Grote Raad*), continually extended its activities as the highest court of justice. It developed its own registry, and in 1449 it appointed a procurator general (procureur-général) and later a special receiver. The number of councillors and secretaries gradually increased to sixteen of each. The Great Council was the court of first instance for cases involving ducal legislation and administrative acts. Litigants could also appeal to it for a review of judgments passed by local aldermen or regional councils. The dukes consciously pursued an aggressive policy of offering contending parties the opportunity of seeking justice from the Great Council in first instance, bypassing the local and regional courts of justice.[7]

The local authorities were well aware that the duke was undermining their traditional position through the systematic intervention of his higher courts of justice. The regional councils, although they too were composed of ducal officials, also felt themselves slighted on occasion. The cities and rural districts were most affected by these measures. Members of the local elites — among them more and more university-educated jurists — made decisions based primarily on their own local privileges and customs. A Flemish jurist, Martin van den Bundere, complained in 1510 that learned judges rejected the dignity and antiquity of local custom by replacing it with law from books, and that it was wiser to let towns enjoy their local customs, rather than imposing new law and causing people to criticize the ruler. This would then lead to civil unrest and suffering, he said, and, with local law abolished, would offer nothing in its place but a law understood only by the learned. On the other hand, the duke's higher magistrates attempted to free themselves from these same local customs through the increasing application of academic law. The practice of learned law came to be regarded as a profession that offered potentially lucrative careers. Learned jurists increasingly thought of the needs of the centralized state in which they pursued their careers, and they thought less and less of the role of local law in local consciousness.[8]

In 1463, the Council of Holland counted as many university-trained councillors as noblemen who were acquainted with customary law. From then onward, lawyers pleading before the court had to be academics.[9] In 1477, the General Privilege (see Chapter 7) similarly prescribed that the newly installed Great Council should have from each principality an equal number of noblemen and academics.[10] The registers of the Great Council show references to learned law mainly in the lawyers' pleadings, as additional arguments by analogy at the end of demonstrations based on customary law for the expressly stated material rights. Procedure and terminology were most influenced by the steady increase of the reception of learned law. Even then, we should not overestimate the rapidity of this reception. The volume of lawyers' pleadings before the Great Council increased by a factor of 5.4, from 1,412 written pages in 1460–1504 to 7,670 pages in 1504–40. The number of allegations of the *Corpus Iuris Civilis, Corpus Iuris Canonici,* and individual authors of works on learned jurisprudence rose by a factor of 3.25, from 342 to 1,113. Cities equally increasingly appointed academics as their main administrators and jurists, without expecting them to apply romano-canonical law as such.[11]

The increasing centralization of the state can also be seen in the number of other areas. In 1433, the duke commemorated the expansion of his territory by minting a new common silver coin, the "fourlander" (*vierlander*), which circulated equally throughout his territories and was called by different names in French- and Dutch-speaking areas. In 1437 he summoned the Estates of Brabant, Flanders, Hainault, Holland, Zeeland, Namur, and Mechelen to a joint deliberation on the currency exchange rate. This type of meeting was repeated in 1438, although without the delegations from Holland and Zeeland, given the harsh economic conflict these counties were involved in with England and the Hanse. There were again meetings in 1441 and 1446, with the cities of Holland once more participating in the negotiations. The agenda for numerous meetings of the cities of the various territories included such common economic problems as coinage, tolls, the English wool export, and whatever protectionist measures should be taken against finished English cloth.[12] This increased scale and intensity of consultation was connected to legislation that began to be enacted more and more often at a supra-regional level, after due consideration of regional points of view and interests. This cooperation made it more difficult for foreign trade partners of a particular region, such as the German Hanse or the English, to play Flanders, Brabant, and Holland against each other.

This extension of central ducal institutions and the reinforcement of their regional counterparts meant an increase in the number of officials. A growing corps of functionaries asserted the ruler's claims at the expense of traditional local authorities, usually the urban aldermen. Like the learned lawyers, these ducal officials developed into a separate class, pursuing their careers without reference to their own region of origin. Although each territory exhibited a marked preference for its own native ducal administrators, an exclusive right that was always proclaimed in the Brabantine Joyous Entries, the dukes were more and more inclined to seek supraregional integration of their administrative corps.[13] To the dukes, personal loyalty was the highest criterion of administrative service, and "foreigners," that is, officials native to one principality who were serving in another, were expected to promote the interests of the central state rather than regional interests. Thus the stadtholders of Holland and Zeeland came from Hainault or Flanders until 1477, and then again after 1480, while many native Burgundians held high offices in the Chambers of Account and the Councils of Flanders and Hainault. In Holland, there were a number of Flemings and Brabanters in official functions. Burgundians were clearly the dominant regional group in the service of the duke; they remained the old, trusted core of his servants and could be put to work everywhere.

Because the majority of them were Francophone, their prominence in ducal service extended the use of French as the language of the central administration. And the French that they used tended to be the language of the French royal court rather than the variants of the language spoken locally in Picardy and Rouchy, or the Walloon French, called *waalsch*, of the eastern part of the Francophone region. The committee of inquiry formed in 1457 to investigate official abuses in all the principalities consisted of five Francophone members and a single Brabanter. The Chamber of Accounts at Lille, which also supervised the finances of Flanders, used French exclusively. The bookkeeping of the Council of Flanders at Ghent was maintained in French, except that the dossiers of individual cases used the language of the parties involved. Litigation before the Great Council took place almost exclusively in French. Individual officers from Flanders, Brabant, or Holland who pursued careers in the central administration adopted the French language and often used a French form of their own names. Ultimately, the gallicization of ducal government occurred at the expense of many non-French-speaking litigants.[14]

The Burgundian territories beyond the "linguistic frontier" spoke variants of the Low Germanic vernacular (besides Frisian) common to the Low Countries, called by its speakers *duitsch* or *dietsch* to distinguish it from High German. The English called it Dutch. Dutch, or Netherlandish, was not a single language, but a set of related dialects of Low German that differed in various regions of the Low Countries and were not often well understood by speakers of similar dialects. Linguistic variations in Dutch did not prevent the development of Dutch as a literary language, and in the fourteenth and fifteenth centuries, a number of cities boasted of having several "chambers of rhetoric" (*rederijkerskamers*), literary associations that composed and presented poetic and dramatic programs on a number of public occasions. Throughout most of the Low Countries in the fifteenth century, although a "language frontier" existed, the two languages did not separate the collective development of the Burgundian state. The chambers of rhetoric flourished in both French and Dutch, and the dukes and their officials were often bilingual. Members of the ducal family often learned the Dutch of the particular territories they administered—Flanders or Brabant, for example—from tutors. The personal motto of the generally Francophone John the Fearless was the Dutch expression *Ik houd* ("I hold"). The personal device of the ducal councillor Lodewijk van Gruuthuse (or Louis de Bruges, as he was also called) was the French *Plus est en vous*, "there is more in you [than there might seem]," which he used in clever combination with his personal emblem, a firing bombard. Both emblem and device can still be seen in the Gruuthuse Palace in Bruges and in the many manuscripts he commissioned. Philip the Good and Charles the Bold both spoke Dutch, and bilingualism was one of the elements that helped to make a Burgundian ruler the "natural prince" (*naturlijke prins*) of his diverse peoples.

The dukes put their officials to work at a variety of tasks. The councillors of a given territory were usually considered the most suitable persons to conduct negotiations with the cities and Estates in the name of the central authority. The duke could, however, also entrust a diplomatic mission to a secretary from his chancery if it suited him.[15] The result was a great flexibility on the one hand, but also a lack of clear definitions of function on the other.

This encouraged integration and centralization, for at the head of the Burgundian administration was the chancellor. The Burgundian Nicholas Rolin held that office from 1422 to 1457, and he worked himself into a position of far-reaching power, although he was seldom allowed to make important decisions without reference to the duke. In addition to power, Rolin acquired in the course of his long career a noble title and a considerable fortune. These enabled him to commission the great altarpiece by Jan van Eyck in which his own portrait as donor appears, and to found the magnificent Hospital of Beaune, with the powerful painting of the *Last Judgment* by Rogier van der Weyden. The hospital still shows the initials of Rolin and his wife on the walls, beams, and stained-glass windows.[16] This extremely successful career could be termed typical of Burgundian officialdom. Those who struggled for advancement, enrichment, and social mobility could hold a career like that of Rolin in mind as they advanced their own careers and learned better how to advance them. It is remarkable that the number of university-trained jurists of bourgeois origin, like Rolin, in the top ranks of the Burgundian administration during the fifteenth century was comparable to that of the clerics and nobles. Expertise, thus, tended to win out over heredity, but the duke — and not he alone — still deemed it necessary to elevate his university-trained chancellor of bourgeois origin to the ranks of the nobility, so that he would have sufficient status to deal with the noble councillors.[17] And on occasion, heredity still won out. Rolin's dismissal from the post of chancellor in 1457 was the result of a power struggle among the duke's leading advisers, from which the noble Croy family emerged victorious.

The longer the Burgundian union existed, the more real it became and the greater grew the number of people with a personal stake in its continued existence and extension. Thus the gap widened between the corps of officials and the rank and file of society, which still thought largely in terms of local, or at most regional identity. A successful public career in the Burgundian working state increasingly required statewide consciousness.

Local Resistance Broken: Flanders

The movement toward centralization was most strongly resisted in Flanders, where the traditions of local autonomy were most deeply rooted. Jurisdictional disputes broke out repeatedly between the duke's highest judicial officer, the sovereign bailiff (*souverain bailli*, or *soeverein-baljuw*), and a city where the former dared to imprison one of its citizens. According to the cities' privileges, only a city's own aldermen could judge its citizens. Violations of this privilege often gave rise to violent conflicts. In 1401, after an escalation of mutual condemnations, the citizens of Ghent succeeded in having the sovereign bailiff, Jacob van Lichtervelde, dismissed from office and sent on a penitential pilgrimage to the Holy Land.[18] For similar reasons, in 1436 Bruges banished the sovereign bailiff, Colard van der Clyte, and the captain of Sluis, Roeland van Uitkerke—both nobles and officials of the duke—from the county for a period of fifty years.

But the revolt of Bruges left the proud city the loser.[19] In May 1437, Philip assembled an army before Bruges, whose citizens forced him to take flight. Jean de Villers, lord of l'Isle-Adam (Lelidam) was killed as he covered the duke's retreat. As Philip continued the siege of Bruges, the effects of the failure of the European grain harvest introduced famine into the city; in late summer or early autumn, plague also struck. The city surrendered in March 1438, and the duke summoned the Estates of Flanders, Artois, and Hainault as witnesses to his condemnation of Bruges at Arras. This was a city outside Flanders, and hence the condemnation was doubly humiliating for the Brugeois. Besides several symbolic penalties, the city lost its hegemony over its outport Sluis and over the surrounding lands (castelries) in western Flanders, and it was sentenced to pay the huge fine of 480,000 pounds. For an idea of the fine's enormity, it can be compared with the 380,000-pound subsidy granted to the duke by the county of Flanders as a whole for the year 1440, to which Bruges contributed 15.7 percent, or 44,000 pounds. Thenceforth the Council of Flanders, as the ruler's regional judicial college, and not the aldermen of Bruges, would be authorized to moderate conflicts and handle appeals between the city and the inhabitants of various lower judicial districts around Bruges.

But the duke had not deliberately provoked the revolt of Bruges in September 1436, a time particularly inconvenient for him, in the midst of his war against England. His original attempts to arrive at a peaceful settlement failed, and the military confrontation in May 1437 placed the duke and his noble following in danger of their lives. The conflict thus escalated into a threat to the duke's prestige. His resounding victory over the rebellious metropolis not only improved Philip's image, tarnished in his defeat by the English, but it also gave him a chance to break the supremacy of the powerful city of Bruges over the western portion of the county. The vacuum thus created provided Philip with the opportunity to extend the authority of his own judges and officials.

In 1447, the government decided to take a decisive step in reinforcing the state's central authority.[20] Following the example of the king of France, the duke decided to establish a permanent consumer's tax on the sale of salt. Salt was an essential product, of course, not only for the preparation of meals, but even more so for the preservation of food. It could be obtained only in a limited number of places, which facilitated the control of its source and distribution. The salt mines of the county of Salins, in the south of the Franche-Comté, were famed. Biervliet, in the north of Flanders on the west branch of the Scheldt, had been an important source of salt since the fourteenth century. At Biervliet, salt was obtained by burning salt-rich peat, a process also commonly used in Zeeland. Finally, salt was imported from the southwest coast of France, where it was obtained from seawater. Much of this was, in turn, shipped from Bruges to the regions around the Baltic Sea. From the point of view of the central government, the initiative to impose a tax on salt was entirely rational; it would render superfluous the delicate negotiations over financial subsidies with the Estates and cities in various regions, and it would replace the uncertain aids and subsidies with a guaranteed regular income. Moreover, it was an objective method of taxation, since it could be applied in the same way in all the regions, in both cities and countryside, and it would, in itself, introduce the number of the inhabitants as a criterion for the distribution of the tax burden, without necessitating a cumbersome census of hearths.

Philip the Good recognized clearly the advantage that the king of France derived from his own salt tax (*gabelle*), and how profitable the king of England found the tolls on his wool export. Philip dreamed of an income that would stream regularly and automatically into his own treasury. He also found it less and less acceptable to have to account to his subjects for his administrative needs, since without satisfactory explanations, his subjects could refuse to pay him taxes or at least could reduce and delay their payments. For precisely these same reasons, Philip's subjects were opposed to the new system, which would undermine their negotiating position and thus diminish their influence over both the ducal administration and their own purse strings.

Philip did not act precipitately; rather, he prepared each step carefully. He first attempted to persuade Flanders, which paid the greatest portion of all the different taxes, to introduce the system. If he could win Flanders over, the other territories were likely to follow suit. He negotiated not with the Estates as a whole, but only with Ghent, the greatest city and potentially the most formidable obstacle in his path. First he contacted several of the deacons from the most important craft guilds, summoning them to him in order to influence the stance of the General Council of Ghent. The meeting of one hundred delegates from the craft guilds and the bourgeoisie, representative of the city's Three Members — the weavers or textile crafts, the "small crafts," which included the smaller professional and artisanal groups, and the poorterij, the propertied bourgeoisie.

Since about 1360, municipal power in Ghent had been based on a careful distribution of all municipal offices among the Three Members. In the General Council and in both of the aldermen's colleges, the craft guilds held a clear majority, but the bourgeoisie retained the most influential positions and enjoyed an overrepresentation that contributed to the stability of the administration. Ghent's system of proportional representation in all public offices, from the highest to the lowest, had a pacifying effect quite different from that of municipal government in Holland. There, throughout the entire fifteenth century, rival parties managed repeatedly not only to exclude one another from power, but also to expel each other from the cities with threats (and not idle ones) of physical violence.

When Philip addressed the General Council of Ghent in 1447 to defend the introduction of the salt tax, he counted on its consent.[21] He argued that his father had left him with huge debts and mortgages on many of his domains, and that he had been forced to wage many expensive wars, including the then-current war in Luxemburg, which was of strategic importance for the defense of Brabant and Flanders. It was a rather thin argument. Rather than new aids, he said, a tax on every measure of salt sold throughout his lands would be appropriate to ease his financial situation, and it would be paid not only by his own subjects, but also by all foreign merchants residing in his lands. According to the duke, this tax would bring in more than the aids currently under consideration, without the average person noticing it. The rich would pay the most, especially the foreigners, clerics, nobles, and well-to-do burghers, and the poor would pay the least. He would ask for the consent of all his lands later, but he would not impose the tax in Flanders if it was rejected elsewhere, for he had no wish to tax this territory more heavily than any other. Such a statement would inevitably lead an attentive listener to conclude that the proposal would indeed raise the tax burden, perhaps even to a level that would hinder trade. Furthermore, it would certainly — given the nature of a tax on the consumption of a staple food item — weigh disproportionately upon the less prosperous.

Contrary to Philip's expectations, the General Council of Ghent refused to give its consent to the imposition of the salt tax. Was the argument from social morality decisive, or was it the fear of losing influence as a representative body? Or were both factors in combination decisive? In any case, the duke left the city of the Arteveldes with bitter feelings. Later he would lay the blame upon the untrustworthiness, perjury, and treachery of a trio of craft deacons whom he mentioned by name, maintaining that they had maligned the duke before the people, with misrepresentations of his proposal. Several months later Philip repeated his experiment at Bruges, where he met with an equal lack of success. A salt tax was never imposed in the Low Countries, and even a full century later, any form of tax on consumption was staunchly resisted.

The cordial relations between the duke and Ghent had been seriously compromised. At the annual renewal of the aldermen's colleges, Philip attempted to prevent his opponents from being appointed to office; this step exacerbated their differences. Judicial harassment of citizens of Ghent and of the Franc of Bruges (the large and fairly wealthy rural district the Free Quarter) further aggravated the situation. The duke was now clearly and deliberately pushing matters to a head in order to undermine the position of Ghent, the greatest city in all his lands and one that—unlike Bruges—still enjoyed all the privileges it had been granted a hundred years before. In 1450, the duke enumerated all his grievances against Ghent before an astonished meeting of the Estates of Flanders. At the same time, he increased the pressure by systematically violating the city's privileges and recalling his bailiff, thus rendering correct legal procedures impossible. Thus provoked, the artisans of Ghent armed themselves in 1451 and called a strike. Various attempts at arbitration ran aground on the duke's uncompromising stance. In the summer of 1451, the city was subjected to a military blockade, and the militia issued forth. In one of the ensuing battles, a favorite illegitimate son of the duke was killed, further increasing his bitterness. The decisive battle was fought in July 1453 at Gavere, where the Ghent militia panicked after the ineptitude of their own men caused a load of gunpowder to explode in their midst.

As in the case with Bruges in 1438, the duke exploited the subjection of Ghent to the fullest, and the punishment imposed was similar. The immense fine of 840,000 pounds — although reduced by 168,000 pounds two years later — was as much as the aid paid by the whole county of Flanders from 1440 to 1443. The judicial authority of the aldermen outside the city was substantially limited, and their sentences could now be appealed before the ducal court, the Council of Flanders. The influence of the craft deacons on the municipal administration was reduced to virtually nothing, and the guilds were required to surrender their banners. Here, too, symbolism played an important role: the aldermen and the craft deacons were required to kneel before the duke bareheaded, barefoot, and in penitential robes, and to offer him the banners of their guilds. During the revolt, the crafts had assembled around their banners at the Friday market square, and during military expeditions, these had also marked the fierce identity of the citizens. Their subjection went so far that some prominent citizens of Ghent, perhaps even aldermen, commissioned for the occasion a luxurious new copy of their book of privileges, containing not only the adjusted—and considerably diminished—version of the city's rights, but also fifteen beautifully executed miniatures. One of these shows a tableau of the Gentenaars' subjection before the duke, seated high on his white horse; another illustrates the battle of Gavere, while others portray earlier glorious accounts of Flanders according privileges to humble Gentenaars. This splendid product of the Ghent school of book illumination was probably offered to the duke on the occasion of his entry in 1458.[22]

The duke doubtless intended the subjection of Bruges and Ghent to serve as examples; if he could tame these, the greatest and most rebellious of his cities, the others would remain docile. And this does, indeed, appear to have been the case in Brabant. There, too, the cities continually complained that the duke violated their privileges, which were also embodied in written form and which the duke had solemnly sworn to uphold on the occasion of his Joyous Entry. As in the other territories, the Council of Brabant was extended to include a procurator (*procureur*) and a fiscal advocate (*advocaat-fiscaal*), and this council continually overrode the judicial decisions of the urban aldermen. In 1459 the duke made use of a conflict between the city of Brussels and the ducal judicial officer, the *amann*, to declare the city's privileges of 1421 void. In 1421 the Estates of Brabant had set aside their duke, John IV (see Chapter 3), for numerous violations of the Joyous Entry and for maladministration, and they had appointed his younger brother, Philip of St. Pol, as regent. Philip of St. Pol had acknowledged their grievances and had also accepted the principle that ducal councillors were accountable to the Estates. The fact that this remarkably early expression of the notion of popular sovereignty and administrative accountability to the representative institutions could be so effortlessly repealed in 1459 bears witness to the increasing success of the monarchical state.[23]

But the often heavy-handed methods that the dukes used to break resistance in their territories also caused such bad blood between the ruler and various groups of his subjects that revolts broke out at the slightest provocation, rolling back—or at least temporarily impeding—the ruler's growing authority. Voices were raised in protest against the increasing authority of the state and its agents on the occasions of both the 1467 and 1477 inaugurations of Charles the Bold and his successor, Mary of Bur-

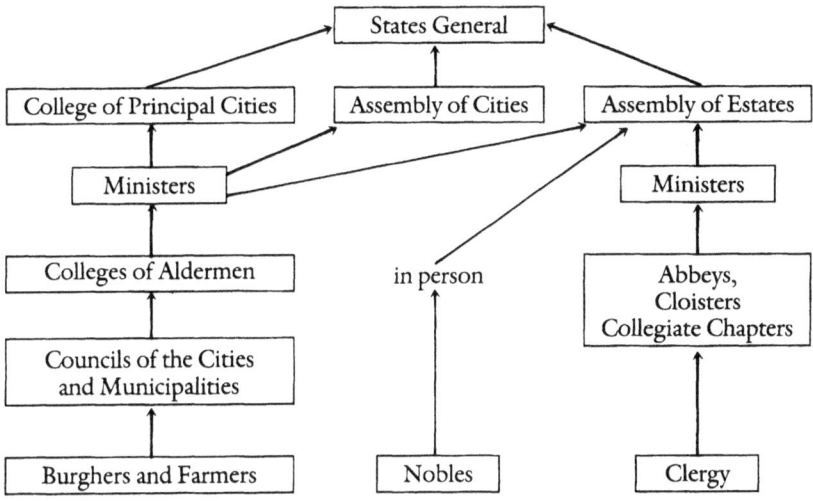

Figure 2. Representative Institutions

gundy. The administrative weaknesses of the Burgundian state, thus, had manifold political consequences. These need to be considered here.

The Working State: Administrative Weaknesses

The continuing friction between the duke and his subjects was the result of the development of an enormous inefficient administrative machine. Judicial officials turned over to the regional receivers only a small portion of the fines they collected, and the regional receivers themselves proved to be just as susceptible to corruption as were the toll collectors, demesnial administrators, court clerks, and chancery secretaries. Supervisory laxity tended to encourage the embezzlement of public monies at all levels.

In 1457, in the context of the power struggle between the Croys and chancellor Nicholas Rolin, the duke commanded a large-scale investigation into administrative irregularities. Numerous cases were soon exposed. The chancellor was forced out of office, as was shortly thereafter the president of the Great Council, Bishop Jean Chevrot of Tournai. But curiously enough, the investigation came to an abrupt halt after both the Four Members of Flanders and the most prominent of the Brabanter towns spontaneously offered the duke a large subsidy to close it. Evidently the interests of the local elites and those of the ducal officials coincided; they belonged to the same families, often rose from the service of the city to that of the ruler, and doubtless conducted at least some business with each other that would not bear up under intense public scrutiny. Midsized cities like Saint-Omer and Lille maintained exclusive relationships with some highly placed Burgundian officials or dignitaries, who would then champion the interests of their "client" city. One good turn deserved another, and those who held power used it preferentially and did not, in so doing, neglect their own self-interest. The idea of public service had not yet taken sufficient root, and power was still too often perceived in personal terms. All of this was alien to the development of a generalized system of professional ethics, meaning that everyone tried to enrich himself at the expense of the state, and that the state itself was powerless to prevent this, despite its constant references to the idea of the public weal.[24]

The state's continual shortage of money was both a result of and a further stimulus for corruption. To acquire revenues rapidly, the government farmed out a great many tolls and judicial offices, and, in general, it paid its officials poorly. As a result, many candidates who were the highest bidders, but not the most qualified, were appointed to an office, clearly intending not to administer the regulations of the office, but to recoup and increase as quickly as possible the capital they had invested. Those who suffered most from such irregularities, since it was they who paid for them, were the ordinary subjects, who could expect normal services only upon payment of bribes, and who encountered abuses wherever they turned. Opposition was no longer simply city against prince, but the people in general against both city administrators and ducal officials, who all belonged to the same ranks and were appointed in the duke's name.

The Joyous Entry of Charles the Bold in 1467 was greeted by a massive outburst of protest. In several cities, riots broke out as a reaction to increased excise taxes. In Ghent the people called for the abolition of the humiliating measures of 1453, such as the closure of one of the city gates. In the confusion, the duke himself barely escaped the mob. An exemplary punishment was again imposed on the city. In January 1468, Charles summoned the aldermen of Ghent and the craft deacons to Brussels (as in the case of Bruges in 1438, a site outside their own county and hence an additional humiliation) to hear his judgment. After several hours of waiting in the snow, they heard the sanction: the craft banners were to be surrendered once again, and the craft deacons were to lose their voice in the appointment of aldermen, who would henceforth be appointed solely in the duke's name. A riot had again resulted in further subjection of the city.[25]

Riots also broke out in Mechelen during Charles's Joyous Entry. It is interesting to note that the duke had a memorandum drawn up in which it was reported how, nearly thirty years earlier, Bruges had been punished, and what sanctions should now be considered appropriate for Mechelen. From this report it is clear that Duke Philip rejected the suggestion made by several councillors that the city be destroyed; the same consideration had been shown for Ghent in 1453. At that time, the duke is reported to have said: "The People of Ghent are my people, the city is mine, and if they were destroyed I know of no living being who could make their equal for me."

In 1467, the duke's advisers pointed out that "It would be better to found a city such as Bruges than to destroy one."[26] Similar sanctions were debated about Mechelen in 1467. But it was recalled that Duke Philip had punished Bruges financially in 1438, had executed or banished the forty guilty parties, and had obliged three hundred citizens to kneel before him; after that, Philip had allowed them to retain most of their rights. Duke Charles was counseled to grant Mechelen the same grace after imposing a substantial fine, because the city had originally been purchased for a huge sum, and it was strategically situated. Centralist thought in government circles was systematic, but also cynical and extremely paternalistic.

At the time, Duke Charles the Bold proved that he considered the destruction of rebellious cities as a real option. In 1467 he was himself formally recognized as their hereditary ruler by the Estates of Liège, but only after he threatened military action. Because the Liégeois cities revolted a few months later, and because the citizens of Dinant had mocked the duke and his mother in effigy, Charles had Dinant destroyed. In 1467 and 1468, there was still fierce fighting and determined resistance. When the Burgundian army, encamped at Liège, was attacked by the legendary "six hundred men of Franchimont," the duke subjected the city to days of plundering, murder, fire, and destruction. As the new procurator and regent of the bishopric, Charles entered Liège triumphantly after a siege of two weeks on November 17, 1467, and pronounced a severe judgment, depriving the proud city of all her privileges, institutions, and fortifications. Visiting the cathedral, Charles made an *offrande* to the relics of her patron saint, Lambert, whom the duke revered as the protector of the church and the diocese. Immediately afterward, he commissioned a golden reliquary with his own kneeling effigy offering the relics. The fresh outbreak of the revolt in 1468 led to a renewed military subjection and the city's destruction. The reliquary was handed over to the cathedral only in 1471, now extended with a standing image of St. George, the patron saint of the Burgundian dynasty, to whom Charles had appealed for intercession before his final battle.[27] This donation in no way diminished the human suffering. Dinant and Liège did not belong to the dynasty's hard-won patrimony, and for that reason, Charles felt fewer qualms about sparing these cities as he had Mechelen. Nevertheless, this fact appears inadequate as the sole explanation of Charles's repeated resort to drastic measures. His irritation over the successive revolts and over the intrigues of Louis XI of France — whom he dragged away from the negotiating table at Péronne to witness the punishment of Liège — must have led the duke to give way to an impulsiveness that he later came to regret.

In order to understand both the waxing of Burgundian power and its administrative weaknesses, we need to take into consideration several decisive elements. Territorial expansion had strengthened the position of the ruler with respect to each region and each city. Only rarely did an uprising take place among his subjects on a scale larger than in a single place, implying that the ruler was able to bring to bear the resources of more and more regions for the subjugation of the rebels. It is remarkable how loyal to the ruler other cities and regions remained in the face of revolts elsewhere. This attitude worked in favor of ducal victories. The Burgundian state had its advantages: the period of peace and relative prosperity from around 1440 to 1475; political careerism in its administration; support of foreign trade; and protection offered to small cities and villages, against the aggression of dominant cities and feudal lords. Military technology brought cannon to the forefront. City walls could be destroyed more easily by bombardment. The amateur militia of the cities, which in the fourteenth century had been able to force the count of Flanders and even the king of France to retreat, now faced the trained, professional troops of the duke, equipped with superior artillery.

This combination of developments formed a stronger state that was able more easily to deprive the great cities of their hegemony. The subjugation of the great cities of Flanders, as well as of Liège and Utrecht, was meant to intimidate the others. In Holland and Brabant gentler pressure was applied, but the goal was the same everywhere, and the means of achieving it were often those of spectacle and display as well as power.

The Theater-State and the Imagery of Power

The Burgundian state expressed itself not only through diplomatic, legal, military, and administrative institutions, but also by the repeated public demonstration of the grandeur of the dukes and the ducal court through the patronage of art, literature, manuscript and tapestry production, music, ceremony, spectacle, and display. In these activities, some historians have seen what is termed the Burgundian theater-state, a useful term that offers yet another perspective on the realities and fictions of Burgundian power.

But the proud and strategic expression of self and power was not invented by the dukes alone. Wealthy citizens of Ghent and Bruges, managers of public institutions and leaders of civil and devotional associations, commissioned, endowed, and donated many artistic works to the institutions they protected. The construction and decoration of public buildings, the commissioning of statues and fountains, as well as the design and materials of banners, all received significant attention and financing. Throughout Flanders, cities had celebrated festivals, religious holidays, and significant political events with processions and tournaments, for a very long time. Thus the Valois dukes found a public display of civic ceremony and artistic expression as soon as they arrived in Flanders.

In the tradition of the French royal house of Valois, Duke Philip the Bold had devoted much attention to the artistic glorification of his young dynasty. Coincidentally, he found in the Low Countries a remarkably original group of painters, wood-carvers, and sculptors whose work was to transform the character of the visual arts in Europe. Klaas Sluter, Jacob de Baerze, Melchior Broederlam, and Klaas de Werve were summoned to Dijon to carve statues and altarpieces for the decoration of the ducal mausoleum in the Carthusian Charterhouse at Champmol. Philip also commissioned the Maelwal brothers to paint miniatures for a splendid manuscript bible. His successors continued this practice, although, with the shift in the governmental center of gravity and operations toward the Low Countries, artists received most of their commissions in those regions.

Because no clear distinction was made among art, artistic crafts, and other crafts during the Middle Ages, princely patronage generally amounted to the reservation for the ruler of the rarest and most expensive products. In this way rulers were able to distinguish themselves from ordinary people, who in their turn desired to emulate the symbols of this princely splendor. This drive, recognizable throughout society, as well as ambitious social climbing, led to the imitation and adoption of the ducal example by those wishing to enhance their own status.

The dukes of Burgundy, more than most European rulers, made use of artistic patronage to enhance their public image both at home and abroad, directing their display as much toward rival rulers as toward their own subjects. Precisely because they belonged to a young dynasty whose power had been only recently established, the dukes were probably more sensitive than were other rulers to the need to emphasize the significance of their many titles through an excess of artistic glory. By the middle of the fifteenth century, Philip the Good and others considered himself worthy of a royal crown, and he compensated for his subroyal ducal status by emphasizing the exceptional splendor of his court on ceremonial occasions.

In the Low Countries, the Burgundian dukes found a virtually inexhaustible supply of artists of the highest quality to whom they could entrust the portrayal of their preeminent political position. On the one hand, the initiative, inspiration, and motivation for this patronage of the arts emanated from the dukes. On the other, the dukes found in their new territories a breeding ground for the nurturing of artistic creativity that, thanks to their support, attained a leading position in Europe. The combination of ducal initiative and the existing artistic traditions of the various cities in the Low Countries provided a spark that ignited an explosion of artistic activity in all fields. This activity is usually — and not very accurately — referred to by the designations "Flemish primitives" and "Brabantine gothic" in painting and architecture, and by "Flemish polyphony" in music. But these terms should be understood as collective ones, embracing some four generations of artists in a number of centers and regions of the Low Countries. The example set by the dukes was imitated by the entire social elite: court nobility, clergy, city administrators, rich merchants, and wealthy monks and nuns. None of the artists of the famed Burgundian-Habsburg period worked exclusively for the rulers; other patrons emulated the ducal model.

The flourishing period of artistic creativity coincides generally, although not precisely, with the period of "the promised lands," the great period of political stability, peace, and prosperity between 1440 and 1470. Already in the fourteenth century, each of the great cities in the southern Netherlands had made noteworthy contributions to the fields of architecture and painting — in architecture by the building of churches, town halls, and luxurious private residences; in painting, on walls, sculptures, panels, and in book illumination. And it was not only religious art, but also banners, placards, and other secular settings that were being produced. The arrival of the dukes of Burgundy gave new impetus to this existing tradition, and activity in certain centers reached new heights. A painter like Roger van der Weyden, a pupil of Robert Campin in Tournai, had no need to await the advent of the dukes to leave his master's atelier for Brussels, where an eager public both at court and among the burghers provided him with more commissions and buyers for his paintings. Indeed, the very invention of an art market may have been one of this period's most enduring contributions to European culture. Jan van Eyck worked in Bruges after completing in Ghent his altarpiece *The Adoration of the Lamb* in 1432. The painters Petrus Christus, Hans Memling, Gerard David, and Pierre Coustain all migrated to Bruges around the middle of the fifteenth century. They were joined by a remarkably talented group of manuscript illuminators, to the extent that Bruges became the only city in Europe that created a guild of all the artisans who worked in the book trade.

Philip the Good's only true court painter was Jan van Eyck, who appeared on the ducal salary lists, from 1425 until his death in 1441, as a valet de chambre. This position, however, did not prevent van Eyck from undertaking and carrying out other artistic projects, such as ambitious altarpieces for a number of prominent citizens and residents of Bruges (canon Joris van der Paele, for example, and Giovanni Arnolfini and Giovanna Cenami in their betrothal portrait of 1434) and Ghent (alderman Willem Vijd and his wife Elizabeth Borluut in the marvelous Ghent altarpiece), as well as for the chancellor Nicholas Rolin in Burgundy. Also to be found in the duke's service were miniaturists, usually from Hainault and Artois. The duke's master builder, Jan van Ruisbroek, was a Brabanter who expanded the ducal palaces, particularly the Coudenberg palace in Brussels. The court also included a group of singers, serving primarily to enhance religious services. But the gap between spiritual and secular music was not great, and such singer-composers as Gilles Binchois, Antoine Busnois, and Guillaume Dufay are known to have worked in various genres. The daily life of fifteenth-century Burgundian cities was consistently punctuated by the ringing of bells, the music of horns and trumpets, the organs and stringed instruments of religious and secular occasions, and the voices of singers.

Besides court artists, the Burgundian dukes and their court commissioned innumerable projects from ateliers in different cities. The most remarkable of these were the tapestries, generally produced at Arras and Tournai. Given their considerable dimensions and price, they were truly gifts fit for a prince. The splendid series of twelve tapestries depicting the destruction of Troy cost the equivalent of the yearly wages of 125 skilled artisans.[28] This high cost can be explained by both the expensive materials used—wool, silk, and gold and silver thread—and the years of labor required for highly skilled and highly paid weavers. Both their enormous size and their rarity contributed to the great impression these tapestries made on the viewer. The dukes made conscious use of this effect by displaying the works in their reception halls, especially on solemn occasions. At the lavish wedding feast of Charles the Bold and Margaret of York at Bruges in 1468, the guests enjoyed a series of tapestries portraying the victory of Duke John the Fearless over Liège at Othée in 1408. The chronicler Jean de Haynin also lists other series of tapestries portraying such subjects as the story of Gideon and the Fleece; the great deeds of Clovis; and those of King Ahasuerus, who was said to have ruled over 127 provinces. All are clear allusions to princely triumphalism. Philip the Good alluded more subtly to this theme by ordering a series representing Alexander the Great. The symbolism of power is apparent in other commissions as well, such as that of the so-called *Tapestry of the Thousand Flowers*, which pictures the coat of arms and device of the duke along with such other dynastic symbols as the Cross of St. Andrew and the fire irons. In the same vein, a tapestry was commissioned linking Gideon with the Golden Fleece, the favorite symbol of grandeur of the Burgundian dynasty.[29]

Tapestries were clearly directed at a particular audience, that is, the many members of and visitors to the court. By means of these magnificent images, that public entered into the self-fashioned Burgundian vision of lordship. More numerous yet were the art works erected in churches, since all Christians would frequently pass through them. These included architectural monuments like the tombs at Champmol and liturgical memorials like those for the murdered John the Fearless, to be performed at the Carthusian Charterhouse at Montereau — founded specifically for that purpose, as stipulated in the Treaty of Arras of 1435. Last, but not least, were the stained-glass windows and altarpieces, although the latter were more frequently commissioned by eminent subjects than by the dukes themselves.

The dukes also devoted special attention to books. They commissioned many translations of Latin works into French: chronicles of the history of their newly acquired principalities, world histories, and heroic tales of Alexander the Great and Charlemagne. A select group of translators rewrote these epic works into more easily readable prose, thereby often altering the meaning and function of the works. A writer such as David Aubert from Valenciennes in Hainault was very active in Brussels on Duke Philip's commission, in the years from 1458 to 1465. In 1468–69 he produced mainly for Anthony the Great Bastard, and in 1475 in Ghent, for Duchess Margaret of York. In later years, he must have found patrons outside the ducal court.[30] The chosen themes often provide politico-ideological support for the dukes' claims. This is clearly discernible in contemporary accounts by such court writers as Enguerrand de Monstrelet, Georges Chastellain, Jean Froissart, and the later disaffected Philippe de Commynes.[31] In 1475, the learned Jean Molinet was appointed as the court *indiciaire et escripvain*, a position he held for thirty years. His historiography as well as his poems display an outspoken political vision and an innovative artistic style.[32]

Even if a particular orientation is perceptible in the subjects of the hundreds of manuscripts that the dukes commissioned—and it should be noted that many purely literary, theological, and philosophical works also fell within their sphere of interest—it was still primarily the form of their manuscripts that engaged their attention. It is no coincidence that there are numerous miniatures depicting Philip the Good or the young Charles the Bold paying a visit to an atelier where books were illuminated. Other scenes portrayed the duke surrounded by officials and nobles, being presented with a new manuscript. It is precisely the emphasis with which this ceremony was treated that underlines the importance that the dukes attached to precious and beautiful books. As patrons, they were visible in text and image in their manuscripts and through their coats of arms, as well as through symbols, devices, mottoes, and presentation scenes. This entire ritual was performed around enormous books that were finished with richly ornamented initials, magnificent border illuminations, and full-page miniatures. These manuscripts were very similar in appearance to liturgical manuscripts. It is striking that Philip the Good chose this opulent format only for his religious and historical books. In this way the glamour of the past, of the dynasty, and the illustrious predecessors with whom the dukes sought comparison were elevated to a quasi-sacral level.

It stands to reason that these magnificent manuscripts were perused by eminent courtiers and that they, too, desired to possess similar treasures. Louis de Bruges—Lodewijk van Gruuthuse of Bruges—for example, was a noted bibliophile. He was a knight of the Golden Fleece and stadtholder of Holland and Zeeland. In his still well-preserved palace at Bruges, he amassed an impressive collection of manuscripts, inspiring the English king Edward IV, who visited during his exile in 1470–71, to order copies of some twenty manuscripts. Imitation led to widespread noble patronage of the production of beautiful manuscripts—with the intellectual messages that they contained.[33]

The Burgundian rulers and patrons made their greatest impression on the larger public by means of their production of mass spectacles. Whether these were Joyous Entries into the cities, marriages, funerals, chapter meetings of the Order of the Golden Fleece, diplomatic journeys, great banquets, or receptions at court, extreme care was taken to achieve the maximum dramatic effect. In spectacles that lasted for days, the court was presented to the people in all its glory. The public could stare in amazement at the magnificent clothing, precious jewelry, and dignified bodily comportment of the gorgeously attired courtiers and their servants. Banners and trumpets contributed their colorful notes to the ensemble. In 1454, a year after his triumph over Ghent and only a few months after his splendid Feast of the Pheasant at Lille, where he and his courtiers solemnly pledged to undertake a Crusade against the Turks who had conquered Constantinople, the duke undertook a long journey abroad. As the most prominent territorial prince within the German Empire, he participated in the Reichstag at Regensburg. The political consequences of Philip's participation were negligible, but the splendor that the Burgundian entourage vaunted before the envious eyes of the imperial princes, who were accustomed to considerably less luxury, greatly enhanced the ducal reputation. Still, there was more than symbolism at stake; this courting of the German Empire ultimately led to the marriage in 1477 of the Burgundian crown princess, Mary of Burgundy, daughter of Charles the Bold, to the future Habsburg emperor Maximilian of Austria.

Cities also developed their traditions of festivals in order to enhance their own reputations, staging elaborate processions and Joyous Entries that outdid those of other cities. Some processions, such as those of the Holy Blood in Bruges, the Corpus Christi at Oudenaarde, or the Virgin's Birth at Louvain, attracted numerous spectators who came to see the giants and the pageants. Urban authorities used the massed spectacle of a ducal entry to convey a message both to the duke and to their fellow citizens. They carefully designed the pageantry in a coherent iconographical program, clarifying some difficult and obscure references to the Bible or to classical or mythological heroes with inscriptions on banderoles and brief oral announcements. Duke Philip's first entry into Bruges after the revolt was held during Advent of 1440. It celebrated the duke in numerous representations as Christ bringing peace and reconciliation. The pageants along the route through the city were built up in a crescendo, from humiliation and sorrow to the joyful images of the Resurrection, showing the ruler accepting his people and the people revering their ruler.[34]

For the entry of Philip the Good into Ghent in 1458, five years after the suppression of a violent revolt, the city administration organized competitions for the most beautiful street decorations and the best-executed theatrical productions and *tableaux vivants*. Themes from the Bible and from classical antiquity, the figures of saints, allegories and displays of heraldry were portrayed in every possible way. *The Adoration of the Lamb*, the vast, privately commissioned altarpiece by Philip's own court painter Jan van Eyck, was dramatized as a tableau vivant, along with other themes dear to the duke such as the myth of Gideon and the Golden Fleece. And there were appropriate biblical parables — the Prodigal Son, the Good Shepherd, the meeting of David (suggesting the duke) and Abigail (the city of Ghent) — and portrayals of the courageous heroes Alexander, Caesar, and Pompey. The images of saints and heraldic emblems were painted on the great canvases, just as the meaningful quotation from Judith (3:6), "Come to us, peacebringing Lord," and music resounded. Again the authorities had devised a gradually built-up climax, from repentence and wrath to wisdom, justice, forgiveness, and the alleviation of penalties.

In Ghent a broader variation on themes was chosen than in Bruges, including especially dramas performed in both Dutch and French, representing the magnanimity of Alexander the Great toward the Sarmatians.[35] The city mobilized all of its artistic creativity to convey the message of affection and devotion to the duke that the entire urban community supported. A form of symbolic language had evolved in which both the duke and his subjects were able to "address" one another very clearly. The whole city celebrated for several days and was lavishly decorated with tapestries and paintings. Along the processional route, theatrical performances were given by seven troupes, poems were recited, and music was played. The city administration had encouraged this display and promised a number of silver dishes embellished with the arms of the city for the most beautiful decorations and the best play. A scant five years after its resounding defeat, Ghent seemed reborn, with the guilds competing for the richest and most beautiful performance offered to the honor and glory of the duke. The duke, in turn, suitably impressed, was finally reconciled to his most rebellious city.

During the wedding feasts of Charles the Bold and Margaret of York in 1468, tournaments were held on the marketplace of Bruges, where the nobility could display their prowess before the fascinated populace. There were week-long festivities at Sluis, where the English bride landed, at Damme, and at Bruges itself. Twice there were evening fireworks. After the marriage ceremony at Damme, the wedding party left for Bruges, where it was met by a procession of clerics (among them the bishops of Cambrai and Utrecht, both half-brothers of Charles the Bold), the local guilds, and dozens of "nations" of foreign merchants: the German Hanse, various Italian cities, Catalans, English, and many others. The high points of these festivities were the banquets, varied by courses featuring special effects, dances, and games.

Dozens of artists were employed for the architectural setting and the decoration of the halls, among them the young painter Hugo van der Goes from Ghent.

Patronage of the arts by the Burgundian dukes had more far-reaching consequences than merely the commissions given directly to artists, for these amounted only to a small percentage of the annual state budget. The artwork of the palaces at Dijon, Arras, Lille, Bruges, Ghent, and Brussels represented the greatest part of this expense. But the most far-reaching consequence was the *Gesamtkunstwerk*, the entire ensemble of courtliness and its public display that captured the imagination of contemporaries, as reflected in the densely descriptive court chronicles and in reports sent to the four corners of Europe by foreign visitors. The ducal style led to imitation among his own people, both of the ostentatiously elegant and luxurious fashions of court dress and of the duke's investment in works of art. A capitalist elite existed in the great Flemish and Brabantine cities, desirous of affirming its status by being portrayed as donors on altarpieces viewed by the entire community. And its imitation of the ducal style extended the influence of a flourishing Burgundian courtly culture far beyond court life.

* * *

The period from around 1440 to approximately 1470 can be considered the central and most characteristic period of the Burgundian hegemony. This period should be characterized as predominantly peaceful. The military campaigns that were undertaken by Philip the Good after 1440 were limited and did not endanger the stability of his lands. He did, however, deal harshly with domestic resistance, even using strong military force against the great and rebellious cities in order to further the state formation that he pursued. Most remarkable of all, despite even the bitterest of conflicts that led to a substantial erosion of the cities' autonomy, namely the Ghent revolt of 1450–53, the duke adopted such paternalistic mildness in the aftermath that a scant few years later, he was once more generally applauded in Ghent, *zeere uutnemende blijdelic ende rijkelic*—"most outstandingly, joyously, and richly," in the words of his contemporaries, and more triumphally and honorably than any other ruler in the previous five centuries.

6

The Promised Lands
1440–1475

The Promised Lands

In the 1470s and 1480s, Philippe de Commynes, a Flemish diplomat in the service of the dukes of Burgundy until his defection in 1472 to Louis XI of France, wrote a chronicle of the events he had witnessed, one of several remarkable narrative accounts that are important sources for the history of the Burgundian rule in the Low Countries. Looking back at the Burgundian complex of Philip the Good over the previous twenty-five years, Commynes wrote: "At that time the subjects of the house of Burgundy lived in great wealth, thanks to the long peace they had known and to the goodness of their ruler [Philip the Good], who imposed few taxes upon them. Therefore it seems to me that these lands, more than any other principality on earth, could be called the promised lands [*les terres de promission, de landen van belofte*]. They overflowed with wealth and lived in great peace, the like of which were afterwards unknown to them. People had money to spend, the clothing of both men and women was luxurious, meals and banquets were larger and more sumptuous than in any other place I know."[1]

Commynes was certainly able to draw comparisons, since he had traveled widely in Europe, including visiting the highly developed city-republics of northern Italy. Although he was tendentious in idealizing the reign of Philip the Good in contrast with that of his son and successor, Charles the Bold (1467–77), with whom Commynes had fallen out, there was much pertinent truth in the chronicler's observation.

From 1440 to 1465, the Burgundian territories had indeed been spared the ravages of war, whereas both before and after this period, they were involved in a number of foreign military operations. The surviving financial data suggest that Commynes was correct, too, in his claim that taxes were less heavy in Philip's time than later. In the county of Flanders under Charles the Bold and Maximilian (1477–94), taxes were roughly three times what they had been under Philip the Good. In Holland, the subsidies (*beden*, or aids) allocated in 1478 were more than double the average imposed since 1428.[2] It is safe to assume that this considerable increase also took place in other regions. The relationship suggested by Commynes was, in general terms, that the absence of war made it possible to keep the tax burden low, and that this enabled the duke's subjects to live in remarkable prosperity.

It is possible, of course, to express some reservations concerning some of Commynes's hyperbole, but his enthusiasm was typical of the way that many other people, both native and foreign, perceived the Burgundian lands during twenty-five years of peace, prosperity, and territorial expansion. At the end of his life, Philip the Good was duke of Burgundy, Brabant, Limburg, and Luxemburg; count of Flanders, Artois, the county of Burgundy (Franche-Comté), Hainault, Holland, Zeeland, Namur, Auxerre, Mâcon, and Ponthieu; seigneur of (West) Friesland, Salins, and Mechelen. He held Picardy as a redeemable pledge until 1463. Eighteen principalities, large and small, had been acquired at various times by various means, and all were diverse in their traditions. His holdings consisted of two principal blocks of land: one was formed by the heartland of Burgundy, the neighboring Franche-Comté and a number of smaller seigneuries, and a second was formed by the principalities of the Low Countries. At first the dukes themselves spoke of these as "our lands over here" and of those "over there," the meaning of "here" and "there" depending on wherever the duke happened to be at the time. After their greatest interests led the dukes to reside more and more in the Low Countries, the Burgundian heartlands gradually became permanently "the lands over there," and the Low Countries the "lands over here."

It is possible to test Commynes's claims in greater detail, by considering the ducal financial complex and then the demography, agriculture, maritime and manufacturing economies, the financial structures, and the standard of living in "the promised lands," the "lands over here."

The Ducal Financial Complex in Burgundy and the Low Countries

It was not easy to pursue a consistent administrative and financial policy throughout the duke's constellation of territories, or even to acquire a clear sense of their motley traditions, rights, and customs. The duke was unable to calculate even approximately the amount of revenue at his disposal.³ There were a number of reasons for this difficulty. In one charter of 1426, Philip the Good accused his financial officials of carelessness and of withholding portions of the taxes they collected for their own use, thereby reducing his net income. But in fact, Philip himself continually resorted to this practice. When he owed a debt that was payable at a particular location, he referred his creditor to one of his receivers — toll collectors or judicial officers — in that locality, who was then required to pay the requisite sum promptly from revenues that were either anticipated or already collected. This practice also took the form of allotting rents or guarantees of payment for a specified period of years, which meant that a substantial portion of the ducal income had already been assigned for local distribution long before it reached the duke. In such cases, any oversight of the entire complex of ducal finances was difficult, although the duke's continual financial needs and the practical advantage of local disbursement of receipts continued to make the practice of withholding portions of all sorts of income very attractive.

After 1435, the territorial acquisitions of the dukes of Burgundy began to assume a greater degree of cohesion, as the duke strove to gain a firmer grip on his finances. In 1433 there were three Chambers of Accounts — one in Dijon, for the lands "over there"; one in Lille, for Flanders, Artois, Hainault, and Picardy; and one in Brussels, for Brabant, Limburg, and, later, Luxemburg. In 1438 Philip the Good formed a special financial commission within his Great Council. From 1438 to 1443, this committee sought to devise methods of gaining a clearer idea of the central government's financial resources. This led to the creation in 1444 of the office of treasurer and general governor of finance (*trésorier et gouverneur général des finances*), entrusted to the Fleming Pieter de Leestmaker, also known as Bladelin, whose palace can still be seen in the Naaldenstraat in Bruges and who commissioned a magnificent altarpiece attributed to Rogier van der Weyden. In 1440 the duke issued detailed regulations for the office of receiver-general. The first results of these reforms became evident in 1445. In March, all the ducal officials who rendered accounts were required to present their accounts and justificatory documentation to three councillors at the Chamber of Accounts at Lille. The councillors, in turn, used these documents to gain a general overview of the total receipts, the expenditures at the local level (including payments to ducal creditors), and the expected net income for the duke's central treasury. In 1447 a Chamber of Accounts was created in the Hague for Holland and Zeeland, consisting of two *maîtres des comptes* and a clerk. In this manner the gross receipts for the year were estimated at 315,000 pounds (at forty groats to the pound), whereas net income amounted to only 171,000 pounds. Thus, 46 percent of the duke's income went to operating expenses and allocations administered by the many local and regional receiverships, and barely half the gross income actually reached the central authorities. In addition, many of these expenses were in fact repayments of debts incurring by earlier rulers. For example, in Holland these expenses accounted for 54 percent of the receipts, in Flanders 57.5 percent, and in Artois, as much as 86 percent.

The territorial distribution of ducal revenues in the duke's role as lord of his domains is particularly enlightening. Most remarkable is the fact that the region of the "lands over there"—Burgundy, Franche-Comté, and the attached territories—represented only 26 percent. These domainal receipts came from the revenue for the duke's own lands (rents in kind and in money, farms), as well as from his income as the lord. This income would most likely have come from fines from jurisdiction, tolls, feudal rights, and a share in the indirect taxes in some cities (in Bruges this amounted to one-seventh).[4] Our source does not give a breakdown between the duchy of Burgundy and the imperial county of Franche-Comté.[5]

Flanders proves to have been the richest territory by far, in terms of income available to the duke. The considerable difference between the gross and net income is indicative of a large amount of expenditure within the county itself, implying a low level of centralization. Thus, more resources flowed into the central treasury from the Burgundian territories proper than from Flanders. Grouping these territories according to the dates of their acquisition, it becomes apparent that the patrimonial lands of Philip the Bold (Burgundy, Franche-Comté, Flanders, and Artois) still accounted for a good 60 percent of the gross income as late as 1445. Philip's marriage to Margaret of Male, heiress to Flanders, Artois, Franche-Comté, Nevers, and Rethel, had brought him many times the income he had enjoyed from the duchy of Burgundy. This block thus remained, even after the later territorial expansion, the chief source of ducal revenues.

Philip the Good's acquisitions in the empire (Namur, Brabant, Limburg, Hainault, Holland, Zeeland) accounted for 27.6 percent of his gross income in 1445, which was substantial but still considerably less than the 34.6 percent contributed by Flanders and Artois (further increased by the undifferentiated portion contributed by Franche-Comté). The Peace of Arras of 1435, with the Burgundian conquest of Picardy and of several smaller territories, must have brought the duke at least an additional 12 percent, considerably augmenting an income that had already increased

TABLE 1. Percentage Distribution of the Ducal Income from Demesne Rights in 1445

	Gross receipts (percentage)	Net receipts (percentage)
Burgundy (duchy, county, and dependencies)	26.0	33.7
Flanders	24.0	18.9
Picardy	11.8	15.9
Artois	10.6	2.8
Holland-Zeeland	9.5	8.0
Brabant-Limburg	7.9	10.7
Hainault	7.6	7.1
Namur	2.6	2.9

substantially. Nevertheless, the amount of additional income provided by territorial expansion would appear to have decreased.

If we examine how these funds were spent, the first thing we observe is that the total expenditures of the central accounts amount to 326,000 pounds, more than the gross revenue and nearly double the net income. This needs to be examined in detail.[6] The costs of the court itself and the personal expenses of the duke, including gifts and remunerations, accounted by far for the greatest part of these central expenditures. Clearly there was still no question of a depersonalized governmental structure. These accounts did not yet draw a sharp distinction between the private finances of the ruler and those of the state. Two observations need to be made: first, by no means were all of the resources of the Burgundian state centralized—many were administered by local and regional receiverships or Chambers of Accounts; second, the duke disposed of nearly four times his net income, since, in addition to the 46 percent of his normal revenues dispensed locally, he could also draw on other, extraordinary revenues. The most important of these were the aids, those occasional subsidies that he requested from his subjects. All the figures we have cited pertain to the so-called demesnial revenues of the ruler: everything he was entitled to as owner of lands and as seigneur. As seigneur he was entitled to receipts from tolls, coinage, fines, feudal levies, taxes on money changers and Lombards, and a share in the excise taxes of certain cities such as Bruges, where he claimed one-seventh of such receipts.

Since the thirteenth century, the rulers had begun requesting that their subjects contribute extraordinary subsidies in addition to normal seigneurial income. Originally these extraordinary subsidies were permitted only in exceptional circumstances: the inauguration of the ruler, his marriage, the knighting of his heir, or his ransom, if he was captured in war. But since the financial needs of rulers, particularly in the fourteenth and fifteenth centuries, were virtually unlimited, the temptation to request such aids increased continually, and a systematic tax levy grew out of this practice. In principle, such requests for aids could be refused by the estates or by the urban representative institutions, and on occasion these refusals held good, usually during periods of strained relations between ruler and subjects. In Flanders, the Third Estate paid no aids whatsoever between 1433 and 1437. At first the duke accepted this situation, as compensation for the damages suffered as a result of the interruption of English trade. In those years the duke contracted considerable loans from Italian bankers, merchants, and courtiers. These lenders were reassured by preemptions on the revenue from his domains.[7] At the request of the duke, however, the urban militia was mobilized in 1436, and the clergy paid a substantial sum. In Hainault, there were only two years in which no aids were granted. In Holland, aids were paid annually and granted for periods of ten years, or, on exceptional occasions, for five or six years. In Zeeland, Artois, and Brabant, aids were granted without interruption for periods of several years. Only in the largely rural areas of Namur, Luxemburg, and Burgundy had tax levies not yet developed a regular pattern by 1445.[8] During the reigns of the first three dukes, the revenue from aids amounted to about 40 percent of the total state revenue. Under Charles the Bold, this share rose to 47 percent.

As a rule, it was more advantageous to both sides to continue negotiating and to seek mutual advantage through these continuing negotiations. Thus the representative institutions were often able to persuade the duke to grant their own demands, often presenting him with a list of requests that soon became a list of grievances. The precise amount granted and the conditions under which it was granted depended, in large measure, on the give-and-take relationship between rulers and subjects and the extent to which both parties were willing to go. But by the fifteenth century, the practice had come to be generally accepted. It must be noted that aids were generally paid by the Third Estate—city dwellers and peasants. The Church considered itself and its clergy exempt from taxation because of its religious mission, although under exceptional circumstances it might occasionally offer the ruler financial support, always upon the explicit condition that this was not to be regarded as a precedent. The nobility was equally exempt from this form of taxation, since, in principle, it was bound to provide feudal service and could thus be called upon to serve in the duke's army.

There has as yet been no detailed study of the duke's total receipts from this sort of extraordinary income. Research into this problem is extremely complex, precisely because accounting practices were so confused and irregular during this period. Negotiations took place in each principality separately for subsidies that differed in their amounts, in the periods for which they were granted, and even in the currency in which they were to be paid. The amount once appropriated, all sorts of agreements were reached informally and often surreptitiously, which might lead to a particular city within the principality contributing little or nothing at all. Bribes to high officials occasionally facilitated such escapes. There was, thus, frequently a substantial difference between the amount theoretically granted to the duke and the real receipts that came into the treasury. In theory, the income from aids (not taking into account exemptions and payments in arrears) from the various territories can be estimated at a maximum of 196,000 pounds for the year 1445. Together with the 171,000 pounds of net revenue from ordinary receipts, this totals 367,000 pounds of gross revenues, and, after subtracting the 326,000 pounds of ducal expenses, it leaves a positive balance of 41,000 pounds.[10]

These figures, obviously, have only a relative value. It is possible, however, to compare them with similar data available for the revenues of the English crown in the years from 1462 onward. Expressed in metric tons of fine silver, for the sake of comparison, King Edward IV (1461–1483) received annually between 12 and 14 tons.[11] Duke Philip's total receipts for 1445 were equivalent to nearly 12 tons of fine silver.[12] Taking into account the 30 percent increase of his income from aids, his receipts may be estimated at 13.6 tons around 1465, which was fairly comparable to that of Edward IV. The average of the aids in the Burgundian Low Countries during the years 1456–65 was equivalent to 8 tons of fine silver, while the *servicios* granted by the Cortes of Castile amounted in those years to about 10 tons.[13] It should be obvious that the financial potential of the Burgundian state made it a competitor on a standing comparable to that of the most prominent kingdoms of the west, although its population was far less numerous.

Viewed as a whole, the finances of the Burgundian state, despite the theoretical surplus, were actually in continual deficit. The duke constantly borrowed money from the Italian merchants and bankers of Bruges, from

TABLE 2. Expenditures of the Central Chamber of Accounts in 1445

Categories	Cost in pounds (of 40 groats)	Percentage
Salaries	47,365	14.5
Ducal household	104,300	32.0
Household of the duchess and the heir apparent	22,096	6.8
Cash payments	68,000	20.9
Gifts and food	35,500	10.9
Ambassadors and messengers	13,500	4.1
Army	5,600	1.7
Stables	4,000	1.2
Furs and clothing	15,000	4.7
Jewelry and plate	6,000	1.8
Alms	1,400	0.4
Pocket money	3,150	1.0
Totals	325,911	100.0

money changers in various cities, and from his own officials. The revenues expected from aids were often pledged as security for these loans, as were jewels and silver. Naturally, credit was very expensive. In 1437 and 1438 the duke financed his military campaign against Bruges by pledging jewels and silver plate as security to a money changer at Tournai at an interest rate of 20 percent. By continually deferring payments and committing revenues anticipated but not yet received, the dukes and their officials often stole from Peter to pay Paul. Thus, they could attain only the vaguest overview of their true financial situation. They regularly made expenditures of sums greater than the amount of cash on hand, and, as a consequence, they paid high prices for the necessary financial means of staying afloat.[14]

The reasons for these deficits were clear, but they were also difficult to resolve. Money was not always available at the time or in the place where expenditures had to be made. This was in part the result of the weak centralization of the finances, and in part of the often unpredictable peregrinations of the ducal court. In 1445, aids produced (theoretically) 15 percent more than the net demesnial income. But income from aids fluctuated enormously—from 338,000 pounds in 1430 to 134,000 pounds in 1444—because they were dependent upon political negotiations with the Estates of the individual principalities.[15] In addition, these sums, once granted, trickled slowly into the treasury, and many cities, in exchange for their consent to these aids, exacted special reductions for themselves. In reality, the picture was far less favorable than would appear. Still, in 1445 the financial situation of the Burgundian state was particularly favorable, thanks primarily to the peace reigning both within and outside its borders.

Recalling the quotation from Philippe de Commynes with which this chapter opened, contending that Philip the Good imposed few taxes on his subjects, we must now examine how these extraordinary taxes evolved. Including all of the territories, these indeed amounted to little more at the end of Philip's reign than they had in 1430, by which time most of the territorial expansion had already taken place. In the decade 1430–1439, the total receipts from aids amounted to an average of 241,737 pounds per year, and in 1456–1465 they rose to an average of 246,933 pounds per year. Receipts varied, however, from one territory to another. In Flanders they averaged 47,300 pounds per year during the decade 1420–1429, and 76,900 pounds from 1456 to 1465, an increase of 63 percent.[16] These figures may appear difficult to reconcile with the vision of Commynes, but for the Burgundian territories as a whole, his assertion was essentially correct. His statement becomes more comprehensible in the light of later increases. At the time Commynes wrote, in the seventies and eighties of the fifteenth century, the rate of taxation had again doubled relative to the sixties. The period from 1430 to approximately 1470 was, from a fiscal point of view, characterized by only a slight overall increase in the tax burden. However, in comparison with the later war years under Charles the Bold, taxation during the reign of Philip the Good could be perceived as moderate. A gradual increase in taxation would have been perceived as bearable, under the circumstances of external peace and increasing general prosperity. In some cases a significant proportion of the increase, particularly in Flanders, was the result of fines imposed as punishment for rebellion. However painful these measures were for the victims, they did not affect the entire population, whose position was, thus, correspondingly more favorable than the raw numbers may indicate.

Beginning in 1471, aids were simultaneously demanded in all of the territories of the Low Countries, and a formula had to be found for their distribution. They could never be spread equitably, precisely because there was no common or objective means of assessment. The trend, however, is clear. Three-quarters of the aids in the Low Countries were contributed by three territories together with their annexes—namely, Flanders, Holland-Zeeland, and Brabant-Limburg, each contributing a quarter. The other

TABLE 3. Distribution of the Ducal Income in the Low Countries

	Domains in 1445 (Percentage of gross receipts)	Aids of 1473 (Percentage)
Flanders	32	25
Picardy	16	—
Artois	14	(2)
Holland-Zeeland	13	25
Brabant-Limburg	11	24
Hainault	10	6
Namur	3	1

territories were of little fiscal importance. In 1473, Hainault contributed barely 6 percent, Luxemburg 2 percent, and Namur 1 percent of the substantial aids raised in that year.[17] These figures by no means accurately reflect the relationship of the territories in terms of what we would today refer to as the gross national product. Such a distribution formula was too much the product of a political debate for it to be closely tied to measurable economic resources. Certain territories considered it a matter of prestige to contribute larger portions. Flanders and Brabant were kept at a 60 : 40 formula in joint ventures, which was not, however, applied to the general distribution. Occasionally one territory was inclined to make a relatively greater contribution because of some direct interest in the matter, for example in the defense of its own borders.

Comparing this 1473 distribution of the duke's extraordinary revenue to the demesnial receipts of 1445 — an imperfect comparison, in view of the changes during this period and the lack of evidence — we can draw a few tentative conclusions.

Without attaching undue importance to these figures, which we have used solely as indicators of relative distribution, it is evident that Flanders was the leader both for the duke's ordinary revenues (from demesnes, tolls, fines, and other sources) and for his extraordinary revenues. The demesnes in Brabant-Limburg and Holland-Zeeland brought in considerably less, while contributing as great a share to the extraordinary revenues. In the more rural territories of Hainault and Namur, the reverse was the case: their smaller contribution to aids was compensated for, to a certain extent, by relatively greater demesnial revenues.

Population and Production

The measurable regional differences in state revenues raise the question of population and the economic activity that led to a greater or lesser amount of taxable surplus. As with all comprehensive quantitative data in the premodern period, uncertainties must be acknowledged: all of the following figures are based on generalizations deduced from partial information. The overview that follows is for the period around 1470, chosen because the administration of the Burgundian state made special efforts at that time to hold a census of the number of hearths (households) in each territory. This valuable documentation offers a relatively solid foundation for estimating population figures. It also distinguishes between the inhabitants of towns and villages. The total population has thus been computed using a multiplication factor, so that it matters a great deal how many persons are counted per hearth. On the basis of sound, if limited, statistical data, we counted five persons per hearth in the countryside and four in the cities. For Holland, the earliest information of this nature does not appear until 1514, which is in itself an indication of the weak administrative integration of this county. An estimation of the population of Zeeland can be deduced from that of Holland using the distribution formula for aids in the two counties, which was 3 : 1 at that time.[18]

There are still some unknowns remaining, for example the population of the Sticht Utrecht. If we add the territories that only came under Habsburg-Burgundian control in the course of the sixteenth century, such as Friesland, Overijssel, and the Tournaisis, and deduct Picardy, which was lost to France in 1477, then the population of the Low Countries must have been around 2.6 million. Here too Flanders was in the lead, even though the seigneury of Mechelen and the districts of Lille, Douai, and Orchies were included despite their constituting separate administrative districts. In the light of these population figures, the question arises as to the per capita tax burden. Holland-Zeeland, Brabant, and Flanders each contributed a quarter of the general aids, even though they differed greatly in population. This results in the following rather surprising figures for the Burgundian state as a whole.

The range in the tax burden from 1 to 10 in the aid burden from one territory to another could certainly be called significant. It is improbable that a difference in per capita income would entirely justify this difference in the tax burden. One of the causes of these discrepancies was certainly a lack

TABLE 4. Population and Urbanization in the Territories of the Low Countries Circa 1470

	Inhabitants	Urban (%)	Inhabitants per km^2	% of total population of the Low Countries
Flanders	705,000	33	72	28.6
Brabant	399,000	29	39	16.1
Holland	254,000	44	63	10.3
Hainault	202,000	28	40	8.2
Picardy	184,000	19	?	7.4
Artois	176,000	20	34	7.1
Luxemburg	138,000	12	?	5.6
Liège	135,500	26	?	5.4
Guelders	133,000	41	?	5.4
Zeeland	[85,000]	?	?	3.4
Boulonnais	31,000	12	34	1.2
Namur	17,500	26	?	0.7
Limburg	16,500	6	21	0.6
Total	2,476,500	32		

of precise knowledge on the part of the ducal administration. Political considerations, such as the desire of the duke to maintain his popularity with the border region of Picardy, assuredly played a role as well. These differences also help us to better understand why the peasants of northern Holland were so often moved to rebellion, and why the towns of Holland encountered such serious liquidity problems toward the end of the century.

The reason for the stubborn resistance of the Flemish cities to a more equitable distribution of the tax burden also becomes apparent. They knew very well that this could only mean that they would have to contribute more.[19] The three leading territories together accounted for 55 percent of all the inhabitants of the Low Countries—Flanders alone for 26 percent, Brabant for 16 percent, and Holland for 10 percent. Together, however, they paid more than 74 percent of the aids, which shows that this form of tax weighed most heavily on the commercialized regions, whereas the demesnial revenues (56 percent of the total revenue at that time) simply continued from the traditional seigneurial rights. The differences between the territories were, in fact, much greater than those that could be deduced from the distribution of ducal revenues. But the tax share contributed by

TABLE 5. Average Contribution Per Capita for Aids in 1444–1467

Holland	6.1 groats
Artois	4.5
Brabant	3.6
Lille-Douai-Orchies	3.6
Flanders	3.4
Hainault	1.9
Picardy	0.6

Hainault and Namur appears to have corresponded reasonably well to the size of their relative populations.

From the dynamic point of view, equating the acquisition of new territories with the procurement of new sources of revenue and human capital, it is evident that such acquisitions varied significantly in value. This variation is undoubtedly related to the socioeconomic structure existing in each of these territories and to the ways and degrees by which the ducal administrative apparatus was introduced in each. The degree of urbanization, in combination with the population density, can provide us with considerable insight into socioeconomic conditions. When judged according to these criteria, Flanders and Holland both score highly. A high percentage of urban dwellers presupposes an intensive, highly developed agricultural economy like that of Flanders, or intense commercial activity like that taking place in both Holland and Flanders. Holland, in this respect, seems to have shown a higher degree of per capita development than Brabant, which had a structure analogous to that of Hainault, although its population was twice as large. The contrast between these territories and distinctly agrarian Luxemburg, very sparsely populated and possessing only the smallest of towns, is especially striking.

These elements were, obviously, important in the formation of a centrally administered state. In the more heavily urbanized regions, the population density was generally greater, and there were a number of cities with populations in excess of ten thousand. In Flanders these were Ghent, Bruges, Ypres, Lille, and Douai. Ghent and Bruges were the second and third largest cities in Europe north of the Alps after Paris. In Brabant, the major cities were Louvain, Brussels, Antwerp, and 's-Hertogenbosch, with the separate seigneury of Mechelen as an enclave in their midst. In Holland, they were Leiden, Dordrecht, Delft, Haarlem, and Amsterdam. In Hainault, or bordering on it, were Mons, Valenciennes, and Tournai. In less urbanized regions that nevertheless enjoyed substantial trade, there was usually only one large town, such as Arras, Liège, Nijmegen, and Utrecht.

Extensively urbanized regions having high concentrations of capital and heavy traffic in various goods were taxed with relative simplicity through the imposition of tolls and excises. In more rural areas, the per capita wealth of the population was more limited and was concentrated primarily in the form of feudal estates, which were mostly exempt from taxation. In such a territory, much less revenue was available to the duke, and he was continually obstructed by local lords. For these reasons, Hainault and Picardy, for example, bore a relatively low tax burden. In the cities, the duke encountered other forms of resistance and autonomy. Precisely because they were large, rich, and walled, the cities could pose formidable obstacles to any expansion of the ruler's power. Thus the toll at Gravelines, where wool imported from England via the obligatory staple at Calais was the primary source of tax revenues, generated some 26,000 pounds of income for the duke in 1445, whereas the entire county of Namur yielded scarcely 16,000 pounds in gross revenues.[20] Thanks to their strong negotiating position with the ruler, the Flemish and Brabantine cities succeeded much better than their counterparts in Holland in keeping the tax burdens relatively bearable; their rate of taxation was more favorable than the rate in Artois and Holland.

Here it is possible to see the fundamental contrast in the economic structures of the Burgundian Low Countries: the contrast between the maritime territories and those regions lying further inland. The former were characterized by a substantially higher degree of urbanization, which, naturally, had an impact on all aspects of production. The urban development that took place along some of the greater rivers before the Burgundian period—for example, along the Maas, the Waal, and the IJssel—stagnated during the period considered here. In contrast to this stagnation, further urban growth took place in northern Brabant, with Antwerp and Bergen op Zoom as its most important centers. It was especially significant in Holland, with a growing Amsterdam at its core. In Holland and also in Flanders, long the site of the greatest cities in the Low Countries, a typical urban economy flourished. Since city dwellers did not produce their own food but had to import it from the surrounding countryside or even from farther away, they needed to produce the equivalent in the form of manufactured goods or services. The majority of the raw materials processed in the cities also came, originally, from the countryside.[21]

Agriculture in the Burgundian Low Countries

The urban demand for foodstuffs and raw materials shifted the orientation of agricultural production toward the urban market. Consequently, in heavily urbanized and densely populated areas, agricultural activity was more intense, more specialized, and more productive than in purely rural, thinly populated areas. In the neighborhood of Brussels, for example, during the second half of the fifteenth century, a net yield of 16.5 hectoliters (100 liters) of wheat per hectare (2.471 acres) could be attained after subtracting seed for the next year's planting. In Artois, net yields of more than 20 hectoliters per hectare were achieved. In Flanders, with sandier soil, net yields ranged from 13.5 to 15.5 hectoliters per hectare. During this period the European average was much lower, and only a combination of rich, loamy soil, intensive plowing, manuring, and crop rotation can explain such high yields. Because the demand in the cities was so great and constant, additional investments, certainly those in labor, were worthwhile. In Artois, as early as the late thirteenth century, agricultural demand and profitability had reached such levels that cattle were kept in barns and fed fodder such as vetch, grown as a second crop on fields that would otherwise have lain fallow. Thanks to the manure thus accumulated, together with that obtained from the cities themselves, and to the high yield of the excellent loamy soil, net yields of as much as 30 hectoliters per hectare could be harvested in the neighborhood of Saint-Omer.[22]

It has been postulated that a city of twenty thousand inhabitants consumed the grain harvest of twenty villages.[23] Given that the people of the fifteenth century consumed an average of one liter of grain per day, it follows that in the Flemish-speaking part of the county of Flanders, some 2,318,000 hectoliters of grain per year were necessary. To obtain this, with a moderate yield of 11 net hectoliters per hectare, some 219,000 hectares were needed — a fourth of the total surface area of the territory. Two-thirds of the agricultural lands either lay fallow or were taken up by pasture, which implies that the total area of effectively used agricultural land extended over 75 percent of the total surface area of the territory. There were, of course, other crops, extensive forests, and wasteland, so that it is understandable that provisioning was precarious and that regular importing of grain from more productive and sparsely populated regions such as Artois, Hainault, and Zeeland — and, in years of crisis, even distant Prussia — was essential.

Artois exported annually the enormous quantity of 1,520,000 hectoliters of bread grains, chiefly wheat, enough to feed the entire population of

Brabant. The majority of this grain went to nearby Flanders. Ghent lay along navigable rivers and was scarcely 100 kilometers from Lille, 115 kilometers from Béthune, 140 kilometers from Aire, and 155 kilometers from Douai. Ypres and Bruges were reached easily by canals from the Lys. Douai alone accounted for half the export, the surplus of a territory of a 3,616 square kilometers extending far to the south of Bapaume. Artesian grain was also shipped to Antwerp and from Saint-Omer downstream, via the river Aa, and thence by sea to Holland and England. Picardy, more distant, shipped considerably less grain to the Low Countries—a maximum of 15,000 hectoliters even in the best of years. For Prussia the figures are only sporadically available, but these also reflect a maximum of 15,000 hectoliters.[24]

Fluctuations in the net grain yield at harvest—that is, the grain yield after the next year's seed grain had been subtracted—and thus in grain prices, were often extreme. The region around Louvain yielded an average of 6.26 kernels of rye per kernel sown. Deviations were, however, from 40 percent lower to 200 percent higher: sometimes double, but also often less than half the average.[25] This uncertainty, for both the producer and the consumer, was therefore great. For this reason, everyone who could possibly afford to do so purchased a piece of land, on the condition that he receive annually a fixed amount of grain from the tenant's harvest. The city administrations also kept vigilant watch over the grain supply, and they did not hesitate to take emergency measures affecting both producers and grain merchants in order to ensure a sufficient supply for their market.

Grain, of course, was not the only foodstuff. The population also needed livestock, vegetables, and dairy products. Some fields were temporarily converted to pasture, providing the advantage of extra manure and thus restoring the quality of the soil after several continuous years of grain production. All sorts of fodder crops were grown to feed the livestock. These were often produced as a second crop, and they offered the double advantage of supporting more livestock and at the same time contributing essential nitrogen to the soil. In the urbanized territories, a variety of plants were cultivated that served as raw materials for urban industry. Plants were also used in making textile dyes. For example, red came from the roots of the madder plant, blue from woad, and yellow from weld. The cultivation of flax and hempseed also increased markedly in such regions as the Lys valley. These fibrous stalks required moist, fertile soil. Increasingly, fine linen was woven from flax, imitating the shimmer of silk but at a much lower price. Ropes were braided from hemp to meet the important needs of

Holland's shipbuilding industry.[26] Hops, needed for brewing beer, was a crop sensitive to weather conditions. Only the larger farms had sufficient capital and labor available for its cultivation, which became important in some regions from the late fourteenth century.[27]

Peat was dug for fuel on a grand scale in low-lying areas. But removing peat in regions with a high watertable had the unfortunate consequence of lowering the ground level, leading to occasional flooding. Moreover, the topsoil left after peat had been removed was frequently of poorer quality. This was a recurrent problem in Holland. Since the peat bogs were reclaimed through drainage projects, the ground level sank as a soft sponge does when it dries. Within a few decades, the level of the land had sunk by several meters. In the course of time, drainage by natural waterways became impossible, necessitating the construction of new dikes and additions to old ones. Drainage was achieved by means of sluices, opened at low tide so that water could escape and closed at high tide to keep the rising water out. At the beginning of the fifteenth century, paddlewheels powered by windmills also came into use. Much of the land thus put into exploitation by human labor or won from the waters could only be retained by continuing investments and by meticulous organization. Nevertheless, storms occasionally destroyed lands, in spite of prolonged and substantial labor, investment, and organization.

Since the thirteenth century, water control had been organized by special water boards known as Waterschappen.[28] These were public institutions that were recognized by the counts but were virtually autonomous. Their autonomy was practical: the construction and maintenance of hydraulic works required continuous participation and effort on the part of the peasants who were their principal beneficiaries, and who had the most experience in such matters. The high cost of this vast system of dikes, sluices, ditches, and canals could only be borne by a strict and rationally devised organization, applying the principles both of fair distribution of costs and of responsibility for the rigorous application of the measures decided upon. The share of each landowner in the costs was calculated according to the surface area of his lands within the protected area, but it also gave him a voice in all related decision making. In such circumstances there was little room or need for the presence of the central government.

A local mentality developed in the coastal and fluvial regions over the centuries, based on the rational consideration of goals and means, the careful administration of goods acquired, and the right of all interested parties to participate in decision making. This mentality has remained characteristic of large groups in the northern Netherlands. It stood in stark contrast to the Burgundian court culture, which tended toward centralized decision making and ostentation even to the point of conscious waste. This difference in mentalities eventually lay at the heart of later violent conflicts in the Low Countries.

In this context, the relative infertility of the silty soil of Holland is of primary importance. The cultivation of wheat was limited or impossible, leaving more possibilities for the cultivation of the less-demanding grains rye and barley. The latter provided the raw material for the breweries that were developing into true export industries in Delft, Gouda, and Haarlem. Hops, which were added to beer both to enhance the flavor and to render it less perishable, had been grown increasingly in the Low Countries since the late fourteenth century. The general unsuitability of the soil of Holland for cultivation, particularly of those cereal grains used for bread, goes far toward explaining both the predominance of stock breeding and brewing in Holland and the high degree of urbanization there. In the cities the standard of living had to be realized by trade and industry, which became increasingly feasible because of their maritime location and a growing merchant navy.[29]

The Maritime Low Countries

A combination of factors favored the inhabitants of Holland and Zeeland in maritime development. The limited possibilities of their agriculture forced them to engage in such other activities as fishing, shipbuilding, and related maritime industries. The art of marine design and the engineering and technology of shipbuilding changed rapidly in northern Europe from the eleventh through the fifteenth centuries, and a common vocabulary of marine technologies developed across the world of the North Sea and the Baltic. The swift, shallow-draft, side-ruddered, sail- and oar-powered ships of the northern seas of the eleventh century gave way before the demands that emerged in the thirteenth and fourteenth centuries: increased cargo volume, reduced numbers of crew, and the consequent need for more sail. By the beginning of the fifteenth century, shipbuilders in northern Europe had increased the depth of their hulls, replaced the side-mounted, oar-like rudder with a permanent centerline stern rudder, and raised the main deck above the waterline, producing greater draft, improved stability in rough weather, and a greater working capacity for both fishing and shipping. The great Dutch herring *buss* could sail across the open North Sea to Scotland, trawling huge nets behind it. Although sizes varied, the average later buss in the sixteenth century carried just under one hundred tons and was nearly twenty-five meters long, five meters in beam, and three meters deep. Its ratio of length to beam made it easy to control and an excellent working ship. It provided the point of development for the later Dutch *fluyt*, the most successful sailing ship of the early modern period. In the late fourteenth century, fishermen from Flanders, Zeeland, and Holland also developed a new method for processing: the fish were cleaned, salted, and packed in barrels immediately after the catch was hauled aboard. With their more efficient methods of fishing and preserving their catch, fishermen from the Low Countries dominated the markets of Europe, including those of the Baltic coast, bypassing the north German Hanse.[30]

The shipbuilders of the northern seas also succeeded in constructing other types of larger, faster, and more maneuverable merchant vessels. Their prototype was the *cog*, a clinker-built (overlapping planking construction, built shell first) ship with a large, flat-bottomed hull, a straight-raked sternpost, and a centerline stern rudder, powered by a single sail. The cog was replaced during the fourteenth century by the larger *hulk*, characterized by a curved bottom, greater structural continuity, and extension of the cargo space closer to the prow and stern.

By the fifteenth century, ships from the Low Countries sailed regularly to England and Scotland, the Baltic ports, and beyond the Bay of Biscay. Shipbuilding activities were localized in countless villages and small towns along the coasts and riverways. Unimpeded by guild regulations, the marine industry was stimulated by the enormous demand for imported grain in Holland itself. Even the wood, tar, pitch, and iron needed as raw materials for the ships had to be imported from Scandinavia, Prussia, and the Rhineland. Thanks to low wages and to the great efficiency of their ships and maritime services, the Dutch played a preeminent role on the western and northern seas.

The Textile Industry

Aside from fish, the great cargo of Dutch and other ships was wool, initially the transshipment of raw wool from England and later the fine merino wool from the Iberian Peninsula. The textile industry was the manufacturing enterprise most typical of medieval European cities. It fulfilled a basic human need and was virtually omnipresent in both villages and cities. What distinguished the textile industry in a great number of cities in the Low Countries was the high quality of the cloth that they began producing very early. Cloth woven in the Low Countries was in great demand throughout Europe, and cloth production reached unparalleled heights. The basic textile requirement per person per year can be estimated at two to three ells (2.7 square yards) of cloth. Yet at the beginning of the fourteenth century, the city of Ypres produced annually per inhabitant somewhere between 69 and 83 ells (84 to 100 yards).[31] Production reached 42 ells (50 yards) per inhabitant in the mid-fourteenth century at Louvain, and at the end of the fifteenth century at Leiden. Such large figures are indicative of massive export, as are the countless references to Flemish, Brabantine, and, later, Leiden cloth throughout Europe.[32]

But domestic wool production was insufficient to sustain such a high level of cloth production. Raw English wool had enjoyed an established reputation for excellence since the twelfth century and was shipped in huge quantities to the Continent, since the English textile manufacturing industry was underdeveloped until the fifteenth century and wool was overproduced. The English organized their export around the staple, a compulsory distribution point at Calais, which long remained a fortified English outpost on the Continent. Gradually, however, the English ceased limiting their activities to the mere provision of raw materials for the finishing industries of others. Cloth was now woven in the English countryside and, though not of the same fine quality as the Flemish cloth nor available in the same range of colors, was considerably cheaper. The heavy tolls imposed by the English crown on the export of wool explain to a degree the difference in price. Another factor was the lower wage scale of the English cottage weavers, compared with those of the urban artisans on the Continent.[33]

The textile trade was complex, and competition was fierce. In Flanders the great cities were able to persuade the duke to ban the import of English cloth altogether. The Brabanters and the people of Holland, however, were not in favor of the ban, since they themselves imported rough English cloth to be finished in their own workshops and then exported under their own trademark.[34] In these territories, the textile workers had always been less numerous and less well organized than in the great Flemish cities, and they could thus bring less pressure to bear on economic policies — even those that affected them most severely.[35] In Flanders the fear of unemployment led to a frantic protectionism, understandable in light of the financial uncertainty of price differences and diverse economic interests.

The following table gives the relationship between the price of fine black English cloth around 1440 and cloth produced in the traditional centers and small towns and villages of Flanders that also produced cheaper, lighter cloth. With the price of English cloth equivalent to 100, the Flemish prices related to it as given in Table 6.[36]

These price relations led to a double shift: first, toward a general differentiation of production using more Spanish, inland, and cheaper English wools; second, a movement of manufacturing away from the traditional production centers in the great Flemish cities and Louvain, and toward places where there was less regulation by craft guilds and anxious urban administrations. The smaller towns, the villages of southwest Flanders, northern Brabant, Leiden, Amsterdam, and smaller Dutch towns were in a much better position to respond vigorously to English competition by bringing coarser, cheaper, and lighter fabrics onto the European market. Linen production then expanded in Hainault, Flanders, Brabant, and Holland and absorbed a good deal of the rural labor force. There was tremendous demand for these products, and the presence of the existing trade network assured their efficient distribution. Members of the confederation of trading cities known as the German Hanse were probably the most important buyers of Flemish cloth, which they purchased at the staple market at Bruges, where they also maintained their main foreign residence. In certain cases, such as that of the West Flemish town of Poperinghe, the German Hanse merchants pledged to purchase all the cloth manufactured there, from Spanish wool, in imitation of the cloth made in Saint-Omer. In the 1430s, the city of Dendermond hoped to stimulate the sale of its cloths by offering them at the fairs of Antwerp and Bergen op Zoom. However, the simple threat by the Hanse merchants in Bruges that they would stop their purchases blocked this venture immediately. For the smaller towns, the Hanse's hegemonic position toward the Flemish drapers had by now become a factual monopoly.[37]

The reaction of the Flemish textile industry to competition from England, Brabant, and Holland was thus by no means limited to protectionist measures. By the middle of the fifteenth century, wool from the Castilian plateau was fully in use in most towns in eastern Flanders and in numerous cloth centers in the southwest of the county. Even a city like Ghent could not avoid responding to changing market conditions, and it, too, offered cheaper textile products for sale. In cooperation with its principal trading

TABLE 6. Indices of the Prices of Flemish Cloth with Respect to English Cloth, Around 1440 (English Cloth = 100; Flemish Prices in Relation Below)

"Traditional"			"Light"		
Ypres	Scarlet	412	Wervik	Fine black	330
	Black	229	Courtrai	Fine black	117
Bruges	Scarlet	382	Menen	Fine black	214
	Black	278	Nieuwkerke	Motley	81
Ghent		268			

partner, the Hanseatic League, Flanders applied itself to the manufacture of new, cheaper, and lighter products. For such products, both the Flemish domestic population and the Baltic territories provided a large market. This comparison shows that the Low Countries had a considerably richer assortment to offer to northwestern Europe.[38] The Hanse's balance of trade with England had a slight deficit in 1479–82 (the only years for which such a reconstruction is possible), 28,500 pounds against 31,600 pounds, while the city of Lübeck had an important advantage in its relations with the eastern Baltic regions. The Low Countries as a whole had a positive balance of trade with the Hanse, tending in the sixteenth century toward a ratio of 38 : 62.[39]

A new source of raw materials was also tapped. By the middle of the fifteenth century, wool from the Castilian plateau was already in current use in most east Flemish cities and in many centers in the southwest of the county. Bruges became the central port for the import of Spanish wool and remained so until the middle of the sixteenth century.[40] Linen also provided an alternative. In the third quarter of the fifteenth century, London and Sandwich imported 107,000 ells of linen, of which 82,000 ells came from the Low Countries. Of this, 34 percent was of Flemish manufacture, 30 percent was Brabantine, 20 percent came from Hainault, and 15 percent came from Holland and Zeeland. In the following decades this export continued to grow, reaching ten times the late fifteenth-century level by 1530.[41]

These structural alterations in the European economy were caused by changes in the relative prices of different products. The most striking feature in this picture is that the great urbanized regions of the Low Countries, principally Flanders, Brabant, and, increasingly, Holland, formed the hub of a larger economic system. This system included those regions in England, Scotland, Castile, and Prussia that produced raw materials and also formed, together with southern and central Europe, the market for finished products. Developments in any given sector of this system had inevitable consequences for the whole. The rising wool prices and increasing domestic cloth production in England decreased the export of English raw wool, providing greater market opportunities for Castilian sheep raisers and exporters. More extensive contact with Spain also brought other easily transportable products onto the European market. The most noticeable of these was leather, often only partially processed. This led to the growth of an important craft guild for workers in cordovan leather, the name of which was derived from the city of Córdoba, a former center of Arabic manufacturing and culture from which originated many designs that were eagerly imitated in northern Europe. Other products were also imported from Spain: exotic fruits; grain, on some occasions; metallic ores; and increasing varieties of colonial products from the eastern and, later, the western Atlantic, notably ivory and cane sugar.

The Metropolis of Bruges

Characteristic of this entire economic system was the axial function of the large towns situated on the coasts and estuaries of the Low Countries. They bought raw materials elsewhere, turned them into high-quality products, and then distributed those products far and wide. In the fifteenth century, only northern Italy was economically stronger. In many respects the Low Countries were economically dependent on that core area, which economically dominated all of Europe and the lands bordering the Mediterranean. In western and northern Europe, however, the towns of Flanders and Brabant indisputably formed the axis around which everything revolved. In the Low Countries, the highly urbanized coastal regions were the key to the economy of western Europe. The more agricultural provinces like Hainault, Artois, Namur, and Luxemburg formed a periphery that functioned as suppliers of raw materials to — and consumed the finished products from — the centers along the coast.

From an economic point of view, the Low Countries, thus, formed a coherent system of districts that complemented each other in their mutual differences. Bruges, at this time the most international mercantile town in northwest Europe, was undoubtedly its beating heart. Hundreds of foreigners had their residence there, protected by the privileges bestowed by successive counts of Flanders and the town government. At least twelve "nations" of foreign merchants enjoyed the right of exercising their own jurisdiction in internal affairs, and of receiving the legal protection of the local authorities in disputes with parties of other jurisdictions. The largest community was the local settlement (known as the Kontor) of the German Hanse, a league of some two hundred mainly north German towns with commercial interests. From the city accounts of Bruges for the period 1363–80, it would appear that forty or fifty Hanse merchants resided in the city throughout the year, a number that doubled for the annual fair in April.[42] The northern Italians together were even more numerous, but they were organized separately according to their home cities—Venice, Genoa, Florence, Milan, and Lucca. There were also the nations of Catalans, Castilians, Portuguese, Basques, Scots, and English. Each had its own consulate in Bruges, a place where they could store their wares, hold their meetings, and reside temporarily. In addition, they held their own religious services in nearby churches, especially those of the Mendicant orders.

All the foreign merchants established their offices and domicile in a district near the hoist that was erected a few minutes' walk from the Grote Markt, the main marketplace, on the side of the canal that brought small ships from Damme to the *waterhal*, the large covered market dating from the thirteenth century (and today, long since disappeared). Every afternoon, all the traders who wanted to exchange securities would meet for that purpose in the square that housed the consulates of Genoa, Florence, and Venice. In time these meetings came to be known as *beurs*, "exchange," after the Bruges family of brokers van der Beurse (literally and appropriately "of the purse"), which had an inn on the square where many Venetian and Hanseatic merchants stayed. Their name, as *beurs*, or *Bourse*, was later used to describe places where similar functions were performed in Antwerp, Amsterdam, and elsewhere.

Bruges was not isolated, but rather the center of a complex network. Italian traders' correspondence reveals that it was not possible to do business in Bruges during the six-week-long Whitsun Fair in Antwerp; all the foreigners left Bruges in a body for the city on the lower Scheldt. But Bruges money changers and spice traders also bought and rented houses in or near the Grote Markt in Antwerp. There they controlled the trade in expensive textiles such as linen and velvet, and in fashionable clothing as well as in goods from overseas like spices, wine, oil, tropical fruits, sugar, and furs.[43] Bruges served as a depot for raw materials, exotic products, and foodstuffs destined for an extensive hinterland that included the provinces of Flanders, Zeeland, Artois, and Hainault. Through the annual fair in Antwerp, these goods found further transit to the Rhine and central Europe. In reverse, Bruges was the port through which products from these areas were exported to European markets. The German Hanse made Bruges its base for all the Low Countries, which meant that all trade had to pass through Bruges. This system was, obviously, detrimental to the northern Low Countries, which became increasingly powerful after 1438 and began to resist, with some success, the monopolistic practices of the Hanse. Thus, we can imagine Bruges at the top of a pyramid, with rapidly growing Antwerp in the second place and dependent on Bruges until about 1480. Slightly lower still were Ghent and Ypres, regional mercantile centers that depended on Bruges for their foreign contacts. Beneath them came a number of medium and small trading centers with a more limited supply of products.[44]

Bruges was the only city in the Low Countries where dozens of Italian trading houses were permanently represented. Many of these also engaged in banking. There were two reasons for the emergence of Bruges as a banking center: First, the Italians in northwest Europe always had a surplus of liquid assets because their balance of payments showed a structural surplus. Second, their companies had a solid structure based on shares, and they employed commercial and financial techniques more progressive than those in use elsewhere in Europe. In other words, they had more money and they knew how to use it. From the thirteenth century on, Italian firms had extended credit to rulers in the Low Countries and had generally profited from the business. The risks of making such loans were compensated for by the favors the rulers extended to them, such as lucrative and honorable positions in ducal service. Duke Philip the Bold had close connections with Dino Rapondi, a banker from Lucca, whose family also had agents in Paris at the court of the French king. Dino settled in Flanders and lent large sums of money to the duke and to the towns, to enable them to pay taxes. He was a guarantor for the duke in dealings with other merchants and advised him on all important financial matters. With a bill of exchange for sixty thousand francs, payable in Venice, and a large loan, Dino provided the ransom for John the Fearless when he was captured by the Turks, after the defeat at Nicopolis in 1396. Dino secured the loan by collecting the incomes of his debtors at source.⁴⁵ Giovanni Arnolfini played a similar role under Philip the Good, as did Tommaso Portinari, who, under Charles the Bold, was the head of the Bruges branch (opened in 1439) of the Medici bank. The wars waged by Charles the Bold swallowed up money, and he overreached his credit limit by three times the amount set out in his contract with the company. Lorenzo de Medici was thus obliged to close the loss-generating Bruges office in 1480.⁴⁶

There was an intensive exchange of goods, information, and payments between the various branches of the Italian business houses in the great commercial cities of the Low Countries. Busy correspondence accompanied a system of financial transfers through bills of exchange. Bruges was the most northerly base of Italian trading and banking houses on the European continent. It was also the meeting place of two commercial systems, one that could be called Mediterranean characterized by its progressive organization and techniques, and the other the smaller-scale and more primitive system that functioned throughout north and central Europe. The difference was due entirely to the volume of trade and payments. The system of resident trading companies with branches linked through correspondence and bills of exchange was only viable when there was a high frequency and large volume of trade and payments. Thus, papal revenues, collected throughout northern Europe, could be used by merchants in the regions where they were collected to buy goods that were later sold in Bruges, whence the balance was credited to Rome by bills of exchange. Through this system, ecclesiastical income — the so-called papal tithes — was thus used to finance trade as an indemnification for the transfer of monies.

In addition to the merchant-bankers of Bruges, of whom the Italians were without doubt the leaders, local money changers worked in Bruges as early as the thirteenth century. Their primary function was to exchange coins in accordance with the duke's regulations. Other banking activities quickly grew out of this: deposit and transfer. Quite a number of money changers and investors went bankrupt because they were too dependent on a limited number of large investors. Nevertheless, some managed to build up substantial fortunes, which led to productive investments in commercial and manufacturing ventures. And finally, it was possible in Bruges, as in many other towns, to take out customer credit with the Lombards, originally northern Italian money lenders, who were allowed to charge high rates of interest (as much as 43.33 percent per year). Bruges was unique in that it was then the only city in northwestern Europe where the entire range of financial services existing at the time was available. Bruges formed the center of a densely populated, prosperous region, and it also served as an outpost of Italian trade in less-developed northern Europe.

Economic Prosperity and the Standard of Living

The most conspicuous features that distinguished the Burgundian Netherlands from the rest of Europe must be sought in Flanders, Brabant, Holland, and Zeeland. The other regions in the Burgundian complex followed what might be termed the general European pattern: predominantly agrarian and, consequently, dominated by the great noble and aristocratic landowners, with only a few cities that functioned chiefly as regional centers. It has been estimated that the volume of trade in the Low Countries doubled between 1400 and 1475.[47] Vigorous growth took place in northern Brabant around the international fairs held twice a year at Antwerp and Bergen op Zoom. Moreover, the shipping industry and transportation in Holland and Zeeland must also have expanded greatly and increasingly dominated the shipping lanes between England and the Baltic and Atlantic coasts. The toll at Sluis, the main outport of Bruges, was farmed out in 1432 and 1440 for 16,800 pounds, whereas in 1384 and 1423, it had been farmed out for 15,600 pounds. In 1464 the farm declined to 13,400 pounds, a downward trend that continued through the rest of the century.[48] Flanders, dominant until the middle of the century, thus gradually lost ground to the new centers of growth in the neighboring territories.

For the most part, wages were stable during the fifteenth century. Wages in the building industry at Bruges increased by 10 percent in 1440 relative to their 1400 level. The employment situation must have been very favorable, particularly in those industries that profited from the expansion of international trade. No fewer than 668 new masters were registered in the coopers' guild at Bruges between 1375 and 1500, that is, an average of 5.3 new masters per year. Of these, no more than 21 percent were the sons of masters, indicating that this craft, associated closely with trade and transport, continued to attract new workers, the preferential entry regulations for masters' sons notwithstanding. In this context, it is significant that during the first half of the fifteenth century, the building industry of Bruges in its recruitment of laborers from outside the city drew only 20–25 percent of them from the county of Flanders. Twenty-five to 30 percent came from Brabant, while a considerable number came from Holland, Zeeland, Guelders, Utrecht, and the remaining principalities of the southern Netherlands. The employment situation in Bruges was clearly less favorable during the second half of the fifteenth century. This trend is evident in the greatly reduced level of immigration: 75 percent to 80 percent of new building workers now came from Flanders, with less than 10 percent from Brabant and scarcely any from elsewhere.[49]

The declining attraction of Bruges is also apparent in the increasingly limited opportunities for journeymen to rise to the rank of master in the textile and building guilds, a promotion that doubled their wages. The established masters reacted to the declining economic opportunities by raising higher financial barriers to the admission into their ranks of men who were not the sons of masters. In practice, this meant that toward the end of the fifteenth century, the rank of master in these guilds became virtually hereditary.

During the entire fifteenth century, wages in Bruges remained relatively high. The thirties, however, brought a series of crises. These began with trade disputes with England, resulting in a full-blown war and a blockade. Then came the revolt against the duke, the siege, the subjection and consequent imposition of an enormous fine, and a trade boycott by the German Hanseatic League. To make matters worse, from 1436 to 1438, there was a serious grain shortage throughout Europe, and an epidemic of plague swept the continent. In Bruges, grain prices rose to three times their normal levels, while in Ghent — where no major revolt occurred — the prices doubled.[50] Jan van Dixmude, the well-informed chronicler, gave the following account of the situation, all the more poignant for its conciseness: "It was said that around St. Bavo's day [October 1, 1438] a fifth of the townspeople of Bruges was diminished through death, that very many people were dead, that some died of poverty, and some abandoned the town of Bruges because of the evil sickness or because of their debts."[51]

As a result of the reconciliatory triumphal Entry into the city during Advent 1440, in which he had been associated with the coming of the Savior, in January 1441 Philip the Good issued an ordinance intended to breathe new life into trade in Bruges after its recent troubles. For a period of four years, he lowered the conditions of registration for those wanting to establish themselves as burghers of Bruges and members of a trade guild. For foreigners and Flemings alike, the fees were temporarily fixed at 300 groats, the wage that a master craftsman could earn in 26.5 days. Before and afterward, the registration fees were set at 626 groats for Flemings and 986 groats for foreigners, which was clearly discriminatory. The duke's measure was remarkably successful: from 1441 to 1445, an average of 403 new master craftsmen were registered per year, compared with 79 before the period and 158 after.[52] From 1440 to 1449, 53 percent of Bruges's new burghers came from outside the county or from farther away than fifty kilometers. This was clearly the period when Bruges exerted its greatest attraction on the labor force: in 1420–39 and 1460–69, that percentage was respectively 46.5 and 44.5, and it was significantly lower both before and afater these periods.[53] The immigrants were most interested in those trades that demanded high qualifications and for which more work could be found in Bruges than elsewhere.

In spite of these changes for the worse, all the available information indicates that around the middle of the fifteenth century, Bruges was still the wealthiest city of the Low Countries. As a rule, it paid 15.7 percent of the taxes of Flanders to the central government, whereas Ghent paid only 13.8 percent.[54] If we take into account the fact that the population of Bruges around the middle of the fourteenth century was 46,000 and that of Ghent 64,000 (these are the only figures available), then the per capita contribution made by a citizen of Bruges was 59 percent higher than that of a citizen of Ghent. The contrast may have been even sharper, since Ghent often negotiated greater reductions in its taxation, and one-seventh of the revenues from indirect taxes in the city of Bruges also flowed into the ducal treasury. The demographic figures further complicate the situation in the fifteenth century; the population may well have been smaller than that of the fourteenth century, and its numbers may possibly have declined more in Ghent than in Bruges. Still, all things considered, a citizen of Bruges paid substantially more tax than did his counterpart in Ghent, and he was thus, in all probability, wealthier.

What can be said about the evolution of the standard of living for an ordinary manual laborer? We do not have sufficient information to be able to answer this question properly. First of all, there was certainly no question of a uniform economic development throughout the Low Countries. There were many regional and local differences in demographic, economic, and political circumstances that influenced the standard of living. In the towns of Flanders and Liège, and, to a lesser extent, in those of Brabant as well, the guilds were well organized and in a position to exert pressure to protect wage levels. Elsewhere, in Namur and Luxemburg, for example, there were great differences in pay for the same work.[55] There is data on wages for a few occupations over a succession of years. These are usually wages in the construction industry, for which there is substantial information from the accounts of cities and other institutions that commissioned work. Our information for the textile sector, for example, is much less complete, because wages were often at piece rate and the private employers left no records of payments made. Thus, for this important branch of industry, we have only regulations and no factual accounts of payments and are often uncertain of the time needed to complete one piece. In addition, we must not forget that a large part of the work was not paid for in wages, but in kind. And, above all, we know next to nothing about the employment situation. The wages about which we do know something relate to daily amounts. How many days per year such amounts could actually be earned, and by how many members of an average family, can only be guessed at. Even large institutional employers, such as town councils or the dean and chapter of Utrecht, made a call upon the labor market extremely irregularly, so that they should be seen as interfering elements rather than reliable indicators. Taking all these reservations into account, we can state that the general trend was for wages to remain stable, with a slight increase around 1440.

Purchasing power fluctuated greatly from year to year, however, because of the variations in the price of grain. Given that a typical family devoted an average of 44 percent of its income to bread, a rise or fall in the price of bread determined how much money remained available for other expenses. In Bruges, during the disaster years 1437–39, a master carpenter's entire annual income would purchase a scant 17 to 18 liters of rye, while six years later, he could purchase from 59 to 72 liters. In the extremely good years 1462–63, with their very low grain prices, his purchasing power rose to more than 100 liters. These figures are the best measure of the true value of wages as contemporaries experienced them.[56]

In Flanders, still the most highly developed region in the Low Countries, purchasing power was considerably greater than in Brabant and Holland. Wages were higher, especially in the metropolis of Bruges, and the provisioning of foodstuffs was better regulated there. In Bruges, in the bumper years 1463–68, the annual income of a master mason could purchase an average of 42.75 liters of wheat, while his counterpart in Leiden could purchase only 25.50 liters, or 40 percent less. During the lean years 1480–83, both had to content themselves with less, but the impoverishment was greater in the already poorer north: 20–25 liters in Bruges versus 11.475 liters in Leiden, or 43 percent less. The difference in wages thus provides an additional explanation for the displacement of the economic center of gravity from Flanders to Brabant, Holland, and Zeeland.[57] Even after the employment situation in Bruges worsened, wages there remained high, raising the price of products and services in Bruges well above those in the surrounding regions.

On the other hand, the relatively high wages in Bruges attracted many workers from a wide hinterland. After the devastating effects of the English and Hanseatic trade boycotts, the revolt, the siege, the famine and the plague, Duke Philip ordered a substantial reduction in the inscription fees for both citizenship and membership in a craft association during the years 1441 to 1445, as a clear incentive to revitalize the city. Foreigners and Flemings would temporarily have to pay the same amount of 300 Flemish groats, while the normal fees mounted up to 986 and 626 respectively. Inscription of new craft masters in Bruges rose from an average of 79 per year to 403; from 1445 it stabilized, under the normal fees, at around 1,589 per year. Among these masters were many skilled craftsmen migrating from places as far away as one hundred kilometers, as did the famous painter Petrus Christus.[58]

Naturally, the price of other products also fluctuated, although not to the same extent as those of rye and wheat. During the years of grain shortages, people purchased fewer products that were not essential; they economized on butter, cheese, meat, clothing, heat, and other expenditures. Good or poor harvests were the primary cause of fluctuations in the price of grain. However, since the demand for this staple foodstuff remained constant, that is to say that everyone had a constant need for it and that substitutes were difficult to obtain, market factors also played a role in setting prices. When the harvest threatened to be poor, merchants bought up huge quantities of grain while it was still in the fields, at a relatively low price. They withheld their supply from the market, which led to shortages in the marketplace that drove prices up as early as September or October. As the year progressed, the situation grew more critical and prices rose further. The grain merchants speculated, to extract the maximum of profit from the situation. Because of the role played by such speculators, and also because of the protectionist measures taken by those regions normally exporting grain, prices did not rise in direct proportion to the actual decline in the harvest, but much more steeply. In order to escape the effects of such price fluctuations at the markets, well-to-do burghers, hospitals, and convents strove to safeguard their own grain supplies by making private arrangements. They purchased land and negotiated fixed prices for the delivery of annual quantities of grain, agreed upon in advance, thus putting the burden of harvest shortfalls on those who worked the land for them and assuring themselves of both a steady supply of grain and reasonably projected costs. This led to the creation of two parallel markets: one for the wealthy, characterized by regular supplies and limited price fluctuation, and another subject to enormous fluctuations and vulnerable to speculation on a local, regional, and even an international level. All those who could not afford to supply themselves with grain through private arrangements in the first market were entirely dependent on the second.[59]

During the fifteenth century, there were a number of years when the market price for grain doubled, and two periods when it even tripled: 1437–38 and 1481–83. These were years of generalized crisis in Europe, with the export of grain forbidden everywhere, even in the "Prussian granary," so that no succor could be expected from that normally helpful quarter. The effects of such huge increases in the price of staple foods were predictable: the middle class made do with a minimum, and the lower classes suffered famine. During the entire fifteenth century, journeyman artisans were in desperate straits in one year out of four, since their wages were only half those of the master craftsmen. Even in prosperous Bruges, where the standard of living was the highest in the entire Low Countries, a journeyman was unable to feed a normal family in 47 of the 126 years between 1360 and 1486 for which data is available. In such years, nearly half the urban population lived in poverty. Since the institutions of poor relief also received less grain from their demesnes and consequently had to purchase it at exorbitant prices on the market, they were equally unable to meet the needs of the poor.[60]

In the period between 1440 and 1475, grain prices were consistently low; even the 1457 shortage caused only a limited price rise. The same held true for the prices of butter and cheese. These thirty-five years were the most prosperous of the entire century. This prosperity was unquestionably related to the high death toll caused by the plague epidemic of 1437–39: there were fewer mouths to feed, and the survivors were correspondingly better off.[61] The wage increase of around 1440 could be explained as the result of the shortage of labor brought on by the ravages of plague. Greater purchasing power, peace on the borders, a reasonable tax burden, stable currency, an increase in the volume of trade — specifically between Holland and the Baltic lands, which also provided new markets for beer, herring, and textiles — all these factors combined to make possible this thirty-five-year period of prosperity in the Burgundian Low Countries. These were also the golden years of Burgundian culture: this particular generation was not only materially better off than the preceding and succeeding generations, but also better off than any generation of workers living in the southern Netherlands before 1800.[62] Thus, Philippe de Commynes's expression describing the prosperity of the Burgundian lands, "the promised lands," quoted at the beginning of this chapter, corresponded accurately to the measurable material reality of the period, even if this gentleman of standing paid no attention to the vulnerable circumstances of ordinary laborers.

The relative peace contributed to the moderate tax burden and to economic prosperity. The standard of living was on the average higher during this thirty-year period than in the half-centuries preceding and following. But in spite of these circumstances, the elegant clothing and banquets became more luxurious primarily for the elites, and structural poverty continued to exist. What Commynes had in mind was the contrast between the Burgundian Low Countries and other principalities in Europe, where the elites were more restricted and the poverty more widespread and abject. Bearing all these nuances in mind, the subjects of Philip the Good could indeed be said, at least for a time, to inhabit the promised lands.

7

War, Crisis, and a Problematic Succession

1465–1492

The Puzzle of Charles the Bold

Flemish painting of the late fourteenth and fifteenth centuries has left reliably accurate portraits of the dukes of Burgundy, many of their courtiers and servants, and many ordinary citizens. During this period it becomes possible to *see* people and life in the Low Countries in a rich, even if somewhat idealized, physical setting, and to see many of their diverse activities in far greater detail. But portraits do not readily reveal personalities. The sharp contrast between the reigns of Philip the Good and Charles the Bold cannot help but raise the question of personality differences as well as that of the differences in the circumstances that both rulers faced. Three decades that were, on the whole, peaceful and prosperous were followed by three decades of external and internal strife. In both sets of circumstances, there is considerable evidence that the characters and individual decisions of the two dukes seem to have influenced the global, sociopolitical, even the economic changes of the mid-fifteenth century more than those of many other princes of the period.

The question of personality also arises out of the very nature of the highly centralized, preindustrial state, precisely because so much of the responsibility for decision making rests squarely upon the shoulders of the ruler. Foreign policy in particular, with its far-reaching impact on domestic finance and the economy, was the exclusive prerogative of the ruler. In these terms, the rule of Philip the Good must be interpreted largely in the light of the complex factors external to his own personality: the results of the marriage policies of his grandfather, Philip the Bold, the vagaries of births and deaths in the competing dynasties, the relative strength or weakness of the

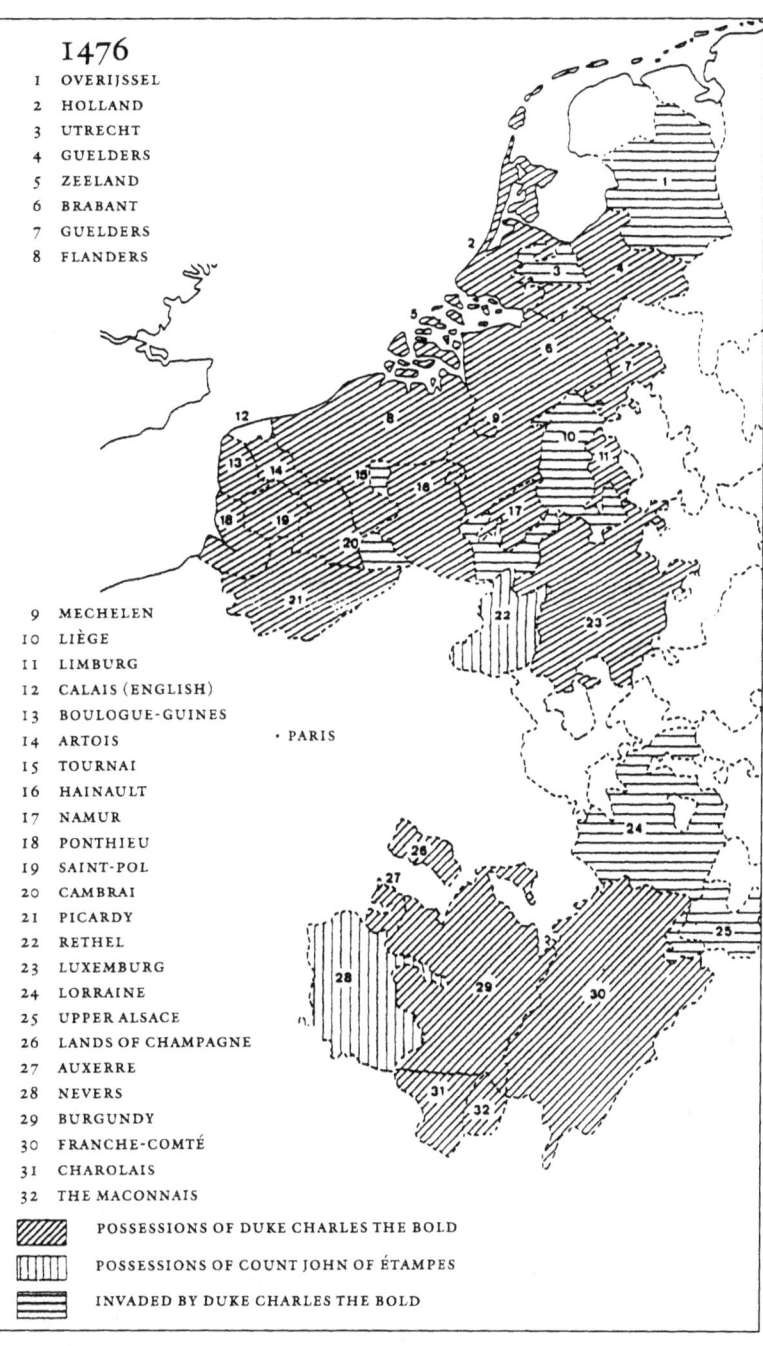

great states adjoining the Burgundian complex, and the influence of centralization on the cities and principalities he ruled. Within this framework the skill and diplomacy of the duke came fully into their own, but they did so in ways that would not have had the same effect in the absence of the general structural conditions.

The personality of Charles the Bold was distinctly different from that of his father. He certainly exhibited a stronger sense of duty, more abundant and deliberately directed energy, and greater physical courage; he was personally devout, generally moderate in his eating and drinking habits, and far less sexually adventurous. But he was also more impulsive and inflexible, was inclined to great ostentation in the self-presentation of both court and manners, often failed to consider the advice of his closest counselors, and was considerably less diplomatic.[1] All of these characteristics had dramatic and far-reaching consequences in the context of the structural elements that framed Charles's own reign, particularly the context of international relations in which he operated. The effects of Charles's personality—sharpened by his resentment at the poor relationship between his parents, Philip and Isabella of Portugal; of the court intrigues involving the Croy family; and of the Franch Dauphin Louis, later Louis XI, who was resident at the ducal court from 1457 to 1461—had led to a breach between Philip and Charles that was never entirely closed.[2] Because of his de facto exile from the court, Charles had been excluded from government from his twenty-fourth year on. Due to these circumstances, Charles prepared for his future role alone and unrelentingly opposed to the policies and personality of his father. He saw from the outside the slow collapse of Philip's rule under the despised Croy influence. Charles regarded the return of Picardy to France—even against the promise of payment—worst of all. By the time his own reign began, he seems to have thought only in terms of mutually exclusive polar opposites, a trait that prevented him from participating fully in the often delicate and compromise-filled deliberations of government.

In spite of the effects of his exclusion from the decision-making process during the last years of his father's reign, however, from the moment he assumed power in the spring of 1465, Charles the Bold developed an initially rational vision that seemed to fit well into the pattern set by his predecessors. On March 12, he published a manifesto in which he severely condemned the disloyalty of the Croy and de Lannoy courtiers, who had, by then, already fled. On April 25, the head of the ducal council, Pierre de Goux, informed the Estates General of Duke Philip's intention to adhere to the Ligue du Bien Public launched by the duke of Berry, and to appoint his son Charles as his *lieutenant général* to conduct his army. Charles had, in turn, promised to behave in the future as Philip's obedient and loyal son. The representatives were urged to recognize Charles as Philip's heir.[3] Politically, these three steps were connected and meant a radical shift from the old duke's former policy. One may interpret them as the definitive restoration of Philip's confidence in Charles. Philip now left the practical orientation of the state in his son's hands, keeping for himself only the formal appearance of rulership.

This decision is apparent not only in the frequent missions of representatives of the cities and Estates to Charles rather than to Philip, but also in the choice of a new chancellor, formally appointed on October 26, 1465, and confirmed by Charles in June 1467. The new chancellor, Pierre de Goux, had been Charles's councillor since 1453 and clearly was his man, rather than Philip's. The choice of such a figure, first as the head of the ducal council and then as the highest government official below the duke, shows the growth of Charles's grip on the government, even if as *lieutenant général* he continued to show due respect to his father.[4] On September 25, 1465, Charles sent an ambassador to Edward IV of England to ask for the hand of Margaret of York, the king's sister.[5] This step represented a considerable reversal in the traditionally French-oriented matrimonial policies of the dukes of Burgundy. The marriage took place in 1468, together with a trading agreement between England and the Burgundian lands.

Like his predecessors, Charles strove to round off his territory by the annexation of regions bordering on the two blocks of land already his. Specifically, he attempted to acquire a territorial link between the "lands over here" and the "lands over there" by gaining control over Alsace and Lorraine. Also like his predecessors, he strove to construct a centralized and administratively homogeneous state. But in both instances, Charles lacked the necessary flexibility and patience in the face of resistance, on the part of the existing centers of power and wealth in the cities and principalities, to the increasingly large demands that he made upon them. During the 1470s, he increasingly closed himself off to all opinions that appeared to challenge his own ideas. These ideas, although often reasonable in themselves, became obsessions from which he refused to depart, even under the relentless pressure of circumstances. A ruler taking such a position becomes a danger to the land he governs.

The essential difference in international relations between the government of Philip the Good and that of his son may be seen in the end of the Hundred Years War and the reemergence of a strong French monarchy bent upon the rapid reconquest of the territory it had lost to Burgundy. Here too, the problem of personality arises: Louis XI was a skillful and patient tactician who knew both the value of persistence and his own limitations. He had observed the Burgundian court from the inside for many years, and, after his accession, he used his knowledge repeatedly to undermine his great rival. Even a more restrained personality than that of Charles the Bold would still have been faced by an aggressive France after 1461, but the situation as it was when Charles took power in 1465 — initially as stadtholder-general but practically speaking with total authority — made a conflict between the two states virtually inevitable and led Charles's personality to determine both the modalities and, ultimately, the disastrous outcome of the conflict.

Other conditions were also very different for Charles the Bold than they had been for his predecessors. At his accession, considerable resentment was already evident among his subjects because of the increasing weight of the bureaucratic Burgundian state. This resentment is apparent in the riots that broke out in several cities during his Joyous Entry in 1467. By rapidly increasing the pace of bureaucratization, Charles created an unbearable degree of strain between his subjects and his government that was barely controlled during his reign and exploded following his death in 1477.

The root of the difficulties of the period 1465–92 lay in the increased tension in both foreign and domestic affairs and in Charles's inability — or indifference — to relax it. The decisive factor was warfare and its costs: this forced a substantial and continual increase in taxation that brought all other conflicts to a head. And the Burgundian state, once committed to war, discovered that it was not possible simply to withdraw. Precisely because the Burgundian lands formed an extensive and discontinuous territory, they had many neighbors who felt potentially threatened by the Burgundian capacity for aggression.

The Return of War: Picardy, Liège, Guelders, Cologne-Neuss

Not surprisingly, Charles's first conflicts took place with Louix XI of France. As early as 1464, Louis's own successful attempts to increase the authority and powers of the French crown at the expense of the higher nobility had incited six of the great French princes into forming a league against the king. The houses of Anjou, Armagnac, Berry, Bourbon, Brittany, and Burgundy, under the leadership of Louis's younger brother Charles, duke of Berry, formed the League of the Public Good (Ligue du Bien Public) and prepared for war. Charles the Bold had ample reason to take advantage of the opportunity offered by the revolt against Louis XI, since in 1463, Louis had taken advantage of a clause in the Treaty of Arras of 1435 and redeemed the Picard territories along the Somme that had been ceded as a pledge to Philip the Good. The old duke had to remain content with a yearly rent of 36,000 francs in exchange for the Somme towns — a rent that remained unpaid.

Louis also affronted Charles the Bold by appointing John of Burgundy, count of Étampes, Nevers, and Rethel and son of the youngest brother of Duke John the Fearless, as his captain over Picardy. John of Burgundy had served Philip the Good faithfully, although he made claims to succeed to the duchy of Brabant following the quarrel between Philip the Good and the young Charles the Bold in 1457. When Charles expelled John of Burgundy from the Burgundian court, along with the hated Croy family, in 1465, John defected to the French king.

The reconquest of strategically and economically vital Picardy — as well as defeating John of Burgundy — was the primary motive for Charles's participation in the battle fought in July 1465 at Montlhéry by the League of the Public Good. During the battle, Charles made a greater show of audacity than of tactical insight, earning himself the sobriquet *le Téméraire*, or *le Hardi* ("the Bold," *de Stoute*). The league won the battle, and Louis XI barely escaped with his life. For Charles the Bold, victory meant the Burgundian reconquest of Picardy and the elimination of John of Burgundy-Etampes. For Louis XI, the defeat taught the king that he had to isolate and destroy his enemies individually, and that diplomacy, rather than war, was his most prudent course of action. Following these principles, and astutely learning from his own mistakes, Louis XI continued to be an active threat to Charles the Bold on many fronts for the rest of Charles's life. Wherever he saw the opportunity, Louis encouraged and supported resistance to Burgundian power: in Liège, in Lorraine, in the Swiss cities, in Guelders, and, later, even in Luxemburg and Flanders.

The difficulties in Liège presented Charles the Bold with his next serious diplomatic and military challenge. Here too, his primary concern was to maintain the status quo created by his father. The prince-bishop of Liège, Louis of Bourbon, had been elevated to that position as an eighteen-year-old with the support of Philip the Good in 1456 (see Chapter 4). But his imperious style of rule succeeded almost immediately in incurring the wrath of his subjects.[6] The burghers of Liège sought and received support from Louis XI, leading Charles the Bold to intervene. In November 1465, Charles arrived in the prince-bishopric with his army, intending to restore Louis of Bourbon to his spiritual authority, while reserving to himself all secular authority in the territory. Persistent strife between the town of Dinant in the region of Liège and the town of Bouvignes on the opposite bank of the Maas in the county of Namur led the duke to renew the siege of Dinant in August 1466. He deployed the most modern of artillery and reduced the city walls to rubble within a week. In an act of revenge for the insults that the townspeople of Dinant had hurled at Charles and his mother, the Burgundian troops were allowed to plunder and burn what was left of the town. Charles considered these insults an act of treason, although to the craftsmen who were fighting for their liberties they had been no more than an expression of their distaste for a foreign and unpopular regime. The destruction dealt a severe blow to the flourishing copper industry of Dinant, and many of its craftsmen emigrated to Mechelen, where they continued their trade.

Resistance to Burgundian and episcopal authority persisted in the city of Liège. With a population of some twenty thousand inhabitants and a centuries-long tradition of social and constitutional turmoil, Liège was once more inflamed by the ineptitude of its prince-bishop, the interventions of Louis XI, and the violent actions of the duke of Burgundy. The prince-bishopric's lack of geographical cohesion and its elongated topography, spread as it was among the Burgundian principalities of Brabant, Hainault, Namur, Luxemburg, and Limburg, made it a difficult territory to defend. Logically, the Burgundian dukes wished to strengthen their grip on it, and it is equally understandable that the independence-minded inhabitants of the Maas valley felt threatened and resisted. Instead of delivering the required hostages to Charles the Bold and paying tribute to him, the craftsmen of Liège executed the mayor of Dinant and other leaders whom they held responsible for the humiliating peace with the Burgundian duke. Their troops raided Limburg and took Huy, where the bishop had ensconced himself with a Burgundian garrison.

By this time, Charles the Bold had begun the mobilization of an army of ten thousand, and he marched on Liège in October 1467. After his troops had plundered a number of towns and villages in the prince-bishopric, the capital surrendered. The duke imposed the usual humiliations: 340 prominent persons were to kneel before him in their underclothing; the city's privileges were rescinded; the craft guilds and the Liège institutions, which had ensured popular participation in government and urban autonomy, were suspended. The symbol of the city, a bronze column called the *perron* in the great marketplace, was carried off to Bruges. The aldermen were thenceforth to be appointed by the bishop, and written rather than customary laws were to be applied. The city lost its gates, fortifications, and weapons, and it was forced to pay a substantial fine. Charles the Bold was once again recognized as the hereditary regent of the Land of Liège and left behind as his stadtholder-general his trusted associate Guy de Brimeu, lord of Humbercourt. This was the most extreme form of subjugation imaginable for the prince-bishopric. Louis of Bourbon had entirely lost all secular authority.

Liège remained restive for months. In September 1468, returning exiles once again seized power, took the town of Tongres, and brought the bishop under their control. When these events took place, Charles the Bold was in Péronne, involved in delicate negotiations with Louis XI. In order to prevent a new war over Picardy, Louis XI had made some concessions concerning the jurisdiction of the Parlement of Paris as a court of appeals for Flanders and Artois and agreed to some conditions for a general truce. He had also stipulated that if he, the king, should violate this treaty, the duke would thereby be released from any form of feudal obligation toward him. Like his father, Charles thus sought recognition of a de facto sovereignty. But when the news of the new revolt in Liège reached the two rulers, the furious Charles forced the king, whom he regarded as the instigator of the revolt, to accompany the Burgundian army while it dealt definitively with the rebels. After the failure of a night raid by the Liègeois on the Burgundian encampment, endangering the lives of both the king and the duke, Charles's thirst for vengeance was unquenchable. On October 30, 1468, Liège was taken by force. The army proceeded, with the duke's consent, to plunder quarter after quarter of the city and afterward to destroy the city systematically.

The tragic events in Liège were symptomatic of Charles's reactions — impulsive, autocratic, and ruthless. One of Charles's counselors strongly urged less drastic measures in dealing with the defeated city, reminding the duke that fortunes could change and that the duke himself might see the day when "all of your past glory, that of you and your house, may be reversed and return to a dream." But Charles brusquely silenced his adviser and proceeded to level the city. After 1468 all resistance in Liège appeared crushed, but the manner in which the prince-bishopric was subdued explains why, immediately after the death of Charles in 1477, it freed itself and preserved its independence until the end of the eighteenth century.

The original goals of the wars in Picardy and Liège were, respectively, to keep and reconquer Burgundian territory. After 1470, Burgundy was in a virtually continuous state of war with France. At issue was the control of territory along the Somme. French tactics consisted of raids that rendered the region unsafe and disrupted the economy. Louis XI also attempted to inflict damage upon his opponents by a trade embargo; he forbade trade with the Burgundian territories and encouraged privateering against ships of the enemy or ships with destinations in enemy territory. Although none of these actions inflicted serious damage, they did hinder economic activity, particularly in the trade-oriented Low Countries, and forced the duke to continue his military efforts in the border areas. The Dutch shippers, therefore, had to turn decisively to the eastern Baltic for their necessary imports of rye.[7]

Besides retaining and reconquering land, however, Duke Charles also intended to pursue a policy of territorial expansion, first by purchase and later by military means. By simply paying off Sigismund of Habsburg, duke of Tirol, Charles acquired a pledge-right in Upper Alsace, including the county of Ferrette, on the left bank of the upper Rhine between Strasbourg and Basel. Ferrette lay just to the east of the Franche-Comté (the imperial county of Burgundy), and this region thus brought Charles's power perilously close to the Swiss cantons, a group of self-governing districts composed of rural areas and small cities furiously resistant to any form of lordship. They had thrown off Habsburg control after the battle of Sempach in 1386, and they remained an independent confederation.

Charles's title to Ferrette, however, did not bring in the income he had expected. The Chamber of Accounts at Dijon pointed out that he did not have rights over a continuous territory that could be annexed, but that he had merely a collection of lordships and rights. At the most, Upper Alsace gave him a base between Burgundy and Luxemburg from which further links might be forged in the future. Even more important may have been the strengthening of Charles's positions along the west banks of the Rhine, where he had earlier secured his influence in the territories of Jülich-Berg, Cleves, Guelders, Liège, and Luxemburg. But any prospect of expanding the authority of the duke of Burgundy in the areas of Upper Alsace and Lorraine was sure to arouse the suspicions of the Swiss Confederation, because it was extremely apprehensive of the sudden appearance of a powerful and autocratic prince on the borders of the upper Rhine.

Charles's ambitions for the annexation of Guelders were more far-reaching, but also continued those of his father (see Chapter 4). Philip the Good's support of Adolph of Egmond against Adolph's father, Arnold, duke of Guelders, enabled Adolph to force his father to abdicate in January 1463, after having roused the old duke from his bed in the middle of the night at

Grave and abducting him, barely clothed, to the secure castle of Lobith. Although Arnold remained in captivity for eight years, his relatives, led by John, duke of neighboring Cleves, now rallied to support his claims, thus keeping alive the factional strife in the duchy. Because both Adolph and his rival, John of Cleves, were knights of the Golden Fleece, Charles the Bold, sovereign of the order, was able to appoint himself as arbitrator between them. Using some of his own troops, he secured the release of Duke Arnold in 1471. With a cynical display of force, Charles also kept his former protégé Adolph under house arrest in his castle at Hesdin. When Adolph attempted to escape, Charles had him actually imprisoned. But Arnold never succeeded in reestablishing his authority over all of Guelders, nor over the cities of Nijmegen, Arnhem, and Zutphen. By the end of 1471, Arnold found no better solution than to offer Charles the Bold a regency over Guelders, a proposal that was rejected by the cities and by some of the nobility. Succumbing more and more to ducal pressure, Arnold first pledged his possessions to Charles, and, just before his death, in February 1473, named Charles as his heir. Charles continued to hold Adolph prisoner, and he bought off the claims of another pretender, the duke of Jülich-Berg. He finally subjugated the duchy in June 1473, with a successful show of military might that reduced all resistance. Only the three-week siege of Nijmegen caused any extensive damage.

In Guelders the new ruler imposed heavy taxes and introduced a central administration, as his father and he had elsewhere. He appointed new aldermen in all districts and introduced new regulations for the ducal judicial officers, expecting to acquire firmer control over the recalcitrant cities. To Guy de Brimeu, the trusted stadtholder-general of Liège, for example, Charles entrusted two districts, with the clear intention of furthering the integration of this new territory into the structure of the Burgundian state.[8]

The annexation of the duchy of Guelders strengthened the duke's already prominent position in the German Empire. It also enhanced his status as a neighbor of Cologne. The archbishop of Cologne, a prince-prelate himself, had also intervened in the struggle in Guelders. By 1473, he was also involved in a violent conflict with the cities of his own territory. An analogy to neighboring Liège was obvious. The archbishop sought support from Charles the Bold, still very much the victorious hero, against his rebellious cities. Charles accepted the role of secular guardian, as he had in Liège, and he lent his support to the archbishop in the hope of further consolidating his own position within the empire. In July 1474, planning first to conquer some smaller cities and then to subjugate Cologne itself,

Charles besieged the town of Neuss, down the Rhine from Cologne. Despite the excellent equipment of the Burgundian army, its great numerical strength, and good supply lines, the siege was not successful. The city defended itself courageously and held out. The German emperor Frederick III saw it as his duty to expel the Burgundian invaders, but not until May 1475 did he succeed in leading an army to Neuss. The imperial army consisted primarily of contingents provided by a wide spectrum of imperial cities, in a show of solidarity for the defense of German territories. After long negotiations and a few skirmishes, both armies, concerned for their honor, reluctantly withdrew.

Charles the Bold had committed himself militarily and politically to this siege to such an extent that his lack of success greatly damaged his prestige. It is surprising that he pursued this small goal so obsessively that he deployed his forces before Neuss for a whole year. One possible explanation is that by 1473, Charles must have been certain that his third wife, Margaret of York, would not provide him with heirs other than his only daughter, Mary of Burgundy. It is remarkable that he spent only twenty days with Margaret of York during the last three years of his life, whereas in the early years of their marriage, they had spent considerably more time together.[9] It remained for Charles to seek out the best possible terms for the future of his hereditary domains through his daughter's hand. He had a royal crown in mind for himself, with the expectation that his son-in-law and grandchildren would wear it after him. In order to exert maximum pressure on the emperor, the only one who could grant him a royal title, it was essential that Charles control as much territory as possible on the western fringes of the empire. After Liège and Guelders there was Alsace, and then, possibly, the vast lands of the archbishopric of Cologne, and eventually Lorraine. Charles's negotiations with the emperor at Trier in November 1473, were unsuccessful. But would they be more fruitful next time, if Charles were to rule over the entire Rhineland?

In April 1474, a revolt broke out in Upper Alsace, pledged to Charles, against his hated *Landvogt* (bailiff), Pierre de Hagenbach, a local nobleman. With the support of the Swiss Confederation, Sigismund of Habsburg, a nephew of the emperor, was called back. After his defeat, it became even more delicate for Charles to withdraw from his protracted siege of Neuss. His honor and his credibility as a candidate for the title of king, perhaps even that of king of the Romans, were at stake.[10]

Louis XI made good use of Charles's prolonged absence at Neuss. From the date on which their truce expired, the first of May 1473, Louis's ships commenced operations off the coast of Zeeland, and he sent two of his armies to attack Charles's territories, one assailing Picardy, Artois, and Hainault, and the other Burgundy. The campaign proved to be a dress rehearsal for the French invasion of 1477. In Picardy and Artois, the French conquered a number of cities. Charles the Bold, who had planned with the English king Edward IV to join forces against Louis, revive the Hundred Years' War, crown Edward king of France at Reims, and split the spoils, missed his rendezvous with Edward because of the entanglement before Neuss. When Charles finally arrived, Edward had already retreated.

Thus Charles's mistaken estimate of his chances against Neuss cost him not only considerable military effort and enormous expense, but also the loss of other hard-won territories, and it dealt a substantial blow to his reputation. Ironically, the stalemate at Neuss occurred at a moment when the administrative apparatus of the Burgundian state had reached its most complete state of development, but had also begun to show serious signs of strain.

The Breakthrough of State Authority

By the same logic with which Charles the Bold pursued the general foreign-policy goals of his father, he also consistently implemented his father's policy of domestic centralization. In both these areas, however, he lacked the necessary tact and flexibility in his relations with his subjects, who gradually came to harbor a growing resentment against his ruthlessly authoritarian actions. Speeches addressed by Charles to the representatives of the Four Members and to the Estates of Flanders abound with the duke's denunciations of his audience as stiff-necked burghers "who devoured his good cities."[11] He considered himself ruler by the grace of God, and he owed his power to God alone: "I do not doubt that I shall remain ruler as long as He wills, in spite of all those who regret it, because God has given me the power and the means, which I would not advise you to test. . . . I would rather prefer that you hate me than despise me, because neither for your privileges — which are in any case worthless — nor for any other reason will I allow myself to be thwarted, nor will I allow anything to detract from my majesty or sovereignty; and I am strong enough to prevent such a thing."[12]

In 1475, after the abortive siege of Neuss, when he requested new taxes to recover Alsace and subjugate Lorraine, the Estates of Flanders at first refused to grant him supplementary funds. To this refusal, the duke responded in fury: "To prove that I have the power to govern as ruler, which power was granted to me by God and not by my subjects, it suffices to read the Book of Kings in the Bible, where God shows in clear language the power of rulers over their subjects. Since I have not been obeyed when I have asked and requested, henceforth I shall command, for I have pleaded long enough. I shall punish the disobedient in a manner which others have already experienced and which I would not recommend."[13]

This is clear language, displaying a paternalistic vision of the ruler's position: the duke's subjects ought to conduct themselves obediently, for if they did, they would find in him a "good shepherd." He left his subjects no room for rights of their own, or even for a significant voice in their own affairs. These ideas, of course, echo a great deal of medieval political theory, from Charlemagne to Frederick Barbarossa, and they were taken up in later European history during the age of absolute monarchy. But they were usually applied to kings and to the emperor. Here again, one sees the self-awareness of sovereign authority and status reflected in the dukes of Burgundy. In his ambition to reign as a true sovereign, recognizing no authority above his, Charles wanted to exclude all foreign jurisdictions within his territories and to organize strongly centralized and homogenized governmental institutions in the whole of his composite "state."

The extension of a centralized administration, the foundations of which had already been laid by his predecessors, fits perfectly into this logic. The basis of centralized administration had to be fiscal. After the failure of Philip the Good's 1447 plan for the creation of a generalized tax on salt, his government limited itself to the traditional negotiations of subsidies with the Estates or cities of the individual territories. The only change was that the period for which these subsidies were granted grew gradually longer, bringing a certain regularity and consistency to the extraordinary revenues.

In 1471 the government addressed for the first time a request for a subsidy to the Estates General, that is, to the assembled Estates of all the territories of the Low Countries. This procedure was regularly repeated in the following decades, but it never entirely replaced the territorial subsidies. The goal was clearly to make the financial situation more manageable, and it coincided with the unsuccessful attempt by the government to standardize the method of taxation throughout the territories. To this end, a census had been taken since 1469 of the number of households, termed "hearths." In each village the number of taxable households was recorded, as well as the number of those that could not be taxed because of poverty or a privileged — ecclesiastical or noble — status. This equitable distribution of the burden would arouse less resistance and thus necessitate fewer negotiations for special reductions. It would increase the revenues available to the government and limit the power of local authorities.[14]

In Holland, there were traditional distribution tables establishing the contributions of each town and village, originally in the form of military service owed to the count, but later converted into monetary payments. In Luxemburg, Hainault, and Brabant, the census of hearths had been taken since the fourteenth century, although it had originally been intended to facilitate the collection of a feudal levy. In Flanders, an attempt was made in 1469 to conduct a census of hearths. This was only partially successful, since the administrations of the great cities were able to retain a powerful tool for themselves by reserving the right to determine the distribution of the tax burden. On later occasions, the government again attempted to impose a uniform system of taxation on all the territories, an example of which was the 1492 tax of one florin per hearth, or a variety of indirect taxes during the sixteenth century. Each time, however, the administrations of the great cities vigorously contested such systems, clearly understanding that their authority to decide on the allocation and distribution of taxes was their most effective lever to retain power.

The immediate pretext for Duke Charles's request for a general subsidy from all the principalities of the Low Countries was the institution of a standing army. Until the late fifteenth century, most European rulers had contented themselves with the mobilization of their vassals and mustering other troops as the occasion arose. The French king had already decided to establish a permanent standing army, however, and this action urged his rival, the duke of Burgundy, to adopt a similar system. In several senses, the project was not initially difficult for Charles the Bold, since he had a flair for military organization and was continually engaged in elaborating increasingly detailed military plans. In July 1471, he issued an ordinance that established a mercenary force of 11,250 men. The army was to be divided into companies of ten lances, each consisting of nine men. The nine, under the command of a heavily armed and mounted knight, consisted of a mounted page, and a *coustillier*: a mounted swordsman, three mounted archers, and three foot soldiers — a crossbowman, a culverineer (a musketeer armed with a primitive handgun), and a pikeman, armed with an iron-tipped, heavy pole. In later proclamations, the duke defined the remaining command structure and regulations that prescribed drills and training exercises; forbade dicing, swearing, and blasphemy; and limited the number of women accompanying the troops to thirty per company of nine hundred men. Despite all these strategic plans, the organization of the standing army did not prove particularly successful. Thereafter, Charles the Bold's great battles generally ended in catastrophic defeats. His rational approach proved inappropriate for fifteenth-century warfare.

The duke attempted to implement a rational centralistic structure of state in other areas as well. Again, his powerful personal influence was apparent. In October and November 1473, he conducted negotiations at Trier with the emperor Frederick III concerning the status of his imperial fiefs. This discussion was a continuation of Philip the Good's negotiations in which the question of the elevation of one or another of the principalities of the Low Countries or of a conglomeration of them to the status of kingdom was the chief item on the agenda. As on earlier occasions, the emperor remained extremely uncertain. Charles was without doubt the most important imperial prince and could thus cherish not only ambitions for a royal crown, but even of being elected king of the Romans, making himself the successor to the emperor. And he certainly represented the greatest financial and military power within the empire.

During the negotiations Charles flaunted Burgundian glory and splendor, but this had the effect of increasing the emperor's uncertainty, rather than convincing him. Of the many possibilities discussed, the emperor and the duke reached agreement concerning only one: the betrothal of the emperor's son Maximilian of Austria to Charles's heiress, Mary of Burgundy. Frederick had already proposed this idea to Philip the Good in 1463, at the time adding the title of king as an inducement to the duke. Ten years later Charles was unable to win a royal concession, and the agreement exclusively benefited the Habsburg emperor, who assured his son a rich Burgundian inheritance while at the same time ensuring the eventual return to direct imperial control of all those territories that had been forged into an autonomous complex in the last half-century. After concluding the agreement, the emperor departed from Trier leaving Charles the Bold noble—not royal—and empty-handed.

But even prospective kingdoms required planning, and Charles, who enjoyed planning, had been devising great plans for his future kingdom. He commissioned his goldsmith, Gérard Loyet, to reshape his crown and to forge a royal scepter.[15] In the tradition of the dukes of Brabant, he claimed the title of duke of Lower Lotharingia (Lorraine), taken from the ninth-century Carolingian idea of a great central European empire. But by the fifteenth century, Lorraine was a petty duchy of limited territory governed by its own ruler, Duke René of Lorraine. Lorraine was also strategically located contiguously to the northwest and west of the county of Ferrette and Upper Alsace, to the southwest of Lower Alsace, and to the south of the county of Bar and the enclave-bishoprics of Metz, Toul, and Verdun, themselves just to the south of Luxemburg. Petty though it may have been, the duchy of Lorraine was a key piece in Charles the Bold's plans for eastward expansion.

Charles first succeeded in wringing from René of Lorraine the right to station garrisons in his cities. The next step was the complete conquest of the duchy, which he could not begin until May–November 1475, because of the long siege of Neuss. At last Charles had built a bridge, binding the "lands over here" and the "lands over there" as a single contiguous territory. Charles's plans included developing the city of Nancy into the capital of a reborn kingdom of Lotharingia, even if the kingdom had to be called Frisia or Burgundy out of consideration for the emperor. Immediately after the failed conference with Frederick III in 1473, Charles proceeded to implement the institutional reforms he had devised for a sovereign state. In December 1473, he made a series of proclamations at Thionville that shed an interesting light on his visions of statecraft. These centralistic reforms explain, in part, the violent reaction in 1477.

Charles the Bold sought complete sovereignty over all of his principalities, regardless of their individual conditions of dependency on other rulers, however nominal. He certainly intended to prevent the possibility of some other monarch claiming authority over them. The Peace Treaty of St. Truiden (December 22, 1465), which was formally still imposed upon the inhabitants of Liège, reveals Charles's complete fascination with a rational legal system. The treaty provided that no Liège court of law could exercise jurisdiction over the duke's subjects in Brabant, Limburg, Luxemburg, Hainault, Laroche, or Chiny.[16] Charles later took further steps to create a tighter hierarchy in the administration of justice within his territories, to the exclusion of external meddling. For the duchy of Burgundy, for Flanders, and for Artois, he was still a vassal of the king of France.

Louis XI did nothing to prevent the exercise of higher jurisdiction in these territories by the Parlement of Paris, the French royal court of justice that had long been a thorn in the side of the Burgundian dukes. In the Treaty of Péronne of 1468, Charles forced Louis XI to suspend the actions of his high court. In his dual struggle to establish complete independence from foreign powers and to centralize judicial power over all his territories, Charles transformed the Great Council, which had functioned since the beginning of the 1440s as a traveling court of higher justice (see Chapter 4), into a Burgundian Parlement with a fixed seat at Mechelen. The use of the term *Parlement* clearly referred to the institution of the king of France and was intended to express the complete equality of the Burgundian state and the kingdom of France. The Parlement of Mechelen was to become the highest and only court of appeal for the Low Countries, excluding them once and for all from the appellate jurisdiction of either the French crown or the imperial German high courts.[17]

To Charles's own subjects, the establishment of the Parlement of Mechelen meant the imposition of a more direct judicial control than they had previously known. In some territories, higher appeal outside the principality itself was not officially possible. In the Golden Bull of 1349, the emperor Charles IV had granted the privilege that a Brabanter could not be issued a summons to appear outside his own duchy. The court of Hainault considered itself equally sovereign. This rule, which became general in parts of northwestern Europe in the following centuries, was known as the *ius de non evocando* — the right not to be summoned outside. For both territories, the Mechelen Parlement meant the violation of their customs and privileges and the loss of territorial independence. But even the Flemings, for whom Mechelen was closer than Paris, protested: for decades they had attempted, with the active support of the dukes, to extricate themselves from the jurisdiction of Paris, but now they were subjected to an even more aggressive high court. This court also received, in addition to its function as a court of appeal, the authority to handle cases as a court of first instance that the local and territorial courts had long considered part of their jurisdiction.

The sentences passed by the ducal Great Council and its successor, the Parlement of Mechelen, in the years from 1470 to 1476 numbered an average of more than sixty-seven per year. During the years following the abolition of the Parlement in 1477 until 1494, this figure fell to two or three sentences per year, clearly showing the deep cleavage between the centralization of jurisdiction under Charles and the breakdown after his death. Even Brabant did not succeed in keeping up its century-old constitution forbidding any jurisdiction over Brabanters outside the duchy or by foreign judges. Under Charles the Bold, ten sentences per year were passed in cases of appeal from Brabant. After 1477, such sentences fell back to only two cases per year. As clear evidence of Charles's grip on jurisdiction, it should be noted that during his reign, and starting in the court of Holland as early as 1464, an increasing number of cases were dealt with by the prosecutor general as *lèse-majesté*, a concept derived from the Roman law of treason that allowed much heavier sanctions against those convicted than any used previously.[18]

Along with the Parlement, Charles also established at Mechelen two central Chambers of Account, one for the ordinary (demesnial) revenues and one for extraordinary (tax) revenues. These replaced the Chambers of Account at Lille and Brussels (at the Hague, it had already been dissolved, in 1463), in order to promote a more efficient and uniform financial administration.

Mechelen now became, in effect, the capital of the Low Countries and was to remain so until 1530. It was not only the central location of Mechelen that led to Charles's choice, but also the fact that although this small seigneury was situated inside Brabant, it was juridically and institutionally entirely autonomous. The duke was thus able to avoid choosing a site in any one of the greater principalities, any of which would have been unacceptable to the others. This sensitivity was particularly important in judicial matters, since his subjects were loath to leave their own principality—especially for legal affairs, which remained one of the strongest signs of local identity. The duke attempted to break this form of particularism by imposing the jurisdiction of the Parlement of Mechelen over his territories, even if Brabant and Hainault were still able to maintain most of their judicial independence.

Wherever possible, Charles also strengthened his grip on the local aldermanic councils. After the revolts of Mechelen and Ghent in 1467 and of Liège in 1468, he reserved the appointment of aldermen in these cities entirely to himself. In practice, this led to a reduction in the number of representatives of the craft guilds and to a larger number of ducal puppets in the councils. In Holland, he was equally indifferent to urban privileges, ending the direct election of aldermen and instead appointing those able to pay the most for the privilege. In this manner, many Hooks forced their way into the city administrations, leading to a flare-up of the old party rivalries.[19] In some cases Charles even named protégés from other cities, or even from "foreign" principalities like Hainault, to the office of mayor or aldermen of, for example, the Franc of Bruges, even though, technically, they had no rights of citizenship.

Favoritism, but more often pure greed, influenced the duke to appoint his partisans to all sorts of urban and ecclesiastical offices over which he had no formal authority. Through such clients, he expected to obtain a firmer hold over the local administrations. But even within his own corps of officials, those who were prepared to pay cash for an appointment were increasingly given priority. The office of judicial officer was sold or farmed out because the government then received from the candidates a substantial sum of money at once. The consequences for the central government were catastrophic. The highest-bidding bailiffs, toll collectors, receivers for rents, and foresters were far less interested in fair judgment or the proper administration of a domain or office than they were in recovering the investment they had made in their office as rapidly as possible, usually by imposing many kinds of extra fees upon the duke's subjects who required their services. There were three general kinds of effects of this traffic in offices. First, officials were increasingly recruited from the wealthy bourgeoisie, since wealth played a greater role than competence in their selection. Second, the duke's subjects were abandoned more and more to the arbitrary actions of officials inclined to abuse their power. The higher authorities could do little to prevent such abuses, since those concerned had paid for their offices and could only be removed by returning to them the money they had invested. Third, the government was a long-term financial loser, not only because the burden borne by the subjects grew heavier, increasing their willingness to revolt, but also because it also enjoyed less and less real income. Moreover, the government was also weakened by the venality of offices, because its role of guaranteeing fair judicial process was no longer adequately fulfilled. Public offices were thus transformed into private hunting grounds, eroding the function and credibility of the state from within.[20]

There are two explanations for this widespread privatization of public office. On the one hand, the state, as noted above, was in constant need of money as a result of its policy of virtually continuous wars. Therefore, more and more stopgap measures were taken to acquire revenues in the short term, even though this method would lead to yet greater losses in the long run. On the other hand, fifteenth-century society had as yet no deeply rooted concept of the abstract state, with officials who were presumed to serve the public interest in accordance with a fixed and generally understood and accepted code of ethics. In the late Middle Ages, people gradually outgrew a framework of thought in which personal loyalties served as the chief basis of authority. Gradually, solidarity grew among groups of greater size, with personal relations playing a weaker role within these structures. Partisan conflict, for example, particularly in Holland and Zeeland, still dominated most cities, and conflict continued between the bourgeoisie and the guilds and between the guilds and the cities. Only a very limited notion of the common good and the rules and behavior required to preserve it existed in the popular consciousness, and private interests or those of a very limited group could continue as the dominant mindset.

The representative institutions protested regularly against these practices, and the duke's reaction to these protests has been described above. And necessity broke law. As his military operations took a less favorable turn beginning in 1474, the duke's financial needs grew, and he exerted increasing pressure for more taxes. From 1466 to 1471, taxes amounted to an annual average of 78,500 pounds (of 40 groats per pound) in Flanders. This was little more than the revenues from taxes during the last ten years of the reign of Philip the Good. From 1472 to 1476, however, the rate of taxation virtually tripled, increasing to an annual average in Flanders of 223,500 pounds. In 1475, the year in which Charles made the furious speech previously quoted, taxation in Flanders reached the highest level of the century — 443,000 pounds, nearly six times the normal amount. The figures for Holland indicate a tripling of the tax burden starting in 1471. Leiden paid an annual average of 4,170 pounds from 1463 to 1470, but it paid 14,025 pounds between 1471 and 1477. In 1475, Charles the Bold issued a general call to arms, imposed virtually uninterrupted military service upon the holders of all property that owed feudal military dues, and demanded that ecclesiastical institutions pay taxes on goods acquired during the previous forty years. All these demands encountered so much resistance that their net yield was certainly not sufficient to outweigh the discontent sown among the vast majority of the populace. It is understandable that in 1476, despite the heavy pressure brought to bear by the chancellor, the Estates General refused to grant the new requests for subsidies to support the reconquest of Lorraine. All the tax money raised in the preceeding years had been squandered in wars that, with the exception of the conquest of Guelders, had shown no positive results whatsoever.[21] Charles the Bold had centralized the Burgundian state as far as he possibly could, but he had done so at the expense of the loyalty among the various classes in the cities and principalities that constituted its base, and he had virtually exhausted the greatest financial reserves of any state in Europe at a terrible price in social discontent.

From a Dream to a Death

After the failed siege of Neuss, his losses along the Somme, and the loss of Ferrette, Charles the Bold turned to Lorraine, which he completely conquered in November 1475. He remained obsessed with the idea of territorial cohesion between the "lands over here" and the "lands over there" with a new capital in Nancy, but his obsession included far more "lands over there" than had any of his predecessors. The campaign in Lorraine again challenged the Swiss, who had already conquered Ferrette in 1474, and, in his attempts to reconquer Upper Alsace, Charles encountered determined resistance from the infantry of the Swiss Eidgenossen. The resolution shown by Charles's armies of professional soldiers and mercenaries proved to be no match for the characteristic determination of the Swiss cantonal armies. In March 1476, the best-equipped army of the fifteenth century was routed by the Swiss at Grandson. Charles could think only of revenge and mobilized all the troops and support that he could muster. In June 1476, this army also was badly defeated by the Swiss, at Murten. The booty captured was enormous, because the entire supply train containing the duke's treasures was abandoned on the battlefield. His silver dishes, tapestries, jewelry, precious clothing, and money were divided up among the participating Swiss towns.

In October 1476, René of Lorraine succeeded in reconquering his duchy. Charles immediately attempted to recover Nancy by laying siege to it, even though it was already winter. Focusing only on the siege, his army weakened by the harsh winter conditions, Charles ignored the vast army of twenty thousand men that the Swiss and his other enemies, including René of Lorraine, dispatched to Nancy in December. In the ensuing encounter, Charles was killed. His badly mutilated and virtually unrecognizable body was left behind in the snow on the battlefield on January 5, 1477, and was only identified several days later—probably by his valet and his physician, who found old battle scars on the body. But according to later folklore, it was his own court jester who located Charles's body. For a long time afterward, as had been the case with other medieval rulers whose deaths had occurred in obscure circumstances and, seemingly at too early an age, in the midst of grandiose plans—Arthur, Frederick II, and, later, Frederick Barbarossa—rumors circulated that he had survived as a captive or a penitent, hidden from the world.

Many of Charles's great nobles were also killed or taken prisoner at Nancy, and the rich ducal supply train was once more looted. For the previous three years Charles had lived as a man obsessed, pursuing limited goals with a determination and commitment of resources and time out of all proportion to their objects, losing sight of his larger interests, especially those of his subjects. During those years, he drove a great many people to senseless deaths and imposed ferociously high taxes on his exhausted subjects. His entire administrative staff lived in mortal fear of the fits of rage that ensued when his demands were not met quickly enough or when alternative advice was offered. A great prince could still exert irresistible and terrible personal influence.

The death of the duke did not, however, bring his subjects any respite. All his former enemies, with Louis XI in the lead, took advantage of the virtual absence of a Burgundian army following three devastating defeats. Even before Charles's death was officially made known to the Burgundian court at Ghent, which did not happen until January 24, three weeks after the battle, French troops invaded Burgundy, Mâcon, Picardy, and Artois.[22] Franche-Comté, Hainault, and Flanders were also threatened. With difficulty, summoned by and in cooperation with both Mary of Burgundy and Margaret of York, who now called herself the Dowager Duchess of Burgundy, the Estates-General mustered a defense. By the summer of 1477, the French attacks had ceased. The conciliatory internal diplomacy of Margaret of York whose loyalty to the house of Burgundy had never wavered and whose personal relations with the twenty-year-old Mary of Burgundy had always been excellent, offered a milder ducal role, cooperation with the Estates, and a remission of taxes. It also played a key role during the spring and early summer of 1477. By August, the hope of the Low Countries could rest as well in the prince-consort Maximilian, the emperor's eldest son and apparent successor. He had been officially betrothed to Mary of Burgundy since 1473. Maximilian only arrived at Maastricht, on the eastern edge of the Burgundian Low Countries, on August 5, 1477. The marriage was celebrated at Ghent on August 19. In 1478 and 1479, Maximilian led military campaigns in Artois that resulted in an advantageous temporary truce with France.

Liège and Guelders, which Charles the Bold had conquered by force, rapidly regained their autonomy. Duke Adolph of Guelders was, however, slain in June 1477 during the struggle against France, fighting voluntarily and as an autonomous prince on the Burgundian side. Confusion followed for decades in Guelders. In Luxemburg, a factional struggle broke out over whether to recognize Mary of Burgundy or another pretender to the ducal title. This struggle ended only in 1480, in Mary's favor.[23] After 1477, the core territories of the Low Countries remained "Burgundian," but the original duchy of Burgundy—with Dijon, Champmol, and the tombs of the dukes—fell definitively into French hands. Most of Artois was occupied by the French until its return, with the Peace of Senlis in 1493. Flanders, Brabant, Hainault, Holland, Zeeland, and Namur, and, after 1480, all of Luxemburg as well, continued to form a unity that grew even more self-conscious in the face of the French threat, which they all resisted vigorously, regardless of the uncertainties of the succession at the center.

Succession, Revolt, and Crisis: The Great Privilege of 1477 and the Death of Mary of Burgundy

Mary of Burgundy was twenty years old in 1477, well educated, fond of riding and hunting, interested in the arts, and personally devout. She was extremely close to her stepmother Margaret of York, and she learned a great deal about court life and the duties of a duchess from Margaret. She was also the most attractive heiress in Europe, and the shifting diplomatic circumstances of the 1460s and 1470s had brought a number of imperial, royal, and noble suitors to Charles the Bold. Perhaps Charles had waited too long to agree to the marriage contract with Maximilian of Austria, for it had been clear for some years that only an imperial marriage could save the Burgundian complex. But the marriage itself seems to have been a happy one, producing three children, two of whom, Philip and Margaret, survived into adulthood.

At the death of Charles the Bold, governmental institutions were in total disarray, diplomatic communications uncertain, subjects shocked, and enemies relieved. The latter, particularly Louis XI, seized the opportunity thus presented. Mary's first task was to convene the Estates General in order to gain formal recognition as Charles's successor. But the recognition was no mere formality; Count John of Étampes and Rethel had already made some claims on Brabant in 1467, and, especially in Luxemburg, some of the nobility refused to recognize Mary until 1480.

It was customary that on the occasion of a succession, as on those when granting requests for subsidies, the Estates presented their complaints about government policy and stipulated that the resolution of these complaints be a condition of their consent. By 1477 the complaints were numerous, serious, and desperate. The Estates General presented a long list of grievances regarding recent governmental policies that they wanted changed. Under pressure of the French invasions, the defections of a number of high nobles to the king of France, and the disarray of governing institutions, Mary and her counselors had no option other than to grant massive concessions. In exchange for granting solemn privileges, Mary was recognized as ruler and the Estates General consented to raise troops to repel the French invasion.[24]

The Great Privilege of 1477, which Mary issued in Dutch, has sometimes been interpreted by historians as a conservative and local-minded reaction to the modern state. But it can be argued that, although many of the measures of centralization were repealed, the Estates General remained cohesive and loyal to the Burgundian dynasty to a substantial degree. The central principalities of the Low Countries did not at any time exhibit the slightest sign of opting in favor of another dynasty. Moreover, the Great Privilege left many other Burgundian institutions intact, namely the territorial councils and Chambers of Account, even the Great Council as a general high court. What the Estates General achieved was an agreement to keep ducal institutions like the Parlement of Mechelen from trampling all existing rights.

The Estates firmly resisted any encroachment upon their own jurisdiction and that of the local governments, and they roundly condemned the widespread abuse of power by ducal officials. Each of the territories enumerated its own grievances, which were resolved by dozens of articles in each of the privileges granted. They summed up in detail precisely which toll collectors had demanded more than they had been entitled to, how many secretaries had issued acts in return for bribes, which offices had been sold only to be exploited for their revenues, how many aldermen had been appointed in return for presents given to the duke's representatives, and other bitterly resented ducal practices. The reaction of the Estates was directed against the forced character of the process of centralization and was directed primarily against excesses that had reached outrageous proportions during the previous few years.

Still, the Burgundian state seems to have attracted and united its subjects more than it repelled them. It is remarkable that the Estates General took only a week or so to reach agreement on the twenty articles in the Great Privilege of February 11, 1477—just a month after the death of Charles the Bold and even less than that since the news had become known in the Low Countries—which reversed all of Charles's recent policies. They entailed the abolition of the central institutions at Mechelen, the formation of a new Great Council with representatives from all the territories, the rights of the Estates General to meet freely, a requirement that the consent of the Estates be obtained before any declaration of war, the limitation of feudal service, respect for all customs and privileges, the use of the language of those concerned in all administrative and judicial affairs, and free trade. The final passage contained the reservation that in the event a duke or his officials undertook anything not in accordance with the privilege, his subjects would no longer be under the slightest obligation to render him any service whatever.[25] Thus, in theory, this clause made any ducal violation of an existing right a legitimate reason for refusing allegiance and service on the part of his subjects.

The Great Privilege can be considered the first constitution for the whole of the Low Countries, and it was often cited during the revolt against Spain in the sixteenth century. Aside from the general privilege, however, a number of territories — Flanders, Holland-Zeeland, Namur, and Brabant — exacted much more comprehensive territorial charters on the occasion of Mary's Joyous Entry and inauguration. In spite of the Great Privilege, in the spring of 1477 riots broke out in innumerable towns, as expressions of popular rage at the oppressive fiscal measures and curbs on urban and guild rights. The local authorities were held responsible for everything that had gone wrong, and heads rolled. In Ghent, where the court, the government, and the Estates General had convened, popular resentment demanded and got not only the heads of several aldermen and the city's treasurer, but also those of the chancellor Hugonet and councillor Guy de Brimeu, lord of Humbercourt and stadtholder of Liège and Luxemburg and of two quarters of Guelders. Overall, sixteen ducal officials were executed. Several ecclesiastical officials successfully pleaded benefit of clergy, while others, like Adolph of Ravenstein, were too widely respected to be tried.

Summer brought the return of internal peace and halted the French incursions as well. Mary's fiancé, the imperial prince Maximilian, finally appeared, looking every inch the *Weisskunig*, the wise king of his later fanciful autobiography. The Gentenaars cheered his arrival, expecting him to rescue the country. But Maximilian, although capable of leading an army and winning battles, had been raised in the Habsburg imperial milieu, which had instilled in him a sovereign contempt for all those outside the nobility and the church. Although he reestablished the Order of the Golden Fleece in 1478 and the office of chancellor with the appointment of Jean Carandolet in 1480, he was unable to summon any understanding of the prominent urban element in the Low Countries, and he cared not a fig for its privileges.[26]

At his inauguration as prince-consort and thus ruling prince, Maximilian took the customary oath to respect the customs and privileges of his lands — which had also been a provision of the Great Privilege as a condition of approving the marriage — but he soon attempted to undermine the concessions that Mary had made in the spring. This naturally resulted in protests on the part of the Estates, but it did not yet lead to the refusal of allegiance and service provided for in the Great Privilege. The leopard has not changed his spots, sighed the Estates of Brabant in 1481.[27] But Maximilian had also repulsed the French — at a high cost. Until 1494, the year that saw the formal end of his personal governance of the Low Countries, the tax burden remained higher even than it had been during the last five years of the reign of Charles the Bold, requiring an average of 231,000 pounds per year in Flanders.[28] The great cities of Holland had borrowed so extensively to pay their taxes that they were unable to pay off the interest on their debts until well into the sixteenth century.[29]

Maximilian was also occupied by his efforts to establish his authority in Luxemburg, Liège, Guelders, and Holland. In Holland, the partisan conflict between Hooks and Cods had broken out again in 1477, chiefly as a reaction to the large number of Hooks appointed to office since 1472. The Hooks seized power completely in Dordrecht, Gouda, Hoorn, Oudewater, and Schoonhoven and expelled their opponents. In compliance with the new territorial charter granted by Mary, the Flemish stadtholder Lodewijk van Gruuthuse was replaced by the Zeelander Wolfert van Borselen. But the latter became totally committed to the Hook party after the Cods plundered his official residence at the Binnenhof in the Hague. Cod noblemen and their partisans from Delft, the Hague, and Haarlem then seized power in Leiden and in turn banished or executed their Hook enemies. They also seized power in Amsterdam.[30]

Faced with so many challenges to his authority and the blatant violations of law and order, Maximilian took action in 1480 and, disregarding the Great Privilege of 1477, replaced the local partisan stadtholder van Borselen with Josse of Lalaing from Hainault. In January 1481, Hook exiles, supported by several nobles from Utrecht and their mercenaries, conducted a successful raid on Leiden. But by April of that year, Josse de Lalaing had managed, with troops from the Cod-dominated cities, to subdue all of the Hook strongholds. Again Maximilian imposed fiscal and judicial penalties, thus assuring a long period of Cod domination.[31]

The discontent stemming from the continuation of the war with France, the heavy taxes, and the violations of privileges reached a constitutional climax in 1482, a year as disastrous as 1477. Mary of Burgundy, who loved to ride and hunt with falcons, rode out in March 1482 to the hunt in the area of Wijnendaele, near Bruges. An excellent rider, she was somehow thrown from her horse and crushed beneath it and was carried in a litter back to Bruges, where she died on March 27. She left Maximilian as the likely prince-regent, but her direct heir was her son, the four-year-old crown prince Philip. It was not the most auspicious of times for a regency, particularly that of Maximilian.

The Troubled Regency of Maximilian, 1482–1494

It is not surprising that Maximilian immediately demanded the regency, but his policies between 1477 and 1482 raised serious objections by many in the Estates General. The Estates of Flanders under the leadership of Ghent went so far as to refuse to accept Maximilian, even after the other territories had somewhat reluctantly agreed to do so. When the Estates of Flanders did agree, they did so under the condition that a peace treaty be finally concluded with France. Formally they were entirely within their rights, but the imperial prince was not the man to acknowledge that he could conceivably accept dismissal from mere Flemish burghers.[32]

The Estates General finally agreed to Maximilian because peace negotiations were opened with France, leading to the Peace of Arras in December 1482. The conditions were particularly favorable to France: Artois, Franche-Comté, and several smaller Burgundian seigneuries — Mâcon, Auxerre, Salins, Bar, and Noyes — were ceded to France as the dowry of Margaret of Austria, the three-year-old daughter of Mary and Maximilian, who was married by proxy to the Dauphin, the future Charles VIII. The legal authority of the Parlement of Paris, which had not been exercised in the French county of Flanders since 1468, was restored.[33]

Louis XI of France died in 1483, and the marriage plans of the new king, Charles VIII (1493–98), were delayed, especially during the regency of his sister Anne and her husband, Pierre de Bourbon, lord of Beaujeu, and then Charles's establishment of his own increasingly personal reign, from 1488 on. In 1491, when the great duchy of Brittany descended to a female heiress, Anne of Brittany, Charles VIII took the opportunity of acquiring the duchy by marrying Anne and returning Margaret of Austria to her father, Maximilian. In compensation, and to prevent Maximilian's possible interference with Charles's plans to invade Italy and enforce his claim to the kingdom of Naples, Charles gave Maximilian both Artois and the Franche-Comté.

The citizens of Flanders, Hainault, and Brabant, who were the chief architects of the peace of 1482, were prepared to pay a high price for it, although it was ultimately accomplished chiefly at the expense of the dynasty. This episode was the second, after 1477, in which the Estates General showed itself to be a vigorous and effective organization, able to impose its own vision of the state over that of the prince without excluding him entirely. Their desire for peace stood in sharp contrast to the prince's desire for more land. The troubles in the dioceses of Liège and Utrecht offered him an opportunity.

In 1482, Guillaume de la Marck had usurped secular authority in Liège, instigated a revolt, and killed the bishop, the hapless Louis de Bourbon. He then attempted to force the cathedral chapter of St. Lambert to elect his own son as Louis's replacement. In 1483, however, Brabant provided Maximilian with an army, and he was able to defeat La Marck and install his ally John of Horne as bishop. But French intervention prevented a final settlement of the Liège question until 1492, when Liégeois neutrality and right to free trade were recognized at the Treaty of Donchéry, bringing the city and its territory more closely into the Burgundian orbit. In 1483 Maximilian also intervened in the war in the prince-bishopric of Utrecht, where Bishop David of Burgundy had been taken prisoner by Hook nobles who were supported by the two most important cities in his territory, Utrecht and Amersfoort. After a successful siege of Utrecht, Maximilian restored David to his ecclesiastical dignity, but he retained for himself the secular authority, thus taking another step toward incorporating Utrecht into the Burgundian territorial complex.[34]

During the Utrecht campaign, Maximilian had consented to the creation in a still recalcitrant Flanders of a regency council composed of relatives of the dynasty and representatives from the three great cities. Despite Maximilian's later dissolution of this council, it continued to administer the county with the open support of France. This episode recalled the events of James of Arteveld's time (1338–45), when the preeminent towns ruled as quasi-states, flagrantly favoring their own interests over those of the surrounding smaller towns and villages.

In 1485 Maximilian's troops, consisting chiefly of German mercenaries, campaigned throughout Flanders and forced one city after another to surrender. In June 1485, he was finally able to be inaugurated as regent of Flanders. A month later, however, Ghent revolted once again, this time against the presence of German soldiers, and Ghent's privileges were once more revoked in retaliation.[35]

Maximilian also went to war over Liège and Artois, again forcing his subjects to finance his operations. In the meantime, he had discovered an alternative source of income by debasing the coinage, without requesting the consent of his subjects. But these currency manipulations soon led to the disruption of the economy, which had already suffered greatly from the military operations of the first half of the decade. Revolts flared up throughout his territories, partly because of the general crop failures that occurred everywhere in Europe at this time, raising the price of grain to three, four, even five times the normal level. Military operations in the countryside contributed to the problem: between 1488 and 1493, huge tracts of agricultural land were abandoned because of the lack of security. It was many years before agricultural productivity again reached normal levels.[36]

Ghent revolted again in November 1487, joined in January 1488 by Bruges. When Maximilian appeared before the gates of Bruges, he was admitted to the city but his troops were not. The citizens of Bruges feared the occupation of their city, probably with good reason. Dukes of Burgundy had been cornered before in Ghent or Bruges, but now Maximilian's situation, for which no one had been prepared, was extremely unusual. The artisans rebelled again against the same abuses that had always led to revolts: the high cost of living, the debasement of the coinage, the exorbitantly high taxes, the economic crisis fueled by Maximilian's ceaseless wars, and the corruption of officials. For three and a half months the Habsburg prince, who had recently been elected king of the Romans (and who anticipated being crowned emperor, eventually, by the pope), was held prisoner by the rebellious citizens of Bruges in the Cranenberg house on the marketplace. From his window, Maximilian could see the executions of those city administrators who had served his cause. The citizens of Ghent also imprisoned a number of powerful councillors. But the rebels had no real aims after the scapegoats had been imprisoned and publicly beheaded. The arrival of an imperial army led the Flemings to release their troublesome prisoners. They wished to be quit of Maximilian, but they could envision no real alternative to the monarchy.

The Estates General did pass a resolution providing for the removal of Maximilian from the regency of Flanders. They entrusted the administration of the county to a regency council, composed of representatives of the Estates of Flanders and blood relatives of the Burgundian house. This arrangement resembled the one that had administered Flanders in 1483–85. Once again, as in 1477 and 1482, the Estates General played an essential role in the resolution of the dynastic conflict. Four territories took the lead: Brabant, Flanders, Hainault, and Holland-Zeeland. They formed a league that drew up the conditions for the release of Maximilian on May 16, 1488. Maximilian swore acceptance of the conditions stipulated by the Estates on the most precious relic in the Low Countries, the Holy Blood at Bruges, and he once more recognized all the customs and privileges of the territory. It surprised no one when, upon his release, he promptly repudiated his oath as having been made under duress and resumed hostilities. French support for Flanders and Liège and the spread of revolt to Brussels and Louvain in 1488 explain why it took Maximilian another four years to restore his authority.[37]

For many years, a dual authority continued to exist in Flanders. The regency council, which was powerful in Ghent, Bruges, and their dependencies, even minted its own gold coin in the name of Maximilian and Mary's son, Archduke Philip the Fair. The stadtholder-general, Albrecht of Saxony, implemented a gradual but systematic strategy of reconquest. He took town after town, first the smaller ones and then the larger, harassing the countryside so that the beleaguered towns were driven to surrender more by hunger than by force. The high taxes imposed during these years, along with the extremely high cost of living and the results of the currency manipulations, led even the remote West Frisian peasants to revolt in 1491–92. They envisioned a league with the Flemings, and Albrecht of Saxony briefly abandoned the siege of Ghent in order to march north and prevent these peasant armies from descending upon the south.[38]

Years of internal warfare inflicted tremendous damage on the economy. Roving bands of soldiers destroyed harvests, livestock, and farms; towns were blockaded, and the trade routes were cut. As a kind of economic warfare, Maximilian ordered foreign merchants to leave Bruges and establish themselves in loyal Antwerp. Because war-torn Flanders was both no longer profitable and highly dangerous, they gradually abandoned it, unquestionably contributing to the economic crisis of the eighties. Although all of Europe was confronted with the highest grain prices of the century and new outbursts of plague, the effects in Flanders were more dramatic and of longer duration than elsewhere. Bruges never recovered its former prosperity after the crisis of the eighties, and this failure hastened Antwerp's replacement of Bruges as the economic metropolis of the north.[39] In all probability, the hellish scenes often painted by Hieronymus Bosch were not entirely the products of his own imagination.[40]

The peace concluded in July 1489 between the empire and France halted the momentum of the revolt. But Ghent did not finally submit until July 1492. The ducal blockade of Sluis lasted until October. The conditions for peace contained the usual stipulations: formal recognition of Maximilian as regent for Philip, the humiliation of the rebels, enormous fines, limitation of the rights of the great cities, and the revocation of the concessions made in the Great Privilege of 1477.[41]

Ruler, State, and People, 1465–1492

From 1465 to 1492, the Burgundian territories suffered from continual wars, and, after 1483, fighting continued within their own borders. After 1481 there were general food shortages, aggravated by military operations.

Trade was at a standstill, and the markets for industry collapsed. The persistently high rate of taxation diverted so much capital from the economy that little remained for investment, resulting in a decline in consumption. Maximilian's currency devaluations increased the confusion and constituted a real bloodletting for the economy.

Renewed French expansion under Louis XI also posed a threat to the Burgundian territories. The exaggerated manner in which both Charles the Bold and Maximilian became absorbed in their rivalry with France undeniably made the problem appear more serious than it was. Their policy of warfare against their own subjects and their inflexibility in the face of widespread resistance from the people over which they ruled rendered the consequences of the general European crisis of the 1480s unusually severe throughout the Low Countries, especially in Flanders.

During the nearly constant confrontations with their rulers, the representative institutions developed their own vision of the organization of the state and its proper function. They showed clearly a feeling of community and unity on a supraterritorial level. In the Great Privilege of 1477 and other privileges, the peace agreement of 1482, and the act of alliance of 1488, they gave form to their ambition to exercise a practical decision-making authority in recognizing the ruler, declaring war, consenting to military policy, establishing tolls, regulating trade, and ordaining judicial procedures. In 1488, the Estates General determined that they would convene annually to discuss such questions, as well as any violation of their privileges. They then agreed that their annual meetings would rotate in Flanders, Brabant, Holland, and Hainault. From these steps and from their confirmation of a supraterritorial high court and regional courts of appeals and Chambers of Accounts, it is clear that the representatives of the duke's subjects—who, naturally, belonged to the political and economic elite and largely represented its interests—did, indeed, wish to preserve several of the fundamental achievements of the Burgundian state.

The period following 1477 was one of reaction to the excessive centralization policies of the dukes and to the proliferating state bureaucracy and its high degree of privatization. The alternatives proposed by the representative institutions became apparent in the period 1477–92, when they took advantage of the opportunities offered by the dynasty's weakness. Their vision was federative in nature rather than centralistic: it did not exclude the ruler, but constrained both the ruler and his officials to work within the existing local and regional customs and privileges, with the Estates General and the Estates of the various principalities guaranteeing their enforcement.

There was special emphasis placed upon protecting the rights of the most vocal groups: the great abbeys, the feudal lords, and the great cities. During this period, the cities consolidated or restored their hegemony over their "quarters," the villages and smaller towns (castelries) in their vicinities. Just as the three great cities of Flanders had done in the time of the Arteveldes, the Flemish regency council pursued a policy that involved curtailing the rural textile industry in favor of that of the great cities. Limitations to the cities' legal power over their respective quarters, such as those imposed by the dukes after unsuccessful revolts, were removed.

In the period from 1477 to 1492, the Estates and the cities greatly expanded their executive power. They organized the territorial defense against France, borrowed money, and devised both a foreign and domestic economic policy. They were emphatically oriented toward peace and showed themselves uninterested in territorial expansion. This alternative to a militaristic and power-hungry ducal state came to full fruition a century later, in the Republic of the United Provinces.

8

The Second Flowering
1492–1530

Internal Peace and the Consciousness of Unity

The rule of the first four dukes of Burgundy was characterized by a continuous effort to form an independent, internally cohesive territory. During the reigns of the first two, however, it was far from apparent that the territorial sway of the Burgundian state would ever grow to the extent that it reached under Philip the Good. In 1477, as a result of the even further-reaching ambitions of Charles the Bold, there was a double reaction to this expansion and to the duke's heavy-handed and authoritarian style of domestic government. The heartland of Burgundy and all of the recently conquered frontier territories in the Low Countries and the east were lost, and local and regional customs and privileges were restored. Until the disasters of 1477, the dukes, by their sheer willpower and relentless ambition, had made their mark on Europe and taken all the advantage they could of the opportunities offered them. The regency of Maximilian was, like theirs, a period of violent power struggles. His ambition was to reconquer the lost territories and reverse the internal decline of ducal power. For their part, his subjects refused to surrender the fruits of their resistance to what they considered a despotic regime. Under the stark conditions of a deep and lasting economic crisis, the inhabitants of the various regions were prepared to use military force to defend the achievements they had won in 1477 — achievements supposedly granted formally, irrevocably, and eternally.

Despite its numerical, logistical, and technological superiority and its support from the empire, Maximilian's professional mercenary army was able to quell the rebellions of his regency after the accidental death of Mary of Burgundy in 1482 only with the greatest difficulty and after several years of fighting. Since the various territories did not adequately coordinate their resistance, they were subdued region by region and city by city. Even between neighboring rebellious cities—Bruges and Ghent, for example—there was much suspicion, and only exceptionally was there any combined effort to resist the ruler. This particularism, in itself a clear reflection of the cities' primarily local and regional sense of identity, facilitated the final victory of the regent's forces. In order to subdue one territory, rebellion was often temporarily tolerated in another.

In terms of state power, the period immediately following this internal strife was primarily one of pacification. The peace with France, established by the treaties of 1489 and 1493, lasted into the 1520s. Adventurous plans of reconquest were shelved, and internal relations at last became peaceful.

At first glance, it seems surprising that the revocation in 1492–94 of all those privileges granted by Mary of Burgundy in 1477 generated so little protest. When Maximilian succeeded his father as king of the Romans and head of the empire in 1493, he was careful to ensure that his son Philip, who had by then reached his majority, confirmed at his inauguration in each territory only those rights that had been acknowledged at the time of Duke Philip the Good. Maximilian thus achieved what he had been fighting for during the whole of his reign in the Low Countries: the restoration of a strong de facto ducal monarchy, unrestricted by the particularistic privileges of 1477. However, Charles's centralizing ordinances were not reintroduced, either. Moreover, as king of the Romans Maximilian did not accept homage from his son, since he intended to retain direct control over the affairs of the Burgundian complex.[1] This was possible only because his subjects were exhausted from the revolt that had lasted a year in Holland in Brabant, but ten years in Flanders. It should be noted that after Maximilian's departure for Germany in 1489, the central government exercised considerably more restraint in its subjugation of the recalcitrant territories. While heavy fines were imposed and privileges revoked, in practice, the day-to-day administration managed to avoid the polarization characteristic of the preceding years. In the city administrations, notables who had chosen the side of rebellion returned, and the government made efforts to consult the representative institutions on a regular basis. The Peace of Cadzand of 1492, which signaled the reduction of Ghent to the control of Maximilian, inaugurated a forty-seven-year period without rebellion on the part of the most historically rebellious city in the county of Flanders.

The Estates General continued to develop into a regular meeting place for the central government and representatives of the various territories. Meetings called to approve or refuse taxes led to more general discussions of public policy, including international relations. The Estates General was also regularly involved in determining monetary policy. Most of the thirty-one meetings held between 1493 and 1506 took place in Brussels or Mechelen, the seigneury enclaved in Brabant, these cities increasingly becoming something like administrative capitals of the Burgundian state. Prior to 1492, such meetings had been held more often in Flanders.[2]

The composition of the delegations varied from session to session. As a rule they consisted of prominent clerics (abbots, and provosts of cathedral or collegiate church chapters), members of the nobility, with the greatest cities of each territory being represented. The particular individuals who actually appeared at these gatherings were determined not only by the circumstances, but also by the balance of power between the different social categories — the Estates — within each territory. The delegation from Hainault, for example, nearly always consisted of high nobles (like the Croy family), along with abbots and representatives of a city or two. The Three Estates normally appeared for Brabant, although the urban constituency was better represented there, and the four major cities — Louvain, Brussels, Antwerp, and 's-Hertogenbosch — were almost always represented. Holland and Zeeland were represented almost exclusively by representatives of cities, often those of the six great cities of Holland and Middelburg, and sometimes a few others as well. Clerics from Holland and Zeeland were almost always excluded (except for the abbot of Middelburg), and only very exceptionally was there a sprinkling of nobles. In Flanders, the picture was more complex. Usually there were several prominent clerics and noblemen present, but the permanent representatives came from the Four Members — Ghent, Bruges, Ypres, and the Franc of Bruges — with delegations participating from as many as twenty smaller towns and up to nine castelries. This representation of the rural population, always from the Franc of Bruges and often other areas as well, was unique in the Estates General.

Altogether, the composition of delegations to a well-attended meeting such as that of April 22, 1493, is shown in Table 7.[3]

If we take into account the fact that the urban delegations consisted of several delegates, it is apparent that the cities must have held an overwhelming numerical majority. The Flemings accounted for approximately half of the participants. Although the votes were taken by land — that is, principality — and by Estate, the concentration in the territory of Flanders and in the Third Estate carried considerable weight in the deliberations. The contrast between urbanized and rural regions is also clearly apparent in these figures. Luxemburg only rarely found it worthwhile to send a delegation on such a long journey. In the Walloon territories, land ownership was dominated by the aristocracy, and this fostered loyalty to the central government.

TABLE 7. Composition of Delegations to Estates General, April 1493

Delegation	Clerics	Nobles	Cities	Countryside	Total
Brabant	6	1+	10	0	17+?
Limburg	0	0	1	0	1
Flanders	10	1+?	16	8	35+?
Artois	1	0	2	0	3
Hainault	2	2	2	0	6
Holland	0	1	9	0	10
Zeeland	0	1	5	0	6
Walloon Flanders	0	0	3	0	3
Namur	1	0	1	0	2
Mechelen	0	0	1	0	1
Total	20	6+?	50	8	84+?

This regional rift between urban and aristocratic interests and the central government later became spectacularly apparent, during the Revolt of the Netherlands in 1579. But even in the 1400s and early 1500s, the delegations representing the nobility consisted partly of counselors and other high ducal officials and thus would hardly function as an opposition party.

The expanding role of the Estates General illustrates two trends: the increasing cohesion of the Low Country territories and the government's increasing inclination toward consultation. This cohesion was no longer imposed by the dynasty; the actions of the Estates General during the period of crisis in 1477–92 showed clearly that the delegates themselves sought territorial unity. Threats to such peripheral territories as Burgundy, Luxemburg, Picardy, Liège, or Guelders had not always been received with great concern, but the Estates were willing to fight for Artois. Even after Artois was partially occupied by France, delegations from the cities of Saint-Omer and Aire continued to appear at the meetings of the Estates General. Between 1400 and 1500, the Burgundian territories had evolved from the personal union of far-flung principalities into a unity perceived by the subjects of the Low Countries themselves.

"The Cradle of All Our Wars": Natural Rulers and the Spanish Marriages

The people's identification with the dynasty, which had gradually come to be considered as autochthonous ("natural," *naturlijcke, naturel*), was typical of this process. In 1478, the dowager duchess Margaret of York displayed her newborn godchild, Philip, at Bruges, "naked to the crowd, holding his bottom in her hand, and said: 'Children, here is your newly born lord, young Philip, of the emperor's seed'; the crowd rejoiced greatly that it was a son."[4] The citizens of Bruges were overjoyed at the birth of a male heir. Philip, who was named after his great-grandfather Philip the Good, was given the title of archduke of Austria, a reminder of the original territory of the Habsburg dynasty. This double dynastic pride is expressed by a contemporary court chronicler who described the first presentation of the new heir to his father, Maximilian, with this dialogue between the parents: "Sir, look at your son and our child, young Philip of imperial seed," said Duchess Mary of Burgundy. Maximilian took the baby in his arms, kissed him, and said, "O noble Burgundian blood, my offspring, named after Philip of Valois."

Philip the Fair ruled from 1494 to 1506 as a ruler beloved in the Low Countries. His will dictated that his heart was to be buried in the mausoleum in the Church of Our Lady (*Onze Lieve Vrouw*) in Bruges, where his mother was entombed. But his father, Maximilian of Austria, always remained a foreigner in the Low Countries, although both his children and even his grandson, the emperor Charles V, were considered autochthonous rulers. Maximilian, who had been king of the Romans since 1486 and succeeded his father as (German) king in 1493, planned and built a grand tomb for himself at Innsbruck in Austria, with large sculptures of both his Habsburg ancestors and the dukes of Burgundy, but in the end, he was buried in Vienna. Philip the Fair's son Charles, when he was the emperor Charles V, declared in 1520 before the Estates General "that his heart had always been in these lands over here," a reference to the old Burgundian ducal term for the Low Countries.[5] In his own will of 1522, Charles specified that he wished to be buried with his Burgundian ancestors in the mausoleum of the Burgundian dynasty at Champmol near Dijon, if the duchy of Burgundy could be recovered from France. If not, Charles wished to be buried at Bruges, next to his grandmother Mary of Burgundy. In the event, however, partly as a consequence of the dynastic marriage that had produced him, Charles was buried in faraway Spain.

Under the influence of their counselors and of the Estates General, and probably because of their own convictions, Archduke Philip the Fair and his sister Margaret of Austria, who was appointed governor-general over the Low Countries for her six-year-old nephew Charles after Philip's death in 1506, resisted pressure from their father, Maximilian. The independent stance of the "natural rulers" enjoyed the warm support of their subjects. Although Maximilian continued to commit himself to the reconquest of Guelders, the Estates General refused his request in 1498 for subsidies to pursue this goal. Even after Maximilian came to Antwerp to plead his cause in person before the meeting of the Estates, the delegates persisted in displaying their preference for peace. Philip's own independent policy also favored a balance of power, and he even went so far as to grant free passage to French troops supporting Guelders's resistance to him. Clearly Philip and Margaret did not consider themselves to be instruments of Habsburg dynastic politics, choosing instead to pursue an independent policy intended to preserve peace in the Low Countries. In 1502–3, Maximilian again requested subsidies from the Low Countries, this time for a Crusade against the Turks and as compensation for the expenses he had incurred for his efforts on behalf of Burgundy and the Low Countries. On this occasion too, the Estates General categorically refused his request. Their views were diametrically opposed to his: whereas they prized peace above all, Maximilian was fascinated by territorial expansion and heroic chivalry.[6]

Peace with France was ensured partly by the fact that King Charles VIII's priorities differed substantially from those of his father. He became militarily engaged in Italy, which occupied his interests throughout the 1490s. When his marriage in 1491 to Anne of Brittany added the duchy of Brittany to France, Charles readily abandoned the frontier territories of Artois and the Franche-Comté, which he had received as the dowry of Margaret of Austria, who in 1482 had been betrothed to Charles. Even with Charles's cooperation, a military campaign was still required to reattach Margaret's dowry territories to the Burgundian domain. This change in French policy contributed substantially to political consolidation and to the restoration of economic prosperity to the Low Countries.[7]

But the failed union of Charles VIII and Margaret of Austria was a considerable blow to the pride of Maximilian, not only because his daughter had been repudiated by the French king, but also because the king's new wife, Anne of Brittany, had formerly been married by proxy to Maximilian himself. It is understandable that the French were unwilling to grant their most powerful rival a new territorial base in Brittany. Nevertheless, the Breton marriage of Charles VIII freed Maximilian's hand to seek out yet other connections for the dynasty through the marriages of Philip and Margaret. The results of Maximilian's negotiations shaped the history of most of Europe for the next three centuries. On November 5, 1495, a double marriage was concluded by procuration between Philip and Margaret and Juana and Juan, the children of Ferdinand of Aragon and Isabella of Castile.[8] The Burgundian-Spanish marriages had more far-reaching consequences than had the double marriage of 1385 that had attached Hainault, Holland, and Zeeland to the Burgundian lands. A third child, Juan's and Juana's sister Isabella, was married to the king of Portugal.

The Spanish royal line was not robust, and Margaret's husband, Juan, died only five months after their marriage, his sister Isabella a year later, and Isabella's son and only child, Don Miguel, in 1500. These premature deaths made Juana, the wife of Philip the Fair of Burgundy, heiress to the kingdoms of Aragon and Castile. In 1500 Juana and Philip and their children became the repositories of all hope of dynastic continuity in the Spanish realms and their overseas colonies. Although Juana was plagued by mental illness during most of her lifetime, and certainly after the death of her husband, she nevertheless provided Philip with healthy children, most of whom married to dynastic advantage. Eleanor married Francis I of France, Isabella married Christian II of Denmark, Catherine married John III of Portugal, Ferdinand I married Anne of Hungary and became king of the Romans in 1531 and emperor in 1556, and Mary married Louis II of Hungary and later served as regent of the Low Countries, from 1531 to 1555. The most successful child of the union of Juana and Philip, however, was Charles (later the emperor Charles V), who at his birth in 1500 was heir-apparent to the Burgundian territories in the Low Countries, the kingdoms of Aragon and Castile, and the Habsburg Austrian lands. He also held the prospect, at least, of the imperial title. Thus, dynastic vagaries placed enormous territories surrounding France under the control of a single ruler. Under Charles V, this situation led to a long conflict between France and Spain, a conflict that ultimately exhausted them both and squandered most of the immense resources at their disposal. There was considerable truth in the remark made by Louis XIV of France when he stood, two centuries later, at the tombs of Mary of Burgundy and Charles the Bold in the church of Our Lady in Bruges: "There is the cradle of all our wars."

After 1500, the policy of Philip the Fair was dominated by the prospect of the Spanish succession. From 1501 to 1503, he made a prolonged journey to his prospective kingdoms and returned to Spain in 1505 after the death of his mother-in-law, Isabella of Castile. From then on, the Low Countries were no longer the most important territories of the princes who ruled them. But Philip's own sudden death in 1506 delayed the decline of the centrality of the Low Countries until his eldest son, Charles, attained his majority in 1515.

The Great Regency: Margaret of Austria and Charles V

During the minority of Charles, from 1506 to 1515, the Low Countries escaped the direct control of the great powers. The Estates General gladly accepted Philip the Fair's sister Margaret of Austria as governor-general. After the death of her husband, Juan, Margaret had remarried, this time to Philibert of Savoy, the ruler of an independent Francophone duchy that was the gateway to Italy and whose fifteenth-century rulers frequently intermarried with the noble and royal dynasties of France. But Margaret was widowed for a second time in 1504, and from that date she turned her considerable talents and interests entirely toward the Low Countries. Margaret's policies and her extensive artistic and devotional patronage were characterized by an adroitness learned from her multifaceted experience at various European courts. She, too, worked for a balance of power between the great neighboring states.

Following a three-year interruption of her regency, from 1515 to 1518, occasioned by Charles's majority and by political intrigues directed against her own person, Margaret resumed her functions as governor-general in the name of the new king of Spain. Together with that of Philip the Bold, her reign was, after that of Philip the Good, the longest of the Burgundian house. Her influence on policy was unquestionably less pronounced than that of the four dukes. Her policies were more moderate and generally in agreement with those of the Estates General. And her goals did not involve new territorial acquisitions, but rather the achievement of a peaceful balance of power.

Her nephew, Charles, however, reopened hostilities with France in 1521. His efforts resulted in the annexation by the Burgundian Low Countries of the Tournaisis, the territory of the bishop of Tournai. Charles also succeeded in imposing himself as the secular authority over the bishopric of Utrecht, so that there remained no enclaves within his territory ruled by spiritual authorities. Little by little, he acquired the territories of Frisia, Overijssel, and Groningen, and the duchy of Guelders. The 1520s also represented another peak in taxation, which had declined to a considerably less burdensome level than that of the years from 1470 to 1492.[9] This territorial expansion stemmed clearly more from Charles's policies than from those of Margaret.

Margaret's talents became apparent in the peace she negotiated in 1529 at Cambrai with Louise of Savoy, the mother of Francis I of France and the sister of Margaret's late husband, Philibert of Savoy. This "Ladies' Peace" brought about a definitive exchange of territories between France and Burgundy. The king recognized the full sovereignty of the former crown territories of the Tournaisis, Artois, and Flanders, which meant that their ruler, Charles, now the emperor Charles V, was no longer his vassal and that the Parlement of Paris would finally cease its interventions in Charles's lands.[10] For his part, Charles relinquished all claims to the duchy of Burgundy, which was now, some fifty years after its actual annexation by France, recognized as indisputably and definitively a part of France. The other Burgundy, Franche-Comté, belonged to the empire, and together with the county of Charolais remained in the hands of the Habsburg dynasty.

From Bruges to Antwerp: The New Low Country Hub of the World Economy

Just as the period of peace between 1440 and 1465 had seen a flourishing of Burgundian society in the Low Countries, the predominantly peaceful years 1492–1520 were also very prosperous. In terms of the economy, these years witnessed a considerable expansion around Antwerp, which soon rose to the status of a metropolis. There was also vigorous economic growth in Holland and Zeeland, which now displaced the German Hanse as leaders in shipping. This growth was associated with a sharp rise in population in these regions, allowing the cities in Brabant and Holland to challenge the former dominance of the cities of Flanders. The economic revival limited the impact of the increased fiscal pressure on the economy and the standard of living of Charles's wars during the 1520s.

The rapid growth of Antwerp was the most remarkable economic phenomenon of the early sixteenth century.[11] The population of this city on the lower Scheldt had increased from 33,000 in 1480 to 55,000 by 1526, and this rate of growth continued during the following decades. Immigration is the only possible explanation for such rapid population growth, and this is borne out by the stagnation or decrease in the population of eastern Brabant and Flanders. What attracted so many immigrants to Antwerp was the prospect of the apparently unlimited opportunities offered by its trade and industry. At the root of this expansion lay the Brabantine fairs, two of which were held yearly at Antwerp and two at Bergen op Zoom, which also offered excellent port facilities on a western branch of the Scheldt. A policy of free trade was in force during these four periods of four to six weeks each, and it offered considerable advantages over the protectionist regulations enforced in Flanders. Gradually, these advantages came to be granted throughout the year.

There has been a great deal of discussion as to why Bruges lost its metropolitan functions to Antwerp. One explanation attributed the loss primarily to the silting up of the Zwin, an inlet of the sea that reached as far inland as Damme and provided a natural outport for Bruges. Against this explanation, it can be argued that even in the days of its prosperity, Bruges had always been obliged to transfer cargo from seagoing vessels to smaller ones at a series of outports, the most important of which were Damme, Sluis, and, later, Arnemuiden, on the island of Walcheren. By the end of the fifteenth century, Bruges made frantic attempts to maintain its accessibility by sea. A pilot service was established and a canal link dug to the sea, to admit tidewater and thus deepen the Zwin channel. But even these substantial investments were insufficient, and it became steadily more difficult for the larger seagoing ships to moor on the Zwin. The ports of Antwerp and Bergen op Zoom were much more accessible, even though they were situated much further inland, and many shippers docked at the outport of Walcheren en route to these destinations.[12]

Other factors played a more decisive role. Not only did the ports of Bruges lose ground to Antwerp, but also, the trade and industrial production of Bruges declined. In the fourteenth and fifteenth centuries, Bruges and Antwerp had complemented each other well. Foreign merchants of the most diverse origins had established themselves at Bruges, which functioned as a center for management and banking, but the annual fairs at Antwerp also offered a temporary economic attraction. Foreign merchants residing in Bruges participated as a body in the yearly Brabantine fairs, to extend their contacts with the Rhineland and with southern Germany. Meanwhile, Bruges suffered increasingly from the disadvantages attached to its corporative organization, which fiercely guaranteed the quality of its products and the standard of living of its artisans, to the detriment of its competitiveness in a changing market. The political conflicts within Bruges were closely related to its protectionist policies; the rebelliousness of the Flemish artisans made the tensions between the cities and the Burgundian and Habsburg monarchs much greater in Flanders than in Brabant. The conflict in Flanders between 1484 and 1492 devastated the county and thoroughly disrupted its trade. Sluis continued to resist Maximilian until October 1492, serving as a base for privateer attacks on commercial shipping. In 1484 and 1488, Maximilian ordered all foreign merchants to abandon rebellious Bruges and establish themselves in the loyal city of Antwerp, where they were also promised greater privileges.

The most important merchants to choose Antwerp over Bruges on account of this freedom were the English. Traditionally, there had existed in

Flanders a protectionist ban on the importing of English cloth (see Chapters 4 and 5). Antwerp, on the other hand, not only circumvented this ban but developed a major industry based on the finishing, dyeing, and resale of rough English cloth. The whole of the Low Countries participated in the annual fairs at Antwerp — both the cities and the countryside. The German Hanse was another of Antwerp's principal trading partners. After a long period of hesitation, in 1553 the Hanse moved its headquarters from Bruges to Antwerp, where in 1468 it had already acquired from the Antwerp city administration a house on the Grain Market. This move shows clearly how vital for the rapidly growing city had become the importation of grain from Prussia. Cologne and the south German cities, particularly Frankfurt, host of an annual fair of its own, were Antwerp's other great trading partners, as were the Portuguese, whose importation of sugar and spice from its worldwide trading network linked Antwerp to the newly discovered Americas and to India and Asia as well.

A Dialogue Between Two Cultures

Two forces of artistic creation met and reinforced each other in the Low Countries. In the heavily urbanized milieus, the rivalry between cities and between different groups within a single city was increasingly expressed in cultural terms. The considerable concentration of wealth and the expanding trade relations provided a stimulus to invest in works of art that was unprecedented in northern Europe. The second force was the stimulus of the vigorous new dynasty of Burgundy, strongly influenced by the tradition of artistic patronage at the French court. The Burgundian dynasty, ambitious to achieve recognition among the royal houses of Europe, chose to assert its status by means of the arts. The Habsburg dynasty continued this tradition until well into the sixteenth century, because it still viewed itself as Burgundian; tradition, once established, continued, and the considerable territorial expansion under the Habsburg dynasty provided yet further stimulus.

The urban and court milieus each had specific functions, and each developed its own forms of cultural expression. Yet the degree of fusion that existed in the form, and, to a considerable extent, also in the content, of the art that was produced for the cities and the dukes justifies the use of the term *Burgundian culture* for the ensemble. Choir music and tapestries, for example, were produced exclusively for the courts (including the episcopal courts), and urban communities chose to invest primarily in architecture.

Manuscripts and stained glass were also commissioned for the most part by the courts, although there was such a wide range in their size, materials, quality, and price that individuals could also commission such works. Already in the fifteenth century, ordinary burghers, either as individuals or as groups, were in a position to commission paintings.

The same artists worked for patrons of varying status. Jan van Eyck's patrons ranged from the duke, his chancellor, and the higher clergy to members of the urban administrative elite and merchants. Hieronymus Bosch received commissions from Philip the Fair, Margaret of Austria, and Henry III of Nassau, as well as from the citizens of 's-Hertogenbosch, his own city. Even in the sixteenth century, there were few court painters, and none of them worked exclusively for the court. Indeed, painters received many equally prestigious commissions from other sources. The strength of "Burgundian" patronage of the arts lay in the way the commissions of the court and those of other social groups complemented and stimulated each other. The increase in demand generated by the two groups gave artists greater opportunities to develop their talents and added to the creativity of the artistic ambience as a whole.

This process was, however, limited to the urban elites, who were also more open to the French language in use at the courts. There was also a considerable interest in literature in the Dutch language, but because Dutch had fallen into disuse at court, such literature did not benefit from the interaction between the court and the other social elites.[13] Middle Dutch literature had begun with the immensely popular thirteenth-century animal epic *Van den Vos Reynaerde* (Reynard the fox) and with the late-thirteenth-century encyclopedic, historical, and moral works of the Fleming Jacob van Maerlant (1225–91). Dutch literature had been cultivated at the court in the Hague in the mid-fourteenth century by Albert of Bavaria, particularly in the genres of lyric poems, chronicles, and devotional works. By the fifteenth century, Brabant produced the most important literature in Dutch, including the miracle play *Mariken van Nieumeghen* and the morality play *Elckerlyc* (Everyman). The Dutch language was also rich in proverbs, and proverbs played an important role in bridging the gap between French and Dutch, even inspiring several painters, including Pieter Bruegel the Elder.

Beginning in the middle of the fifteenth century, there was a remarkable increase in cultural production. The number of artists increased, and works of art were no longer produced exclusively on commission. Painters now began to produce a surplus of pictures and thus created a true art market for anonymous purchasers. The production of some works in series was actually directed specifically at a bourgeois public. In this way the content and forms of cultural expression, if not always its intrinsic quality, came to be more widely distributed and consequently more of a common cultural property. The common ground between court and city gradually grew greater than their differences. Collective exhibitions of the type represented by a Joyous Entry into a city contributed greatly to a direct exchange of expressive media. It should also be noted that the rulers did not seek to establish a monopoly on any particular artistic form. On the contrary, they perceived imitation by other groups in the community as a supreme token of the success of their cultural message. Originality was not a preoccupation; the subject represented and the technical expertise of the artist, even when he remained unknown, were considered far more important.[14]

The Burgundian dynasty's favorite means of exhibiting itself to the outside world, especially to its subjects, involved opulent displays of luxury. The innumerable and magnificent feasts, attended by eminent guests, created an ambience that exerted a powerful attraction upon the nobility of the various territories and, in turn, contributed to the cohesion of all the heterogeneous elements that made up the Burgundian state. This language of collective symbolism furnished a formidable medium for communication with subjects, a medium oriented toward the strengthening of ties between ruler and subjects. The dynasty utilized every possible occasion to display its splendor and at the same time accentuate mutual solidarity. Following the precedent set by French kings beginning in the fourteenth century, formal entries into cities were foremost among the occasions used by the dukes to transmit a political message by many forms of cultural expression.[15]

A tapestry and a colorful collection of illuminations were fabricated for the Joyous Entry of Philip the Fair into Louvain and his spouse, Juana's, entry into Brussels in 1496. A manuscript featuring a series of color pictures and a printed account in French, with illustrations of the Joyous Entry of Charles into Bruges in 1515, was produced for that occasion, and a rhetorician from Bruges composed a similar account in Dutch. A mourning cortege was organized in Brussels in 1516 for King Ferdinand of Aragon, grandfather of Prince Charles. One of the floats was designed by Jan Gossaert in Renaissance style, complete with naked putti, a classical warrior, trophies, and inscriptions. By such artistic magnificence, the city also projected a favorable image of itself.[16] Joyous Entries, weddings, banquets, and funerals, thus, were all occasions at which the rulers and their subjects were able to demonstrate something of a communal bond, cemented by a dynamic artistic and cultural expression.

Urban Centers of Cultural Production

In the fifteenth century, before the largely itinerant dukes had a fixed residence, various cities functioned as centers of artistic production. Tournai, for example, a small episcopal city and an important regional market, was the site of significant activity in tapestry weaving, calligraphy, and the production of paintings and miniatures. Louvain also had workshops for painting and for sculpture in wood, and it attracted the Haarlem painter Dirk Bouts, whose *Last Supper* still hangs in the collegiate church of St. Peter. Bruges was by far the most important artistic center, because there the stimulus of the frequent presence of the ducal court was added to that of the great trading metropolis. The urban centers were also the sites of considerable artistic innovation. In the 1420s and 1430s, Hubert and Jan van Eyck, as well as Roger van der Weyden, made radical innovations in the techniques of painting that were recognized in their own time as *ars nova*, "a new style." They combined a microscopic realism with rich coloring and a clear composition. The elaboration of what was still a primarily religious symbolism did not impede van der Weyden's expression of an extremely personal emotionalism.

The "new style" of these painters appealed to both the court and burghers, to foreign merchants, and to local clergy. The Florentine Tommaso Portinari, head of the Bruges branch of the Medici bank and a financier of Charles the Bold, was a typical example of this sort of patron. Around 1467 Hugo van der Goes painted the triptych *The Adoration of the Shepherds*, now in the Uffizi Museum in Florence, with Portinari's entire family and their patron saints portrayed on the side panels. Later, Portinari's own portrait was painted by Hans Memling. In 1467 another Florentine financier, Portinari's predecessor in Bruges and his later colleague in London, Angelo Tani, commissioned a triptych of *The Last Judgment*, also from Memling. *The Adoration of the Shepherds* had made such an impression on Florence that Tani intended to send the second triptych there as well, but, because of a trade dispute, the ship carrying *The Last Judgment* to Florence fell into the hands of a privateer in the service of Hanseatic merchants and went off to Danzig (now Gdansk). There, in spite of protests from the duke of Burgundy and the pope, it still hangs in Our Lady's Church. Wealthy Italian merchants and bankers, religious fraternities, and patrician families from Flanders were among the most avid consumers of artistic and artisanal products. Their patronage spread the art of the Low Countries all the way across Europe.[17]

And that art made a powerful impression, even in wealthy Florence, where Italian contemporaries had already introduced classical forms and begun to move pictorial art in a direction that appeared quite different from the art of the north. The Flemish painters of the fifteenth century still worked exclusively in Gothic style, a style that never developed a significant appeal in Italy. The northern style implied a clear, rather static apportionment of the surface, with the emphasis on vertical lines. The innovations of each succeeding generation brought more movement and dramatic expressiveness to the figures, which were clearly distinguished from the background. Around 1460, Petrus Christus was the first to introduce in Bruges perspective painting with sight lines converging to a single point.[18] Today, the close relationship between the painting of miniatures on parchment and of larger pictures on wooden panels has been increasingly acknowledged. This interaction can, perhaps, explain the contemporary fascination for detail. Every plant, every jewel, the least ripple on the surface of water, all were depicted with consummate precision and with a refined attention to the play of light. The effect of distance for background landscapes was achieved by the use of color values that ranged from brilliant tints in the foreground to vague, bluish hues in the background. This taste for detail also explains a predilection for secondary backgrounds using vistas viewed through an open window or an arcade, or even as a mirrored reflection. The northern painters' supreme technical mastery in oils lent a magnificent luster and depth to the bounteous creations of nature and of the human hand and spirit. Whereas Italy was still dominated by mural painting, the Flemish panels developed along totally different stylistic lines. Their material form varied from imposing triptychs, intended as altarpieces, to intimate portraits for the home, to miniatures worn in lockets. With this variety, the Netherlandish painters created a marvelous merchandise that proved marketable to a broad spectrum of the public all across Europe.

The dukes repeatedly offered commissions to artists who operated independent ateliers. This was the case for such painters as Rogier van der Weyden in Brussels, the miniaturists Simon Marmion at Valenciennes and Lieven van Lathem in Ghent, and the tapestry weavers Robert Dary at Tournai and Pieter van Aalst of Brussels. Jewelry and luxury textiles were also purchased from craftsmen and dealers in various cities.[19]

For the urban communities, the town halls had great symbolic value in addition to their evident utility. The façade of the Gothic town hall of Bruges (1376–1420) was decorated with statues of the counts and countesses of Flanders. In this way the city, an ancient and favored residence of the counts, expressed its connection to the prince as well as reiterating its claim to be the capital city of the dynasty's expanded territory.

Urban prestige was even more clearly at stake in the construction of the town halls of Brussels and Louvain, undeniably the high points of secular Brabantine Gothic architecture. In 1402, Brussels began construction of a façade embellished with no fewer than two hundred statues, among them those of the dukes and duchesses, all set in lavishly ornamented niches. Not only did Brussels surpass its model at Bruges in its show of loyalty to the rulers, but it clearly intended to thus proclaim its primacy as the leading city of Brabant. A broad balcony was constructed at the second-floor level, where the annually renewed city magistrature could be presented to the populace assembled on the great marketplace. At the same time, this balcony provided an ideal place from which the dukes could proclaim their Joyous Entry into Brabant, a blow aimed at the declining capital, Louvain, where this ceremony had traditionally taken place. Even today, Louvain still has a street named Blijde Inkomststraat. Work at Brussels was begun in 1444 upon the right wing and the tower, which was completed in 1454. Ninety-seven meters in height, the tower overlooked the unfinished towers of the Church of St. Gudula and the ducal palace of the Coudenberg, on a neighboring hilltop. Crowning the tower was a five-meter bronze statue of St. Michael, patron saint of Brussels, who thus visibly triumphed not only over the dragon, but also over the other towers of the city. Louvain understood the message and reacted promptly by beginning construction in 1447 on a new town hall, with yet more niches for statues of rulers and other worthies recommended by theologians at the University of Louvain, founded by papal charter in 1425 and the only university in the Low Countries until the establishment of Leiden, later in the sixteenth century.

Between 1480 and 1530, several other cities built town halls that complemented the profusion of Gothic ornamentation with elements already expressing the new architectural style of the Renaissance. Ghent carried out only in part and with the utmost difficulty its grandiose plan for the construction of what was to have been the greatest town hall of the Low Countries. Between 1482 and 1539–years signaling dramatic changes in the political regime – a flamboyant Gothic wing was added to the older aldermen's halls, under the direction of the Brabantine master builders Rombout and Laureins Keldermans and Domien de Waghemakere. The ground floor consisted of a spacious rectangular hall, where the Estates General later concluded the Pacification of Ghent, in 1576. The project included plans for a much larger building, finally begun in 1580 and constructed in Renaissance style. Oudenaarde (1526–36) and Middelburg in Zeeland completed more modest pearls of flamboyant civic architecture.

The care of souls was also a component of civic identity and responsibility. Each city in the Low Countries had one or more parochial churches, often a collegiate church housing a group of Canons Regular and, occasionally, a cathedral. There was no archbishopric in the Low Countries until the erection of Mechelen to that status in 1559, and the highest provincial authorities were thus the remote archbishops of Cologne, Trier, and Reims for various parts of the Low Countries. Except for Utrecht, the dioceses, and hence the cathedrals, of the Low Countries prior to the reorganization of the bishoprics in 1559 were all located in the francophone, southern periphery of the Burgundian Netherlands. The construction of churches — whether cathedral, parish, or collegiate — primarily a concern of the local community — was thus also a matter of civic pride. The peaks of Brabantine Gothic ecclesiastical architecture were attained by St. Peter's collegiate church in Louvain, St. Gudula at Brussels, St. John's at 's-Hertogenbosch, and countless larger and smaller churches both in Brabant and far beyond its borders. A single case must suffice: the Church of Our Lady at Antwerp, the largest in the Low Countries, built between 1352 and 1518.[20] Generations of master builders participated in its construction, among them members of the de Waghemakere and Keldermans families. Until 1477 all of Antwerp was included in a single parish; consequently, the church assumed immense proportions. It had five aisles and numerous chapels constructed for guilds and fraternities. All these organizations contributed financially to the construction of the church and used its chapels for their altars and religious services. Only one of the two planned towers was completed, and its height of 123 meters made it unique in the Low Countries. St. Rombout's Church at Mechelen, never entirely completed as planned, "only" reached 97 meters. Churches were, thus, by no means the least significant means by which urban communities expressed their self-image.

Artistic dynamism did not necessarily wax and wane with the general economy. When the economic status of Bruges began to decline after 1480, artistic activity in the city did not immediately cease. The painters' ateliers retained their reputation and their allure, and there were still plenty of wealthy patrons to be found. During the sixteenth century, several important masters, such as Pieter Pourbus, worked there. Nevertheless, the center of artistic activity slowly shifted to Antwerp in the wake of prosperity. In 1515–16, Gerard David moved to Antwerp.[21] Although artistic vitality did not precisely follow the economy, painters too were inclined to adapt to new and more favorable circumstances. Materialistic opportunism was certainly not unknown to these artists.

Nor did all of the arts necessarily follow the court. From about 1490 until 1530, Mechelen, stimulated by the presence of the court of Philip the Fair and Margaret of Austria, played a leading role in artistic production. When the capital was transferred to Brussels after Margaret's death in 1530, the principal production center of many art forms shifted accordingly, particularly for those arts most closely associated with court life—metalwork, stained glass, tapestry, and music. The illuminated manuscript experienced a brief resurgence at Ghent and Bruges, but by 1530 this form was finally superseded by the arts of printing and engraving, which had a great future in the Low Countries.[22]

The greatest artistic activity of the second flowering, however, was reserved for Antwerp. There was an enormous increase in the production of paintings, for example. Nearly three hundred new members applied for admission to the painters' guild of St. Luke between 1500 and 1520, virtually the same number as had applied in the entire preceding half-century. Evidently there was also a correspondingly sharp increase in the number of paintings sold. This growing supply led to the further development of a market for objects of art. Artistic production was stimulated by the assurance of a public eager to purchase works of art that were modest in both dimension and price, and these were produced in series, freeing painters from the necessity of producing only individually commissioned works. The client became more typically a bourgeois, often with international and business interests, which was not surprising in a commercial metropolis.[23]

Chief among the artistic merchandise exported on a large scale were the retables produced in Brabant and more especially in Antwerp. These were polychromed or gilded altarpieces, with figurines carved in wood. Brabantine sculpture in wood also met with success in the production of smaller, individual statuettes and groups of figures.[24] This was also true of Brussels tapestries, entire series of which were ordered by all of the royal courts of Europe. Dirk Vellert, a stained-glass painter from Antwerp, received a commission to provide stained-glass windows for King's College Chapel at Cambridge. Of the countless other specialties that had flourished in the Flemish and Brabantine cities during the fifteenth century, two more should be noted: organ building and bell casting, the latter primarily at Mechelen. The oldest mention of a carillon with a keyboard is that from the town hall at Oudenaarde in 1510, and in the years following, a keen rivalry between the cities of this region developed.

Ecclesiastical Organization and Devotional Life in the Low Countries

The hierarchy of the late medieval Church was closely linked to temporal power. Like the kings of France, the dukes of Burgundy tried to control the appointment to high ecclesiastical offices in their domains. Direct manipulation of the chapters of canons who were the electors of bishops and lobbying the popes led to the appointment of ducal favorites to episcopal sees. Thus Philip the Good could — in exchange for 12,000 ducats — have one of his father's natural sons appointed to the bishopric of Cambrai in 1439. In 1441 he was able to establish his own right of nomination, in a concordat with the pope. In this way, he appointed his own illegitimate son, David, first to the bishopric of Therouanne, and in 1456 to that of Utrecht. In 1517 the bishopric of Utrecht was given to another, much younger, illegitimate son of the same duke; this son, also called Philip of Burgundy, had previously held the office of admiral — a title that surely indicates the extent of his spiritual motivation.

Most of these political creatures also held high office in the service of the duke. The ducal chancellor, Jean Canard, was elevated to the prestigious position of bishop of Cambrai in 1391 and dean of the Chapter of St. Donatian in Bruges in 1397. From 1410 to 1483, all the successive bishops of Tournai filled the office of chairman of the ducal council, the second-highest state office after that of chancellor. Abbots of distinguished and wealthy monasteries were also chosen through the duke's intervention; Philip the Good's own illegitimate son, Raphael de Mercatel, for example, was appointed abbot of St. Bavo's monastery in Ghent. In 1515 the pope confirmed that he would not appoint any abbot without the approval of the young Prince Charles. In this way the ruler managed to give his favored servants the extra reward of church revenues, and at the same time he could, through them, bring his influence to bear on yet other appointments. Hundreds of lower ecclesiastical functions (including the appropriate prebends that accompanied them) could, thus, be given to the duke's supporters. The ecclesiastical hierarchy evolved to become an extension of the machinery of state, and its primary religious functions faded into the background.

Studies of devotional history indicate that during the fourteenth and fifteenth centuries, the ordinary faithful began to play a more religiously active role than they had earlier. The preaching of the Franciscans and Dominicans, specialized religious orders with explicitly pastoral functions, certainly contributed to this. The vernacular languages were increasingly in evidence in devotional expression, as was the outward display of faith in the form of processions and pilgrimages and in the extremely emotional and concrete veneration of particular saints. The towns saw the formation of many confraternities in which men and women devoted themselves to the veneration of a particular saint. In Ghent alone there were thirty-seven of these confraternities in 1500.[25] They furnished an altar or even an entire chapel in a church, sometimes embellishing them with a carved or painted altarpiece, often by the greatest sculptors and painters of the Low Countries. In this way they could express their specific devotions to, for example, the Sacred Blood, the Sacred Heart, St. Anne, or St. Joseph. The Bruges painter Hans Memling decorated the great shrine of St. Ursula, today in Bruges, and he painted the *Mystical Marriage of St. Catherine of Alexandria* for the Hospital of St. John, using Margaret of York and Mary of Burgundy as models for Saints Catherine and Barbara.

Marian devotion in diverse forms also gained ground. In 1470 the pope recognized the prayer cycle for the Rosary, for which brotherhoods were established in Douai and Cologne and very soon elsewhere, in part because of the prospect of a special indulgence. Devotion to the Seven Sorrows of Mary by a special brotherhood was permitted in 1495. Papal indulgences were also sold on a wide scale, originally as a result of the Holy Year first declared in 1300. Because of its success, other Holy Years were proclaimed with increasing frequency — in 1475 and again in 1500. After 1400, the faithful did not have to go to Rome in order to derive the spiritual benefits of the Holy Year, since indulgences could also be bought in Mechelen. Here the Church was clearly responding to the concern for divine clemency, but it also helped to further the formalization and, superficiality of the devotion. By creating the impression that grace and ecclesiastical office were for sale, churchmen, already the creatures of political powers, lost much of their spiritual authority.

Monastic life was subjected to fierce criticism, that of Erasmus being the most famous but by no means the only one. In Erasmus's *Praise of Folly* of 1509, the satirist devoted the fifty-fourth paragraph to the foolishness and rudeness of monks and other religious: "As if it weren't enough to be called Christians. Most of them rely so much on their ceremonies and petty man-made traditions that they suppose heaven alone will hardly be enough to reward merit such as theirs. They never think of the time to come when Christ will scorn all this and enforce his own rule, that of charity."[26]

The relaxation of monastic discipline inspired few potential donors to make benefactions to the older cloisters, which had grown into immensely wealthy foundations with an extravagant lifestyle. Only the strict Carthusians and the newly formed order of the Clares still fulfilled the ideal of purity within the framework of the religious life. For this reason, both these orders attracted the special attention and patronage of the Burgundian court. Partly under the influence of the movement known as the Modern Devotion, there was nevertheless a tendency for traditional monastic communities to adhere more strictly to their rule and to expel unworthy monks. The dowager duchess Margaret of York, together with Henry of Bergen, bishop of Cambrai and an early patron of Erasmus, did her best to bring about this sort of reform in the monasteries of her domains. But this wave of reform did little to put an end to the decreasing influence of the older religious houses.

From the thirteenth century, and starting in the diocese of Liège, the Beguine movement grew rapidly. Women who did not want to bind themselves to the strict monastic vows of poverty, chastity, and obedience but wished to live in a religious community, some of whose members produced a vibrant and profound religious literature, were viewed initially with suspicion by ecclesiastical authorities. At the end of the fourteenth century, the movement found further expression in the wake of the Modern Devotion. In 1374 one of the initiators of this women's movement, Geert Groote (who died in 1384), placed his parental house in Deventer at the disposal of poor, single women who aspired to a spiritual life and supported themselves with the proceeds of their own handiwork, usually spinning and weaving. Little by little, the initiative developed into larger communities of women and spread so quickly that in 1419, there were already 150 sisters and brothers "Of the Common Life" in various towns, the men supporting themselves chiefly by copying manuscripts.

By the beginning of the sixteenth century, there were probably 10,000 religious women within the borders of the present-day Netherlands, of whom 8,000 were in some way followers of the Modern Devotion.[27] Besides the sisters of the Common Life, there were also communities that lived in accordance with the Third Rule of St. Francis—Franciscan Tertiaries—and others who proceeded to cloister themselves under the rule of St. Augustine. The congregation formed in 1395 at the Windesheim cloister in Zwolle, which by 1500 comprised one hundred establishments of Canons Regular, counted no more than thirteen cloisters for women. It also included the seven cloisters grouped in the Groenendaal chapter, of which Jan van Ruusbroec (1293–1381), one of the greatest of the Brabant mystics, had been prior.[28] Ruusbroec had been a great inspiration to Geert Groote.

The Modern Devotion aspired to a sober, inner religious experience, in contrast to the secularization and formalism of the Church and the irregularities of the monasteries. To this end its followers made use of devotional works in the vernacular, so that devout reading matter could be widely disseminated to both religious and lay people.[29] One of its most influential works was the *Imitation of Christ*, written by Thomas à Kempis (1380–1471), one of the most widely read devotional works in the history of Christianity. The movement constituted a powerful countercurrent to the external and often excessively materialistic display of the Church. In its outlook and methods, the Modern Devotion looked beyond even the message of the religious reformers of the sixteenth century to the movement of internalizing religion that developed in the modern world. But the ample response that met the sixteenth-century reformers so quickly and enthusiastically in the large towns of the Low Countries cannot be separated from the devotional trailblazing of the followers of the Modern Devotion.

Court Culture and the Capital at Mechelen

Until about 1530, the regent's court remained the most dynamic force for cultural activity; it took the greatest initiative and was usually the first to introduce innovations. The clearest indication of the court's progressive patronage was its reception of humanism and Renaissance style. A renewed interest in classical authors and ancient history was already apparent in the choice of literature for Duke Philip the Fair's library and in the subjects he had depicted on his tapestries. The court stimulated the importation of Renaissance forms from Italy, where the trend had been under way since the fourteenth century. The painter Jan Gossaert (1478–1532) traveled to Rome with Philip of Burgundy, the illegitimate son of Duke Philip the Good, admiral of Burgundy and later bishop of Utrecht, and steeped himself in ancient culture. About the same time, Quentin Metsijs from Antwerp was deeply influenced by the art of Leonardo da Vinci. With such extensive exposure to international influences, beginning in 1530 the metropolis began to overtake the court.

Architecture, however, had never been the chief investment of the Burgundian dukes. Because they did not retain a permanent residence, traveling continually through the various lands they held, the dukes were among the last itinerant rulers of Europe. As their territories accumulated, it became even more necessary for the dukes to show themselves regularly in each region in order to exercise their authority. Although the dukes possessed castles in such cities as Dijon, Bruges, Ghent, Lille, Arras, Hesdin, and Brussels, it was not until around the middle of the fifteenth century that Philip the Good decided to renovate the palace on the Coudenberg in Brussels and enhance its splendor. But his successor, Charles the Bold, decided to establish the central institutions of his government at Mechelen.

Mechelen remained the official residence of the governors-general until 1530, and in the reorganization of the Church in the Low Countries in 1559, Mechelen became the seat of the first archbishopric. Several fascinating structures have survived from this period, built in a style combining the early Renaissance with flamboyant Gothic. Margaret of Austria's palace and the hall of the Great Council of Mechelen are the most notable. Margaret also built outside of her capital. Between 1513 and 1532, Louis of Bodeghem was commissioned by Margaret of Austria to construct a memorial cloister at Brou (near Bourg-en-Bresse and Mâcon) for her prematurely deceased husband, Philibert of Savoy, his mother, and herself. This exceptionally homogeneous church and its monuments represent a bridge between the *gisants* of Champmol and the funeral churches in pure Renaissance style typical of the ensuing decades. This mausoleum might be considered the high point of an infinitely varied architectural style, ironically located back in the original territories of the dukes of Burgundy.

Because the Burgundian court initially had no fixed residence, its image was not reflected in any single building, but in a varied assortment of buildings of different dates and sites. The court itself, however, was an institution with a solid, permanent structure. From the perspective of investment in the arts, the ducal chapel occupied the leading place, with its group of musicians whose duty it was to embellish the daily religious services as well as the great feasts and such dynastic occasions as weddings, christenings, funerals, victories, peace treaties, and memorial services. By around 1500, this court chapel consisted of the *petite chapelle*, of some ten choirboys, and a *grande chapelle*, with from twenty-three to twenty-eight singers, twelve wind players, an organist, and a tambourine player. Dozens of singers and composers of international reputation spent at least some part of their careers in the service of the ducal court during these decades. The best known among them were Guillaume Dufay, Gilles Binchois, Josquin des Prés, Jacob Obrecht, Heindric Isaac, Adriaan Willaert, and others, whose professional reputations brought them to other European courts as well. Antoine Busnois was choirmaster under Charles the Bold, and Pierre de la Rue under Philip the Fair. The so-called Flemish polyphonists (many of whom were of Walloon origin) revitalized European music by their more harmonious use of the various melodic lines for voices and supporting instruments, by increasing emotional expressiveness, and by granting added unity to the successive parts of a large choral work—like a mass—through the repetition of certain passages.[30]

Many musical manuscripts were produced in careful calligraphy during the reigns of Philip the Fair and Margaret of Austria, as a byproduct of the court's musical interests. No fewer than fifty such works have survived, many of them luxuriously executed, some on black parchment with silver musical notation, others playfully illuminated by such artists as Petrus Alamire.[31]

The regent's court of Margaret of Austria at Mechelen (1507–30) became under her influence a progressive center of artistic patronage where the Italian-inspired Renaissance made its earliest appearance in the Low Countries. In addition to Jan Mostaert from Haarlem, Margaret also had in her service the Venetian painter Iacopo de Barbari and the sculptor Conrad Meit from Worms, who established himself at Mechelen in 1512. In 1517, through the intermediary of her contacts abroad, Margaret arranged for the Brussels tapestry weaver Pieter van Aalst to execute Raphael's cartoons (presently in the Victoria and Albert Museum in London) for the series of ten tapestries depicting scenes from the *Acts of the Apostles*, commissioned by Pope Leo X. Bernard of Orley entered Margaret's service in 1518 as court painter and designer of such tapestries as *Maximilian's Hunting Parties* (now in the Louvre, Paris).[32] Following the example set by the rulers, members of their family and councillors also regularly employed artists. Both the painter Jan Gossaert and the sculptor Conrad Meit were active in the service of Philip of Burgundy, the admiral and later bishop of Utrecht. After Philip's death, Gossaert worked for several other noble patrons.

The members of the Great Council of Mechelen imitated the artistic patronage of their rulers. The Busleyden family of Mechelen welcomed many humanist scholars, including Erasmus, to their home. Erasmus himself illustrates the level of academic culture that could be achieved in the Low Countries during the last quarter of the fifteenth century. Born in the small city of Rotterdam in 1466, he attended the school at Deventer that had been established by the Brothers of the Common Life, took the vows of an Augustinian canon in 1488, and was ordained a priest in 1492 by the bishop of Utrecht. Traveling through the Low Countries and France in the service of Henry van Bergen, bishop of Cambrai, Erasmus became the greatest classical scholar of his age. As titular councillor of Prince Charles,

Erasmus wrote his treatise *On the Education of a Christian Prince* in 1515, and in 1517 he wrote the *Complaint of Peace, Who is Scorned by All Nations*. In 1518, Jerome Busleyden founded the College of the Three Languages (Collegium Trilingue) at Louvain, with Erasmus at its head. But Erasmus withdrew from court life after several years' participation in 1521. His passionate pleas for peace no longer heeded, he became again a private scholar.[33] Erasmus was the most learned scholar of his age, but he was not the only one in the Low Countries. Margaret of Austria appointed Adriaan van Boyens of Utrecht as tutor to the young Charles. Van Boyens served the prince and king-emperor as both tutor and minister, and he was elected pope in 1522, taking the name Adrian VI (1522–23), the only pope ever to come from the Low Countries.

Charles V and the "Low Countries by the Sea," 1506–1530

Charles, count of Luxemburg — and later duke of Burgundy, king of Castile and Aragon, and emperor — was born at the Prinsenhof in Ghent in February 1500. Six years old when his father died in 1506, he was raised at Mechelen chiefly by Margaret of Austria, Guillaume de Croy, seigneur of Chièvres, and Adriaan of Utrecht, under the regency of his grandfather Maximilian and then under that of his aunt Margaret and Chièvres. Named after his great-grandfather Charles the Bold, Charles (in 1519 elected emperor as Charles V) marks the transition of the Burgundian Netherlands from the central part of the dynastic complex to the periphery of a continental and eventually worldwide empire. History inclines to identify Charles V with that later empire, with Spain, Italy, Austria, and the new worlds, but it must also remember that he was born in Ghent and was first of all the "natural prince" of the lands that by 1500 were coming to be called collectively, thanks in part to the work of the Valois and then the Valois-Habsburg dynasty of Burgundy, the "Low Countries by the Sea," although the southern parts were still termed *Fiandria* and Flanders until well into the seventeenth century. Charles's childhood and the fifteen years after his coming of age in 1515 mark the end of the Burgundian Netherlands and a new period in the history of the Low Countries.

At the death of Philip the Fair in 1506, the council of the rulers of Burgundy was divided into pro-French and pro-English groups, but its leaders and the staffs of the main divisions of government were retained, allowing for a relatively smooth transition in governance. Maximilian made only two visits to the Low Countries during Charles's minority, in 1508–9 and again in 1513. The work of keeping the provinces together and satisfying the demands for peace from the Estates General fell to Margaret of Austria. Although Louis XII of France (1498–1515) attempted to regain control of several territories and interfered in the affairs of Guelders, Liège, and Friesland, the regent and the cooperation of the Privy Council and the Estates General preserved the integrity of the Burgundian inheritance. The Peace of Cambrai in 1508 successfully averted the main French threat, and Charles was declared legally of age at Brussels in January 1515.

Charles's majority marked a resurgence of Burgundian government and style, chiefly under the influence of Chièvres. Jean le Sauvage was created chancellor of Burgundy, and representatives from the Low Countries filled the ducal councils. In 1515 Charles commenced a tour of his entire realm, beginning in Holland and Zeeland and moving through five of the six great cities of the counties. Upon the death of his grandfather Ferdinand of Aragon in 1516, Charles was proclaimed king of Spain in Brussels. Ties between Spain and the Netherlands had developed readily since the late fifteenth century, and at the chapter meeting of the Order of the Golden Fleece in 1516, ten places were even reserved for Spanish nobles. Charles departed for Spain in 1517, and Margaret of Austria once again became governor-general of the Low Countries. In 1518 Charles convened a chapter of the Order of the Golden Fleece in Barcelona, where the stalls of the choir in the cathedral still display the arms of the knights who attended. Charles returned to the Low Countries in 1520, and on the way to his coronation at Aachen, he reminded his subjects in the Low Countries that in spite of the Spanish and imperial crowns, "his heart had always been in these lands over here," echoing the old Burgundian ducal phrase for the Low Countries. And his subjects had no reason to disbelieve him.

Under Charles and Margaret, the central governmental institutions were restored to working order with far greater ease than they had been created by Charles the Bold. Charles was universally recognized as the common and natural ruler of the Low Countries, operating a state that possessed the unusual features of a monarchic constitution ruling over a federal structure, a federative union on a supraregional scale. Each of the principalities retained its own identity and institutions, but all took increasing pride in their common culture and administrative organization, including the Order of the Golden Fleece, which became something of a symbol of their political unity. The nobility was turned into a nobility of service, dependent on the prince and devoted to administrative and diplomatic work. By the middle of the sixteenth century, the nobility considered itself the natural spokesmen of the Low Countries, defenders of its interests, and servants of its prince. After the last revolt in Ghent in 1537–39, the towns were tamed and their former role was taken over by the nobles.

Charles, Margaret, and Chièvres also paid considerable attention to local sentiments and to senses of local rights and privileges. Whenever he could, Charles appointed local officials, even in the area of water control. This attention and sensitivity to local identity gave a much more peaceable texture to the centralizing process, which proceeded apace at the same time as Charles was able, finally, to round out the Burgundian state in the Low Countries. By the Treaty of Cambrai of 1529, Margaret and Charles permanently secured the detachment of the counties of Flanders and Artois from France. By the Treaty of Venlo of 1543, Charles finally gained control over Guelders and Zutphen, the last territories to be included in what now became labeled as the Seventeen Provinces.

At the death of Maximilian in 1519, Charles, supported by the immense loans of 543,000 florins from the Fugger family of Augsburg, purchased election as emperor of the Romans. In 1520 he was crowned emperor at Aachen, and in 1530 formally by the pope at Bologna, the last emperor of the Romans to be crowned by a pope. His Burgundian subjects took pride in this election too, and they displayed their pride by subscribing considerable sums for the coronation expenses. As part of his reorganization of the empire in 1548, Charles formally designated the seventeen Low Countries provinces he now ruled as the *Bourgondische Kreits*, "Burgundian Circle," a self-contained part of the empire. By 1559, the Burgundian Circle acquired its first archbishop at Mechelen. At last—and only briefly—a Burgundian state had come into existence in fact, although it had been in the process of formation since the early fifteenth century. And its ruler had at last acquired a crown, although it was the crown of Spain and not that of Burgundy, Frisia, or Lorraine for which his ancestors had unsuccessfully negotiated. He also became emperor, as his great-grandfather Charles the Bold had once dreamed of making himself.

Mechelen to Brussels: 1530

The Burgundian state was indeed governed, but its component territories were not passive, and it had never been governed easily. The regency of

Margaret of Austria and the early years of the reign of Charles V scaled down both the ruler's ambitions and the tendency toward resistance on the part of his various domains. Unity was easier to achieve when the rulers exploited the "natural" character of their rule over their different subjects and the mystique of their persons, supported by broad networks of patronage and a willingness to negotiate with their subjects in representative bodies. The territories, in their turn, jealous of their own privileges and of each other, nevertheless worked into the habit of regarding each other as parts of a single complex, a habit encouraged by the ruling dynasty. And their loyalty to the dynasty was remarkable, most dramatically in the crucial year 1477, but also in 1506 and 1515. The regency of Margaret of Austria succeeded not only because of the regent's own skill and the pro-Burgundian policies of Chièvres, but also because she governed in the name of a prince whom all the territories gladly accepted.

But Charles V was also a prince with more than one kingdom. His father had died too soon, after going to Spain in 1505, for the Burgundian state to concern itself with competition from Castile and Aragon for its ruler's attention. And from 1507 until 1530, Charles V was effectively represented in the Low Countries by his aunt Margaret of Austria, with only a brief interval in 1515 to 1517. After Margaret's death in 1530, however, it became clear that Charles's rule was based in Spain, rather than in Mechelen or Brussels. He spent only fifty-five months in the Low Countries between 1517 and his final retirement in 1555, usually in blocks of a year or two — for example, from June 1520 to May 1522 (the coronation journeys), January 1531 to January 1532, and September 1548 to May 1550. In the ruler's absence, the Low Countries were governed by the regent, now Charles's sister Mary of Hungary, and a Privy Council, a Council of State, a Council of Finance, the Great Council (which had been reestablished as the high court at Mechelen in 1504), and noble stadtholders, as well as the Estates General and the regional Estates.[34] The Estates General became more able to speak for the provinces as an ensemble, more confident in their ability to deal with the problems of governance, and more efficient in their administrative machinery. These features gave the Burgundian state a very high credit rating when it needed to borrow.

But Spain occupied more and more of Charles's time and his mind, as did the renewed conflict with France, which saw itself surrounded by a personal empire that extended from Spain to the Low Countries, included much of Italy and Sicily, and held extensive territories in Germany. The traditionally pro-French policy of Charles's Burgundian advisers ended with the death of Chièvres in 1521 and the increasing influence of Charles's Savoyard chancellor Mercurino de Gattinara. Gattinara's influence was particularly strong amid the increasing friction between Charles and Francis I of France over the control of the Mediterranean, particularly the kingdom of Naples and the entire Italian peninsula. In 1525, the armies of Charles V crushed the French army at the battle of Pavia, leading Francis I away as a prisoner. From this point on, the problems of Spanish administration and the Turkish threat in the Mediterranean, as well as the administration of the Spanish territories in the Americas, increasingly made Spain the focus of Charles's attention. The regencies of Margaret of Austria and Charles's sister Mary of Hungary (1531–55), under whom the center of government moved from Mechelen to Brussels, somewhat made up for the ruler's absence and lack of attention to the Low Countries. But Charles did not raise his own son, Philip II, in the Low Countries, and when Philip himself became the ruler, in 1555, he could neither speak nor understand French and Dutch. Philip's authoritarian background did little to make him more than formally acceptable to his northern European subjects.

Finally, the great religious revolution that broke out in 1517, and resulted in both the Protestant and Catholic Reformations, preoccupied Charles increasingly from 1521 on. This revolution increased his deficits and his wars and shaped the rest of his imperial and royal rule. With new religious divisions added to the existing social divisions, internally in the Low Countries it became less and less easy to maintain the cherished *stadsvrede*, the "urban peace" that had characterized Burgundian and Habsburg rule until 1530.

9

The Burgundian Legacy

The cycle that had led from monarchical wars through heavy taxation and authoritarian rule to economic ruin was repeated later in the sixteenth century. From 1520 to 1559, the Habsburg empire and France were at war with each other practically without interruption, so that both empires were weakened and their peoples and resources exhausted. The counterbalance to ducal power that was repeatedly found in the Burgundian period in urban ambitions for self-government had, in the meantime, in the framework of the Estates General, grown into a federative union on a supraregional scale. The authoritarian government of Philip II later broke down in the face of this resistance, as had happened earlier with the governments of Charles the Bold and Maximilian.

The Order of the Golden Fleece is today an antique ornament whose insignia adorn the ruling houses of Europe. Philip II was its last master. The Low Countries took little notice of the loss of their dynasty's ancestral land, the duchy of Burgundy, which the French acquired definitively in 1477. But its ruler did. In 1548, when Emperor Charles V drew up a settlement to offer the Low Countries in their entirety a place within the empire, he called the region the "Burgundian Circle."

From a territorial point of view, with his conquest of Guelders in 1543, Charles V formed a link with the military takeover of that duchy by his great-grandfather, Charles the Bold, in 1473. In the intervening seventy years, Guelders had been a destabilizing factor, whence military expeditions into Holland and Brabant were repeatedly undertaken. On the other hand, it was understood that the dukes of Guelders felt threatened by the superior strength of the surrounding Habsburgs, and for this reason, they sought support from the Habsburgs' great rival, the king of France. The definitive annexation of Guelders by the Low Countries thus cost a great deal of time and effort and shows that such association could by no means be taken for granted.[1]

For generations, the dukes of Guelders had striven to be a counterweight to their aggressive neighbors by entering into alliances with the lower Rhine principalities of Jülich and Cleves. By cutting these lines of support and absorbing Guelders but not going any farther east, Charles established a lasting border in what until then had been an ill-defined frontier region. Guelders itself consisted of areas with little mutual cohesion, into which the union with its western neighbors was gradually to bring more structure. In 1581, Guelders and Overijssel refused to side with those provinces that had repudiated their oath of loyalty to Philip II and declared him forfeit of his principalities, accepting the duke of Anjou as their new prince. This attitude did not so much indicate a stronger loyalty to the Habsburg dynasty as it did the width of the gap between the coastal provinces and the interior.

The initiators of the 1581 "Act of Secession" were, after all, the Estates of Flanders, Brabant, Holland and Zeeland, provinces that traditionally had had the largest population, biggest cities, and strongest commercial and industrial development. Sixty percent of the people lived in these four provinces, and all the major towns were situated there. Together, in 1548 they raised 80 percent of the central taxes of the Seventeen Provinces; in 1543–45, Antwerp alone was responsible for more than three-quarters of all exports. This new metropolis was able to grow far larger than its predecessor, Bruges, because of the growth of the world economy in general; its hinterland now even stretched to other continents. After Paris, Antwerp was the first city in transalpine Europe with more than one hundred thousand inhabitants; by about 1560, Amsterdam had grown to thirty thousand but was still smaller than both Ghent and Brussels. Antwerp's leading position and the expansion of Amsterdam brought about changes in their mutual relations. Just as in the fifteenth century Antwerp had grown because it complemented dominant Bruges, so from 1530 onward Amsterdam developed, thanks in part to capital from Antwerp, into the largest grain market of Europe. During the sixteenth century the coastal provinces maintained an overwhelming position of superiority, both in the Low Countries and in the entire European economic system. Their power was in the towns: they refused to be governed from Spain, especially since the Reformation found its strongest support in their populations.

The economic weight of the towns and regions found its political expression in the assemblies of the provincial Estates and the Estates General. The four capitals of Brabant (Louvain, Brussels, Antwerp, 's-Hertogenbosch) and the Four Members of Flanders (Ghent, Bruges, Ypres, and the Franc of Bruges) not only had the most authority in the Estates General: at their own initiative, they very frequently held separate meetings at which they informally made decisions for their entire province. They were able to do this because their joint share of the provincial taxes was decisive, and the smaller towns and rural areas were largely dependent on them. Similarly, in Holland the nobility played a very limited part, and the monasteries played none at all. The self-interest of the civic town governments was often in conflict with the ruler's efforts to rationalize the machinery of state. They kept the raising and sharing of taxes as far as possible in their own hands, in order to safeguard their foreign trade and to preserve their own wealth. Holland was successful in refusing to place its fleet — the largest in the Low Countries — under the command of the admiral or to levy a tax on grain exports.[2] Since the thirteenth century, these provinces had developed a system of decision making in representative assemblies that sought consensus on the basis of mandates given by the local administrative bodies. This institution was deeply rooted in their political culture, and in the early modern period, the assemblies seemed to be a most suitable and flexible instrument for looking after the political and commercial interests of the trading middle class. Thanks to their centuries-old traditions, the assemblies of cities and the Estates appeared to be the obvious mouthpiece of the opposition to a state whose pressure was felt to be excessive.

From the time of the first dukes of Burgundy, state power exhibited an entirely logical and consequential effort to strengthen central government. As the number of principalities falling under the same dynastic authority grew, rulers felt the increasingly pressing need for this centralized government, but the possibilities of resistance to it also grew. After all, each town, each province had its own system of rights, privileges, and customs and insisted on preserving its autonomy. The rulers' attempts at centralization took place in the areas of finance, administration of justice, local government, and legislation. Since they had come to power, the Burgundians had established Chambers of Accounts (*Chambres des Comptes, Rekenkamers*) in their most important provinces that inspected the accounts of the civil servants and the taxes that cities and towns were required to levy. In 1473, Charles the Bold attempted to bring these provincial Chambers of Accounts, in their turn, under the control of a central Chamber in Mechelen. The Estates General abolished this institution in 1477, but another attempt was made later. A separate Council of Finance reappeared in different guises after 1496, and in 1531, it became a definite government organ under the governor-general Mary of Hungary.[3]

The organization of the higher levels of the administration of justice paralleled that of state finances. When they came to power, the Burgundians installed regional courts (*Chambres du Conseil, Raadkamers*) in Flanders, Brabant, and Holland; after the 1440s, a separate section of the ducal Great Council (*Great Conseil, Grote Raad*) gradually became the central supreme court. Charles the Bold reformed this in 1473 into the Parlement at Mechelen, which disappeared in 1477 under the pressure of the Estates General. But it reappeared before long, under the name Great Council, formally established in Mechelen in 1504. The importance to litigants of impartial and expert administration of justice explains the growing success of this central institution. The number of arrests made grew from an annual average of 40 to 170 between 1500 and 1550.[4]

Centralization, however, proved to be a more difficult matter where government and legislation were concerned. Local governments and autochthonous nobles who had traditionally belonged to the household and council of the sovereign were not prepared to give up their powers and voices. They strongly resisted all governmental efforts to remove tax levies from the negotiations of the Estates' assemblies by having the levy automatically expressed as a percentage on certain transactions. In 1542, the Estates agreed to finance the conquest of Guelders and the war against France with a short-lived tax of 10 percent on the income from property and trading profits. The tax was removed in 1545, but a tax of 1 percent on exports remained until 1554.[5] After that there was a return to the old system of tax demands for a certain length of time. In 1571, despite resistance from the Estates General, the duke of Alva as governor-general forced through the introduction of a tax of 1 percent on capital and 10 percent on trade. He thus reduced the taxation of property from 10 percent, as it had been in 1542, to only 1 percent. These levies were abolished within a year, also because of vehement opposition from the people. Later, in the Republic of the Seven United Provinces, the tax system continued to remain a matter for the towns and individual provinces.

The initiative launched by the government in 1531 to codify the rights of cities and boroughs and thus to lead them to accept a more centralist view of the law also encountered direct opposition from local authorities. In 1579, the Secret Council (*Conseil Privé, Geheime Raad*), the highest governmental organ under the governor-general, had been able to ratify the privileges of only about twenty places and bring them into law. Central legislation remained very limited until the end of the eighteenth century. Only in the area of criminal law could the governor-general enact a coherent system of laws in 1570, under the name *Criminele Ordonnantiën*.

Out of the state's administration of criminal justice came the famous ordinances or proclamations (*placards, plakaaten*) that Charles V and Philip II issued in order to suppress the "heresy" that led the way to the various movements for religious reformation. This gave a very concrete twist to the old connection between Church and state. In implementing the decisions of the Council of Trent, Charles V also paved the way for a reorganization of the bishoprics in the Low Countries, which was eventually proclaimed in 1559. The existing structure dated from the early Middle Ages and no longer had any bearing on demographic reality. Utrecht was the only episcopal see in the region where Dutch was spoken. The Counter-Reformation Church had a tighter organizational structure in mind, and the emperor wanted church administrative borders to coincide with those of the state. The interrelation between Church and state was personified in the newly appointed archbishop of Mechelen, cardinal Granvelle, who was also the most senior state councillor in the Low Countries. Because of his direct link to the king, he was outside — and actually above — the Council of State, the official governmental body to which the important, autochthonous nobles belonged. On the grounds of tradition and the Brabantine Joyous Entry, which reserved the government in the duchy for autochthonous officials, there was resentment at the choice of Granvelle, who came from the Franche-Comté. At his instigation, heretics were dealt with harshly. Between 1521 and 1550, the Inquisition condemned an average of thirteen people a year to the stake. That number rose to sixty in the period 1551–60, and to 264 in 1561–64.

It has been ascertained that Calvinism, especially, enjoyed a marked growth in the cities of the southern Low Countries. A survey made in Antwerp in 1583 showed that one-third of the people said they were followers of Protestantism in some shape or form, while no more than one-third referred to themselves as convinced Catholics; the other third had no view. Calvinist preachers and writers from Huguenot France settled in the towns of Tournai, Valenciennes, Lille, and, shortly afterward, Ghent and Antwerp.[6] Half of the wage earners adopted the "new religion," which also found wide support among prosperous burghers and a part of the lower nobility. Religious freedom became the central issue between the government in Madrid and the elites in the Low Countries. Protestants were certainly not revolutionaries, but the stubborn imposition of Catholicism, which Philip II continued to pursue by every means available, drove them into the camp of those who were opposed to the power of government as such.

In this way, the religious chasm became the all-embracing theme that united a diversity of sources of revolt, varying from dissatisfaction with the economic depression and the crushing tax burden to frustration over the violation and restriction of political rights to real religious motives. The repressive measures that Church and state together took against the Protestants mobilized a broad resistance movement that found its largest support in the large towns and surrounding areas. As the state increased the level of repression with the introduction of a large foreign military force, it drove even the moderates into the arms of rebellion.

During the 1570s, four groups of provinces could be distinguished in the Seventeen Provinces. The first four—Flanders, Brabant, Holland, and Zeeland—formed the nucleus. They were the most populous, urbanized, commercialized, industrialized, open and modern society, where Protestantism could, therefore, find its greatest response. There also the tradition of political autonomy was strongest, the greatest number of Protestants could be found, and the rebellion grew. In 1581, this resulted in the refusal to recognize Philip II as ruler any longer. Artois and Hainault formed the second group of provinces; under the hegemony of nobles and clerics, they chose the side of the king. Third were the recently conquered provinces of Guelders, Overijssel, and Groningen, which continued to adopt an independent attitude. Protestantism had as yet hardly reached them, but the violence of the rebellion aroused more resistance than sympathy. Finally, Namur and Luxemburg were scarcely touched by all these upheavals and remained traditionally feudal and Catholic. Eventually they were lastingly torn apart by military demarcation lines in a north-south division, and the centuries-old socioeconomic relationships were shattered. That was the reason why some two hundred thousand people—11 percent of the south's population—left the southern Low Countries when their land once again came under Spanish rule. Most of them moved to the liberated north, with which they apparently felt most affinity and where they made a substantial contribution to a new "Golden Age." But in the Republic as well as in the Spanish Netherlands, the basic patterns of the Burgundian period remained evident for a long time.

* * *

The essence of the Burgundian period had been the forced interaction between princely power and the urban elites. At stake was the wealthiest segment of northern Europe and a dynamic culture. The princes tried to weave their spell in order to draw in the elites, which resisted just enough to allow room for the realization of their own political and economic goals. After the separation caused by the successful revolt of the Seven United Provinces in the late sixteenth century, the prince's power (now that of Philip II of Spain) reigned supreme in the southern Low Countries, which eventually became Belgium and Luxemburg. The urban elites' power reigned in the north, which became the United Provinces, later the Netherlands. But each part of the old Burgundian Low Countries continued for a long time to feel the loss of a unity whose roots lay in the Burgundian past. From the late sixteenth century, we must trace separate histories. And thereafter, nothing was quite the same as before.

Abbreviations

AGN	*Algemene Geschiedenis der Nederlanden*
	AGN, J. A. van Houtte, J. F. Niermeyer, J. Presser, J. Romein, and H. van Werveke, eds. (Haarlem, 1949–52). Vol. 3.
	AGN, D. P. Blok, A. Verhulst, H. P. H. Jansen, R. C. van Caenegem, A. G. Weiler, and W. Prevenier, eds. (Haarlem, 1980–1982). Vols. 2 and 4.
ASEB	*Handelingen Annales Société d'Emulation de Bruges*
ASRAB	*Annales de la Société royale d'archéologie de Bruxelles*
BCRH	*Bulletin de la Commission Royale d'Histoire — HKCG*
BMGN	*Bijdragen en Mededelingen voor de Geschiedenis der Nederlanden*
BTFG	*Belgisch Tijdschrift voor Filologie en Geschiedenis*
EHR	*Economic History Review*
HKCG	*Handelingen van de Koninklijke Commissie voor Geschiedenis*
HMGOG	*Handelingen Maatschappij voor Geschiedenis en Oudheidkunde van Gent*
JMH	*Journal of Medieval History*
MA	*Le Moyen Age*
PCEEB	*Publication du Centre Européen d'Etudes Bourguignonnes, XIVe–XVIe siècles*
RBPH	*Revue Belge de philologie et d'histoire — BTFG*
RN	*Revue du nord*
SL	*Standen en Landen, Anciens Pays et Assemblées d'Etats*
TG	*Tijdschrift voor Geschiedenis*
TSG	*Tijdschrift voor Sociale Geschiedenis*

Notes

Preface

1. The most recent general overview in Dutch of the history of the Low Countries is D. P. Blok, W. Prevenier, et al., *Algemene Geschiedenis der Nederlanden*, vols. 2, 4 (1980–82). Still useful and more comprehensive for political issues is the older version, J. A. Van Houtte et al., *Algemene Geschiedenis der Nederlanden*, vol. 3 (1951).

2. On the general problem of the formation of the Burgundian state and its continuation under the Habsburg dynasty, see W. Prevenier and W. Blockmans, *The Burgundian Netherlands*, 198–213, 362–72. For its later evolution, the best general work is Ernst H. Kossmann, *The Low Countries, 1780–1940* (Oxford, 1978). A short but excellent synthesis from the Middle Ages to the twentieth century is Johanna A. Kossmann-Putto and Ernst H. Kossmann, *The Low Countries: History of the Northern and Southern Netherlands* (Rekkem, 1987). The most recent overview is Jonathan Israel, *The Dutch Republic: Its Rise, Greatness, and Fall, 1477–1806* (Oxford, 1995).

3. Edward Peters and Walter Simons, "The New Huizinga and the Old Middle Ages" *Speculum* 74 (1999) (forthcoming).

Chapter 1. Perspectives on the Burgundian Dynasty in the Low Countries

1. Jean Favier, *Philippe le Bel* (Paris, 1978), 206–49.

2. The painter Hieronymus Bosch represented such struggles in his *The Haywain*, an allegory of the social struggle precipitated by greed. Roger H. Marijnissen and Peter Ruyffelaere, *Hiëronymus Bosch*, English ed. (Antwerp, 1987), 52–83; Walter Gibson, *Hieronymus Bosch* (New York, 1985), 69–82.

3. W. P. Blockmans and Walter Prevenier, "Poverty," 39–40, 53–57. For a general thesis on this connection, see Catharina Lis and Hugo Soly, *Poverty and Capitalism in Pre-Industrial Europe* (Hassocks, 1979), 215–222. On charity and religious motivations: William K. Jordan, *Philanthropy in England, 1480–1660* (London, 1959); Michel Mollat, *Etudes sur l'histoire de la pauvreté*, vol. 1 (Paris, 1974); translated in English as *The Poor in the Middle Ages: An Essay in Social History* (New Haven, 1986); critical reaction by Miri Rubin, *Charity and Community in Medieval Cambridge* (Cambridge, 1987), 54–98.

4. Walter Prevenier, "La Démographie," 271. Although the basic evidence remains relevant, we are now convinced that a new method of calculating population has to be applied. See comments in Chapter 6.

5. Raymond van Uytven, "La Flandre et le Brabant," 281; Walter Prevenier and W. P. Blockmans, *The Burgundian Netherlands*, 191–196.

6. François Louis Ganshof, "La Flandre," 344–355.
7. Claude Gaier, *L'Industrie et le commerce.*
8. Hans van Werveke, "Industrial Growth in the Middle Ages: The Cloth Industry in Flanders," *EHR* second series 6 (1954): 237–245; John H. Munro, "Industrial Transformations in the North-West European Textile Trades, c. 1290–c. 1340: Economic Progress or Economic Crisis?" in *Before the Black Death: Studies in the Crisis of the Early Fourteenth Century*, ed. B. M. S. Campbell (Manchester, 1991), 110–148; Patrick Chorley, "The Cloth Exports of Flanders and Northern France during the Thirteenth Century: A Luxury Trade?" *EHR* second series 40 (1987): 349–379; M. Boone and W. Prevenier, eds., *La Draperie ancienne*, 15, 164–165, 167–205.
9. Gérard Sivery, *L'Economie du Royaume de France au siècle de Saint Louis* (Lille, 1984), 220–248; Robert H. Bautier, "Les Foires de Champagne," in *La Foire* (Brussels, 1953), 97–147.
10. R. Haepke, *Brügges Entwicklung*; Philippe Dollinger, *La Hanse, XIIe–XVIIe siècles* (Paris, 1964), English trans. D. S. Ault and S. H. Steinberg, *The German Hansa* (London, 1970); Albert d'Haenens, *Europe of the North Sea and the Baltic: The World of the Hanse* (Antwerp, 1984), 174–181.
11. Prevenier, "La Démographie," 255–257; for Ghent, David Nicholas (*Medieval Flanders*, 305–306) prefers lower estimates.
12. Henri Berben, "Une Guerre économique au moyen âge: L'Embargo sur l'exportation des laines anglaises, 1270–1274," in *Etudes d'histoire dédiées à la mémoire de H. Pirenne par ses anciens élèves* (Brussels, 1937), 1–17.
13. Hans van Werveke, "La Famine de l'an 1316 en Flandre et dans les régions voisines," *RN* 41 (1959): 5–14; H. S. Lucas, "The Great European Famine of 1315, 1316, and 1317," *Speculum* 5 (1930): 343–377; William C. Jordan, *The Great Famine: Northern Europe in the Early Fourteenth Century* (Princeton, 1996).
14. On the perturbations before 1350 in general, see B. M. S. Campbell, ed., *Before the Black Death: Studies in the "Crisis" of the Early Fourteenth Century* (Manchester, 1991).
15. On the Black Death, see Philip Ziegler, *The Black Death* (New York, 1971); Willem P. Blockmans, "The Social and Economic Effects," 860–861; Hans van Werveke, *De Zwarte Dood in de zuidelijke Nederlanden* (Brussels, 1950); Daniel Williman, ed., *The Black Death* (Binghamton, 1982).
16. On the English case, see W. Ormrod, *The Reign of Edward III: Crown and Political Society in England, 1327–1377* (New Haven and London, 1990), and Scott Waugh, *England in the Reign of Edward III* (Cambridge, 1991).
17. Malcolm Vale, *The Angevin Legacy and the Hundred Years War, 1250–1340* (Oxford, 1990).
18. On the origins of the war, see H. S. Lucas, *The Low Countries and the Hundred Years' War, 1326–1347* (Ann Arbor, 1929); and Jonathan Sumption, *The Hundred Years War: Trial By Battle* (Philadelphia, 1990). On the war itself, see Jean Favier, *La Guerre*; R. Neillands, *The Hundred Years War*; A. Curry, *The Hundred Years War.*
19. William H. Tebrake, *A Plague of Insurrection: Popular Politics and Peasant Revolts in Flanders, 1323–1328* (Philadelphia, 1993), 15–17, 26–29.

20. Etienne Marcel appealed to the Flemings for help in his Paris rebellion. J. d'Avout, *Le Meurtre d'Etienne Marcel* (Paris, 1960), 303–10.

21. There is no recent monograph on Hainault-Holland for this period; the most recent overviews are those of Maurice Vandermaesen, "Het graafschap Henegouwen, 1280–1384," in AGN, vol. 2, D. P. Blok, W. Prevenier, et al., eds. (Haarlem, 1982), 441–451; Fritz Quicke, *Les Pays-Bas*, 86–102, 221–238. On the role of Albert of Bavaria in Holland, see Dick De Boer, "Een vorst trekt noordwaarts," 283–309.

22. Ria van Bragt, *De Blijde Inkomst*.

23. Quicke, *Les Pays-Bas*, 41–53.

24. Quicke, *Les Pays-Bas*, 41–53, 103–121, 177–257, 395–408. On the first half of the fourteenth century in Brabant, see Piet Avonds, *Brabant tijdens de regering van hertog Jan III, 1312–1356: De grote politieke crisissen* (Brussels, 1984), and *Land en instellingen* (Brussels, 1991).

25. Quicke, *Les Pays-Bas*, 239–57; Jean Lejeune, *Liège et son pays*; Jean Baerten, "Luik en Loon, 1100–1390," in AGN, vol. 2, 486–488.

26. John H. Munro, "Industrial Protectionism," 229–267; Mark de Laet, "De Vlaamse aktieve handel op Engeland in de eerste helft van de 14de eeuw, aan de hand van de Custom Accounts," in *Economische Geschiedenis van Belgie: Behandeling van de bronnen en problematiek*. Handelingen van het colloquium te Brussel, 17–19 November 1971, Algemeen Rijksarchief (Brussels, 1972), 223–231.

27. Hans van Werveke, *Jacques van Artevelde* (Brussels, 1942); Paul Rogghé, *Vlaanderen en het zevenjarig beleid van Jacob van Artevelde*, 2 vols. (Brussels, 1942); David Nicholas, *The van Arteveldes*, 1–71; Walter Prevenier and Marc Boone, "Fourteenth and Fifteenth Centuries: The City-State Dream," 85–87.

28. Quicke, *Les Pays-Bas*, 75–85, 258–271; Paul Rogghé, "De politiek van graaf Lodewijk van Male," 388–441.

29. On the geographical and political position of Walloon Flanders, see François Louis Ganshof, "La Flandre," 354; Léon Vanderkindere, *La Formation territoriale des principautés belges au moyen-age*, vol. 1 (Brussels, 1902), 243–247.

Chapter 2. A New European Power in the Making, 1363–1405

1. Detailed biographies of Philip the Bold were written by Ernest Petit (*Les ducs de Bourgogne: Philippe le Hardi*) in 1909 and Otto Cartellieri (*Philipp der Kühne*) in 1910. The latest work, less strictly biographical, is that of Richard Vaughan (*Philip the Bold*) in 1962 (paperback ed., 1979). For a short overview, see Walter Prevenier, "Filips de Stoute," *National Biografisch Woordenboek* 1 (1964): 499–524.

2. J. J. N. Palmer, "England, France, the Papacy, and the Flemish Succession," 339–394.

3. On the external events of the marriage, see J. J. Vernier, "Philippe le Hardi, duc de Bourgogne: Son mariage avec Marguerite de Flandre en 1369," *Bulletin de la Commission Historique du département du Nord* 22 (1900): 119–25. On the diplomatic background, see C. A. J. Armstrong, *England*, 237, and Quicke, *Les Pays-Bas*, 145–160.

4. J. J. N. Palmer, *England, France, and Christendom*, 1–25.

5. On the personality of Charles V, see Françoise Autrand, *Charles V le Sage* (Paris, 1994); Richard Delachenal, *Histoire de Charles V*, 5 vols. (Paris, 1909–1931). On Charles's interest in art and science, see Etienne Dennery, *La Librairie de Charles V* (Paris, 1968), xv–xvi, 5–6. On the connection with Philippe de Mézières, see G. W. Coopland, *Philippe de Mézières, Chancellor of Cyprus: Songe du Vieil Pelerin*, vol. 1 (Cambridge, 1969), 6–8, 38–60. On Oresme, see Susan M. Babbitt, "Oresme's 'Livre de Politiques' and the France of Charles V," *Transactions of the American Philosophical Society*, 75, part 1 (1985).

6. Françoise Autrand, *Charles VI*, 69–74.

7. On the jurists in the service of the French kings, see Franklin J. Pegues, *The Lawyers of the Last Capetians* (Princeton, 1962); and Joseph R. Strayer, *The Reign of Philip the Fair* (Princeton, 1980), 36–99.

8. Vaughan, *Philip the Bold*, 151–167.

9. Quicke, *Les Pays-Bas*, 407.

10. A. Leguai, "Les Ducs Valois et les villes du duché de Bourgogne," *PCEEB* 33 (1993): 21–33.

11. On the turbulent nobles, see J. J. Vernier, "Une Page d'histoire bourguignonne: Hostilités entre les deux Bourgognes au XIVe siècle," *Revue champenoise et bourguignonne* 1 (1904): 1–23, 183–203.

12. On this peace treaty, see J. J. Vernier, "Traités entre le comte de Savoie Amédée VI et la maison de Bourgogne en 1369 et 1379," *Mémoires de l'Académie des Sciences, Belles-Lettres, et Arts de Savoie* 4 (1893): 493–507.

13. On the Parlement of Paris, see F. Aubert, *Histoire du Parlement de Paris, de son origine à François I, 1250–1515*, 2 vols. (Paris, 1894). There are more recent syntheses by James Shennan, *The Parlement of Paris* (London, 1968); and, for a social analysis of the officials, Françoise Autrand, *Naissance*.

14. J. Rauzier, *Finances et gestion d'une principauté au XIVe siècle: Le duché de Bourgogne de Philippe le Hardi, 1364–1384* (Paris, 1993), 699.

15. Georges Bigwood, "Gand et la circulation," 397–460. On the problems of grain supply in general, see Marie Jeanne Tits-Dieuaide, *La Formation des prix céréaliers*.

16. Roger Demuynck, "De Gentse Oorlog," 305–318.

17. Roger Degryse, "De Vlaamse Westvaart," 116–133.

18. Prevenier and Boone, "City-State Dream," 90–93.

19. Walter Prevenier, *De Leden*, 45–50.

20. David Nicholas, *The van Arteveldes*, 120–159.

21. On the traditional monopoly of the cities, see Raymond Monier, *Les institutions judiciaires*, 212–37; A. van Zuylen van Nyevelt, "Cès de loi du France de Bruges au XVe siècle," *ASEB* 66 (1923): 114–46; Prevenier, *De Leden*, 210–218.

22. Jan Buntinx, *De Audiëntie*, 45–53; Vaughan, *Philip the Bold*, 128–135.

23. E. Giard, "Jean Canard," Positions des thèses de l'Ecole des Chartres (Paris, 1902), 23–28.

24. Marc Boone, *Gent en de Bourgondische hertogen*, 201–207.

25. Walter Prevenier, "Les Perturbations," 477–497; Marc Haegeman, *De Anglofilie*, 189–228.

26. On the Western Schism in general, see E. Delaruelle, E. R. Labande, and P. Ourliac, "L'Église au temps du Grand Schisme et la crise conciliaire, 1378–1449," in *Histoire de l'Eglise, depuis les origines jusqu'à nos jours*, vol. 14 (Paris, 1962), 3–200; Hans-Georg Beck, Karl August Fink, Josef Glazik, Erwin Iserloh, Hans Wolter, *From the High Middle Ages to the Eve of the Reformation*, vol. 4 of *History of the Church*, Hubert Jedin and John Dolan, eds. (New York, 1980), 401–25; Francis Oakley, *The Western Church in the Later Middle Ages* (Ithaca and London, 1979), 25–81; Walter Brandmüller, *Papst und Konzil im grossen Schisma, 1378–1431* (Paderborn, 1990). For the impact in the Low Countries, see Gerard van Asseldonk, *De Nederlanden en het Westers Schisma, tot 1398* (Uterecht-Nijmegen, 1955); Jan van Herwaarden, "De Nederlanden en het Westers Schisma," *AGN*, vol. 4: 379–386.

27. On the idea of the royal crown, see Marjoke de Roos, "Les Ambitions royales de Philippe le Bon et Charles le Téméraire: Une Approche anthropologique," *PCEEB* 36 (1996): 71–88.

28. H. David, "Jeunesse de Jean, second duc Valois de Bourgogne: Le Double mariage de Cambrai," *Miscellanea Prof. dr. D. Roggen* (Antwerp, 1957), 57–76.

29. Vaughan, *Philip the Bold*, 86–88. Many poets and authors of chronicles told of the events: Georges Doutrepont, *La Littérature française à la cour des ducs de Bourgogne* (Paris, 1909).

30. The evidence of the expenses of Albert is taken from the master's thesis work of Klaartje Pompe, Leiden University, 1988.

31. André Uyttebrouck, *Le Gouvernement*, vol. 1, 476–490.

32. Robert Stein, "Een vergeten crisis: Over een conflict tussen hertog Antoon en de Staten van Brabant in 1407," in J. M. Duvosquel et al., *Les Pays-Bas bourguignons*, 413–433.

33. Autrand, *Charles VI*, 75–88.

34. B. A. Pocquet du Haut-Jussé, "Les Dons du roi aux ducs de Bourgogne," *Annales de Bourgogne* 10 (1938): 261–289; and *Mémoires de la Société de l'Histoire du Droit et des Institutions Bourguignons* 6 (1939): 113–114; 7 (1940–41), 95–129.

35. Autrand, *Charles VI*, 88–104.

36. Ibid., 181–213.

37. R. Delachenal, *Histoire des avocats au Parlement de Paris, 1300–1600* (Paris, 1885), 331–89; Vaughan, *Philip the Bold*, 142–144.

38. Ronald Famiglietti, *Royal Intrigue*.

39. Jean Favier, "Paris au XVe siècle," *Nouvelle historie de Paris* (Paris, 1974), 141–142.

40. L. Batiffol, *Jean Jouvenel* (Paris, 1894), 109–125.

41. E. Jarry, *La Vie politique de Louis de France, duc d'Orléans, 1372–1407* (Paris, 1889).

42. Serge Dauchy, "Un Aperçu de la litigiosité," 45–77; Walter Prevenier, "Violence against Women in a Medieval Metropolis: Paris around 1400," *Law, Custom, and the Social Fabric in Medieval Europe: Essays in Honor of Bryce Lyon*, Bernard S. Bachrach and David Nicholas, eds. (Kalamazoo, 1990), 269, 274–275.

43. Claude Gauvard, "Christine de Pisan a-t-elle eu une pensée politique?" *RH* 508 (1973): 417–30; Sandra L. Hindman, *Christine de Pizan's "Epistre Othea": Painting and Politics at the Court of Charles VI* (Toronto, 1986).

44. E. Hoepffner, *Eustache Deschamps* (Strasburg, 1904).
45. A. J. Vanderjagt, *Qui sa vertu anoblist*, 45–74.

Chapter 3. Burgundian Interests in France and the Low Countries, 1404–1425

1. A. S. Atiya, *The Crusade of Nicopolis* (London, 1934); Norman Housley, *The Later Crusades, 1274–1570: From Lyons to Alcazar* (Oxford, 1992).
2. This text comes from a letter of John the Fearless to Philip the Bold. Archives départementales du Nord, Lille, B 18.822, f° 171, n° 23.270.
3. B. A. Pocquet du Haut-Jussé, "Le Retour de Nicopolis et la rançon de Jean sans Peur," *Annales de Bourgogne* 9 (1937): 296–302; Otto Cartellieri, *Philipp der Kühne*, 77–80; J. Calmette, *Les Grands Ducs*, 86–87.
4. B. A. Pocquet du Haut-Jussé, "Les Pensionnaires fieffés des ducs de Bourgogne de 1352 à 1419," *Mémoires de la Société pour l'Histoire du Droit et des Institutions des Anciens Pays-Bas Bourguignons* 8 (1942): 127–150.
5. Bernard Guenée, *Un Meurtre*, 166.
6. M. Nordberg, *Les Ducs et la royauté*, 215–224.
7. E. Jarry, *La Vie politique de Louis de France*, 335–336; Lucien Mirot, "L'Enlèvement du dauphin et le premier conflit entre Jean sans Peur et Louis d'Orléans, juillet–octobre 1405," *Revue des questions historiques* 95 (1914): 329–355; 96 (1914): 47–68, 369–419.
8. On the youth of Isabela, see M. Thibault, *Isabeau de Bavière, reine de France: La Jeunesse, 1370–1405* (Paris, 1903).
9. Guenée, *Un Meurtre*, 170–172.
10. Maurice Rey, *Les Finances royales sous Charles VI: Les Causes du déficit, 1388–1413* (Paris, 1965).
11. On the ideology of the medieval kingdom, see S. Hanley, *The Lit de Justice of the Kings of France: Constitutional Ideology in Legend, Ritual, and Discourse* (Princeton, 1983). Cf. Elizabeth A. R. Brown and R. C. Famiglietti, *The Lit de Justice: Semantics, Ceremonial, and the Parlement of Paris, 1300–1600* (Sigmaringen, 1994).
12. Guenée, *Un Meurtre*, 171.
13. On Gerson, see J. B. Morrall, *Gerson and the Great Schism* (Manchester, 1960); P. Glorieux, "La Vie et les oeuvres de Gerson," *Archives d'histoire doctrinale et littéraire du Moyen Age* 18 (1950–51): 149–192.
14. Noël Valois, *Le Conseil du roi au XIVe, XVe, et XVIe siècles* (Paris, 1888), 113–115.
15. On the murder of the duke of Orléans, see Guenée, *Un Meurtre*, 176–179; Louis Douet d'Arcq, "Document inédit sur l'assassinat de Louis, duc d'Orléans," *Annuaire-Bulletin de la Société de l'Histoire de France*, part 2 (1864): 6–26.
16. E. Collas, *Valentine de Milan, duchesse d'Orléans* (Paris, 1911).
17. On the Duke of Berry, see F. Lehoux, *Jean de France, duc de Berri: Sa vie, son action politique (1340–1416)*, 4 vols. (Paris, 1966–68).
18. On Jean Petit's *"Justification,"* see A. Coville, *Jean Petit: La Question du tyrannicide au commencement du XVe siècle* (Paris, 1932); Stanley Cutler, *The Law of*

Treason and Treason Trials in Later Medieval France (Cambridge, 1981); Guenée, *Un Meurtre*, 180–201.

19. On the conflict between Armagnacs and Burgundians, see J. d'Avout, *La Querelle des Armagnacs et des Bourguignons: Histoire d'une crise d'autorité* (Paris, 1943); J. Schoos, *Der Machtkampf zwischen Burgund und Orleans* (Luxemburg, 1956); Nordberg, *Les Ducs et la royauté*; Autrand, *Charles VI*, 451–469.

20. A. Coville, *Les Cabochiens et l'ordonnance de 1413* (Paris, 1888).

21. Richard Vaughan, *John the Fearless*, 208–209.

22. Guenée, *Un Meurtre*, 270–272.

23. On the murder at Montereau, see Paul Bonenfant, *Du Meurtre de Montereau*, 1–16; A. Mirot, "Charles VII et les conseillers assassins présumés de Jean sans Peur," *Annales de Bourgogne* 14 (1942): 197–210; Autrand, *Charles VI*, 566–576.

24. Prevenier, *De Leden*, 204–208.

25. C. A. J. Armstrong, "The Language Question," 386–409.

26. Vaughan, *John the Fearless*, 14–15.

27. Marc Haegeman, *De anglofilie*, 226–228.

28. Victor Fris, "Het Brugsch Calfvel van 1407–1411," *Bulletin de l'Académie Royale d'Archéologie de Belgique* (1911): 183–274.

29. On the notion of *bien commun*, see Vanderjagt, *Qui sa vertu anoblist*.

30. Marc Boone, *Gent en de Bourgondische hertogen*, 226–235.

31. Prevenier, *De Leden*, 57–84; Willem Blockmans, *De volksvertegenwoordiging*, 161–169; Walter Prevenier, "Les Etats de Flandre," 28–34.

32. On the notion of *heimgefallen*, see Robert Stein, "Philip the Good and the German Empire: The Legitimation of the Burgundian Succession to the German Principalities," *PCEEB* 36 (1996): 33–48.

33. Raymond van Uytven and Willem Blockmans, "Constitutions," 402–410.

34. S. Mund, "Les Relations d'Antoine de Bourgogne, duc de Brabant, avec l'empire," *PCEEB* 36 (1996): 21–32.

35. André Uyttebrouck, *Le Gouvernement*, vol. 1, 476–490.

36. Ibid., 490–496.

37. Haydroit, the name of a political faction, was in fact a critical allusion in a text of 1328: "Liège, qui tire son nom de la loi (*a lege*), a maintenant changé son nom en haine de loi (*in legis odium*)" [Liège, which takes its name from law, has now changed its name into a hatred of law]. Lejeune, *Liège et son pays*, 348.

38. F. Schneider, *Herzog Johann von Baiern*.

39. Paul Bonenfant, *Du Meurtre de Montereau*, 117–179.

40. G. du Fresne de Beaucourt, *Histoire de Charles VII*, 2 vols. (Paris, 1881–1882).

41. Robert Stein, *Politiek en historiografie: Het ontstaandsmilieu van Brabantse kronieken in de eerste helft van de vijftiende eeuw* (Leuven, 1994).

42. Uyttebrouck, *Le Gouvernement*, vol. 1, 503–511.

43. Ibid., 546–50; Stein, *Politiek en historiografie*.

44. Willem P. Blockmans, "The Economic Expansion of Holland and Zeeland."

45. On this party conflict, see Hans Brokken, *Het ontstaan van de Hoekse en Kabeljauwse twisten*; H. P. H. Jansen, *Hoekse en Kabeljauwse twisten*; Fredericus J. W. van Kan, *Sleutels tot de macht*, 126–168.

46. J. W. Marsilje, *Bloedwraak, partijstrijd en pacificatie*.

47. J. A. M. Y. Bos-Rops, *Graven op zoek naar geld*.

48. On these marriages, see E. le Blant, *Les Quatre mariages de Jacqueline, duchesse en Bavière* (Paris, 1904); on her career, see F. von Loeher, *Jacobäa von Bayern und ihre Zeit*, 2 vols. (Nördlingen, 1862–69); R. Putnam, *A Medieval Princess* (New York, 1904); Richard Vaughan, *Philip the Good*, 32–52.

49. C. Monget, *La Chartreuse de Dijon*, 3 vols. (Montreuil sur Mer-Tournai, 1898–1905).

50. Frits P. van Oostrom, *Court and Culture: Dutch Literature, 1350–1450* (Berkeley and Los Angeles, London, 1992), 294–301.

51. Elisabeth Dhanens, *Hubert and Jan van Eyck*, 78–81, 193, 215, 238, 266–69.

Chapter 4. The Decisive Years, 1425–1440

1. C. A. J. Armstrong, "La Politique matrimoniale," 12–14.

2. W. H. James Weale, *Hubert and John van Eyck, Their Life and Work* (London and New York, 1908), plates XXVII–LI; L. Dimier, "Dessin du portrait d'Isabelle de Portugal par Van Eyck," *Bulletin de la Société Nationale des Antiquaires de France* (1921): 116.

3. C. Looten, "Isabelle de Portugal, duchesse de Bourgogne et comtesse de Flandre," 1397–1471," *Revue de littérature comparée* 18 (1938): 5–22.

4. R. Mullally, "The So-Called Hawking Party at the Court of Philip the Good," *Gazette des Beaux-Arts* 119 (1977): 109–112.

5. Armstrong, "La Politique matrimoniale," 13.

6. M. Sommé, "Isabelle de Portugal, duchesse de Bourgogne: Une Femme au pouvoir au XVe siècle." Thèse de doctorat, Lille (Lille, 1995), 19–20.

7. J. Rychner, *La Littérature et les moeurs chevaleresques à la cour de Bourgogne* (Neuchâtel, 1950). The same technique was used in France: see J. Krynen, *Idéal du prince et pouvoir royal en France à la fin du Moyen Age, 1380–1440: Étude de la littérature politique du temps* (Paris, 1981).

8. F. A. T. de Reiffenberg, *Histoire de l'ordre de la Toison d'Or* (Brussels, 1830); Luc Hommel, *L'histoire du noble ordre de la Toison d'Or* (Brussels, 1947); Françoise de Gruben, *Les Chapitres de la Toison d'Or*; D'A. J. D. Boulton, *The Knights of the Crown: The Monarchial Orders of Knighthood in Later Medieval Europe, 1325–1520* (Woodbridge, 1987).

9. Yves Renouard, "L'Ordre de la Jarretière et l'ordre de l'Étoile: Étude sur la genèse des ordres laïcs de chevalerie et sur le développement progressif de leur caractère national," *MA* 55 (1949): 281–300.

10. Johan Huizinga, *The Waning*, 83–90.

11. Pierre Cockshaw and Christiane van den Bergen-Pantens, eds., *L'Ordre de la Toison d'Or, de Philippe le Bon à Philippe le Beau, 1430–1505* (Brussels, 1996), 87, 104–105.

12. C. A. J. Armstrong, "Had the Burgundian Government a Policy for the Nobility?" *England, France, and Burgundy*, 213–236.

13. J. G. Dickinson, *The Congress of Arras*.

14. Régine Pernoud, *Vie et mort de Jeanne d'Arc* (Paris, 1953).

15. Raoul C. van Caenegem, *Les Arrêts et jugés du Parlement de Paris sur appels flamands conservés dans les registres du Parlement, 1320–1521*, 2 vols. (Brussels, 1966–77); Serge Dauchy, "Quelques Remarques sur les amendes prononcés par le Parlement de Paris au Moyen Age pour 'fol appel' provenant de Flandre," *Revue d'Histoire du Droit* 55 (1987): 49–55.

16. Serge Dauchy, *De processen*, 78, 314.

17. Vaughan, *Philip the Good*, 57–58.

18. Dauchy, *De processen*, 301–302.

19. M. Houtart, *Les Tournaisiens et le roi de Bourges* (Tournai, 1908).

20. E. C. Williams, *My Lord of Bedford, 1389–1435* (London, 1963), 97–105; Armstrong, "La Politique matrimoniale," 245.

21. See Vaughan, *Philip the Bold*, 24–25, for the translation of this letter.

22. On the Council of Basel, see J. Helmrath, *Das Basler Konzil*; H. Müller, *Die Franzosen, Frankreich, und das Basler Konzil*.

23. On the Council of Constance, see J. Gill, *Constance et Bâle-Florence*, Histoire des Conciles oecuméniques, 9 (Paris, 1965); Walter Brandmüller, *Der Konzil von Konstanz, 1414–1418* 2 vols. (Paderborn, 1991, 1997).

24. On this tradition, see A. Leman, "La Politique religieuse de Philippe le Hardi en Flandre," *Compte-rendu Congrès Archéologique et Historique* (Bruges, 1903), 437–449; Walter Prevenier, "Les Triangles 'eglise, etat, société' et 'eglise, famille, société laïque' dans les Pays-Bas bourguignons du XVe siècle," in F. Alvares-Péreyre, ed., *Le Politique et le religieux* (Jérusalem, 1995), 119–137.

25. J. Toussaint, *Les Relations diplomatiques de Philippe le Bon avec le Concile de Bâle, 1431–1449* (Louvain, 1942).

26. Yvon Lacaze, "Jean Germain," Positions des thèses de l'Ecole des Chartes (Paris, 1958).

27. L. Stouff, *Contribution à l'histoire de la Bourgogne au Concile de Bâle* (Dijon, 1928).

28. Helmrath, *Der Basler Konzil*; Müller, *Die Franzosen, Frankreich, und das Basler Konzil*.

29. Yvon Lacaze, "Philippe le Bon et le problème hussite: Un Projet de croisade bourguignon en 1428–1429," *Revue Historique* 241 (1969): 69–98; Guenée, *Un meurtre*, 251; Howard R. Kaminsky, *A History of the Hussite Revolution* (Berkeley, 1967); F. M. Bartos, *The Hussite Revolution (1424–37)* (Boulder, 1986).

30. A. Perier, *Nicolas Rolin, 1380–1461* (Paris, 1904); R. Berger, *Nicolas Rolin. Kanzler der Zeitwende im Burgundisch-Französischen Konflikt, 1422–1461* (Freiburg, 1971); Herta-Florence Pridat, *Nicolas Rolin, 1376?–1462, Kanzler von Burgund* (Berlin, 1995).

31. Marie Rose Thielemans, "Les Croij Conseillers des Ducs de Bourgogne. Documents extrairs de leurs archives familiales," *BCRH* 124 (1959), 1–141.

32. Dickinson, *The Congress of Arras*; text of the treaty of E. Cosneau, *Les Grands traités de la Guerre de Cent Ans* (Pris, 1889), 143.

33. On this institution, see Jan van Rompaey, *De Grote Raad*, 54–60.

34. John H. Munro, *Wool, Cloth, and Gold*, 93–126.

35. On the career of Gloucester, see Kenneth H. Vickers, *Humphrey, Duke of Gloucester* (London, 1907).

36. Jacques Paviot, *La Politique navale des ducs de Bourgogne*, 69–83.

37. R. H. Bainton, *Christian Attitudes toward War and Peace* (London, 1961).

38. The original text is in J. Kervyn de Lettenhove, "Programme d'un gouvernement constitutionnel en Belgique au XVe siècle," *Bulletin de l'Académie Royale de Belgique* 2, 14 (1862): 218–250; English translation in Vaughan, *Philip the Good*, 102–107. On Hugh of Lannoy, see B. de Lannoy, *Hugues de Lannoy* (Brussels, 1957); H. Potvin, "Hugues de Lannoy, 1384–1456," *BCRH* 2, 6 (1879): 117–138.

39. Marie Rose Thielemans, *Bourgogne et Angleterre*, 116–133; Munro, *Wool, Cloth, and Gold*, 117–121.

40. Paviot, *La Politique navale des ducs de Bourgogne*, 59–60.

41. On the conflict between Burgundy and Jacqueline of Bavaria, see Huub P. H. Jansen, *Jacoba van Beieren* (The Hague, 1976).

42. R. van Marle, *Le Comté de Hollande sous Philippe le Bon* (The Hague, 1908); M. van Gent, "*Pertijelike saken*," 23–26.

43. T. S. Jansma, *Raad en Rekenkamer*, 60–69.

44. On the van Borselen family, see Henri Obreen, "Het geslacht van Borselen," *Nederlandsche Leeuw* 45 (1927): 242–249, 294–306, 321–336, 363–366; 46 (1928): 11–13, 58–59; van Gent, "*Pertijelike saken*," 23–26.

45. K. Spading, *Holland und die Hanse*.

46. Uyttebrouck, *Le Gouvernement*, vol. I, 512–523.

47. J. C. M. Warnsinck, *De zeeoorlog van Holland en Zeeland tegen de Wendische steden der duitsche Hanze, 1438–1441* (the Hague, 1939).

48. Paviot, *La Politique navale des ducs de Bourgogne*, 229–233.

49. Robert Wellens, *Les Etats Généraux*, 89–101.

50. Marc Boone, "Simon van Formelis," *Nationaal Biografisch Woordenboek* 13 (1990): 286–292.

51. Marc Boone and Hanno Brand, "Vollersoproeren en collectieve actie in Gent en Leiden in de 14de en 15de eeuw," *TSG* 19 (1993): 168–192.

52. Marc Boone, *Geld en macht*, 213–218.

53. Jan Dumolyn, *De Brugse opstand*.

54. Marc Boone, *Gent en de Bourgondische hertogen*, 163–198.

55. Myriam Greilsammer, "Rapts de séduction et rapts violents en Flandre et en Brabant à la fin du moyen âge," *Revue d'Histoire du Droit* 56 (1988): 49–84; Walter Prevenier, "Geforceerde huwelijken en politieke clans in de Nederlanden," in Hugo Soly and René Vermeir, eds., *Liber Amicorum M. Baelde* (Gent, 1993), 299–307.

56. Walter Prevenier, "Officials in Town," 1–17; Prevenier, "Les Triangles," 119–137. For the interesting case of a particular noble family, see Bertrand Schnerb, *Enguerrand de Bournonville et les siens: Un Lignage noble du Boulonnais aux XIVe et XVe siècles* (Paris, 1997).

57. For France, see Bernard Guenée and F. Lehoux, *Les Entrées royales françaises de 1328 à 1515* (Paris, 1968). The idea of theater-state was used by the authors of this

book in *The Burgundian Netherlands*, 223–227; since then, Peter Arnade worked it out in his *Realms of Ritual*.

Chapter 5. The Difficult Path Toward an Integrated State, 1440–1465

1. A. M. Bonenfant and P. Bonenfant, "Le Projet d'érection."
2. A. Lafortune-Martel, *Fête noble en Bourgogne au XVe siècle: Le Banquet du Faisan, 1454: Aspects politiques, sociaux, et culturels* (Montréal, 1984); M. Stanesco, "Le Banquet du Faisan," *Rencontres Médiévales* 2 (Reims, 1992): 47–67; Werner Paravicini, "Philippe le Bon en Allemagne (1454)," *RBPH* 75 (1997), 967–1018.
3. A. G. Jongkees, *Staat en Kerk*, 133–145; S. Zilverberg, *David van Bourgondië*; B. van den Hoven van Genderen, *Het kapittel-generaal en de Staten*.
4. De Gruben, *Les Chapitres de la Toison d'Or*, 224, 242–243.
5. M. R. Thielemans, "Les Croij, conseillers des ducs de Bourgogne," *BCRH* 124 (1959): 1–141; J. Bartier, *Légistes et gens de finances*.
6. J. Bartier, *Charles le Téméraire*, 32–51.
7. Van Rompaey, *De Grote Raad*, 39–44; John Gilissen, "Oprichting en evolutie."
8. Van Rompaey, *De Grote Raad*, 162–163, 167–168.
9. Jansma, *Raad en Rekenkamer*, 151–155.
10. W. P. Blockmans, ed., *1477*, 90.
11. A. A. Wijffels, *Qui millies allegatur: Les Allégations du droit savant dans les dossiers du Grand Conseil de Malines (causes septentrionales, ca. 1460–1580)* (Amsterdam, 1985), 285–286, 304, 427–441.
12. Peter Spufford, "Coinage, Taxation, and the Estates General"; Wellens, *Les Etats Généraux*, 89–101; Munro, *Wool, Cloth, and Gold*, 127 ff.
13. Raymond van Uytven, "1477 in Brabant," in Blockmans, ed., *1477*, 272.
14. Bartier, *Légistes et gens de finances*, 44–56, 83–93, 138–79; J. Bartier, "Une Crise de l'état bourguignon: La Réformation de 1457," *Hommage au Professeur Paul Bonenfant* (Brussels, 1965), 501–11; J. van Rompaey, *Het grafelijk baljuwsambt*, 461–470; W. Blockmans, "Corruptie."
15. P. Cockshaw, *Le Personnel de la chancellerie*, 173–181; C. de Borchgrave, *Diplomaten en Diplomatie*, 107–63.
16. H. Kamp, *Memoria und Selbstdarstellung: Die Stiftungen des burgundischen Kanzlers Nicholas Rolin* (Sigmaringen, 1993).
17. P. Cockshaw, *Le personnel de la chancellerie*, 1–58.
18. M. Boone, "Particularisme gantois, centralisme bourguignon, et diplomatie française," *BCRH* 152 (1986): 49–114.
19. There is an excellent account in Vaughan, *Philip the Good*, 86–91; see W. P. Blockmans, *De volksvertegenwoordiging*, 346–353.
20. Boone, *Gent en de Bourgondische hertogen*, 27–160.
21. There is a full account of the events in Vaughan, *Philip the Good*, 303–333; see also Blockmans, *De volksvertegenwoordiging*, 353–363; Boone, *Gent en de Bourgondische hertogen*, 226–236.
22. Arnade, *Realms of Ritual*, 95–142; E. Dhanens, "De Blijde Inkomst van

Filips de Goede in 1458 en de plastische kunsten te Gent," *Actum Gandavi*, 53–112; J. C. Smith, "Venit Nobis Pacificus Dominus: Philip the Good's Triumphal Entry into Ghent in 1458," in B. Wisch and S. S. Munschower, eds., "'All the world's a stage' . . . Art and Pageantry in the Renaissance and Baroque," *Papers in Art History from the Pennsylvania State University* 6 (1990): 259–290.

23. Uyttebrouck, *Le Gouvernement*, 2:503–512.

24. Blockmans, "Patronage, Brokerage, and Corruption"; Bartier, *Légistes et gens de finances*, 138–179; A. Derville, "Pots-de-vin, cadeaux, racket, patronage: Essai sur les mécanismes de décision dans l'Etat bourguignon," *RN* 56 (1974): 341–363.

25. Vaughan, *Charles the Bold*, 6–9.

26. W. Blockmans, "La Répression de révoltes urbaines comme méthode de centralisation dans les Pays-Bas bourguignons," *PCEEB* 28 (1988): 5–9.

27. H. van der Velden, "Gerard Loyet en Karel de Stoute: Het votiefportret in de Bourgondische Nederlanden," dissertation, University of Utrecht (1997), 58–96; Vaughan, *Charles the Bold*, 12–37.

28. In 1471 the city and the Bruges Free Quarter (the Franc) each paid 400 pounds *groten* for the tapestry offered to the duke. See L. Gilliodts-van Severen, ed., *Inventaire des archives de la ville de Bruges*. Section Première: Inventaire des Chartes (Table analytique et Glossaire Flamand par E. Gaillard) 9 vols. (Bruges, 1871–85), 432. Eight hundred pounds *groten* amount to 192,000 *groten*. In 1471, a journeyman carpenter earned 5 *groten* per day in winter and 6 in summer, which could bring him a yearly salary of 1,350 *groten* (J. P. Sosson, *Les Travaux publics*, 226, 303).

29. Vaughan, *Charles the Bold*, 47–53; D. Quéruel, "Olivier de la Marche ou 'l'espace de l'artifice,'" *PCEEB* 34 (1994): 55–70; M. Cheyns-Condé, "L'Adaptation des 'Travaux d'Hercule' pour les fêtes du mariage de Marguerite d'York et de Charles le Hardi à Bruges en 1468," *PCEEB* 34 (1994): 71–85.

30. R. E. F. Straub, *David Aubert, escripvain et clerc* (Amsterdam and Atlanta, 1995), 144–161.

31. Graeme Small, "Chroniqueurs et culture historique au bas Moyen Age," in L. Nys and A. Salamagne, eds., *Valenciennes aux XIVe e XVe siècles: Art et histoire* (Valenciennes, 1996), 271–296; Graeme Small, "Qui a lu la chronique de George Chastellain?" *PCEEB* 31 (1991): 101–1111; Graeme Small, *George Chastellain and the Shaping of Valois Burgundy* (Woodbridge, 1997); D. Boucquey, "Engueran de Monstrelet, historien trop longtemps oublié?" *PCEEB* 31 (1991): 113–125; Joël Blanchard, *Commynes l'européen: L'Invention du politique* (Geneva, 1996).

32. J. Devaux, *Jean Molinet, indiciaire bourguignon* (Paris, 1996).

33. M. P. J. Martens, ed., *Lodewijk van Gruuthuse*; see also the contributions on Simon Marmion and miniature painting by A. Châtelet, D. Vanwynsberghe, and A. M. Legaré in L. Nys and A. Salamagne, *Valenciennes aux XIVe et XVe siècles*, 151–224.

34. G. Kipling, "Entering the City, Bruges 1440: Theatre, Civic Ritual, and the Representation of the Burgundian State," paper delivered at Groningen (the Netherlands), December 1996, forthcoming in M. Gosman, ed., *Power and Creativity*.

35. E. Dhanens, "De Blijde Inkomst van Filips de Goede in 1458 en de plas-

tische kunsten te Gent," *Actum Gandavi*, 53–89; J. C. Smith, *"Venit nobis pacificus Dominus*: Philip the Good's Triumphal Entry into Ghent in 1458," in B. Wisch and S. S. Munschower, eds., "'All the world's a stage . . . ?'": Art and Pageantry in the Renaissance and Baroque, *Papers in Art History from the Pennsylvania State University* 6 (1990), 259–290; Arnade, *Realms of Ritual*, 127–142.

Chapter 6. The Promised Lands, 1440–1475

1. B. de Mandrot, ed., *Mémoires de Philippe de Commynes* (Paris, 1901), 15, as quoted by R. van Uytven, "La Flandre et le Brabant," 281.
2. W. Blockmans, "Finances publiques," 83–85; J. W. Marsilje, *Het financiële beleid*, 300–316; J. A. M. Y. Bos-Rops, "Van incidentele gunst," 26–29.
3. A. van Nieuwenhuysen, *Les Finances du duc*; J. A. M. Y. Bos-Rops, *Graven op zoek naar geld*; A. Zoete, *De beden*; M. A. Arnould, "Une Estimation."
4. M. Martens, *L'Administration du domaine ducal en Brabant au Moyen Age, 1250–1406* (Brussels, 1954), 137–161. E. van Cauwenberghe, *Vorstelijk domein*, 52–105; M. Baelde, *De domeingoederen van de vorst in de Nederlanden onstreeks het midden van de zestiende eeuw, 1551–1559* (Brussels, 1971), 36–43.
5. Arnould, "Une Estimation," 214.
6. Ibid., "Une Estimation," 215.
7. E. van Cauwenberghe, *Het vorstelijk domein*, 320–322.
8. Blockmans, *De volksvertegenwoordiging*, 434–439, 610–635; Blockmans, "Finances publiques," 83–85; M. A. Arnould, *Les Dénombrements de foyers*, 89–95, 114–155; D. D. Brouwers, *Les "Aides" dans le comté de Namur au XVe siècle* (Namur, 1929), iii–v; A. Moureaux-van Neck, "Les Aides accordées aux ducs de Brabant entre 1356 et 1430," *ASRAB* (1984): 501–502; Marsilje, *Het financiële beleid*, 302–309; Bos-Rops, "Van incidentele gunst," 26–29; A. Zoete, *De beden*.
9. E. Van Cauwenberghe, *Vorstelijk domein*, 286.
10. Arnould, "Une Estimation," 157–158; A. Zoete, *De beden*, 151–167.
11. W. M. Ormrod, "The West European Monarchies in the Later Middle Ages," in R. Bonney, ed., *Economic Systems and State Finance* (Oxford, 1995), 151.
12. From 1434 to 1465, a Flemish groat weighed 1.70 grams and had a purity of 0.479 and thus contained 0.8143 grams of fine silver. See H. Enno van Gelder and M. Hoc, *Les Monnaies des Pays-Bas bourguignons et espagnols, 1434–1713* (Amsterdam, 1960), 14.
13. Ormrod, "The West European Monarchies in the Later Middle Ages," 153.
14. Boone, *Geld en macht*, 57–79; D. Clauzel, *Finances et politique*, 195–197; C. Dickstein-Bernard, *La Gestion*, 180–185; Marsilje, *Het financiële beleid*, 300–316; Blockmans, "Finances publiques," 85–87.
15. Zoete, *De beden*, annex 3, 142–200.
16. Blockmans, *De volksvertegenwoordiging*, 632.
17. Ibid., 421–423, 636–637.
18. The figure of four persons per hearth is based on the 1574 population census of Leiden. See D. E. H. de Boer and E. van Maanen, *De bevolkingstelling van*

Leiden in 1574 (Leiden, 1987), correcting W. P. Blockmans et al., "Tussen crisis en welvaart," in D. P. Blok and W. Prevenier, eds., *AGN* 4 (1980): 42–56, and W. Prevenier, "La Démographie des villes."

19. Blockmans, *De volksvertegenwoordiging*, 414–32.

20. Arnould, "Une Estimation," 151, 208.

21. P. M. M. Klep, "Long-Term Developments in the Urban Sector of the Netherlands, 1350–1870," in *Le Réseau urbain en Belgique, 1350–1850: Approches statistique et dynamique* (Brussels, 1992), 205–215.

22. M. J. Tits-Dieuaide, *La Formation*, 98; A. Derville, "Le Grenier"; E. Thoen, *Landbouwekonomie*, 810–20.

23. R. van Uytven, "L'Approvisionnement."

24. Derville, "Le Grenier"; Tits-Dieuaide, *La Formation*, 156–66.

25. Tits-Dieuaide, *La Formation*, 299–306.

26. E. Sabbe, *De Belgische vlasnijverheid* (Bruges, 1943), 72–73; Thoen, *Landbouwekonomie*, 980–1,020.

27. Thoen, *Landbouwekonomie*, 704–33; P. C. M. Hoppenbrouwers, *Een middeleeuwse samenleving: Het Land van Heusden*, 258–62; R. W. Unger, *Dutch Shipbuilding*.

28. H. vander Linden, "Les Communautés rurales en Hollande, de la fin de l'époque mérovingienne à la Révolution Française," *Les Communautés rurales,* Receuils de la Société Jean Bodin 44 (1987): 477–84; W. Blockmans, "La lotta dell'uomo contra l'acqua in Ollanda," in A. Paravicini Bagliani and J. C. Maire Vigueur, eds., *Ars et Ratio* (Palermo, 1990), 55–70.

29. J. L. van Zanden, *The Rise and Decline of Holland's Economy* (Manchester, 1993); Blockmans, "The Economic Expansion"; R. van Uytven, "Haarlemmer hop, Goudse kuit en Leuvense Peterman," *Arca Lovaniensis* 4 (1975): 334–342.

30. Unger, *Dutch Shipbuilding*.

31. H. van Werveke, "De omvang van de Ieperse lakenproduktie in de XIVe eeuw," *Mededelingen Kon: Vlaamse Academie* (Antwerp, 1947); R. van Uytven, *Stadsfinanciën en stadsekonomie*, 353–358; N. W. Posthumus, *De geschiedenis van de Leidsche Lakenindustrie*, vol. 1, 370–371; E. Scholliers, *Loonarbeid en Honger*, 159–161.

32. P. Chorley, "The Cloth Exports of Flanders and Northern France during the Thirteenth Century: A Luxury Trade?" *EHR* 40 (1987): 349–379; M. Boone and W. Prevenier, *La Draperie ancienne*.

33. Munro, *Wool, Cloth, and Gold*, 125 ff; M. Boone, "Nieuwe teksten over de Gentse draperie: wolaanvoer, productiewijze en controlepraktijken, ca. 1456–1468," *BCRH* 154 (1988): 1–62.

34. Thielemans, *Bourgogne et Angleterre*, 47–163, 365–424.

35. M. Boone and H. Brand, "Vollersoproeren en collectieve actie in Gent en Leiden in de 14e en 15e eeuw," *TSG* 19 (1993): 168–192. For Leiden, see M. Howell, *Women, Production, and Patriarchy*.

36. J. H. Munro, "Industrial Protectionism in Medieval Flanders: Urban or National?" 261–263.

37. H. van Werveke, "Die Stellung des hansischen Kaufmanns dem flandrischen Tuchproduzenten gegenüber," in H. van Werveke, *Miscellanea Mediaevalia* (Ghent, 1968), 123–130; P. Stabel, *Dwarfs*, 156.

38. E. Sabbe, *De Belgische Vlasnijverheid* (Bruges, 1943), 72–73; Thoen, *Landbouwekonomie*, 980–1,020; M. Boone, "Nieuwe teksten over de Gentse draperie," *HKCG* 154 (1988), 1–62, at 19–21.

39. M. North, *Geldumlauf und Wirtschaftskonjunktur im südlichen Ostseeraum an der Wende zur Neuzeit, 1440–1570* (Sigmaringen, 1990), 138–172.

40. W. Brulez, "Bruges and Antwerp."

41. E. Sabbe, *De Belgische Vlasnijverheid* (Bruges, 1943), 270–271; Thielemans, *Bourgogne et Angleterre*.

42. W. Paravicini, "Bruges and Germany," in V. Vermeersch, ed., *Bruges and Europe*, 101–102.

43. W. Blockmans, "Bruges as a European Commercial Centre," in V. Vermeersch, ed., *Bruges and Europe*, 41–55.

44. P. Stabel, *De kleine stad*, 92–100; Stabel, *Dwarfs*, 156–173.

45. A. van Nieuwenhuysen, *Les Finances du duc de Bourgogne Philippe le Hardi, 1384–1404: Economie et politique*, 49–51, 342–344.

46. E. Aerts, "Money and Credit: Bruges as a Financial Centre," in Vermeersch, ed., *Bruges and Europe*, 57–67.

47. Van Uytven, "La Flandre et la Brabant," 290.

48. Ibid., 282.

49. Sosson, *Les travaux*, 205–216, 236–256, 333–336; J. P. Sosson, "La Structure sociale de la corporation médiévale: L'Exemple des tonneliers de Bruges de 1350 à 1500," *RBPH* 44 (1966): 470.

50. W. Blockmans, "Die Niederlande vor und nach 1400: Eine Gesellschaft in der Krise?" In F. Seibt and W. Eberhard, eds., *Europa 1400: Die Krise des Spätmittelalters* (Stuttgart, 1982), 130.

51. J. J. de Smet, ed., *Corpus cronicorum Flandriae* (Brussels, 1856), III, 103.

52. W. Blockmans, "The Creative Environment: Incentives to and Functions of Bruges Art Production," in M. W. Ainsworth, ed., *Petrus Christus in Renaissance Bruges* (New York and Turnhout, 1995), 13–14.

53. E. Thoen, "Immigration to Bruges in the Late Middle Ages," in *Le Migrazioni in Europa sec. XIII–XVIII: Atti della 20a Settimane de Studi dell'Istituto di storia economica Francesco Datini* (Prato, 1993), 337, 347–348.

54. W. Prevenier, "De Beden in het graafschap Vlaanderen onder Filips de Stoute, 1384–1404," *RBPH* 38 (1960): 365; Prevenier, "La Démographie."

55. J. P. Sosson, "Les XIVe et XVe siècles: Un Age d'or de la main-d'oeuvre?" 24.

56. Ibid., 28; W. Blockmans et al., "Tussen crisis en welvaart," *AGN* 4, 73; W. P. Blockmans and W. Prevenier, "Poverty," 26–27; J. P. Sosson, "Corporation et paupérisme aux XIVe et XVe siècles: Le Salariat du bâtiment en Flandre et en Brabant, et notamment à Bruges," *TG* 92 (1979): 557–75, especially 560.

57. Blockmans, "The Economic Expansion of Holland and Zeeland," 47–48.

58. Blockmans, "The Creative Environment," 13.

59. Van Uytven, "L'Approvisionnement," 95–96; Thoen, *Landbouwekonomie*, 595–604, 935–937.

60. Blockmans and Prevenier, "Poverty," 49–50.

61. W. Prevenier and W. P. Blockmans, *The Burgundian Netherlands*, 393;

E. Scholliers, "Le pouvoir d'achat dans les Pays-Bas au XVIe siècle," in *Album Charles Verlinden* (Ghent, 1975), 305–330; esp. 318; Blockmans, "Social and Economic Effects," 861–863.

62. Scholliers, "Le Pouvoir d'achat," 318, 330; Sosson, "Les XIVe et XVe siècles," 26.

Chapter 7. War, Crisis, and a Problematic Succession, 1465–1492

1. J. Bartier, *Charles le Téméraire*, 252–269. For the epithet the Bold, see J. M. Cauchies, *Louis XI et Charles le Hardi*, 147–159.
2. P. M. Kendall, *Louis XI*.
3. Wellens, *Les Etats Généraux*, 102–124, 421–424.
4. Wellens, *Les Etats Généraux*, 120–21; P. Cockshaw, *Le Personnel de la chancellerie*, 50–51; W. P. Blockmans, "'Crisme de leze majesté': Les Idées politiques de Charles le Téméraire," in J.-M. Duvosquel et al., *Les Pays-Bas bourguignons*, 79–81.
5. Vaughan, *Charles the Bold*, 45.
6. J. Lejeune, *Liège et Bourgogne*, 64 ff.
7. M. van Tielhof, *Koren op Amsterdams molen: De Hollandse graanhandel*, 18–30.
8. W. Paravicini, *Guy de Brimeu*, 382–97; J. Kuys, *De ambtman*, 57–60; R. W. M. van Schaïk, *Belasting, bevolking en bezit*, 67–71; J. Kuys, "Het hertogdom Gelre in de periode 1339–1543," *Van Gelre tot Gelderlands* (s. 1, 1989).
9. Vaughan, *Charles the Bold*, 158–59; W. P. Blockmans, "The Devotion of a Lonely Duchess," 29–46.
10. Cauchies, *Louis XI et Charles le Hardi*, 95–102.
11. L. P. Gachard, ed., *Collection de documens inédits concernant l'histoire de la Belgique*, vol. 1 (Brussels, 1833), 221–223.
12. Ibid., 223.
13. Ibid., 257–58.
14. Wellens, *Les Etats Généraux*, 129–142; Blockmans, *De volksvertegenwoordiging*, 414–423; Arnould, *Les Dénombrements*, 159–61; Bos-Rops, *Graven op zoek naar geld*, 248–54.
15. H. van der Velden, "Gerard Loyet en Karel de Stoute: Het votiefportret in de Bourgondische Nederlanden," dissertation, University of Utrecht (1997), 55–56, 274–277.
16. J.-M. Cauchies, "Ducs de Bourgogne et tribunaux Liégeois: Contribution à l'étude de la technique législative, 1465–1470," in Duvosquel et al., *Les Pays-Bas bourguignons*, 136.
17. Van Rompaey, *De Grote Raad*, 54–72.
18. Blockmans, "'Crisme de leze majesté';" M. C. le Bailly, "Un Cas particulier de lèze-majesté: Injures verbales contre la Cour de Hollande en tant que collège, 1428–1491," *Revue d'histoire du droit* (1998); W. P. Blockmans, "Die Hierarchisierung der Rechtsprechunginstanzen in Flandern und Holland im 15. Jahrhundert," *Zeitschrift für Historische Forschung* (forthcoming).

19. Van Gent, *"Pertijelike saken,"* 135-138.

20. Blockmans, "Corruptie"; Bartier, *Légistes et gens de finances*, 138-79; Van Rompaey, *Het grafelijk baljuwsambt*, 359-399; M. Boone and H. Brand, "De ondermijning van het Groot Privilege van Holland, Zeeland, en West-Friesland volgens de instructie van 21 December, 1477," *Holland* 24 (1992): 2-21.

21. Wellens, *Les Etats Généraux*, 144-52; Blockmans, *De volksvertegenwoordiging*, 614-15, 632-33; Marsilje, *Het financiële beleid*, 232-309; Jongkees, *Staat en Kerk*, 214-40.

22. M. A. Arnould, "Les Lendemains de Nancy," in Blockmans, ed., *1477*, 1-18; Wellens, *Les Etats Généraux*, 153-178.

23. R. Petit, "Le Luxembourg et le recul du pouvoir central après la mort de Charles le Téméraire," in Blockmans, ed., *1477*, 373-400.

24. Arnould, "Les Lendemains de Nancy," 13-23; W. Blockmans, "Breuk of continuïteit?" in Blockmans, ed., *1477*, 97-109.

25. Blockmans, ed., *1477*, 94; W. Blockmans, "La Signification 'constitutionelle' des privilèges de Marie de Bourgogne, 1477," in Blockmans, ed., *1477*, 495-516.

26. H. Wiesflecker, *Kaiser Maximilian I*, vol. 1, 113 ff.

27. Literally, it said, "It is as white-washing a Moor." R. van Uytven, "1477 in Brabant," in Blockmans, ed., *1477*, 277.

28. Blockmans, *De volksvertegenwoordiging*, 437.

29. J. W. Marsilje, "Les Modes d'imposition en Hollande, 1477-1515," *PCEEB* 28 (1988): 159-171.

30. Van Gent, *"Pertijelike saken,"* 154 ff; J. W. Marsilje, "Ordeverstoring en partijstrijd in laat-middeleeuws Holland," in Marsilje, ed., *Bloedwraak*, 55-59.

31. Van Gent, *"Pertijelike saken,"* 281-309.

32. W. Blockmans, "Autocratie ou polyarchie?"

33. Wellens, *Les Etats Généraux*, 186-96; Wiesflecker, *Kaiser Maximilian I*, vol. 1, 165-67; Dauchy, *De processen in beroep*, 178, 209-211.

34. Van Gent, *"Pertijelike saken,"* 360-69; S. B. J. Zilverberg, *David van Bourgondië*, 50-66; Wiesflecker, *Kaiser Maximilian I*, vol. 1, 168-171.

35. Wiesflecker, *Kaiser Maximilian I*, vol. 1, 171-180.

36. Spufford, "Coinage, Taxation, and the Estates General," 80-88; Tits-Dieuaide, *La Formation*, graphs 1-11; E. Thoen, "Warfare and the Countryside," *Acta Historiae Neerlandicae* 13 (1981): 25-38.

37. R. Wellens, "La Révolte brugeoise de 1488," *ASEB* 102 (1965): 5-52; Wellens, *Les Etats Généraux*, 199-213; Blockmans, "Autocratie ou polyarchie?" 293-302; Wiesflecker, *Kaiser Maximilian I*, vol. 1, 207-218.

38. J. Scheurkogel, "Het Kaas- en Broodspel," *BMGN* 94 (1979): 189-212.

39. Brulez, "Bruges and Antwerp."

40. Recent works on this important painter include R. H. Marijnissen and P. Ruyffelaere, *Bosch* (Antwerp, 1986); P. Vandenbroeck, *Jheronimus Bosch: Tussen volksleven en stadscultuur* (Berchem, 1987); Walter Gibson, *Hieronymus Bosch* (New York, 1985).

41. Blockmans, "Autocratie ou polyarchie?" 304-6.

Chapter 8. The Second Flowering, 1492–1530

1. Blockmans, ed., *1477*, 55, 117, 189–191; Wiesflecker, *Kaiser Maximilian I*, vol. 1, 382–385.
2. Wellens, *Les Etats Généraux*, 235–279, 309, 366–369, 468–525.
3. Ibid., 472–475.
4. W. J. Alberts, ed., *Dit sijn die wonderlijcke oorloghen van den doorluchtighen hochegeboren Prince keyser Maximiliaen* (Groningen, 1957), 50, 58.
5. C. Terlinden, *Charles Quint, Empereur des Deux Mondes* (Brussels, 1965), 53.
6. Wellens, *Les Etats Généraux*, 244–251, 258–262; Wiesflecker, *Kaiser Maximilian I*, vol. 2, 140–146.
7. Wiesflecker, *Kaiser Maximilian I*, vol. 1, 318–344.
8. Wiesflecker, *Kaiser Maximilian I*, vol. 2, 27–43.
9. James Tracy, *Holland under Habsburg Rule, 1506–1566*, 75; N. Maddens, *De beden in het graafschap Vlaanderen*, 426–428; Blockmans, "Finances publiques," 86.
10. W. Blockmans, "La Position du Comté de Flandre dans le royaume à la fin du XVe siècle," in B. Chevalier and Philippe Contamine, eds., *La France à la fin du XVe siècle* (Paris, 1985), 71–89; Dauchy, *De processen*, 286–304.
11. H. van der Wee, *The Growth of the Antwerp Market*.
12. Brulez, "Bruges and Antwerp"; W. Brulez and J. Craeybeckx, "Les Escales."
13. M. Martens, *The Bruges Art Market*; J. Wilson, "Marketing Painting in Late Medieval Flanders and Brabant," in X. Barral Altet, *Artistes, artisans, et production artistique au Moyen Age* (Paris, 1990), 621–627; L. Campbell, "The Art Market in the Southern Netherlands in the Fifteenth Century," *Burlington Magazine*, 118 (1976): 188–198; J. M. Montias, "Le Marché de l'art aux Pays-Bas, XVe et XVIe siècles," *Annales, Economies: Sociétés, Civilisations* 48 (1993): 1,545–1559.
14. M. Ainsworth, "Implications of Revised Attributions in Netherlandish Painting," *Metropolitan Museum Journal* 27 (1992): 72.
15. W. P. Blockmans, "Le Dialogue imaginaire entre princes et sujets: Les Joyeuses Entrées en Brabant en 1494 et en 1496," *PCEEB* 34 (1994): 37–53; W. P. Blockmans, "The Creative Environment: Incentives to and Functions of Bruges Art Production," in M. Ainsworth, ed., *Petrus Christus in Renaissance Bruges: An Interdisciplinary Approach* (New York and Turnhout, 1995), 11–20; W. P. Blockmans, "The Burgundian Court and the Urban Milieu as Patrons in 15th Century Bruges," in M. North, ed., *Economic History and the Arts* (Cologne, Weimar, and Vienna, 1996), 23–25.
16. On the cultural interaction between court and burghers, see H. Pleij, *De sneeuwpoppen van 1511*, 327–356.
17. R. de Roover, *The Rise and Decline of the Medici Bank, 1397–1494* (Cambridge, Mass., 1963), 343–347.
18. M. W. Ainsworth and M. P. J. Martens, *Petrus Christus* (New York, 1994), 43–49.
19. Kren, ed., *Margaret of York*; L. Nys and A. Salamagne, eds., *Valenciennes aux XIVe et XVe siècles*.

20. W. Aerts, ed., *La Cathédrale d'Anvers* (Antwerp 1993).

21. J. J. van Miegroet, *Gerard David* (Antwerp 1990).

22. *De Habsburgers en Mechelen* (Brussels, 1987); M. Smeyers and J. van der Stock, eds., *Flemish Illuminated Manuscripts, 1475-1550* (Ghent, 1996).

23. Jan van der Stock, ed., *Stadtbilder in Flandern: Spuren bürgerlicher Kultur, 1477-1787* (Brussels, 1991), 141-156, 219-254.

24. E. Vandamme, *De polychromie van gotische houtsculptuur in de Zuidelijke Nederlanden* (Brussels, 1982).

25. Paul Trio, *De Gentse broederschappen (1182-1580)* (Ghent, 1990).

26. A. H. T. Levi, ed., *Collected Works of Erasmus*, vol. 27, *Praise of Folly (Moriae Encomium)*, Literary and Educational Writings 5 (Toronto, Buffalo, and London, 1986), 131.

27. R. P. Post, *Kerkelijke verhoudingen in Nederland vóór de Reformatie van ±1550 tot ±1580* (Utrecht, 1954), 160-67.

28. A. G. Weiler, *Volgens de norm van de vroege kerk: De geschiedenis van de huizen van de broeders van het Gemene Leven in Nederland* (Nijmegen: Centrum voor Middeleeuwse Studies, 1997).

29. T. Mertens, "The Devotio Moderna and Innovation in Middle Dutch Literature," in E. Kooper, ed., *Middle Dutch Literature in its European Context* (Cambridge, 1994), 226-243; T. Mertens, "Mystieke cultuur en literatuur in de late middeleeuwen," in *Grote lijnen: Syntheses over Middelnederlandse letterkunde* (Amsterdam, 1995), 117-135, 205-217.

30. G. van Doorslaer, "La Chapelle musicale de Philippe le Beau," *Revue belge d'archéologie et d'histoire de l'art* (1934); I. Bossuyt, *Adriaen Willaert (ca. 1490-1562)* (Louvain, 1985).

31. M. Picker, "The Chanson Albums of Marguerite of Austria," *Annales musicologiques* (1958, 1963); R. W. M. de Beer, "Petrus Alamire, muziekschrijver en calligraaf," in A. M. Koldeweij, ed., *In Buscoducis. Bijdragen* (The Hague, 1990), 505-512.

32. A. Balis et al., *Les Chasses de Maximilien* (Paris, 1993).

33. W. P. Blockmans, "Die politische Theorie des Erasmus und die Praxis seiner Zeit," in J. Sperna Weiland et al., eds., *Erasmus von Rotterdam: Die Aktualität seines Denkens* (Hamburg, 1988).

34. L. V. G. Gorter-van Royen, *Maria van Hongarije, regentes der Nederlanden*, 131-161.

Chapter 9. The Burgundian Legacy

1. James D. Tracy, *Holland under Habsburg Rule 1506-1566*, 64-89; Jonathan Israel, *The Dutch Republic: Its Rise, Greatness, and Fall, 1477-1806* (Oxford, 1995), 1-128.

2. Van Tielhof, *Koren op de Amsterdamse molen*, 132-38; Louis Sicking, *Zeemacht en onmacht: Maritieme Politiek in de Nederlanden, 1488-1558* (Amsterdam, 1997).

3. Gorter-van Royen, *Maria van Hongarije*, 129-145.

4. H. de Schepper, *"Belgium nostrum," 1500–1650: Over integratie en desintegratie van het Nederland* (Antwerp, 1987), 10–17.

5. Tracy, *Holland under Habsburg Rule*, 138–146.

6. Guido Marnef, *Antwerp in the Age of Reformation: Underground Protestantism in a Commercial Metropolis, 1550–1577* (Baltimore, 1996).

Bibliography

This bibliography only contains works of general interest. Other titles are cited in full in the notes.

Alberts, W. J. *De Staten van Gelre en Zutphen tot 1459* (the Hague, 1950).
———. *Geschiedenis van Gelderland tot 1492* (Zutphen, 1978).
———. *Overzicht van de geschiedenis van de Nederrijnse territoria tussen Maas en Rijn, 2: 1288–c. 1500* (Assen, 1982).
Algemene Geschiedenis der Nederlanden, 1st edition J. A. van Houtte et al., eds., vols. 3, 4 (Utrecht, 1951–1952); 2d edition D. P. Blok, W. Prevenier, et al., eds., vols. II–V (Haarlem, 1980–82).
Allmand, C. *The Hundred Years' War: England and France at War, c. 1300–c. 1450* (Cambridge, 1988).
Anrooij, W. van, ed. *Holland in wording: De ontstaansgeschiedenis van het graafschap Holland tot het begin van de vijftiende eeuw* (Hilversum, 1991).
Armstrong, C. A. J. "La Double monarchie France-Angleterre et la maison de Bourgogne, 1420–1435: Le Déclin d'une alliance," *Annales de Bourgogne* 37 (1965): 81–112.
———. "The Language Question in the Low Countries: Administration," in *Europe in the Middle Ages*, J. R. Hale, J. R. L. Highfield, and B. Smallay, eds. (London, 1965), 386–409.
———. "La Politique matrimoniale des ducs de Bourgogne de la maison de Valois," *Annales de Bourgogne* 40 (1968): 5–58, 89–139.
———. *England, France, and Burgundy in the Fifteenth Century* (London, 1983).
Arnade, P. *Realms of Ritual: Burgundian Ceremony and Civic Life in Late Medieval Ghent* (Ithaca, N.Y., and London, 1996).
Arnould, M. A. *Les Dénombrements de foyers dans le comté de Hainaut, XIVe–XVIe siècles* (Brussels, 1956).
———. "Le Hainaut: Evolution historique d'un concept géographique," in *Le Hainaut français et belge* (Mons, 1969), 15–42.
———. "Une Estimation des revenus et des dépenses des Philippe le Bon en 1445," in *Recherches sur l'histoire des finances publiques en Belgique: Acta Historica Bruxelensia* 3 (1973): 131–219.
Autrand, F. *Naissance d'un grand corps d'Etat: Les Gens du Parlement de Paris, 1345–1454* (Paris, 1981).
———. *Charles VI* (Paris, 1986).
———. *Charles V, le Sage* (Paris, 1994).
Bartier, J. *Légistes et gens de finances au XVe siècle: Les Conseillers des ducs de Bourgogne Philippe le Bon et Charles le Téméraire* (Brussels, 1955).

———. *Charles le Temeraire* (Brussels, 1970).
———. *Karel de Stoute* (Brussels, 1970).
Bigwood, G. "Gand et la circulation des grains en Flandre, du XIVe au XVIIIe siècles," *Vierteljahrschrift für Sozial- und Wirtschaftsgeschichte* 4 (1906): 397–460.
Bittmann, K. *Ludwig XI und Karl der Kühne: Die Memoiren des Philippen de Commynes als historische Quelle*, 2 vols. (Göttingen, 1964).
Blockmans, W. P. "Autocratie ou polyarchie? La Lutte pour le pouvoir politique en Flandre, d'après des documents inédits, 1482–1492," *BCRH* 140 (1974): 257–368.
———. "A Typology of Representative Institutions in Late Medieval Europe," *JMH* 4 (1978): 189–215.
———. *De volksvertegenwoordiging in Vlaanderen in de overgang van Middeleeuwen naar Nieuwe Tijden, 1384–1506* (Brussels, 1978).
———. "The Social and Economic Effects of Plague in the Low Countries 1349–1500," *RBPH* 60 (1982): 833–863.
———. "Corruptie, patronage, makelaardij en venaliteit als symptomen van een ontluikende staatsvorming," *TSG* 11 (1985): 231–47.
———. "Finances publiques et inégalité sociale dans les Pays-Bas aux XIVe–XVIe siècles," in *Genèse de l'état moderne: prélèvement et redistribution*, J. P. Genet and M. Le Menée, eds. (Paris, 1987), 77–90.
———. "The Devotion of a Lonely Duchess," in *Margaret of York, Simon Marmion, and the Visions of Tondal*, T. Kren, ed. (Santa Monica, 1992), 29–46.
———. "The Economic Expansion of Holland and Zeeland in the Fourteenth–Sixteenth Centuries," in E. Aerts et al., eds., *Economic Growth and Development in an Historical Perspective: Liber Amicorum Herman van der Wee* (Leuven, 1993), 41–58.
———, ed. *1477. Het algemene en de gewestelijke privilegiën van Maria van Bourgondië* (Heule and Kortrijk, 1985).
Blockmans, W. P., and W. Prevenier. "Poverty in Flanders and Brabant from the Fourteenth to the Mid-Sixteenth Century: Sources and Problems," *Acta Historiae Neerlandicae* 10 (1978): 20–57.
Boer, D. de. *Graaf en grafiek: Sociale en economische ontwikkelingen in het middeleeuwse Noordholland tussen 1345 en 1415* (Leiden, 1978).
———. "Een vorst trekt noordwaarts: De komst van Albrecht van Beieren naar de Nederlanden, 1358," in D. de Boer and J. W. Marsilje, *De Nederlanden in de late middeleeuwen* (Utrecht, 1987), 283–309.
Bonenfant, A. M. and P. Bonenfant. "Le Projet d'érection des états bourguignons en royaume en 1447," *MA* 45 (1935): 10–23.
Bonenfant, P. *Du Meurtre de Montereau au traité de Troyes* (Brussels, 1958).
Boone, M. *Geld en macht: De Gentse stadsfinanciën en de Bourgondische staatsvorming (1384–1453)* (Ghent, 1990).
———. *Gent en de Bourgondische hertogen* (Brussels, 1990).
Boone, M., T. de Hemptinne, and W. Prevenier. "Fictie en historische realiteit: Colijn van Rijsseles, 'De Spieghel der Minnen,' ook een spiegel van sociale spanningen in de Nederlanden der late Middeleeuwen?" *Jaarboek de Soevereine Hoofdkamer van Retorica "De Fonteine" te Gent* 4 (1984): 9–33.

Boone, M., and W. Prevenier, eds. *La Draperie ancienne des Pays-Bas: Débouchés et stratégies de survie (14e–16e siècles)* (Drapery production in the late medieval Low Countries: Markets and strategies for survival (14th–16th Centuries)) (Leuven and Apeldoorn, 1993).

———. *Finances publiques et finances privées au bas Moyen Âge* (Public and private finances in the late Middle Ages) (Leuven and Apeldoorn, 1996).

Borchgrave, C. de. *Diplomaten en Diplomatie onder hertog Jan zonder Vrees* (Kortrijk and Heule, 1992).

Bos-Rops, J. A. M. Y. "Van incidentele gunst tot jaarlijkse belasting: de bede in het vijftiende-eeuwse Holland," in *Fiscaliteit in Nederland* (Zutphen and Deventer, 1987), 21–32.

———. *Graven op zoek naar geld, De inkomsten van de graven van Holland, 1389–1433* (Hilversum, 1993).

Bragt, R. van. *De Blijde Inkomst van de hertogen van Brabant Johanna en Wenceslas* (Leuven, 1956).

Brand, H. *Over macht en overwicht: Stedelijke elites in Leiden, 1420–1510* (Leuven and Apeldoorn, 1996).

Brokken, H. *Het ontstaan van de Hoekse en Kabeljauwse twisten* (Zutphen, 1982).

Brulez, W. "Engels laken in Vlaanderen in de 14ᵉ en 15ᵉ eeuw," *ASEB* 108 (1971): 5–25.

———. "Bruges and Antwerp in the 15th and 16th Centuries: An Antithesis?" *Acta Historiae Neerlandicae* 6 (1973): 1–26.

Brulez, W., and J. Craeybeckx. "Les Escales au carrefour des Pays-Bas, Bruges et Anvers, 14ᵉ–16ᵉ siècles," *Recueils de la Société Jean Bodin* 31 (1975): 417–74.

Buntinx, J. *De Audiëntie van de graven van Vlaanderen: Studie over het centraal grafelijk gerecht, c. 1330–c. 1409* (Brussels, 1949).

Byl, R. *Les juridictions scabinales dans le duché de Brabant des origines à la fin du XVe siècle* (Brussels, 1965).

Calmette, J. *Les Grands Ducs de Bourgogne* (Paris, 1956).

Carlier, M. "De sociale positie van de bastaard in het laat-middeleeuwse Vlaanderen," *TSG* 13 (1987): 173–97.

Carlier, M., A. Greve, W. Prevenier, and P. Stabel, eds. *Core and Periphery in Late Medieval Urban Society. Hart en marge in de laat-middeleeuwse stedelijke maatschappij* (Leuven and Apeldoorn, 1997).

Cartellieri, O. *Philipp der Kühne* (Leipzig, 1910).

Cauchies, J. M. *La Législation princière pour le comté de Hainaut: Ducs de Bourgogne et premiers Habsbourg (1427–1506)* (Brussels, 1982).

———. *Louis XI et Charles le Hardi, de Péronne à Nancy, 1468–1477: Le Conflit* (Brussels, 1996).

Cauwenberghe, E. van. *Het vorstelijk domein en de overheidsfinanciën in de Nederlanden, 15de–16de eeuw* (Brussels, 1982).

Cazaux, Y. *Marie de Bourgogne* (Paris, 1967).

Cinq-centième anniversaire de la bataille de Nancy, 1477 (Nancy, 1979).

Clauzel, D. *Finances et politique à Lille pendant la période bourguignonne* (Dunkerque, 1982).

Cockshaw, P. "A propos de la circulation monétaire entre la Flandre et le Brabant, de 1384 à 1390," *Contributions à l'histoire économique et sociale* 6 (1970): 105–41.

———. *Le Personnel de la chancellerie de Bourgogne-Flandre sous les ducs de Bourgogne de la maison de Valois* (Kortrijk and Heule, 1982).
Coornaert, E. *Un Centre industriel d'autrefois: La Draperie-sayetterie d'Hondschoote, XIVᵉ–XVIIIᵉ siècles* (Paris, 1930).
Craeybeckx, J. *Un Grand Commerce d'importation: Les Vins de France aux anciens Pays-Bas, XIIIᵉ–XVIᵉ siècles* (Paris, 1958).
Curry, A. *The Hundred Years War* (Basingstoke, 1992).
Danneel, M. *Weduwen en wezen in het laat-middeleeuwse Gent* (Leuven and Apeldoorn, 1995).
Dauchy, S. *De processen in beroep bij het Parlement van Parijs, 1320–1521. Een rechtshistorisch onderzoek naar de wording van staat en souvereiniteit in de Bourgondisch-Habsburgse periode* (Brussels, 1995).
Decavele, J., ed. *Ghent: A Rebellious City* (Antwerp: Mercatorfonds, 1989).
Degryse, R. "De Vlaamse Haringvisserij in de XVe eeuw," *ASEB* 88 (1951): 116–33.
———. "De Vlaamse Westvaart en de Engelse represailles omstreeks 1378," *HMGOG* 27 (1973): 193–239.
Demey, J. "Proeve tot raming van de bevolking en de weefgetouwen te Ieper van de XIIIᵉ tot de XVIIᵉ eeuw," *BTFG* 28 (1950): 1,031–48; reprinted in O. Mus en J. A. van Houtte, eds., *Prisma van de Geschiedenis van Ieper* (Ypres, 1974).
Demuynck, R. "De Gentse Oorlog, 1379–1385: Oorzaken en karakter," *HMGOG* 5 (1951): 305–18.
Derville, A. "Les Draperies flamandes et artésiennes vers 1250–1350: Quelques considérations critiques et problématiques," *RN* 54 (1972): 353–70.
———. "Le Grenier des Pays-Bas médiévaux," *RN* 69 (1987): 267–80.
———. "La Fiscalité d'état dans l'Artois et la Flandre wallonne avant 1569," *RN* 74 (1992): 25–52.
Dhanens, E. *Actum Gandavi: Zeven bijdragen i.v.m. de Oude Kunst te Gent* (Brussels, 1987).
———. *Hubert en Jan van Eyck* (Antwerp, 1980); *Hubert and Jan van Eyck* (New York, 1980).
Dickinson, J. G. *The Congress of Arras, 1435* (Oxford, 1955).
Dickstein-Bernard, C. *La Gestion financière d'une capitale à ses débuts: Bruxelles, 1334–1467* (Brussels, 1977).
Dieperink, F. H. J., ed. *Studiën betreffende de geschiedenis van Oost-Nederland van de dertiende tot de vijftiende eeuw* (Groningen, 1953).
Dumolyn, J. *De Brugse opstand, 1436–38* (Kortrijk-Heule, 1997).
Dupont, G. *Maagdenverleidsters, hoeren en speculanten: Prostitutie in Brugge tijdens de Bourgondische periode, 1385–1515* (Bruges, 1996).
Duvosquel, J.-M., et. al., eds. *Les Pays-Bas bourguignons, histoire et institutions: Mélanges André Uyttebrouck* (Brussels, 1996).
Famiglietti, R. C. *Royal Intrigue: Crisis at the Court of Charles VI, 1392–1420* (New York, 1987).
Favier, J. *La Guerre de Cent Ans* (Poitiers, 1980).
Favresse, F. *L'Avènement du régime démocratique à Bruxelles pendant le Moyen Age, 1306–1423* (Brussels, 1932).
Formsma, W. J., ed. *De wording van de Staten van Stad en Lande tot 1536* (Assen, 1930).

———. *Historie van Groningen: Stad en Land* (Groningen, 1976).
Gaier, C. *L'Industrie et le commerce des armes dans les anciennes principautés belges du XIIIe à la fin du XVe siècle* (Paris, 1973).
Ganshof, F. L. "La Flandre," in F. Lot and R. Fawtier, eds., *Histoire des institutions françaises au Moyen Age*, vol. 1 (Paris, 1957), 343–426.
Ganshof, F. L., and A. Verhulst. "Medieval Agrarian Society in Its Prime: France, the Low Countries, and Western Germany," in M. M. Posran and H. J. Habakkuk, eds., *The Cambridge Economic History of Europe: I. The Agrarian Life of the Middle Ages* (Cambridge, 1966), 291–339.
Genicot, L. *L'Economie rurale namuroise au bas Moyen Age, 1199–1429*, vol. 1 (Namur, 1943); vol. 2 (Leuven, 1960); vol. 3 (Brussels, 1982).
Gent, M. J. van. *"Pertijelike saken": Hoeken en Kabeljauwen in het Bourgondisch-Oostenrijkse tijdperk* (the Hague: Stichting Hollandse Historische Reeks, 1994).
Gilissen, J. "Oprichting en evolutie van het Parlement/De Grote Raad van Mechelenc," in *Concilium Magnum, 1473–1973* (Brussels, 1977), 11–24.
Gorissen, P. *Het Parlement en de Raad van Kortenberg* (Leuven, 1956).
Gorter-van Royen, L. V. G. *Maria van Hongarije, regentes der Nederlanden* (Hilversum, 1995).
Gruben, F. de. *Les Chapitres de la Toison d'Or à l'époque bourguignonne (1430–1477)* (Leuven, 1997).
Guenée, B. *Un Meurtre, une société: L'Assasssinat du duc d'Orléans, 23 novembre 1407* (Paris, 1992).
Haegeman, M. *De anglofilie in het graafschap Vlaanderen tussen 1379 en 1435: Politieke en economische aspecten* (Kortrijk-Heule, 1988).
Haepke, R. *Brügges Entwicklung zum mittelalterlichen Weltmarkt* (Berlin, 1908).
Helmrath, J. *Das Basler Konzil, 1431–1449* (Cologne and Vienna, 1987).
Herwaarden, J. van. "Stedelijke rivaliteit in de middeleeuwen: Toscane, Vlaanderen, Holland," in P. Blaas and J. van Herwaarden, eds., *Stedelijke naijver: De betekenis van interstedelijke conflicten in de geschiedenis* (The Hague, 1986), 38–81.
Hoppenbrouwers, P. C. M. *Een middeleeuwse samenleving: Het Land van Heusden, ca. 1360–ca. 1515*, 2 vols. (Wageningen, 1992).
Houtte, J. A. van. *An Economic History of the Low Countries, 800–1800* (London, 1977).
Hoven van Genderen, B. van den. *Het kapittel-generaal en de Staten van het Nedersticht in de 15de eeuw* (Utrecht, 1987).
Howell, M. *Women, Production and Patriarchy in Late Medieval Cities* (Chicago, 1986).
Huizinga, J. *The Waning of the Middle Ages: A Study of the Forms of Life, Thought, and Art in France and the Netherlands in the Fourteenth and Fifteenth Centuries* (London, 1924).
Immink, P. W. A. *De wording van Staat en souvereiniteit in de middeleeuwen. Een rechtshistorische studie in het bijzonder met betrekking tot het Nedersticht*, vol. I (Utrecht, 1942).
Janse, A. *Grenzen aan de macht: De Friese oorlog van de graven van Holland omstreeks, 1400* (The Hague, 1993).

Jansen, H. P. H. *Hoekse en Kabeljauwse twisten* (Bussum, 1966).
Jansma, T. S. *Raad en Rekenkamer in Holland en Zeeland tijdens Hertog Philips van Bourgondië* (Utrecht, 1952).
Janssen, W. "Niederrheinische Territorialbildung," in E. Ennen and K. Flink, eds., *Soziale und wirtschaftliche Bindungen im Mittelalter am Niederrhein* (Cleves, 1981), 95–113.
Jean, M. *La Chambre des Comptes de Lille. L'Institution et les hommes, 1477–1667* (Paris and Geneva, 1993).
Jongkees, A. G. *Staat en Kerk in Holland en Zeeland onder de Bourgondische hertogen, 1425–1477* (Groningen and Batavia, 1942).
———. *Burgundica et Varia* (Hilversum, 1989).
Joris, A. "Der Handel der Maasstädte im Mittelalter," *Hansische Geschichtsblätter* 79 (1961): 15–33.
Kalma, J. *Geschiedenis van Friesland* (Drachten, 1968).
Kalveen, C. A. van. *Het bestuur van bisschop en Staten in het Nedersticht, Oversticht en Drenthe, 1483–1520* (Groningen, 1974).
Kan, F. J. W. van. *Sleutels tot de macht: De ontwikkeling van het Leidse Patriciaat tot 1420* (Hilversum, 1988).
Kastner, D. *Die Territorialpolitik der Grafen van Kleve* (Düsseldorf, 1972).
Kendall, P. M. *Louis XI: The Universal Spider* (New York and London, 1971).
Kerling, N. J. M. *Commercial Relations of Holland and Zeeland with England, from the Late Thirteenth Century to the Close of the Middle Ages* (Leiden, 1954).
Kokken, H. *Steden en Staten: Dagvaarten van steden en Staten van Holland onder Maria van Bourgondië en het eerste regentschap van Maximiliaan van Oostenrijk (1477–1494)* (the Hague, 1991).
Kruse, H. *Hofambt und Gagen: Die täglichen Gagenlisten des burgundischen Hofes (1430–1467) und der erste Hofstaat Karls des Kühnen, 1456* (Bonn, 1996).
Kuys, J. *De ambtman in het kwartier van Nijmegen (ca. 1250–1543)* (Nijmegen, 1987).
Lambrechts, P., and J. P. Sosson, eds. *Les Métiers au Moyen Age: Aspects économiques et sociaux* (Louvain-la-Neuve, 1994).
Laurent, H. *La Loi de Gresham au Moyen Age: Essai sur la circulation monétaire entre la Flandre et le Brabant à la fin du XIVe siècle* (Brussels, 1933).
Lejeune, J. *Liège et son pays: Naissance d'une patrie (XIIIe–XIVe siècle)* (Liège, 1948).
———. "Introduction historique," in *Liège et Bourgogne* (Liège, 1968), 15–92.
Lemmink, F. H. J. *Het ontstaan van de Staten van Zeeland en hun geschiedenis tot het jaar 1555* (Nijmegen, 1951).
Maddens, N. *De beden in het graafschap Vlaanderen tijdens de regering van keizer Karel V (1515–1550)* (Heule, 1978).
Marechal, G. *De sociale en politieke gebondenheid van het Brugse hospitaalwezen in de middeleeuwen* (Kortrijk and Heule, 1978).
Maris, A J. *Van voogdij tot maarschalkambt: Bijdrage tot de geschiedenis der Utrechtsbisschoppelijke staatsinstellingen, voornamelijk in het Nedersticht* (Utrecht, 1954).
Marsilje, J. W. *Het financiële beleid van Leiden in de laat-Beierse en Bourgondische periode, c. 1390–1477* (Hilversum, 1985).
———, ed. *Bloedwraak, partijstrijd, en pacificatie in laat-middeleeuws Holland* (Hilversum, 1990).

Martens, M. P. J., ed. *Lodewijk van Gruuthuse* (Bruges, 1992).
Monier, R. *Les Institutions judiciaires des villes de Flandre, des origines à la rédaction des coutumes* (Lille, 1924).
Mueller, H. *Die Franzosen, Frankreich, und das Basler Konzil (1431–1449)* (Paderborn, 1990).
Munro, J. H. *Wool, Cloth, and Gold: The Struggle for Bullion in Anglo-Burgundian Trade, 1340–1478* (Brussels and Toronto, 1973).
———. "Industrial Protectionism in Medieval Flanders: Urban or National?" in H. A. Miskimin, D. Herlihy, and A. L. Udovitch, eds., *The Medieval City* (New Haven, 1977), 229–67.
Mus, O., and J. A. van Houtte, eds. *Prisma van de Geschiedenis van Ieper* (Ypres, 1974).
Neillands, R. *The Hundred Years War, 1337–1453* (London, 1990).
Nicholas, D. *Town and Countryside: Social, Economic, and Political Tensions in Fourteenth-Century Flanders* (Bruges, 1971).
———. *The Metamorphosis of a Medieval City: Ghent in the Age of the Arteveldes, 1302–1390* (Lincoln and London, 1987).
———. *The van Arteveldes of Ghent: The Varieties of Vendetta and the Hero in History* (Ithaca, N.Y., 1988).
———. *Medieval Flanders* (London and New York, 1992).
———. *The Growth of the Medieval City: From Late Antiquity to the Early Fourteenth Century* (New York, 1997).
———. *The Later Medieval City, 1300–1500* (London and New York, 1997).
Nieuwenhuysen, A. van. *Les Finances du duc de Bourgogne Philippe le Hardi (1384–1404): Economie et politique* (Brussels, 1984).
———. *Les Finances du duc de Bourgogne Philippe le Hardi (1384–1404): Le Montant des ressources* (Brussels, 1990).
Nordberg, M. *Les Ducs et la royauté: Etudes sur la rivalité des ducs d'Orléans et de Bourgogne, 1392–1407* (Uppsala, 1964).
Nüsse, K. *Die Entwicklung der Stände im Herzogtum Geldern bis zum Jahre 1418 nach den Stadtrechnungen von Arnheim* (Cologne, 1958).
Oostrom, F. P. van. *Court and Culture: Dutch Literature, 1350–1450* (Berkeley and Los Angeles and Oxford, 1992).
Overvoorde, J. C., and J. G. C. Joosting. *De gilden van Utrecht tot 1528* (The Hague, 1897).
Palmer, J. J. N. "England, France, the Papacy, and the Flemish Succession, 1361–1369," *JMH* 2 (1976): 339–64.
Paravicini, W. *Guy de Brimeu: Der burgundische Staat und seine adlige Führungsschicht unter Karl dem Kühnen* (Bonn, 1975).
———. *Karl der Kühne* (Göttingen, 1976).
———. "Expansion et intégration: La Noblesse des Pays-Bas à la cour de Philippe le Bon," *BMGN* 95 (1980): 298–314.
———. "The Court of the Dukes of Burgundy: A Model for Europe?" in R. G. Asch and A. M. Birk, eds., *Princes, Patronage, and the Nobility: The Court at the Beginning of the Modern Age, c. 1450–1650* (Oxford, 1991), 69–102.
———. "Die Residenzen der Herzöge von Burgund, 1363–1477," in H. Patze and

W. Paravicini, eds., *Fürstliche Residenzen im spätmittelalterlichen Europa* (Sigmaringen, 1991), 207–63.

Paviot, J. *La Politique navale des ducs de Bourgogne, 1384–1482* (Lille, 1995).

Peteghem, P. P. J. L. van. *De Raad van Vlaanderen en staatsvorming onder Karel V (1515–1555)* (Nijmegen, 1990).

Petit, E. *Les Ducs de Bourgogne de la maison de Valois*, vol. 1: *Philippe le Hardi, 1363–1380* (Paris, 1909).

Pirenne, H. *Early Democracies in the Low Countries: Urban Society and Political Conflict in the Middle Ages and the Renaissance* (New York, 1963).

Pleij, H. *De Gilde van de Blauwe Schuit: Literatuur, volksfeest, en burgermoraal in de late Middeleeuwen* (Amsterdam, 1979).

———. *De sneeuwpoppen van 1511: Literatuur en stadscultuur tussen middeleeuwen en moderne tijd* (Amsterdam and Leuven, 1988).

———. *Dromen van Cocagne: Middeleeuwse fantasieën over het volmaakte leven* (Amsterdam, 1997).

———, ed. *Op belofte van profijt: Stadsliteratuur en burgermoraal in de Nederlandse letterkunde van de middeleeuwen* (Amsterdam, 1991).

Posthumus, N. W. *De geschiedenis van de Leidsche Lakenindustrie*, vol. 1 (The Hague, 1908).

Prevenier, W. *De Leden en de Staten van Vlaanderen (1384–1405)* (Brussels, 1961).

———. "Les Etats de Flandre, depuis les origines jusqu'en 1790," *SL* 33 (1965): 15–59.

———. "De Verhouding van de Clerus tot de locale en regionale overheid in het Graafschap Vlaanderen in de late Middeleeuwen," in *Sources pour l'histoire religieuse de la Belgique: Moyen Age et temps modernes* (Leuven, 1968), 9–45.

———. "Financiën en boekhouding in de Bourgondische periode: Nieuwe bronnen en resultaten," *TG* 82 (1969): 469–481.

———. "Les Perturbations dans les relations commerciales anglo-flamandes entre 1379 et 1407: Causes de désaccord et raisons d'une réconciliation," in *Economies et sociétés du Moyen Age: Mélanges E. Perroy* (Paris, 1973), 477–497.

———. "Officials in Town and Countryside in the Low Countries: Social and Professional Developments from the Fourteenth to the Sixteenth Century," *Acta Historiae Neerlandicae* 7 (1974): 1–17.

———. "En marge de l'assistance aux pauvres: L'Aumônerie des comtes de Flandre et des ducs de Bourgogne (13e–début 16e siècle)," in *Recht en Instellingen in de Oude Nederlanden tijdens de middeleeuwen en de nieuwe tijd: Liber Amicorum J. Buntinx* (Leuven, 1981), 97–128.

———. "La Démographie des villes du comté de Flandre aux XIVe et XVe siècles," *RN* 65 (1983): 255–275.

Prevenier, W., and W. P. Blockmans. *The Burgundian Netherlands* (Cambridge, 1986).

Prevenier, W., and M. Boone, "Fourteenth and Fifteenth Centuries: The City State Dream," in J. Decavele, ed., *Ghent: A Rebellious City* (Antwerp: Mercatorfonds, 1989), 80–105.

Quicke, F. *Les Pays-Bas à la veille de la période bourguignonne, 1356–1384* (Paris and Brussels, 1947).

Ramakers, B. A. M. *Spelen en Figuren: Toneelkunst en processiecultuur in Oudenaarde tussen Middeleeuwen en Moderne Tijd* (Amsterdam, 1996).

Ridder-Symoens, H. de. "Possibilités de carrière et de mobilité sociale des intellectuels-universitaires au Moyen Age," in *Proceedings of the First Interdisciplinary Conference on Medieval Prosopography held at Bielefeld, 3–5 December 1982* (Kalamazoo, 1986), 1–15.

Rogghé, P. "De Gentse Klerken in de XIVe en XVe eeuw: Trouw en Verraad," *Appeltjes van het Meetjesland* 11 (1960): 5–142.

——. "De politiek van graaf Lodewijk van Male," *Appeltjes van het Meetjesland* 15 (1964): 388–441.

Rompaey, J. van. *Het grafelijk baljuwsambt in Vlaanderen tijdens de Boergondische periode* (Brussels, 1967).

——. *De Grote Raad van de Hertogen van Boergondië en het Parlement van Mechelen* (Brussels, 1973).

Roover, R. de. *Money, Banking, and Credit in Mediaeval Bruges* (Cambridge, Mass., 1948).

——. *The Bruges Money Market Around 1400* (Brussels, 1968).

Rutgers, C. A., ed. *De Utrechtse bisschop in de middeleeuwen* (the Hague, 1978).

Schaïk, R. W. M. van. *Belasting, bevolking en bezit in Gelre en Zutphen (1350–1550)* (Hilversum, 1987).

Schneider, F. *Herzog Johann von Baiern: Erwählter Bischof von Lüttich und Graf von Holland (1373–1425)* (Berlin, 1913).

Schnerb, B. *Les Armagnacs et les Bourguignons: La Maudite guerre* (Paris, 1988).

Scholliers, E. *Loonarbeid en Honger: De levensstandaard in de XVe en XVIe eeuw te Antwerpen* (Antwerp, 1960).

Seifert, D. *Kompagnons und Konkurrenten: Holland und die Hanse im späten Mittelalter* (Cologne and Vienna, 1997).

Sivéry, G. *Les Comtes de Hainaut et le commerce du vin au XIVe siècle et au début du XVe siècle* (Lille, 1969).

——. *Structures agraires et vie rurale dans le Hainaut à la fin du moyen âge*, vol. 1 (Villeneuve d'Ascq, 1977).

Slicher van Bath, B. H., ed. *Geschiedenis van Overijssel* (Deventer, 1970).

——. *Een samenleving onder spanning, geschiedenis van het platteland in Overijssel* (Utrecht, 1972).

Smit, J. G. *Vorst en Onderdaan: Studies over Holland en Zeeland in de late middeleeuwen* (Leuven, 1995).

Sosson, J. P. *Les Travaux publics de la ville de Bruges, XIVe–XVe siècles: Les Matériaux, les hommes* (Brussels, 1977).

——. "Die Körperschaften in den Niederlanden und Nordfrankreich: Neue Forschungsperspektiven," in K. Friedland, ed., *Gilde und Korporation in den nordeuropäischen Städten des späten Mittelalters* (Cologne and Vienna, 1984), 79–90.

——. "Les XIVe et XVe siècles: Un Age d'or de la main-d'oeuvre?" *PCEEB* 27 (1987): 19–37.

Spading, K. *Holland und die Hanse im 15. Jahrhundert* (Weimar, 1973).

Spufford, P. "Coinage, Taxation, and the Estates General of the Burgundian Netherlands," *SL* 40 (1966): 61–88.

———. *Monetary Problems and Policies in the Burgundian Netherlands, 1433–1496* (Leiden, 1970).
Stabel, P. *De kleine stad in Vlaanderen (14de–16de eeuw)* (Brussels, 1995).
———. *Dwarfs among Giants: The Flemish Urban Network in the Late Middle Ages* (Leuven and Apeldoorn, 1997).
Stein, R. *Politiek en historiografie: Het ontstaansmilieu van Brabantse kronieken in de eerste helft van de 15de eeuw* (Leuven, 1994).
Sterk, J. *Philips van Bourgondië (1465–1524), bisschop van Utrecht, als protagonist van de renaissance* (Zutphen, 1980).
Straeten, J. van der. *Het Charter en de Raad van Kortenberg*, 2 vols. (Brussels and Leuven, 1952).
Strohm, R. *Music in Late Medieval Bruges* (Oxford, 1985).
Struick, J. E. A. L. *Gelre en Habsburg, 1492–1528* (Utrecht, 1960).
Stuip, R. E. V., and C. Vellekoop, eds. *Utrecht tussen kerk en staat* (Hilversum, 1991).
Taal, G. "Het graafschap Zeeland en zijn verhouding tot Holland in de landsheerlijke tijd," *Archief Zeeuwsch Genootschap der Wetenschappen* (1965), 51–96.
Thielemans, M. R. *Bourgogne et Angleterre: Relations politiques et économiques entre les Pays-Bas bourguignons et l'Angleterre, 1435–1467* (Brussels, 1966).
Thoen, E. *Landbouwekonomie en bevolking in Vlaanderen gedurende de late Middeleeuwen en het begin van de moderne tijden: Testregio, de Kasselrijen van Oudenaarde en Aalst (eind 13de–eerste helft 16de eeuw)*, 2 vols. (Ghent, 1988).
Tielhof, M. van. *Koren op Amsterdams molen: De Hollandse graanhandel, 1470–1570* (The Hague, 1995).
Tits-Dieuaide, M. J. *La Formation des prix céréaliers en Brabant et en Flandre au XVe siècle* (Brussels, 1975).
Töpfer, B. "Die Rolle von Städtebunden bei der Ausbildung der Ständeverfassung in den Fürstentümern Lüttich und Brabant," in B. Töpfer, ed., *Städte und Ständestaat: Zur Rolle der Städte bei der Entwicklung der Ständeverfassung in europäischen Staaten vom 13. bis zum 15. Jahrhundert* (Berlin, 1980), 113–154.
Toussaert, J. *Le Sentiment religieux en Flandre à la fin du Moyen Age* (Paris, 1960).
Tracy, J. D. *A Financial Revolution in the Habsburg Netherlands: Renten and Renteniers in the County of Holland, 1515–1565* (Berkeley, 1985).
———. *Holland under Habsburg Rule, 1506–1566: The Formation of a Body Politic* (Berkeley, 1990).
Unger, R. W. *Dutch Shipbuilding before 1800* (Assen, 1978).
Uyttebrouck, A. *Le Gouvernement du duché de Brabant au bas moyen âge (1355–1430)*, 2 vols. (Brussels, 1975).
Uytven, R. van. "La Flandre et le Brabant, 'terres de promission' sous les ducs de Bourgogne?" *RN* 43 (1961): 281–317.
———. *Stadsfinanciën en stadsekonomie te Leuven van de XIIde tot het einde der XVIde eeuw* (Brussels, 1961).
———. "Plutokratie in de 'oude demokratieën der Nederlanden,'" *Handelingen Koninklijke Zuidnederlandse Maatschappij voor Taal — en Letterkunde en Geschiedenis* 16 (1962): 373–409.
———. "What Is New Socially and Economically in the Sixteenth-Century Netherlands," *Acta Historiae Neerlandicae* 7 (1974): 18–53.

———. "La Draperie brabançonne et malinoise, du XIIe au XVIIe siècles," in *Produzione, Commercio, e Consumo dei Panni di Lana* (Florence, 1976), 85-97.

———. "Vorst, adel, en steden: Een driehoeksverhouding in Brabant van de twaalfde tot de zestiende eeuw," *Bijdragen tot de Geschiedenis* 59 (1976): 93-122.

———. "L'Approvisionnement des villes des anciens Pays-Bas au Moyen Age," in *L'Approvisionnement des villes de l'Europe occidentale: Flaran* 5 (1983): 75-116.

Uytven, R. van, and W. P. Blockmans. "Constitutions and Their Application in the Netherlands During the Middle Ages," *RBPH* 47 (1969): 399-424.

Vanderjagt, A. J. *Qui sa vertu anoblist: The Concepts of Noblesse and Chose Publique in Burgundian Political Thought* (Groningen, 1981).

Vaughan, R. *Philip the Good: The Apogee of the Burgundian State* (London, 1970).

———. *Charles the Bold: The Last Valois Duke of Burgundy* (London, 1973).

———. *Valois Burgundy* (London, 1975).

———. *John the Fearless: The Growth of Burgundian Power* (London, 1979).

———. *Philip the Bold: The Formation of the Burgundian State* (London, 1979).

Verhulst, A. "De inlandse wolhandel in de textielnijverheid van de Nederlanden van de 12e tot de 17e eeuw: Produktie, handel, en verwerking," *BMGN* 85 (1970): 6-18.

———. *Précis d'histoire rurale de la Belgique* (Brussels, 1990).

Vermeersch, V., ed. *Bruges and Europe* (Antwerp, 1993).

Vries, O. *Het Heilige Roomse Rijk en de Friese Vrijheid* (Leeuwarden, 1986).

Waale, M. J. *De Arkelse oorlog, 1401-1412: Een politieke, krijgskundige, en economische analyse* (Hilversum, 1990).

Watson, W. B. "The Structure of the Florentine Galley Trade with Flanders and England in the Fifteenth Century," *RBPH* 39 (1961): 1,073-91.

Wee, H. van der. *The Growth of the Antwerp Market and the European Economy (Fourteenth-Sixteenth Centuries)*, 3 vols. (The Hague, 1963).

———. "Structural Changes and Specialization in the Industry of the Southern Netherlands, 1100-1600," *EHR* 27, 2d series (1975), 203-221.

———, ed. *The Rise and Decline of Urban Industries in Italy and in the Low Countries (Late Middle Ages-Early Modern Times)* (Leuven, 1988).

Weightman, C. *Margaret of York, Duchess of Burgundy, 1446-1503* (Gloucester and New York, 1989).

Wellens, R. *Les Etats Généraux des Pays-Bas, des origines à la fin du règne de Philippe le Beau (1464-1506)* (Heule, 1974).

Werveke, H. van. *Gent: Schets van een sociale geschiedenis* (Ghent, 1947).

Wiesflecker, H. *Kaiser Maximilian I*, 4 vols. (Munich, 1970-1979).

Zilverberg, S. B. J. *David van Bourgondië, bisschop van Terwaan en van Utrecht, ±1427-1496* (Groningen, 1951).

Zoete, A. *De beden in het graafschap Vlaanderen (1405-1467)* (Brussels, 1994).

Index

Aa, river, 156
Aachen, 231
Aalst, Pieter van, 220, 229
Abigail, 139
Act of Secession, *1581*, 236
Adolf, duke of Cleves, 110–11, 182
Adolf of Egmond, duke of Guelders, 110, 182, 195
Adolf of Mark, bishop of Liège, 12
Adolf of Ravenstein, 110–11
Adrian VI, pope (Adriaan van Boyens), 230
Agincourt, 43, 56, 61, 104
Agriculture, 155–58
Ahasuerus, 136
Aire, 156, 179, 232
Alamire, Petrus, 229
Albert of Bavaria, count of Hainault, Holland, and Zeeland, 11, 29, 30, 32, 70, 72, 217
Albrecht, duke of Saxony, 203
Alençon, 113
Alexander the Great, 136, 139
Alkmaar, 88, 108
Alphen, 88
Alsace, 176, 182, 184–85, 189, 194
Alva, duke of, 238–39
Amersfoort, 201
Amiens, 40
Amsterdam, 66, 107, 108, 154, 155, 161, 165, 199, 236
Anjou, duke of, dynasty of, 32, 178, 236
Anne of Brittany, 200–201, 211
Anne of Burgundy, wife of John, duke of Bedford, 63
Anthony of Burgundy, duke of Brabant, xvi, 31, 35, 38, 39, 43, 45, 54–56, 57, 91, 104
Anthony the Great Bastard. *See* Burgundy, dynasty
Antwerp, 1, 11, 13, 24, 67, 154–55, 156, 162, 165, 167, 203, 211, 214, 216, 222, 223, 227, 236, 239

Apanage, 15
Aquitaine, 9
Aragon, 211, 230
Argonauts, 74
Aristotle, 6, 17
Armagnac, party, 41–44, 50–51, 53, 58, 61–62, 70
Arnemuiden, 215
Arnhem, 110, 183
Arnold of Egmond, duke of Guelders, 82, 110, 182–83
Arnolfini, Giovanni, 135, 166
Arras, ix, 18, 37, 42, 51, 60, 63, 81, 115, 135, 140, 154, 228; Congress of, 81–82, 85, 113, 179; Peace of, *1482*, 200; Treaty of, 81–82, 85, 95, 115, 136, 145, 178
Artevelde, 99, 127, 205; Philip of, 24; James of, 2, 10, 12, 23–24, 201
Artois, 1, 5, 6, 22, 24, 35, 60, 63, 81, 85, 102, 112, 124, 135, 142–46, 150–56, 164, 185, 195, 201, 209, 211, 214, 232, 240
Ath, treaty of, 11
Aubert, David, 136
Autun, 16, 20
Auxerre, 20, 77, 81, 142, 200
Auxonne, 19
Avesnes, dynasty, 10–11
Avignon, 9, 17–18, 21–22, 27, 33, 39, 62, 101

Baerze, Jacob de, 28, 71, 133
Balkans, 35
Bapaume, 156
Bar, 63, 189, 200
Barbari, Iacopo de, 229
Barbarossa. *See* Frederick Barbarossa
Barcelona, 231
Basel, 79–80, 81, 182
Bavaria, duchy, dynasty of. *See* Wittelsbach
Beaujolais, 53
Beaune, 2, 17, 18, 19, 123
Beauvais, 43

Bedford. *See* John, duke of Bedford
Beguines, 226
Benedict XIII, pope, 38, 39, 41, 59
Berg, 105
Bergen op Zoom, 155, 162, 167, 214
Berghe, Jan van der, 140
Berghe, Tielman van der, 22
Besançon, 105
Béthune, 69, 156
Beurse, Van der, 164–65
Biervliet, 125
Binchois, Gilles, 135, 228
Biscay, 159
Black Death, 9
Bladelin. *See* Leestmaker
Blois, 30
Bodeghem, Lodewijk van, 228
Bohemia, king of, 104
Bonne of Artois, countess of Nevers, xvi, 73
Bonne of Luxemburg, wife of King John II of France, 14
Borluut, Elisabeth, 73, 135
Borselen, Frank van, 90
Borselen, Wolfert van, 199
Bosch, Hieronymus (Jerome), 203, 217
Boulogne, 113
Bourbon, duke of, 31, 412
Bourg-en-Bresse, 228
Bourges, 44, 76
Bousse, David, 55
Bouts, Dirk, 219
Bouvignes, 180
Boyens, Adriaan van. *See* Adrian VI, pope
Brabant, ix, 1, 6, 8, 11–12, 13, 22, 28, 30–31, 39–40, 50, 53–56, 59, 63, 64–65, 69, 71, 83, 86, 87, 91–92, 97, 104, 110, 115, 122, 126, 128, 142–46, 150–55, 161–68, 180, 187, 189, 195, 198, 200–202, 208–9, 214, 221–23, 235–38, 240
Brederode, Gijsbrecht van, 110–11
Brederode, Reinoud van, 108, 111
Brétigny, treaty of, 18
Brielle (Den Briel), 88
Brimeu, Guy de, lord of Humbercourt, 181, 183, 198
Brittany, duchy of, 63, 73, 113, 129, 178
Broederlam, Melchior, 28, 71
Broquière, Bertrandon de la, 106
Brouwershaven, 87
Bruegel, Pieter the Elder, 217

Bruges, ix, 6, 7, 17, 18, 21, 22, 24–25, 26, 27, 48, 49, 50–51, 71, 73–74, 87, 92, 97–99, 115, 122, 124–29, 130–31, 135, 135–40, 143, 144, 148, 154, 146, 161–69, 180, 199, 202, 203, 207–8, 210, 214–25, 218, 220, 221–23, 228, 236
Bruges Free Quarter (Franc), 46, 127, 191, 208, 237
Bruges, Jan van, 17
Brussels, 35, 67, 87, 90, 115, 130, 134, 140, 143, 154, 155, 202, 208, 218, 220–23, 228–29, 231–33
Bulgaria, 35
Bundere, Martin van den, 119
Burgundian Circle, 232, 235
Burgundy, dynasty: Anna, daughter of John the Fearless, wife of John duke of Bedford, 63; Anthony, the "Great Bastard," 136
Busleyden, Jerome, 229–30
Busnois, Antoine, 135, 228

Cabochiens, 42
Cadzand, treaty of, 207
Caesar, 139
Calais, 13, 15, 38, 39, 68, 82–85, 93, 97, 98, 154, 160
Calfvel, 46, 47, 50–51, 98
Cambrai, 29, 32, 112, 139; Peace of, 213, 232
Cambridge, 13, 223
Campin, Robert, 134
Canard, Jean, 25, 224
Carolingian Empire, 6, 28
Carondolet, Jean, 198
Cassel, 77
Castelries, 22
Castile, 162–63, 171, 183–85; Cortes of, 148
Catalans, 92, 139
Cateau-Cambrésis, treaty of, 116
Catherine de Bourbon, 110, 164
Catherine of Cleves, 110
Catherine of France, xvi, 44, 63
Cenami, Giovanna, 135
Chalons-sur-Saône, 16, 20
Chambers of Accounts, 20, 25, 52, 55, 101, 118, 121, 143, 145, 182, 191–97, 203, 237
Chambéry, 77
Champagne, county of, 6, 16, 38, 62
Champagne Fairs, 6
Champmol, 28, 35, 70, 71, 75, 133, 136, 195, 210, 228

Index

Charlemagne, 73, 80, 92, 136, 165, 186
Charles IV of Luxemburg, emperor, 11, 190
Charles V, duke of Burgundy and emperor, viii, xi, xii, xvii, 3, 209, 212–18, 229, 230–36, 239
Charles V, king of France, xvi, 1, 16–18, 20, 23, 26, 28, 31, 34
Charles VI, king of France, 29, 31–33, 37–44, 61–63, 72, 76
Charles VII, king of France, 39, 41, 42, 43–44, 61, 63, 76–78, 79, 80, 86, 93, 104, 113, 115
Charles VIII, king of France, 200, 211
Charles the Bold, xvii, 73, 106, 114–16, 129, 130, 136–37, 139, 141, 142, 147, 166, 174–98, 206, 212, 219, 228, 232, 235, 237, 238
Charles, duke of Berry, 176–78
Charles, duke of Bourbon, 113
Charles, duke of Orleans, 38, 41
Charles the Good, count of Flanders, 7
Charlotte of Savoy, 115
Chartres, 43; Peace of, 41
Chastellain, Georges, 61, 67, 136
Chevrot, Jean, 114, 129
Chiny, county, 189
Christus, Petrus, 135, 171, 220
Clairvaux, Bernard of, 33
Clement VII, pope, 27
Cleves, duchy of, 105, 110, 181–82, 236
Clisson, Olivier de, 32
Clothilde, 33
Clovis, 136, 159
Clyte, Colard van der, 124
Cobham, Eleanor, 68, 89
Cod, party, 66–67, 86, 88, 89–90, 107–9, 199
Collegium Trilingue, 230
Cologne, 178, 183–84, 216, 222
Commynes, Philippe de, 5, 136–37, 141–42, 149, 173
Compiègne, 78
Conciliarism, 79
Conflans, treaty of, 115
Constance, council of, 27, 60, 79
Constantinople, 106
Copenhagen, 91
Córdoba, 163
Council of Flanders, 46–48
Courtrai, 161
Coustain, Pierre, 135

Crécy, 14
Crotroy, Le, 83
Croy, family of, 81, 113–16, 123, 129, 176, 208, 230
Croy, Anthony of, 105, 113, 115
Croy, Guillaume of, lord of Chièvres, 230–31
Croy, Jan of, 113
Croy, Johanna of, 108
Croy, Philip of, 113
Crusade, 35–36, 45, 106, 111, 138

Dalmatia, 9
Damme, 139, 164, 215
Danzig, 219
Dary, Robert, 220
Dauphin, 115
David of Burgundy, bishop of Utrecht, 111, 201, 224
David, Gerard, 222
Delft, 88, 154, 158; Treaty of, 88, 89, 90, 107, 111
Delft, Dirc van, 93
Dendermonde, 162
Denmark, 91
Deschamps, Eustache, 33
Deventer, 226, 229
Dijon, 20, 21, 25, 28, 36, 37, 52, 59, 60, 62, 87, 140, 181, 195, 210, 228
Dinant, 6, 131, 179, 180
Dixmude, Jan van, 168
Donchéry, 201
Dordrecht, 67, 107–8, 154, 199
Douai, 13, 152–54, 156, 225
Drenthe, 110
Dufay, Guillaume, 135, 228

Edmund Langley, 13
Edward III, king of England, 13, 18, 73
Edward IV, king of England, 137, 148, 176, 185
Egmond dynasty, 110
Eleanor of Aquitaine, wife of the English king Henry II, 9
Elizabeth of Austria, 105
Elizabeth of Görlitz, duchess of Luxemburg, xvi, 56, 104
Empire, Holy Roman, xi, 3, 5–6, 10–11, 54–56, 57, 60, 79–86, 104–7, 138, 182–83, 188–89, 198, 207, 212, 232, 233

Engelbert of Mark, bishop of Liège, 12
England, xii, 12–18, 23–28, 36–39, 42, 44–45, 63, 78, 83, 85–86, 156, 162, 168
Erasmus, 229–30
Estates-General, 94, 95, 124–25, 186, 195–96, 200, 202, 204, 207–9, 210, 211, 213, 221, 231, 233, 235, 236
Étampes, 202
Eugenius IV, pope, 79, 81, 89
Eyck, Hubert van, 71, 93, 98, 162, 219
Eyck, Jan van, 71, 73, 75, 98, 123, 135, 139, 162, 217, 219

Famine, 9
Ferdinand, king of Aragon, 212, 218, 231
Ferrette, county of, 182, 189, 193–94
Finance. *See* Chambers of Account
Flanders, ix, 1–2, 5, 6–10, 19–27, 35, 37, 83, 85, 94, 112, 122, 123–29, 141–49, 150–53, 155–56, 158, 159, 161–62, 164, 170, 179, 187, 193, 195, 198, 200–209, 214–25, 230, 232, 236, 238, 240
Formelis, Simon van, 55, 94
Four Offices (Vier Ambachten), 109
France, chapters 1–3 passim, 76–77, 85–86, 112–26, 195, 200–207, 211, 235
Franche-Comté (Free County of Burgundy), 1, 18–19, 20, 24, 25, 105, 142, 144–45
Francis I, king of France, 212, 234
Frankfurt, 216
Frederick Barbarossa, emperor, 186, 194
Frederick III, emperor, 104–7, 184–89
Frederick IV, duke of Austria, 80
Frederick of Meissen, duke of Saxony, 104
Frisia, 88, 105, 116, 122, 142, 152, 203, 213, 231, 232
Froissart, Jean, 136
Fugger family, 232

Gattinara, Mercurino de, 234
Gavere, 127–28
Genoa, 5, 6, 7, 164
Geraardsbergen, 96
Germain, Jean, 79
Gerson, Jean, 33, 39
Ghent, ix, 2, 3, 7, 10, 12, 13, 21–26, 46, 68, 69, 71, 83, 94, 96, 99–100, 106, 121, 124–29, 130, 133–40, 154, 156, 161–62, 165, 168, 169, 191, 193, 195, 198, 200–203, 207–8, 220–25, 228, 230, 232, 236, 239

Ghent-Bruges school, 128
Gideon, 74, 136, 139
Gloucester, Humphrey, duke of. *See* Humphrey
Goes, Hugo van der, 140, 219
Golden Fleece, Order of the, 73–75, 83, 106, 110, 111, 113, 136–39, 183, 193, 198, 231, 235
Gorkum, 114
Gossaert, Jan, 218, 227, 229
Gouda, 66, 69, 87, 158, 199
Goux, Pierre de, 176–77, 238
Grandson, 194
Granvelle, cardinal, 239
Gravelines, 154, 185
Great Council, 101, 112, 118–20, 129, 143, 189–90, 197, 233, 238
Great Privilege of *1477*, 196–99, 203–4
Great Schism, 9, 27, 49, 59, 101
Gregory XI, pope, 17
Groenendaal, 226
Groningen, 4, 110, 213, 240
Groote, Geert, 226
Gruuthuse, Lodewijk van, 122, 137, 199
Guelders, 4, 30, 35, 109–12, 152, 168, 179, 182, 184, 195, 199, 209, 211, 213, 231–32, 235–36, 238, 240
Guines, 13
Guyenne, 9, 10, 43, 78

Haarlem, 28, 108, 154, 158, 199, 219
Habsburg dynasty, 107
Hagenbach, Pierre de, 184
Hague, The, 30, 70, 71, 72, 143, 199
Hainault, ix, 6, 10–11, 13, 22, 29–30, 32, 39, 40, 53–59, 64–65, 69, 72, 76, 82, 83, 88–89, 93, 97, 105, 112, 113, 124, 135, 142–46, 150–53, 154, 156, 163–64, 180, 185, 187, 191, 195, 200, 202, 208, 209, 212, 240
Hal, 35
Hanse, 50, 90, 92, 107, 120–21, 139, 159, 162–64, 168, 214
Haydroits, 59–60
Haynin, Jean de, 136
Henry II, king of England, 9
Henry III, king of England, 13
Henry V, king of England, 42–44, 61–63, 67, 68, 72, 76
Henry VI, king of England, 63, 78, 81
Henry III of Nassau, 217

Henry of Bergen, bishop of Cambrai, 226, 229
's-Hertogenbosch, 154, 208, 217, 222, 236
Hesdin, 183, 228
Holland, 6, 10–11, 13, 22, 28, 29–30, 32, 39, 40, 43, 50, 53–59, 65–67, 72–73, 76, 83, 85, 86, 88–89, 90, 93, 95, 97, 99, 101, 107–9, 110, 119, 126, 142–46, 150–53, 154–59, 162–63, 187, 191, 193, 195, 198–99, 202, 207–9, 212, 214–16, 231, 235–38, 240
Holy Ghost Tables, 4
Holy Land, 124
Holy Year, 225
Hook, party, 66–69, 86, 88, 89–90, 107–9, 191, 199, 201
Hoorn, 199
Hops, 157–58
Horne, John of, 201
Hugonet, Guillaume, 198
Humbercourt. *See* Brimeu
Humphrey, duke of Gloucester, 68, 71, 78, 82, 83, 86, 87, 89
Hungary, 16
Hunyadi, John, 106
Hussites, 80
Huy, 12

IJssel, river, 110, 154, 155
Innocent VII, pope, 39
Innsbruck, 210
Isaac, Heinric, 228
Isabela of Bavaria, queen of France, 32, 33, 36–37, 38, 41–44, 56, 58–59, 62, 72
Isabella, queen of Castile, 21
Isabella of Bourbon, wife of Charles the Bold, xvii, 113
Isabella of Portugal, wife of Philip the Good, xvi, 73–79, 81, 97, 114
L'Isle Adam (Lelidam), Jean de Villiers, lord of, 99, 124
Israel, 97
Italy, Italians, xii, 6, 9, 24, 38, 139, 141, 146, 164–65, 167, 219–20

Jacqueline of Bavaria, countess of Hainault, Holland, and Zeeland, xvi, 41, 43, 56, 58–59, 64–69, 71, 78, 82, 86–91, 104, 107
Jan van Mechelen, 30
Jason, 74
Jean de Touraine, dauphin, 41, 43, 56

Joan of Arc, 76, 78
Joan, duchess of Brabant, 11–12, 30, 35, 54
Johanna van Luxemburg, xvi
John II, king of France, xvi, 1, 14–16, 19–20
John the Fearless, xvi, 29, 35–62, 70, 72, 75–76, 122
John, duke of Bedford, 42, 63, 68, 73, 78, 80, 82, 87
John, duke of Berry, 29, 31, 32, 40, 41
John III, duke of Brabant, xvi, 11
John IV, duke of Brabant, xvi, 11, 35, 56–59, 64–68, 86, 87, 88, 91, 104
John, duke of Cleves, 183
John of Gaunt, duke of Lancaster, 15, 73
John III, count of Namur, 69
John of Bavaria, bishop-elect Liège, 57–59, 66, 68, 70, 86–104, 107
John of Bruges, miniaturist, 17
John of Burgundy, bishop of Cambrai, 112
John of Burgundy, count of Etampes and Nevers, xvi, 179, 196
Josquin des Prés, 228
Jouvenel, Jean, 33
Joyous Entry, 7, 11, 18, 30–31, 45–46, 48, 51, 54, 55, 64–65, 70, 91, 121, 128, 130, 138, 178, 198, 218, 221, 239
Juan de Castile, 212, 213, 235
Juana of Castile, wife of Philip the Fair, xvii, 212, 218
Jülich, county of, 105, 236
Jülich-Berg, 182–83

Keldermans, Laureins, 221, 222
Keldermans, Rombout, 221, 222
Kempis, Thomas à, 227
Kennemerland, 88, 95, 116
Königsberg, 5
Kontor, 164
Kossovo, 35

Ladislas, Polish prince, 17
Lalaing, Joost van, 199–200
Lalaing, Willem van, 108
Lalaing, Yolanda van, 108
Langres, 16, 227
Language, 31, 46, 47, 70–71, 121–22, 139, 196, 217, 222
Languedoc, 144
Lannoy, 176, 201
Lannoy, Hugh of, 84–85, 90, 108

Lannoy, Jean of, 108
Laroche, 189
Lathem, Lievin van, 220
Law, 116–20, 189–91
Leestmaker, Pieter de, alias Bladelin, 143
Leiden, 66, 108, 109, 154, 160, 161, 171, 193, 221
Leie/Lys, river, 22, 156
Leo X, pope, 229
Leonardo da Vinci, 227
Levant, 5, 9
Lichtervelde, Jacob van, 55, 124
Liège, city and prince-bishopric, 4, 6, 8, 12, 40, 53, 57, 59–60, 70, 110, 111–12, 113, 131, 136, 152, 154, 170, 179, 180–84, 189, 195, 199, 200, 209
Ligue du Bien Public, 176, 179
Lille, 13, 25, 46, 55, 60, 90, 106, 121, 129, 138, 140, 143, 152–53, 154, 156, 228, 239
Limburg, duchy of, 30, 31, 38, 56, 92, 104, 105, 142–43, 150–52, 180, 209
Limburg, brothers, miniaturists, 32
Lisbon, 73
Lithuania, 6
Lobith, 183
Lodewijk van Grunthuse, 122, 137, 199
Lombardy, Lombards, 30, 145, 167
Lorenzo de'Medici, 166
Lothar I, 92
Lotharingia, kingdom/duchy, 6, 63, 92, 177, 184–85, 188–89, 193, 232
Louis the Pious, emperor, 92
Louis of Bavaria, emperor, 10, 11
Louis IX, saint, king of France, 9
Louis XI, king of France, 15, 114–16, 131, 141, 176, 178, 179, 184, 195, 196, 204
Louis XII, king of France, 231
Louis XIV, king of France, 212
Louis, duke of Anjou, 31, 32
Louis of Bourbon, bishop of Liège, 113, 133, 136, 179, 200, 203, 204
Louis of Guyenne, dauphin, husband of Margaret of Nevers, 42, 43
Louis, count of Hessen, 83
Louis of Male, count of Flanders, xvi, 1, 2, 8, 11, 12, 13, 16, 19, 21, 24
Louis of Nevers, count of Flanders, xvi, 10
Louis of Orleans, duke of Touraine, 32, 33, 37–41, 44, 57, 59, 60, 70
Louise of Savoy, queen of France, 213

Louvain/Leuven, ix, 91, 138, 154, 156, 160, 161, 202, 208, 219, 221–22, 232, 236; university of, 221
Loydet, Gerard, 188
Lubeck, 92, 162
Luxemburg, duchy of, viii, ix, 8, 60, 65, 66, 104–5, 113, 126, 142–46, 150–52, 154, 164, 170, 179, 180, 182, 189, 195, 209, 240–41
Lyon, 16, 77

Maas, river, ix, 6, 110, 155, 180
Maastricht, 195
Macedonia, 35
Mâcon, 16, 20, 81, 142, 185, 195
Maelwel brothers, 133
Maerlant, Jacob van, 217
Mantes, 43
Marcel, Etienne, 10
Marck, Guillaume de La, 200–201
Margaret, countess of Artois, wife of Louis of Nevers, count of Flanders, 1, 18, 19
Margaret of Austria, regent, xii, xvii, 200, 210, 211, 213–14, 223, 225, 228–33
Margaret of Avesnes, wife of Louis of Bavaria, emperor, 10
Margaret of Bavaria, wife of John the Fearless, xvi, 29, 40, 45, 50, 52–53, 72
Margaret of Burgundy, wife of William VI, count of Hainault and Holland and duke of Bavaria, 29, 88–89, 91
Margaret of Male, countess of Flanders, wife of Philip the Bold, 1, 13, 16, 19–20, 24, 35, 37, 54, 55, 145
Margaret of Scotland, mother of Louis XI of France, 115
Margaret of York, duchess of Burgundy, 136, 139, 177, 184, 194–95, 210, 225
Marmion, Simon, 220
Mary, duchess of Burgundy, 106–7, 195–99
Mary of Hungary, regent, 212, 231, 233–34
Maximilian, xi, xvii, 106–7, 138, 195–214
Mechelen, ix, 1, 11, 13, 24, 67, 120, 130, 142, 191, 208–9, 222, 223, 227–30, 232–33, 237–39; Parliament of, 81, 189–90
Mechelen, Jan van, 30
Medici, 166, 219. *See also* Lorenzo
Meit, Conrad, 229
Members of Flanders, 21, 24, 46, 48, 49–50, 51, 88, 95, 185, 208, 236, 236–37

Memling, Hans, 135, 219, 225
Mendicant orders, 164, 224, 226
Menen, 161
Mercatel, Raphael de, 224
Metsijs, Quentin, 227
Metz, 189
Mézières, Philippe de, 17
Michelle of France, xvi, 72–73
Middelburg, 208, 222
Milan, 17
Modern Devotion, 226–27
Moerbeke, William of, 6, 17
Molinet, Jean, 137
Mons, 68, 86, 154, 187
Mons-en-Vimeu, 61
Monstrelet, Enguerrand de, 136
Montdidier, 50, 97
Montereau, 44, 62, 63, 78
Monthléry, 179
Mostaert, Jan, 229
Murten, 194
Music 228–29

Naaldwijk, Willem van, 101
Namur, county, ix, 8, 69, 86, 91, 102, 105, 113, 120, 142, 146, 150–52, 154, 164, 170, 180, 195, 198, 209, 240
Nancy, 189, 193–94
Naples, 32–33
Navarre, 62
Neuss, 183–85, 189, 193
Nevers, 1, 10, 13, 19, 20, 24, 25, 34, 35, 38, 39, 40, 51, 145, 178
Nicholas V, pope, 111
Nicopolis, 36, 45, 62, 166
Nieuwkerke, 161
Nieuw Regiment, 66
Nijmegen, 28, 110, 154, 183
Normandy, 43

Obrecht, Jacob, 238
Odo IV, duke of Burgundy, 19–20
Orchies, 13, 152–53, 158
Oresme, Nicolas, 17
Orley, Bernard van, 229
Othée, Treaty of, 36, 60, 88, 98, 136
Oudenaarde, 46, 138
Oudewater, 199
Overijssel, 110, 152, 213, 236, 240
Oversticht, 110

Paele, canon Joris van der, 71, 135
Papacy, 9, 13, 36, 166
Paris, 7, 9, 21, 33, 36–37, 38, 40, 41–50, 54, 61–62, 63, 69, 78, 154, 166, 189–90, 236; Parlement of, 20, 25, 31, 33, 37, 39, 76–77, 81, 94, 190, 200; University of, 27, 31, 37, 39
Pavia, 16
Peloponnesus, 35
Péronne, 80, 81, 131, 182, 189
Perron, 180
Petit, Jean, 41, 42
Petrarca, 33
Pheasant, Vow of the, 106, 138
Philibert, duke of Savoy, xvii, 213, 228
Philip IV the Fair, king of France, 1, 18
Philip VI, king of France, 10
Philip I the Fair, king of Spain, prince of the Low Countries, xvii, 199, 203, 207, 210–12, 217–18, 223, 227, 228–30
Philip II, king of Spain, 11, 234–36, 239, 240–41
Philip the Bold, duke of Burgundy, xi, xvi, 1–2, 8, 12, 13, 14–34, 35, 37, 45, 46, 54, 55, 72, 145, 165, 213
Philip the Good, duke of Burgundy, xvi, 40, 45, 50, 61–175, 186, 188, 193, 205–7, 210, 213, 224, 227, 228
Philip of Rouvres, duke of Burgundy, 13, 15, 19
Philip of Saint-Pol, duke of Brabant, xvi, 64, 91, 128
Philip, count of Nevers and Rethel, xvi, 38, 43, 91
Philip of Burgundy, admiral, bishop of Utrecht, 224, 227
Picardy, 113, 121, 142–46, 152, 154, 156, 176, 177–79, 183, 195, 209
Pisan, Christine de, 33
Pius II, pope, 106
Plague, 9
Poelgeest, Van, 108
Poitiers, 2, 14, 15, 36, 62
Poland, 17
Pompey, 139
Ponthieu, county of, 13, 81, 142
Pontoise, 14
Poorterij, 99, 126
Poperinghe, 83, 162
Portinari, Tommaso, 166, 219

Portugal, 71, 73
Pourbus, Pieter, 222
Prague, 11
Praguerie, 114
Provins, 43
Prussia, 156, 160, 164, 187

Quesnoy, Le, 114

Raphael, 229
Rapondi, Dino, 166
Receiver-General, 118
Rederijkerskamers, 122, 132
Regensburg, 105–6, 107, 138
René, duke of Lotharingia, 189, 194
Rethel, county of, 1, 19, 24, 35, 38, 145
Revolts, urban, 22–24, 96–99, 123–29, 140, 191, 195–205, 209, 232
Reynard the Fox, 217
Rheims, 78
Rhône, 17
Roermond, 110
Rolin, Nicolas, 62–63, 71, 80, 114, 123, 129, 135
Rome, 17, 27, 62, 166
Rosary, 225
Rotterdam, 101
Rouen, 80
Rudolf van Diepholt, 89, 91, 111
Rue, Pierre de la, 228
Ruisbroek, Jan van, 135
Ruusbroec, Jan van, 226

Saint-Denis, 78
Saint-Donatian Chapter of Bruges, 111
Saint-Omer, 129, 155–56, 162
Saint-Truiden, 12; Treaty of, 189
Saint-Vaast, abbey, 81
Saintes, 108
Salins, 125, 142
Salisbury, count of, 39, 61
Salt-tax (*gabelle*), 125–26, 186
Sandwich, 163
Savoy, 63
Scandinavia, 6, 160
Scheldt, river, 5, 6, 10, 22, 125, 165, 214
Schism. *See* Great Schism
Schlick, Kaspar von, 105
Scotland, 80, 115, 159, 163–64
Scutelaere, Lubrecht, 26

Sempach, 182
Senlis, 43, 195; Peace of, 195
Shipping, 158–60
Sigismund, emperor, 56, 58, 60, 64, 66, 80–86, 91, 104
Sigismund of Habsburg, 182, 184
Sluis, 6, 73, 139, 167, 203, 215
Sluter, Klaas, 28, 35, 71, 73, 75, 133
Somme, 81, 83, 115, 179, 182, 193
Sont, 90
Spain, 3
Staple, 22, 154, 160
Stephen, duke of Bavaria, 32
Sticht of Utrecht, 110, 152
Strasbourg, 182
Sweden, 96
Switzerland, 179, 182, 184, 194–95

Tani, Angelo, 219
Thérouanne, bishopric, 109, 111, 112, 224
Thionville, 189
Tirol, 181, 205
Tonnerre, 53
Toul, 189
Touraine, duchy of, 15
Tournai, 77, 112, 129, 134, 135, 149, 152, 154, 213, 219, 220, 239; Peace of, *1385*, 26–27
Trent, Council of, 239
Trier, 106, 184, 188, 222
Trojans, 74, 80
Troy, 73, 74, 135
Troyes, 44, 61–63; Treaty of, 44, 63, 68, 72, 77–78
Turks, 35–36, 106, 138

Uitkerke, Roeland van, 97, 124
Urban VI, pope, 27
Utrecht, 4, 89, 91, 109–12, 139, 154, 168, 170, 199, 200, 201, 213, 222, 224, 227, 229, 239

Valenciennes, 136, 154, 220, 239
Varna, 106
Varsenare, Morisses van, 98
Vellert, Dirk, 223
Venice, 36, 164–66
Venlo, treaty of, 232
Verdun, 189
Vijd, Joos, 93

Vijd, Willem, 135
Visconti, 17
Visconti, Galeazzo, 16
Visconti, Valentina, 40–41
Vottem, 12

Waal, river, 10, 101, 154–55
Waghemakere, Domien de, 221, 222
Walcheren, 215
Waterschappen, 157
Wenceslas, husband of Johanna, duke of Brabant, 66
Wendish Hanseatic cities, 93
Werve, Klaas van de, 133
Westrozebeke, 24, 26
Weyden, Roger van der, 123, 134, 143, 219, 220
Willaert, Adriaan, 228
William V, count of Holland, 11
William VI of Bavaria, count of Hainault, Holland, and Zeeland, 29, 39, 41, 43, 57–59, 66, 70, 86
Windesheim, 226
Wittelsbach, dynasty, 10, 11, 32, 56–58, 72
Woudrichem, treaty of, 58, 65, 67

Ypres, 7, 21, 24, 25, 36, 46, 154, 156, 161, 165, 208, 236

Zeeland, 10–11, 29, 32, 39, 40, 43, 53–59, 65–67, 72, 73, 76, 83, 85, 86, 89, 90, 93, 95, 97, 104, 107–9, 142–3, 146, 150–52, 156, 158, 159, 163, 185, 195, 198, 202, 208, 209, 212, 214, 222, 231, 240
Zevenbergen, 88, 98
Zierikzee, 94
Zutphen, 110, 183, 232
Zwieten, Van, 108
Zwin, 97, 215
Zwolle, 226